MURDERESSES IN GERI
1720–186(

The way deviant women – murderesses, witches, vampires – are perceived and represented reveals much about what a society considers the norm for acceptable female behaviour. Drawing on extensive archival records and published texts, Susanne Kord investigates the stories of eight famous murderesses in Germany as they were told in legal, psychological, philosophical and literary writings. Kord interrogates the role of representation in legal judgment and the way the emancipation of women was perceived to be linked to their crimes. She demonstrates how perceptions of normal and criminal women permeated not only legal thought but also seemingly unrelated cultural spheres – from poetry, philosophy and physiognomy to early psychological profiling. A major work of German cultural history, this highly original book raises thought-provoking questions about eighteenth- and nineteenth-century gender norms in ways that continue to resonate today.

SUSANNE KORD is Professor of German at University College London.

CAMBRIDGE STUDIES IN GERMAN

GENERAL EDITORS
H. B. Nisbet
University of Cambridge
Martin Swales
University of London

ADVISORY EDITOR
Theodore J. Ziolkowski
Princeton University

Also in the series

MURDERESSES IN GERMAN WRITING, 1720–1860

Heroines of Horror

SUSANNE KORD

CAMBRIDGE
UNIVERSITY PRESS

CAMBRIDGE UNIVERSITY PRESS
Cambridge, New York, Melbourne, Madrid, Cape Town,
Singapore, São Paulo, Delhi, Mexico City

Cambridge University Press
The Edinburgh Building, Cambridge CB2 8RU, UK

Published in the United States of America by Cambridge University Press, New York

www.cambridge.org
Information on this title: www.cambridge.org/9781107412606

First published 2009
First paperback edition 2012

A catalogue record for this publication is available from the British Library

Library of Congress Cataloguing in Publication Data
Kord, Susanne.
Murderesses in German writing, 1720–1860 : heroines of horror / Susanne Kord.
p.   cm. – (Cambridge studies in German)
Includes index.
ISBN 978-0-521-51977-9
1. Women murderers – Case studies.   2. Murder in literature.   3. German literature –
18th century – History and criticism.   4. German literature – 19th century – History and criticism.
I. Title.   II. Series.
HV6517.K67   2009
364.152´30820943–dc22
2009006832

ISBN 978-0-521-51977-9 Hardback
ISBN 978-1-107-41260-6 Paperback

Contents

Contents

Illustrations

Acknowledgments

To everyone who offered their help:

Jürgen Barkhoff, Wolfgang Braungart, Alexander Košenina, Julie Koser, Betsy Li, Mary Lindemann, Nicholas Saul and Maria Stehle sent me those parts of their work that intersected with this project.

Mary Lindemann shared her notes and knowledge about the Wächtler case. Franklin Kopitzsch sent me documents about Wächtler.

Laura Ambrós, Dennis Báthory-Kitsz, Jürgen Howaldt, Toni Tasić, the Gleim-Haus Halberstadt, the Stiftung Klassik Weimar, the Focke-Museum in Bremen and the Staatsarchiv Hamburg kindly allowed me to publish images in their possession.

Jürgen Barkhoff, Clare Griffin, John Landau and W. Daniel Wilson were generous first readers of parts of the manuscript and offered useful criticisms.

Pointers towards important literature came from Johannes Birgfeld, Susan Cocalis, Helen Fronius, Howard Gaskill, Clare Griffin, Karl Härter, Christina von Hodenberg, Kathrin Hoffmann-Curtius, Alexander Košenina, Julie Koser, Maria Lange, Mary Lindemann and W. Daniel Wilson.

Helen Fronius chased up some last-minute page references for me when the submission deadline loomed.

Ritchie Robertson offered advice about possible publishers. I was lucky to work with Linda Bree, Maartje Scheltens, Kay McKechnie and Tom O'Reilly at Cambridge University Press.

My colleagues in the UCL German Department heard of many cases in this book in hallway conversations and always listened supportively and patiently.

The German Academic Exchange Service (DAAD) and the Graduate School at UCL funded part of the initial research for this book in December 2005.

Gretlies Haungs hosted me for a month of library research in Germany and supported my work with her kind curiosity about the project.

Outstanding expertise and support came from the staff at the Staatsarchiv Hamburg, the Bodleian Library in Oxford, the Staatsbibliothek zu Berlin Preußischer Kulturbesitz, the Staats- und Universitätsbibliothek Bremen, and especially Mr Paget Anthony and the staff at the Rare Books Reading Room at the British Library, my home away from home for three years.

Nothing spurs a writer on like an enthusiastic future reader. Christine Ezell's excited anticipation was a wonderful incentive to get it done. Christine, you can read it now.

As ever, I owe thanks to John Landau, my 'partner in crime', without whose love and support I'd never get anything written.

CHAPTER I

Criminal women: on bodies, paradoxes, performances and tales

A GAME IN THE DARK: THE PRINCIPLE OF PARADOX

In one of the earliest German journals of psychology, Karl Philipp Moritz's *Know Thyself or Journal of Psychology. A Reader for Scholars and Amateurs* (1783–93), an anonymous contributor describes how close he came to murdering his brother.[1] He bore his brother no grudge or ill will; he had no reason to kill him; he had not even, as emerges in the course of his tale, made a *decision* to kill him. All that was needed to arouse a bloodlust that he describes as virtually irresistible was a state of complete exhaustion, his letter opener just slightly out of reach on the desk, and his brother sleeping and defenceless in the same room. In the beginning, there was opportunity; from the opportunity arose his fear of availing himself of it, and 'from the fear of doing it, of having to do it, arose the sudden determination to do it'.[2]

Instead of committing fratricide, the narrator reflects on two questions that trouble him and undoubtedly also, at this point, his readers. The first is the question how the idea of murder even occurred to him and how it grew, apparently without any cognitive input from him, from vague fear to firm determination in a matter of seconds. In answer, he offers a suspicion:

Any idea of the present has an analogy that has always been there … this energy of the soul was perhaps aroused by an old idea slumbering within me, or fashioned from several similar ones which raised it to this high degree of vividness. Without finding enjoyment in this I was often present when animals were slaughtered; perhaps I had even attended this act on that very evening … My soul copied this image and played its game with it in the dark. Is a clear awareness truly necessary to form ideas, particularly when their main features are imprinted on our souls? Their

---

[1] 'Ueber meinen unwillkührlichen Mordentschluß', in *Gnothi sauton oder Magazin zur Erfahrungsseelenkunde als ein Lesebuch für Gelehrte und Ungelehrte herausgegeben von Carl Philipp Moritz*, III 3, 61–81. The contribution is credited to 'J. Gottfr. V..w.g. in Bschwg.' (81).

[2] 'So entsprang aus der Furcht es zu thun, es thun zu müssen, plötzlich der Entschluß' ('Ueber meinen unwillkührlichen Mordentschluß', 66).

building blocks are certainly already there; all that is missing is their proper assembly and order to form a whole.[3]

In a twenty-page contribution to a journal of psychology, this is the sole passage describing psychological processes. Everywhere else, the physical reigns supreme. The idea of murder, mediated in its analogous idea of slaughter, may well have been 'already there', but it is brought to the fore by the narrator's physical condition at the time, his exhaustion, coupled with the physical arrangement of objects – the paper knife, the sleeping brother – in the room. Throughout his treatise, physical processes are the determining factor in life-and-death decisions, with the soul utterly dependent on the body and the mind nowhere in evidence:

Clearly, this decision to commit murder was the effect of many combined motivations; it most likely originated more from physical than moral causes. Precisely the involuntariness of these thoughts, the paradox of simultaneously wanting to and not wanting to, argue loudly enough in favour of the … dependence of the soul, which is weakened and overpowered by the body.[4]

This argument also sums up his answer to the second question troubling his readers, namely, why he ultimately resisted the temptation. As he describes it, it was not a conscious decision that saved his brother's life, but a simple sequence of events: he stood up to reach for the knife; the movement caused his blood to flow more regularly and his circulation to settle, and with increased blood flow to the brain rationality returned.[5] Again, these are almost entirely physical processes; the broad spectrum of moral contemplation, emotional expression or rational reflection we might expect here – anguish, shock, horror, relief, gratitude and ultimately the reassertion of moral balance and rational thought – do not enter into the

---

[3] 'Von einer gegenwärtigen Idee ist immer schon ein Analogon da gewesen … diese Energie der Seele erweckte vielleicht eine alte schlummernde Idee in mir, oder bildete aus mehrern ähnlichen eine, die sie zu den hohen Grade von Lebhaftigkeit erhob. Ohne ein Vergnügen daran zu finden, war ich oft zugegen, wenn geschlachtet wurde, vielleicht hatte ich dieser Handlung noch an demselben Abend, zu welcher Zeit sie gewöhnlich vorgenommen wurde, beigewohnt. Dieses Bild kopirte meine Seele und trieb ihr Spiel damit im Dunkeln. Sollte immer ein deutliches Bewußtseyn bey unsern Vorstellungen, insonderheit wenn sich ihre Grundzüge in unserer Seele mahlen, nöthig seyn? Die Materialien dazu sind freilich schon vorhanden, es fehlt nur an schicklicher Anordnung und Zusammenfügung, um das Ganze zu übersehen' ('Ueber meinen unwillkührlichen Mordentschluß', 68–9).

[4] 'Augenscheinlich war dieser Mordentschluß eine Wirkung sehr zusammengesetzter Triebfedern, und muß ursprünglich wohl mehr aus physischen als aus moralischen Ursachen hergeleitet werden. Eben das Unwillkührliche bei diesen Gedanken, eben der gleichzeitige Widerspruch zwischen Wollen und Nichtwollen, reden laut genug für die enge Verbindung und Abhängigkeit der Seele, die von dem körperlichen geschwächt und übertäubt wurde' ('Ueber meinen unwillkührlichen Mordentschluß', 74).

[5] 'Ueber meinen unwillkührlichen Mordentschluß', 75.

equation. Cognitive powers, mental responses and moral decisions – in the narrator's view not merely his own, but those of humanity at large – are compelled by such coincidental and uncontrollable outside forces as, say, the weather. 'Without question', the narrator muses, 'the climate has a considerable influence on every murderer: he will act differently in a warmer or colder climate. The latter will proceed more slowly and deliberately; to the former, the thoughts 'I want to' and 'I have to' are one and the same: … He thinks it and commits murder.'[6] In his addendum on 'the power of involuntary thoughts', the narrator admits that he nearly committed suicide by jumping out of the window, a decision he relates not to emotional anguish or even the unbearable heat, but simply to the fact that his bedroom window was high off the ground: 'the height of my bedroom caused [!] my fear that I might take a fatal plunge out of the window in the heat'.[7] And fear, as we know from the tale of his involuntary homicidal impulse, does not shield him against the urge but, paradoxically, increases his temptation to yield to it.

This story of irrational impulses, written at the end of the period we now call the 'Age of Reason', is, like this book, a study of paradoxes. Published in a well-known psychological journal, the anonymous author participates in the debate on the inner workings of humans that was one of the overriding concerns of the enlightened age. And yet, the text itself, with its matter-over-mind stance, seems to break with its own context. It also seems to invite interpretations indebted simultaneously to 'ancient' (for our purposes: pre-Enlightenment) and 'modern' (post-Enlightenment) ideas. We might be tempted, for example, to read this tale as an early expression of the modern cliché that every human being is a potential killer, or as a prefiguration of psychoanalytic insights, such as the discovery of the subconscious. Or we might read it just as easily in the context of the late Middle Ages. Both the author's designation of his compulsion as an 'energy of the soul' and his strict distinction between this and the mind evoke the theories of Paracelsus (1493–1541), who famously conceptualised humans as composed of body, soul and mind/spirit (*corpus, anima, spiritus*).[8] Other aspects, too, raise doubts about the text's 'modernity', such as its assertion of

---

[6] 'Ohne Zweifel hat das Klima auf jeden Mörder beträchlichen [sic] Einfluß; anders handelt er unter einem wärmern, anders unter einem kältern. Der letztere geht langsamer und bedächtiger zu Werke, bey jenen ist der Gedanke: ich will, ich muß Eins, ein Ton, ein Ruf, von dem er sich auf- oder abgefordert glaubt. Er denkt's und mordet' ('Ueber meinen unwillkührlichen Mordentschluß', 76).

[7] '… die Höhe meines Schlafzimmers erzeugte die Furcht, in der Hitze einen tödtlichen Sprung aus dem Fenster zu thun' ('Anhang einiger Erfahrungen von der Gewalt unwillkührlicher Ideen', Moritz, *Gnothi Sauton*, III 3, 78–81, the quotation 78).

[8] See Kaemmerer.

the supremacy of the physical during a period that propagated the power and autonomy of the human mind.

Taking this tale and the interpretive possibilities it offers as a parable for my own project, I would describe my interest in it – and in other murder cases analysed further on – as an interest in the principle of paradox, exemplified here in the text's puzzling inconsistencies and in the uncomfortable questions it raises. Puzzling inconsistencies and uncomfortable questions will recur throughout this book, which aims to examine rather than 'explain' them. A perfectly sensible explanation for the paradoxical tale by our not-quite-murderer might be, for example, to view it as the product of a 'transitional period'. Such a statement, however, would itself adopt an enlightened stance in its assumption that there are two distinct time periods, that they are not only distinct but hierarchically organised (one is considered more 'rational' than the other), and that for this reason, the transition from one to the next represents a form of progress (or, in this case, regression). This kind of implicit hierarchisation is a common approach to the time period under consideration, the period between about 1720 and about 1860, or – in epochal terms – from Enlightenment to Empire, with the Enlightenment – in hierarchical terms – occupying pride of place as the philosophical and intellectual foundation of Modernity. Positivist historians of social and political life, philosophy and literature have tended to interpret the Enlightenment as the era in which rationalism obtained its final victory over medieval and Baroque superstitions. Among the developments that are often cited as indicative of this victory are the end of the witch trials,[9] the advance of new intellectual and philosophical thought systems such as Cartesianism[10] and Pantheism,[11] the emancipation of the bourgeoisie and its replacement of the aristocracy as the culturally dominant class,[12] and a new concern with human rights (Kant's philosophy,[13] the French and American revolutions[14] and the reform of the penal system[15]). To this day, the 'long' eighteenth century is overwhelmingly interpreted as the period during which order is first established, and the ordering principles attributed to this time are commonly accepted as the basis for those of

[9] See the following chapter.   [10] See the contributions in Hans Wagner's anthology.
[11] See Christophe Bouton, Heinrich Scholz and Gérard Vallée's introduction to *Die Hauptschriften zum Pantheismusstreit*, i–vi.
[12] See Blackbourn and Evans; Vierhaus; and Kocka, *Bürger und Bürgerlichkeit*.
[13] Among many others, Deligiorgi; Gerhardt, Horstmann and Schumacher; Kopper; Cassirer; and Durant.
[14] See Dippel; Saine, *Black Bread, White Bread*; Rürup; and Mason.
[15] See Ju; Ebel; Beirne; and Häntzschel, Ormrod and Renner.

the modern age.[16] In Germany, these ordering principles have been variously imagined as an epoch (the 'Age of Enlightenment', the 'Classical Age', 'Romanticism'), a philosophy (the 'Age of Reason'), or even a mere individual (the 'Age of Goethe'). Two further classifications that are relevant in this context are the establishment of a literary canon (a nineteenth- and twentieth-century construction that often refers back to Johann Christoph Gottsched's literary reforms of the 1730s[17]), and the modern interpretation of the sexes as diametrically opposed rather than complementary, which also, or so twentieth-century philosophers have told us, developed in the course of the eighteenth century.[18]

Surely, these categories of high and low, male and female, elite and uncultured, balanced and absurd, have their uses; they enable us to classify, contextualise, rank and file. And surely, they have also limited our thinking. Since this book is concerned – invariably, given its subject matter, but also unapologetically – with the subordinate, the trivial, the uncanny, the irrational, the scandalous, the sensationalistic, the lowbrow, the unsubtle and the inexplicable, its investigations and conclusions will necessarily be at odds with a literary and social history that has privileged the highbrow, the sophisticated, the aesthetically valuable and the rational.[19] This book investigates not only criminal cases, but also the ordering principles and hierarchies that we as readers so often impose upon texts and contexts, stories and histories. It takes as its subject not only the criminal women of the past, but also the gender codes, reading behaviours and aesthetic and moral judgments of the present.

THE GENDER OF CRIME: TESTIMONIES

The tale of near-fratricide published in Moritz's journal prefigured later thinking about the nature of crime in significant ways. Particularly the idea that the body controls the mind became a staple of later writing on criminality in general and female criminality in particular. In writing about crime, whether criminal stories or criminological studies, it is indeed 'bodies that matter';[20] in writing about crime and women, what matters

---

[16] See Saine, *The Problem of Being Modern*; Mah; and Kocka, *Geschichte und Aufklärung*.

[17] For a broad history of reading and reading behaviours in Germany, see Jost Schneider.

[18] See the Laqueur, *The Making of the Modern Body* and *Making Sex*; and Honegger, *Die Ordnung der Geschlechter*.

[19] On literary and aesthetic hierarchies, see, among others, Goddard and the contributions in Kord and Whittle.

[20] See Judith Butler on the discursive limits of 'sex'.

most is the body's gender. Moritz's contributor already assumed this when he wrote that 'the female imagination is more excitable and excessive than the male imagination',[21] suggesting that a woman in his situation would not have been able to resist the murderous impulse that nearly consumed him. His twofold theory that crime originates 'more from physical than moral causes' and that women make likelier killers was taken up in grand style almost exactly one hundred years later, in Cesare Lombroso and Guglielmo Ferrero's seminal work *Criminal Woman, the Prostitute, and the Normal Woman* (*La donna delinquente, la prostituta, e la donna normale*, 1893).[22] Lombroso and Ferrero proposed that the nature of female crime is fundamentally biological in origin, that female criminals are less evolved than both male criminals and law-abiding women, and that criminal women are more masculine than 'normal' women, a theory that resulted in countless studies, from the early 1900s on, attempting to prove that women's criminality was on the rise because women were becoming more 'like men'. Most perniciously, Lombroso and Ferrero claimed, based on physical evidence such as cranial measurements and other physiological experiments, that there was very little physical difference between criminal women and normal women, whereas male lawbreakers displayed a wealth of abnormalities that distinguished them from normal men. The physical evidence confirmed their view that both normal and criminal women were defined by the same characteristics, namely cruelty, immorality, vanity, dishonesty and affectability. From this they concluded that normal women, like criminal women, are inherently deviant, 'walking bundles of pathology, which can at any moment unravel into criminality'.[23] Far from letting statistical evidence (which showed then, as now, that women committed far fewer crimes than men) stand in the way of their theories, Lombroso and Ferrero argued that women's empirically low criminality was, in fact, further proof of their inferiority. In a word, 'women are less criminal than men because they are too weak and stupid to be bad'.[24]

Like the tale of barely averted fratricide, *La donna delinquente* is a study in contradictions. On the one hand, its central claim is that criminality, for women, is normal; on the other, female criminals are described as anything but ordinary. 'The born female criminal is, so to speak, doubly exceptional,

---

[21] '… daß weibliche Imagination reitzbarer und ausschweifender als Männer-Imagination ist' ('Anhang einiger Erfahrungen von der Gewalt unwillkührlicher Ideen', 79).
[22] On Lombroso and Ferrero's work, see Gibson; Hahn Rafter and Gibson's introduction to their translation of Lombroso's *La donna delinquente*, 3–33; Hart, particularly 12–13; and Weiler 84–91.
[23] Hahn Rafter and Gibson 29.   [24] Hahn Rafter and Gibson 14.

first as a woman and then as a criminal. This is because criminals are exceptions among civilized people, and women are exceptions among criminals ... As a double exception, then, the criminal woman is a true monster.'[25] With the benefit of hindsight, we might consider this one of the most significant passages of the work. It formulates a paradox that has ever since been reiterated in writings on women and crime without being recognised as such: all women are natural criminals, but female criminals are no longer natural women. What, then, is the true gender of the female criminal? Lombroso and Ferrero's cranial measurements of normal women, criminal women and normal men answers the question, producing a conclusion that has haunted literature on female delinquency to the end of the twentieth century: 'Many abnormal characteristics in the skulls of female criminals are almost normal characteristics in men.'[26] Criminal women, then, are unlike women; they are like men, but not *quite* normal. They display what Lombroso and Ferrero termed man's 'virile' traits, but on a lower level of development. For this reason, 'female born criminals', although 'fewer in number than male born criminals ... are often much more savage'; their crimes 'are more intense and perverse even than those of their male counterparts'.[27]

We might dismiss *La donna delinquente* as the ravings of eloquent bigots, or, more charitably, as an exercise in what its translators have termed 'tortured logic',[28] were it not for its unrivalled impact on later writers.[29] The book's central theories were reproduced *ad infinitum* by German criminologists in the early twentieth century.[30] Nor did its influence end there. Both the idea that women are biologically predestined for crime and the view that criminal women are really 'like' men have, apparently without violating each other's turf, enjoyed nearly undiminished popularity throughout the twentieth century. In 1969, Hildegard Damrow attributed violent crimes committed by women to hormonal causes, particularly menstruation and menopause. In the 1970s and 1980s, politicians and journalists routinely explained the high percentage of female members in terrorist groups like the Red Army Faction (*Rote Armee Fraktion*) by stating

---

[25] Lombroso and Ferrero 183, 185.   [26] Lombroso and Ferrero 115–16.

[27] Lombroso and Ferrero 183, 182 respectively; discussion in Naish 75–6.

[28] Hahn Rafter and Gibson 10.

[29] Hahn Rafter and Gibson 23: 'No other study can rival *La donna delinquente* in its influence on subsequent thinking about women and crime.'

[30] Some examples: Erich Wulffen, *Das Weib als Sexualverbrecherin* (orig. 1924); Hans Schneickert, *Das Weib als Erpresserin und Anstifterin* (1919); Otto Weininger, *Geschlecht und Charakter* (1903); Richard Krafft-Ebing, *Psychosis Menstrualis* (1902); and Wilhelm Gustav Liepmann, *Psychologie der Frau* (1920); discussion of many of these texts in Dornhof.

that terrorism was a logical outgrowth of women's emancipation.[31] 'The concomitant features and aftereffects of women's emancipation', wrote *Der Spiegel* in 1977, 'are also discernible in traditional … criminality, where women, more and more frequently, do men's work.'[32] And as late as the year 2000, Christian Bolte and Klaus Dimmler have described what happens when 'Women Become Men and Seek Adventure': 'Either they became prostitutes, acting out their femininity in such a life but remaining passive … Or they decided in favour of the asexual lifestyle of active masculinity. In this role it could happen very easily that they became criminal and brutal.'[33]

Studies alleging women's biological predestination for crime are more than evenly matched by those asserting the exact opposite. 'Criminality is presumed to be the quintessential domain of men. Men are perpetrators, women victims … When people speak of "criminal activity", they mean that of men.'[34] Seen from this perspective, femininity is the very antithesis of criminality: of all factors used to predict crime, from regional differences and religion to class or economic backgrounds, gender has been historically the most reliable.[35] This view does have the empirical evidence on its side. That the statistical average of women's criminal activities from the eighteenth century until today was, and is, considerably lower than that of men has never been disputed. For the period under discussion, various authors have offered estimates ranging from about 10 to

---

[31] This is an argument that recurs near-obsessively in coverage of the terrorist movement in *Der Spiegel* and other print media (see Stehle). Günter Nollau, later President of the Bundesamt für Verfassungsschutz, is quoted as wondering out loud why so many 'girls' had joined the terrorist movement, and answering his own question: 'Perhaps this is an excess of women's emancipation' ('Vielleicht ist das ein Exzeß der Befreiung der Frau', cited in Aust 176). And Ingeborg Hauschildt, in an unpublished paper decrying the evils of feminist theology, stated in 1980: 'Unfortunately, women are somewhat fanciful. Otherwise I could not explain why … there are so many women among terrorists. Here they achieve a complete perversion of femininity' ('Leider neigen Frauen etwas zum Schwärmertum. Anders kann ich es mir nicht erklären, daß … es auch unter den Terroristen nicht wenige Frauen gibt. Hier kommen sie zu einer völligen Perversion fraulichen Wesens', 10).

[32] 'Begleit- und Folgeerscheinungen der Emanzipation zeigen sich auch in der herkömmlichen … Kriminalität, wo Frauen immer häufiger Männerarbeit verrichten' ('Frauen im Untergrund – Etwas Irrationales', 23).

[33] 'Entweder sie wurden Prostituierte, gaben sich mit einem solchen Leben zwar weiblich, blieben aber passiv … Oder sie entschlossen sich für die asexuelle Lebensweise des Männlich-Aktiven. In dieser Rolle konnte es leicht geschehen, daß sie kriminell und brutal wurden' (Bolte and Dimmler, in a chapter segment entitled 'Frauen werden Männer und suchen das Abenteuer', 131).

[34] Ulbricht, 'Einleitung' to *Von Huren und Rabenmüttern*, 1–37: 'Kriminalität gilt als ureigenstes Gebiet des Mannes. Männer sind Täter, Frauen Opfer; diesen Eindruck vermittelten kriminologische Studien; dieser Eindruck herrscht auch in der Öffentlichkeit vor. Wenn von "Kriminalität" gesprochen wird, ist Männerkriminalität gemeint' (5).

[35] Ulbrich 281, citing Lutz Gero Leky's essay on female crime rates (1988).

42 per cent,[36] with the percentages over 25 invariably including crimes for which only women could be sentenced, such as infanticide,[37] abortion and prostitution. The only category in which women ever reached the 50 per cent mark was sex offences,[38] which may tell us more about contemporary moral codes and their legal consequences than about women's criminal behaviour. Violent crime, on the other hand, seemed antithetical to women, both statistically[39] and in the popular imagination. How antithetical is documented by a variety of anecdotes which do not have to be true to make the point, such as the one of the man who, ambushed by a highwaywoman in eighteenth-century England, did not understand that he was being held up.[40] Of course, the statistical fact that men far outnumber women as criminals added grist to the mill of those claiming that female criminals are masculinised women.

Yet another paradox permeating the writing about women and crime is the following: on the one hand, crime is nearly universally presumed to have a gender – in writing, it is either quintessentially male or archetypally female. On the other hand, the law judging crime is often described as gender-neutral. Schnabel-Schulte has pointed out that the *Carolina* (the Penal Code of Emperor Charles V of 1532, by which crimes were judged in eighteenth-century Germany) was couched in gender-neutral terms like 'the accused', 'perpetrators' and 'victims', adding that

[w]omen, like men, could be victims or perpetrators, they could, given the same advantageous conditions, expect as fair a treatment as men; under less favourable conditions, they could be sanctioned harshly in the course of the criminal procedure, just like men. The penal system treated both sexes equally, that is, equally capable of guilt.[41]

---

[36] Statistics on women's crimes are cited, among others, by the following authors: Ulbricht, 'Einleitung' to *Von Huren und Rabenmüttern*, 18 (10–20%); Behringer, 'Weibliche Kriminalität', 70 (13.5% of those executed in Munich for violent crimes between 1749 and 1759 were women); Ulbrich 281 (10%); Härter, *Policey*, II 539–70 (25–42% in the principality of Kurmainz).

[37] Infanticide was legally defined as a woman-specific offence; men killing children, including infants, would have been sentenced for murder, not infanticide (see chapter 5).

[38] Härter, *Policey*, II 540; Schwerhoff, 'Geschlechtsspezifische Kriminalität', 102 and 104; Ulbricht, 'Einleitung' to *Von Huren und Rabenmüttern*, 20; Wunder, 'Weibliche Kriminalität', 41.

[39] See Ulbricht, 'Einleitung' to *Von Huren und Rabenmüttern*, 21; Schwerhoff, 'Geschlechtsspezifische Kriminalität', 98–9.

[40] The story is cited by Ulbricht, 'Einleitung' to *Von Huren und Rabenmüttern*, 10.

[41] Schnabel-Schulte 191 and 198: 'Frauen waren gleichermaßen Opfer wie Täterinnen, sie konnten bei gleich günstigen Rahmenbedingungen eine ebenso faire Behandlung erwarten wie Männer; sie konnten bei ungünstigen Voraussetzungen aber auch ebenso wie die Männer den Sanktionsdruck des Strafverfahrens mit aller Härte zu spüren bekommen. Das strafrechtliche Verfahren behandelte die Geschlechter als gleichwertig, d.h. auch im selben Maße als schuldfähig.' On the gender-neutrality of the law, see also Hull, *Sexuality* and 'Sexualstrafrecht'.

And yet, the 'conditions' governing this measure of equality before the law, which could include local differences in the way in which the law was applied, could translate into considerable differences in the legal treatment of men and women. The Bavarian Penal Code of 1751, for example, stated that since women were not legally responsible, they could not be charged with capital crimes.[42] Women could serve as witnesses at a trial,[43] but in many cases not as accusers; as legal dependents, they had to rely on their fathers, brothers or husbands to initiate judicial proceedings on their behalf.[44] Just as there were crimes with which only women could be charged, such as infanticide and prostitution, there were gender-specific methods of execution: breaking on the wheel or impaling for men; drowning or live burial for women.[45] More women than men were accused of sex crimes; their sentences more frequently included an element of public humiliation; and some crimes, such as adultery, were punished more harshly if committed by a woman.[46] Some studies claim that women, even when guilty of the same crimes as men, were less often subject to the death penalty.[47]

Even ignoring, for the moment, the absurdity of speaking of gender equality before the law at a time when women had no vote and thus no hand in choosing public officials, including the magistrates who then judged them at trial, it seems that the view of eighteenth- and nineteenth-century law as a gender-neutral space could do with some modifications. Both crimes and punishments, as we shall see in the course of this book, were often thought of in gender-specific terms. Ideas of crime and its gender – its quintessential masculinity or femininity – permeated philosophical, psychological, criminological and legal writings, reformist debates and literary works. Various convincing interpretations are possible about the interaction between these various writings and court decisions. To suppose, however, that legal rulings were immune to this discourse[48] is patently absurd.

To think about criminal women means to consider them empirically – their crimes and punishments – in the context of the ubiquitous discourse

[42] Schnabel-Schulte 192.   [43] Schnabel-Schulte 191.   [44] Göttsch 11.
[45] Schnabel-Schulte 192–3; Harms-Ziegler 326; Göttsch 10. In the eighteenth century, many of these methods were still in use – with some gender-crossover, as we shall see – ; in the legal practice of the nineteenth century, both women and men were usually executed either by hanging or beheading (see chapter 7 for a more extensive discussion of executions).
[46] Hull, *Sexuality*, 222–9; Göttsch 10.
[47] For example Schwerhoff, 'Geschlechtsspezifische Kriminalität', 102.
[48] As does Baerlocher in his 'Nachwort' to Wahl's edition, 396.

on crime and its gender. Whether criminal women are thought of as rare exceptions or the inevitable rule naturally makes a difference to the discussion. One reason why this book focuses on violent women is that they embody the principle of paradox. In philosophy and literature, Woman most often appears as a victim, not a perpetrator.[49] If she is a perpetrator, she is downgraded to the status of an accomplice of the 'real' (male) criminal – his 'helpmeet', even in crime.[50] If she undeniably acted alone, she is presented as committing her crime in as furtive, cowardly and non-violent a fashion as possible – this is why the 'classically female' form of murder is presumed to be murder by poison.[51] 'In essence, women's criminality seems far less spectacular than men's; it appears as rather banal, mundane, downright "conformist".'[52] If she is irrefutably violent, she is seen as transgressing not only against humanity – as a man would be – but also against gender norms. Writings about women and crime have been, as Otto Ulbricht has pointed out, 'extremely prone to ideologies'; they have been 'the ideal stomping ground for prejudices, ideologies and myths about the female sex. Thus [this research] now constitutes an outstanding source for ideas about gender.'[53] Perhaps the day-to-day 'normality' of gender discourse can be best assessed through the distortion mirror of abnormality; perhaps – paradoxically – this distortion mirror shows us a clearer image than the comparatively polite contemporary discourse on what Lombroso and Ferrero called 'normal women'. When eighteenth- and nineteenth-century gender ideologues write about 'respectable' women transgressing gender norms (writers, actresses, the occasional 'scholarly' woman, or, *horribile dictu*, adulteresses or women who eloped), they touch the subject with the kid-gloves mandated by the contemporary discourse on morality, women's education, or the disastrous consequences of women's reading behaviour.[54] When they write about murderesses, the gloves come off.

---

[49] I am distinguishing here between 'Woman', a discursive concept, and empirical women (who are also, and have been historically, more often the victims than the perpetrators of crimes). On women as victims, see particularly Bronfen, *Over Her Dead Body*; Weigel, 'Die geopferte Heldin'; Huyssen; von Hoff; Geitner; and Richards.

[50] See the materials and discussion in Göttsch, who has made the point on 19.

[51] See chapter 6.

[52] Otto Ulbricht, 'Einleitung' to *Von Huren und Rabenmüttern*: 'Im Prinzip erscheint die Kriminalität von Frauen als weit weniger spektakulär als die von Männern, eher als gewöhnlich, als alltäglich, geradezu als "konformistisch"' (19).

[53] In his 'Einleitung' to *Von Huren und Rabenmüttern*, he speaks of the 'extreme Ideologieanfälligkeit' of research on the subject, adding: 'Es war in der Vergangenheit der ideale Tummelplatz für Vorurteile, Ideologien und Mythen über das weibliche Geschlecht ... so daß sie [diese Forschungen] sich jetzt geradezu als vorzügliche Quelle für das Denken über die Geschlechter anbieten' (25).

[54] See, among others, the texts by Campe, Fichte, Humboldt, Hegel, Kant, Knigge and Pockels.

Since my assumption here is that writings about extreme cases are most eloquent on the subject of gender normality, my thematic focus is on murderesses, the most extreme variety of criminal woman and therefore the least likely to be the subject of conciliatory representations. I have intentionally excluded from discussion women who acted in concert with someone else and who might therefore be represented as coerced, intimidated or misled.[55] Equally absent from this volume are female killers whose acts allow for sentimental interpretations as heroic deeds, self-defining acts, grand gestures or noble self-sacrifice: the shield-maidens, female warriors, amazons, political assassins and suicides. Nearly all of the 'heroines' of this book were, historically, on trial for murder (with the exception of Anna Göldi, who was tried for attempted murder), and many of the sources informing my analysis are sociological and historical. The main point of the book, however, will be cultural. If I involve a variety of different sources (including, but not limited to, philosophical, psychological, legal, literary, historical, sociological and anthropological), it is not to argue that literature should be measured against or compared with a social or historical 'reality', however perceived. Rather, I am writing from the conviction that the social, historical, legal and other sources describing events experienced as 'reality' by their authors are themselves highly literary. I hope to show that both forms of literature, the literary text that lays claim to historical accuracy and the one that admits to its own fictionality, have shaped how we think of people and the past: particularly the people we fear the most (for example, killers, or women), and particularly the past we revere the most (for example, the Enlightenment as the time where our ideas about freedom, equality and human rights originated, or the Age of Goethe, now commonly considered Germany's most glorious cultural period). This book hopes to provide some insights into the history of ideas about women and their cultural expression by examining this principal paradox: that criminal women, while empirically rare, are discursively ubiquitous, and that 'women' are, as Lynda Hart has put it, 'paradoxically constructed as both inherently violent and incapable of aggression'.[56]

IN THE HALL OF MIRRORS: THEORIES OF INVESTIGATION

In the eighteenth century, there was not yet a strict distinction between juridical and literary ideas about crime; the line between the 'facts of the case' and fiction was not firmly drawn until the professionalisation of both

---

[55] *Der neue Pitaval* tells many such stories (see Hitzig and Häring).   [56] Hart x.

law and literature around 1850.[57] Until then, even 'literary' crime writers
such as Meißner and Schiller were likely to emphasise that their stories were
based on actual court cases, and nothing in their reception indicates that
they were read as describing a world distinct from juridical practice.[58] The
Pitaval stories, which enjoyed great popularity in both centuries, have been
perceived as both a juridical and a literary phenomenon, by both scholars
and amateur readers.[59] Legal training in the eighteenth century usually
included the 'relation' of a criminal case, which had to incorporate both
juridical and poetical rules.[60] Although there were constant warnings
against overly 'fanciful' (*romanhaft*) portrayals, the *Pitaval* or *Pitaval*-type
collections were an integral part of the legal curriculum; they served 'to
increase judiciousness at trial', to educate magistrates on the law, even to
hone arguments proposing or opposing legal reform.[61] The great debates on
torture and the death penalty, reform debates, and new ideas in criminal
anthropology, psychology and sociology took place in fiction long before
they were given their day in court.[62] Ideas of right and wrong were the
terrain of literature, not law.

For the analysis of crime narratives written at a time that made little
distinction between legal and literary genres, the opposites fact and fiction,
authenticity and fabrication, cause and effect are extraordinarily blunt
analytical tools. Clearly, '"fictional literature" does not simply absorb
what is "secreted" from juridical theory and practice'.[63] Even the

---

[57] See, among others, Luhmann; Schönert, 'Zur Ausdifferenzierung', III; Schönert, Naucke and Imm, 'Zur Einführung', 17; Weiler 11–12.

[58] See, among others, Meyer-Krentler, particularly 119–20, and Dainat on Meißner and the *Pitaval* tradition. The crime stories of August Gottlieb Meißner (1753–1807) have recently been re-edited by Alexander Košenina.

[59] François Gayot de Pitaval's collection of *Causes célèbres*, originally published in 1734–43 in twenty volumes, was translated into German in the late eighteenth century. One hundred years later, its successor, *Der neue Pitaval*, had mushroomed to sixty volumes; the original author's name had become synonymous with the genre; and dozens of *Pitaval* imitations vied for a share of the market. On the *Pitaval* tradition, see particularly Linder, 'Deutsche Pitavalgeschichten'.

[60] Schild, 'Relationen und Referierkunst: Zur Juristenausbildung', 170.

[61] Rückert lists dozens of late eighteenth- and nineteenth-century *Pitaval*-type collections of criminal cases, many of which were recommended to and used by students of law or cited in books on jurisprudence (the quotation 'zur Vermehrung der Klugheit im Verfahren', 295).

[62] See the materials and discussion in Schönert, Naucke and Imm ('Zur Einführung'), who come to the same conclusion: 'Literarische Darstellungen des Verbrechens überschreiten seit dem Ausgang des 18. Jahrhunderts entschlossen die Perspektiven, die im tatorientierten Ermittlungs- und Strafverfahren gesetzt sind. So können in nicht-fachlichen "Erzählungen" über Kriminalität Diskussionen und Ergebnisse der Kriminalanthropologie, der Kriminalpsychologie, der Psychiatrie und Kriminalsoziologie Gewicht erhalten, ehe sie juristische Relevanz gewinnen' (35).

[63] Schönert, Naucke and Imm, 'Zur Einführung', 35: '[Es] wird deutlich, daß die "schöne Literatur" nicht einfach nur aufnimmt, was aus dem Bereich von juristischer Theorie und Praxis "abgegeben" wird.'

(undoubtedly true) statement that crime narratives, fictional or otherwise, were central in shaping both social ideas of criminality[64] and the legal discourse that responded to them[65] does not adequately describe the complex relationship between the various different text types I will discuss in this book. Certainly, (mimetic) art imitates life (Goethe's *Werther* may well have been 'inspired' by the suicide of his fellow student Karl Wilhelm Jerusalem), and quite possibly, life also imitates art (Goethe's *Werther* may well have 'inspired' some of his more impressionable readers to commit suicide). Neither statement, however, tells us much about Goethe's novel, his time, or, for that matter, contemporary ideas on suicide. To presume that the only possible relationship between a text and a context is causal is, to modify Joel Black's sardonic comment, to blame Homer for Alexander the Great;[66] it simultaneously diminishes the text and oversimplifies the context to the point of one-dimensionality. These thoughts are hardly original, but perhaps worth reiterating in a book that aims to point to connections between seemingly disparate things – belief in witchcraft and physiognomy (chapter 2), vampire fiction and gender theory (chapter 3), social thought and 'trivial' literature (chapter 4), the infanticide debate and bourgeois tragedies (chapter 5), psychology and poetry (chapter 6), and the literary and legal/social manifestations of executions (chapter 7). My goal is to accomplish this *without* reducing the discussion to the dissatisfying divide between 'literature' and 'real life', and without having to make the undoubtedly true but profoundly uninteresting claim that 'real life' is described in literature or that literature shapes 'real life'. To do so would be doubly inappropriate for the analysis of texts written during the period under discussion, a time before the professions of law, psychology, criminology and literature were clearly and irrevocably demarcated, and a time when 'the twofold aspect of transcript-based juridical reporting and the literary portrayal of the strange and psychologically remarkable'[67] could grace any text, whether it perceived itself as 'fact' or 'fiction'. To assume the literariness of texts is not, however, to say that there is no such thing as 'real

---

[64] 'Über die Erzählform wird Kriminalität gesellschaftlich hergestellt' (Seibert 85). See also Weiler, who has read the nineteenth-century *Pitaval* collection as fulfilling a medial function, namely, to define criminality for readers who had little personal experience with it (14).

[65] See Ludger Hoffmann, who cites Bennett and Feldman's *Reconstructing Reality in the Courtroom*: 'gegen einschlägige rechtssoziologische Auffassungen zur ausschlaggebenden Bedeutung von Faktoren wie Rasse, Schicht, Geschlecht, strategischem Geschick des Verteidigers etc. setzen sie die Plausibilität der *story*' (90–1).

[66] Black 11.

[67] 'der doppelte Aspekt von aktenmäßig-juristischem Referat und literarischer Darstellung des Merkwürdigen und psychologisch Besonderen' (Schönert, 'Zur Ausdifferenzierung', 111).

life'. It is rather to question the text's – any text's – ability to describe reality. My basic interpretive attitude throughout this study will be that there is a distinction between the history of events and the history of ideas, and that at times, although there may be serious discontinuities between them, the latter is mistaken for the former.[68]

My thinking about women and crime has been influenced, broadly speaking, by the fields of anthropology, social history, psychology, and feminist social and literary theories, and – in more specific terms – by Victor Turner, Judith Butler, Jacques Lacan, Sigrid Weigel, Michel Foucault and Norbert Elias (although I will not cite all of these authors all of the time). I owe my greatest intellectual debts to the anthropologist Victor Turner, whose ideas I am adapting for my purposes, and the social historian Michel Foucault, who has painted the largest and most impressive philosophical canvas on the subject to date (although I would quibble with him over some of his broader brushstrokes). Central for my understanding of the relationship between literary and non-literary, or less literary, genres is Turner's concept of 'modes of symbolic action', which he defines as 'the peculiar relationship between the mundane, everyday sociocultural processes (domestic, economic, political, legal and the like) found in societies … and what may be called … their dominant genres of "cultural performance"'.[69] His thesis is that this relationship is 'not unidirectional and "positive" – in the sense that the performative genre merely "reflects" or "expresses" the social system or the cultural configuration, … but that it is reciprocal and reflexive – in the sense that the performance is often a critique, direct or veiled, of the social life it grows out of, an evaluation (with lively possibilities of rejection) of the way society handles history'.[70] If authors, as he puts it,

'hold the mirror up to nature', they do this with 'magic mirrors' … The mirrors themselves are not mechanical, but consist of reflecting consciousnesses and the products of such consciousnesses formed into vocabularies and rules, into meta-linguistic grammars, by means of which new unprecedented performances may be generated … The result is something like a hall of mirrors – magic mirrors, each interpreting as well as reflecting the images beamed to it, and flashed from one to the others.[71]

---

[68] For a discussion of this phenomenon, see chapters 5 and 7.

[69] Turner, *Anthropology*, 21.

[70] Turner, *Anthropology*, 22. Eakin has proposed a similar process for the act of autobiographical writing, arguing that autobiographical writing is collaborative and that the self is 'made' in the act of narrating.

[71] Turner, *Anthropology*, 22, 24.

Throughout this book, I will read eighteenth- and nineteenth-century tales of women and murder – regardless of their genre or their degree of 'fictionality' – as 'magic mirrors', in the sense that I will assume them to 'interpret as well as reflect the images beamed into them'. Tales of murderous women – witches, vampires, husband-killers, child-killers and poisoners – told in court records, legal reform texts, press articles, broadsheets, ballads, poems, novels, crime stories, biographies and many other text genres will be examined for their potential to generate new 'unprecedented performances'. Turner's 'hall of mirrors' allows us to think of tales rooted in 'real life' (for example, interrogation reports or psychological profiles) and in 'literature' (for example, ballads and novels) not in terms of origin and influence, cause and effect, but as drawing water from the same well, the well in this case being contemporary ideas about crime and, more importantly, about women. In the hall of mirrors, all tales are more or less fictional, and in the act of interpretation, reflection and beaming back, they all participate in a cultural performance. My primary interest in these tales lies not in the chicken-and-egg question, but in the tenacity of these tales and the perniciousness of their meanings: how they reflect and interpret contemporary ideas about women and crime, what they add to this store of ideas when they are 'beamed back', why they persist, how they mutate, how they cross or cheerfully ignore genre borders between 'fact' and 'fiction' and between the legal and literary (or psychological, aesthetic, theological, etc.) realms. Throughout, I will presume that the cultural performers who add to the lore of women and crime incorporate both 'rehearsed' and 'spontaneous' elements into their performance. 'Rehearsed' elements describe the cultural heritage of ideas, passed down in tales and traditions until they become the things 'we have always known' about women: that they are too cowardly to use violence, for example, or that their cruelty, immorality, vanity, dishonesty etc. predestine them for crime. 'Spontaneous' elements would describe what cultural performers then do with this knowledge.[72]

Michel Foucault's *Discipline and Punish* has famously described *The Birth of the Prison* at the outset of modernity, which he places into the eighteenth and nineteenth centuries. This development takes place in the stages of torture (physical punishment), punishment ('gentle' and generalised punishments), discipline (the creation of a 'docile' body) and prison (modern life under incessant supervision from the 'network' of

---

[72] Helmut Walser Smith has taken a similar approach to his 'cameo history' of antisemitism, told through the lens of the murder of Ernst Winter in 1900 (see 177 on rehearsed and spontaneous elements of cultural performance).

schools, hospitals, factories and military institutions). Foucault's book pays more attention to the big philosophical picture than to historical detail. My agreements with Foucault are largely philosophical, my disagreements largely historical. Whereas Foucault claims that there is a transition in the eighteenth century from punishing the body to converting the soul,[73] I would argue that throughout the eighteenth century (and certainly earlier), the punishment of the body could only proceed once the soul had been 'converted', that is: once the culprit's submission, even joyous consent, to his or her own execution had been secured. Foucault, then, views the punishment of the body and the conversion of the soul as successive events; I view them as concurrent and related. Foucault sees the punishment of the body as a public spectacle and the conversion of the soul as a surreptitious act; I would argue that the conversion of the soul was *part* of the public spectacle that ended in the punishment of the body (expressed in the 'poor sinner's' final words from the scaffold, for example). Foucault reads crimes and punishments as social and political events and texts, including literary texts, as social signs; I consider the literary aspects of social and political events, including executions, and read all texts as more or less 'literary', no matter what their provenance or self-presentation. Foucault's watchwords are 'political technology';[74] mine are 'cultural coding'.

Like Foucault, however, I am as concerned with social and cultural ideas as I am with the changes in the penal system. And like Turner, I am interested in showing that these ideas are created in 'cultural performances', which I would define, for the purposes of this project, as the telling of tales: tales whose relationship with each other may be causal, contrastive, or simply parallel, all of them reflecting, interpreting, mutating, creating and recreating the same thought system on women and crime.

SEARCHING THE SCENE OF THE CRIME: MODUS OPERANDI

Not all heroines described in this book were German. Not all main authors discussed in this book were German. But all sources, both literary and historical, discussed here were either written in German and/or in German-speaking lands, thus participating in and shaping a German cultural debate. This book examines gender codes in German culture during a time when Germany as a political unit did not exist. By German 'culture' I mean both a language community and a desire to identify with a cultural 'Germany' that

---

[73] Foucault 16–19.   [74] Foucault 24.

is clearly recognisable in the German/Austrian, Swiss and Hungarian sources I have used.

The chapters are essayistic in nature; each can stand alone or be read in conjunction with its neighbours. Each professes an interest in what Walser Smith has termed 'cameo history'[75] as well as larger philosophical, social, political or aesthetic contexts. The cases of the 'witch' Anna Göldi (chapter 2), the 'vampire' Elizabeth Báthory (chapter 3), the husband-killers Maria Katharina Wächtler and Christiane Ruthardt (chapter 4), the infanticides Dorothea Altwein and Johanna Höhn (chapter 5), and the poisoners Anna Margaretha Zwanziger and Gesche Gottfried (chapter 6) will be discussed in their own rights, not merely as exemplifications of a larger point. They will also, however, serve as the catalyst for difficult questions about the interaction of cultural spheres. How did the belief in witchcraft of the seventeenth century resurface in eighteenth-century art (aesthetic theories) and science (physiognomy)? How did the spectre of the female vampire arise in history and myth, how did it mutate in literature, and what do female vampires have to do with contemporary gender ideology and aesthetic hierarchies? Why were some of the most important legal reform debates not waged in the legal but in the literary realm? Why can infanticide be read both as the utter repudiation and the classic exemplification of 'femininity'; why did ideas on gender rather than class set the terms of the infanticide debate, and how did literary images of infanticide complicate court cases? What is the link, if any, between a woman's class and her 'character', and between female criminality and female normality? And finally: what do their theatrical and literary aspects tell us about executions, and what do executions tell us about gender, humanity and civilisation? As is readily apparent, these questions contain not only historical, social and cultural ramifications, but also what Kant would have called an ethical charge. We may not be able to answer them all, but we are required, for reasons both intellectual and ethical, to consider them.

Since my conclusions rely on many obscure sources – some of which exist only in handwritten form and others in difficult-to-obtain rare copies – and since I would like readers to be able to draw their own conclusions, I quote extensively. All English translations of German, French, Italian and Latin primary or secondary sources throughout the book are my own unless otherwise indicated.

Each chapter represents an investigation of a case and a (legal, literary, social, political, psychological) context. At the end of the investigation,

[75] For his discussion of the term, see 21–2.

readers may find something as solid as a verdict or something as insub-
stantial as a suspicion. My attitude towards conclusions has been shaped
significantly by two great writers on the subject of eighteenth-century
crime: Michel Foucault on the one hand and the historian Richard Evans
on the other. Foucault tends to make sweeping – if extremely persuasive and
elegantly expressed – statements about humanity at large based on very little
historical evidence, leaving his readers in a state of excited suspicion. Evans
tells his readers every single story, fact and anecdote unearthed in his
painstaking historical research, and draws only sparing conclusions from
this vast amount of material, leaving his readers in admiring exasperation.
One deprives us of the material that would enable us to follow his grand
claims, nodding along in agreement, as it were; the other deprives us of his
own expertise as an interpreter, as the mediator between the material and
the reader. Both Foucault and Evans are titans shouldering a mountain. I
am someone standing on the side of the mountain, someone who has picked
up some interesting, if misshapen, pebbles. The ultimate goal of this study is
to ask, and entice readers to wonder, what the pebbles can tell us about the
mountain. Sometimes concrete conclusions can be drawn. In other cases, I
found that I had enough evidence for a search warrant, but not enough for a
conviction.

What this book sets out to do, more than anything else, is search the
scene of the crime. For this reason, it is more prone to asking questions than
answering them, more likely to complicate matters than to resolve
complications.

CHAPTER 2

The evil eye: witches

By common accord, the eradication of the belief in witchcraft is one of the most important ways in which the Enlightenment practised progress. It was the age when experimental and mathematical sciences began to form the basis of new philosophies; mechanistic processes supplanted the spiritual as a method of explaining the world; belief in witchcraft and other super-stitions began to lose their validity, and – accordingly – witch-hunts, trials and executions became a thing of the less enlightened past.[1] But much evidence indicates that contrary to established wisdom, the old superstitions were not abandoned during the Age of Reason, but co-existed comfortably alongside new intellectual and philosophical thought systems like Cartesianism and Deism. The belief in witchcraft weathered the Enlightenment in two ways: out in the open – in the form of eighteenth-century witch-hunts and executions – and underground, sublimated not only in the fairy tales of Romanticism, as is so often claimed,[2] but in physiognomy, a discipline embraced or at least condoned by the best and brightest of the enlightened age, including Goethe, Herder, Lenz, Nicolai and Mendelssohn.[3] Throughout, I will take a look at an organ that has not only played an important role in both the belief in witchcraft and physiog-nomy, but is also at the centre of the enlightened credo 'seeing is believing': the eye.

---

[1] See Martin Pott, *Aufklärung und Aberglaube*, 193 and 'Aufklärung und Hexenaberglaube'; Harmening, *Zauberei*, 18–19, 126. Most recently, Alexander has placed the time 'the witch executions ... ceased in Germany' around 1700 (330). And Hauser, writing about the witch trial of Anna Göldi towards the end of the Enlightenment, nevertheless maintains that the Enlightenment brought witch trials to an end ('Der Hexenwahn fand erst ein Ende, als im Zeitalter der Aufklärung die menschliche Vernunft und das damit zusammenhängende Denken den Glauben an Hexen und Teufel verdrängten', 51). A more differentiated account of the belief in witchcraft during the Enlightenment can be found in Porter. – This chapter is a revised and updated version of my earlier article 'Ancient Fears and the New Order', *German Life and Letters* 61.1 (2008), 61–78.
[2] For example Geyer-Kordesch 145.   [3] Gray, *About Face*, xxxvi.

WHEN LOOKS COULD KILL: THE CASE OF ANNA GÖLDI
(GLARUS, 1782)

The belief in witchcraft, far from being relegated to the scrap heap of historical superstitions, was a subject of intense debate during the Enlightenment. The most renowned thinkers of the age, including Montaigne, Descartes, Althusius, Hobbes and Thomasius, wrote seriously about demonology.[4] Throughout the eighteenth century and the two centuries that followed, the supernatural found vigorous defenders against the encroaching tide of enlightened scepticism.[5] Medical advances aside,[6] there were still enough doctors claiming that most diseases were a direct result of demonic possession or bewitchment, among them the prominent Halle medical professor Friedrich Hoffmann, who claimed that the devil acted upon witches through animal spirits,[7] and the magical healer and exorcist Johann Joseph Gassner, who linked all diseases to witchcraft, attracted a considerable following in the 1770s and counted the renowned physiognomist Johann Caspar Lavater among his disciples.[8] Early in the century, Christoph and Hermann Anton von Chlingensperg, both professors of law at the University of Ingolstadt, confirmed the validity of witch prosecutions in keeping with the methods described in Kramer and Sprenger's *Malleus Maleficarum* (1486),[9] and Ernst Johann Friedrich Mantzel, a professor at the University of Halle, famously defended the prosecution of witches on the grounds that they, 'having denied God and made a pact with the Devil, should be punished with death in accordance with divine command'.[10] Ferdinand Sterzinger's 1766 speech to the Bavarian Academy of Sciences, in which he contemptuously repudiated the belief in witchcraft, led to an uproar of fury and a flurry of publications, many of which undertook to prove the existence of witches and legitimise continued witch trials and executions.[11] The legal basis for such trials remained in place in nearly all German states throughout the century,

---

[4] Behringer, *Hexenverfolgung in Bayern*, viii.

[5] A few examples of many, one from each century since the eighteenth: *Evidences* and Elworthy describe contemporary supernatural occurrences and incidents of witchcraft in various countries. Friend offers magical remedies for anything from demon possession to toothache and informs readers about animal magic, charms and the elixir of life. In *Verbotene Künste*, Labouvie has documented the continued existence of the belief in magic in the Saar region until deep into the nineteenth century.

[6] For a discussion of eighteenth-century medicine and its relation to magic, see Geyer-Kordesch.

[7] Porter 230.   [8] Behringer, *Hexenverfolgung*, 394–7.

[9] Behringer, *Hexenverfolgung*, 341.

[10] See Mantzel; the citation is taken from Levack, 'Decline', 44.

[11] Behringer, *Hexenverfolgung*, 371–84; Harmening, *Zauberei*, 114. For an account of this debate, see Behringer, 'Der "Bayerische Hexenkrieg"'.

despite some evidence of progress.[12] The edicts of King Friedrich Wilhelm I of Prussia (1714) and Empress Maria Theresia (1766), for instance, are often cited as irrefutable signs that witchcraft was decriminalised during the enlightened age. Neither edict, however, denied the existence of witches or banned witch trials; rather, they sought to control them: both edicts required that all judicial decisions either to torture or execute witches be submitted to the king or empress for confirmation before implementation.[13]

The most significant indication that the belief in witchcraft was alive and well during the Age of Enlightenment is, of course, the persistence of witch trials and executions throughout the age.[14] Such trials occurred too frequently to be considered aberrations. Wolfgang Behringer has documented 113 witch executions during the eighteenth century, not in Germany, but in Bavaria *alone*, and considers this number a low estimate.[15] In the Austro-Hungarian Empire, the last witch execution took place in 1777, eleven years after Maria Theresia's edict.[16] Death sentences for witches were carried out in Prussia in 1714, the year of Friedrich Wilhelm's edict; in Augsburg and in Westphalia in 1728, the year of Thomasius's death; in Würzburg in 1749, the year of Goethe's birth; in Württemberg in 1749 and 1751, the year in which Diderot and d'Alembert published the first volume of their *Encyclopédie*; in Schleswig-Holstein in 1752, the year in which Benjamin Franklin invented the lightning rod; in Kempten in 1775, the year after the publication of Goethe's *Werther*; in Glarus in Switzerland in 1782, the year after Lessing's death.[17] In Bavaria, the most active German state in terms of witch-hunting, there were single executions in 1740, 1745, 1749, 1750, 1751, 1752, 1754, 1755 and 1756 and recurring mass trials during which between sixty and 200 persons were accused of witchcraft and dozens were executed.[18] Numerous cases besides these are known of women who were

---

[12] On the legal situation in general, see Trusen.

[13] For Friedrich Wilhelm I's edict, see Levack, 'Decline', 76. For Maria Theresia's edict, see Behringer, *Hexenverfolgung*, 385; Porter 214–16; and Klaniczay, 'The Decline' and 'Historische Hintergründe'.

[14] Georg Conrad Horst discusses a number of eighteenth-century witch trials in his *Zauber-Bibliothek* (see II 147–250, 351–75; III 161–202; IV 201–18; V 231–5). See also Roper's discussion of the case of the Württemberg villager Catharina Schmid and her daughter Maria Dornhauser, executed for witchcraft in 1746 ('A Witch in the Age of Enlightenment').

[15] See his list of trials and executions in the appendix of *Hexenverfolgung*, 462–9; see also his *Witches and Witch-Hunts*, 188–95, for eighteenth-century witch executions in Europe. Another interesting case, that of the 'child witches' in Augsburg in the 1720s, is related by Alexander, who reads the case as evidence that 'the old symbolic economy of witchcraft was crumbling' (330–5, the citation 334).

[16] Gijswijt-Hofstra 161.

[17] Gijswijt-Hofstra 162–3, 168, 172–3; Levack, 'Decline', 8, 77–8.

[18] Behringer, *Hexenverfolgung*, 342–54, 359. Specific cases are described in the following sources: Behringer, *Hexenverfolgung*, 357–69; Roper, 'A Witch'; Lorenz; Bösken; Bader; Hasler; Hauser; Lehmann; and Memminger.

accused as witches and died in prison as a result of torture.[19] Torture, despite growing doubts about its efficacy and the reliability of confessions extracted under torture, continued to be used[20] and remained the principal means of exhorting confessions in witch trials.

Eighteenth-century believers in witchcraft recognised a witch by the same mark as their forefathers did: the evil eye. 'All witches possess the evil eye, and that is one of the ways they produce their maleficia ... Germans look with suspicion on those with red eyes ... Often it is a glaring or piercing eye that is to be feared.'[21] The belief in the evil eye as a reliable indication of witchcraft endured until the end of the century: in 1793, two women were sentenced to be burned as witches because their eyes were inflamed and their neighbour's cattle fell sick.[22] Since the *Malleus Maleficarum*, the evil eye has been indelibly connected with witchcraft and sexual passion[23] (which the authors of the *Malleus* famously attributed particularly to women[24]). Learned eighteenth-century dissertations proclaimed the injurious powers of the witch's evil eye even at great distance:

In this manner, old malicious crones or other women of evil complexion, who gaze upon the moon while menstruating, send the poisonous spirits or rays of their eyes streaming up towards it, and in so doing they cast the evil eye on other, healthy people who simultaneously, at that very moment, look at the moon, and do them considerable harm.[25]

Unmistakable owners of the evil eye were women with rolling eyes, doubled or lengthy pupils (cat eyes), red or inflamed eyes, dry (unweeping)

---

[19] Examples are cited by Grießhammer 107–9; Behringer, *Hexenverfolgung*, 355.

[20] See Levack, 'Decline', 21–2; Lorenz; Helbing; Zagolla; Zelle, 'Autorität'; and most recently the contributions in Helmut Jacobs's anthology. For a more extensive discussion of torture in the eighteenth century, see chapter 4.

[21] Louis C. Jones 152. See also Coss and Elworthy.   [22] See Helbing II 157.

[23] Robbins 24. For relevant passages on the evil eye in the *Malleus*, see Sprenger and Institoris 29–34.

[24] All witchcraft, according to Kramer and Sprenger, 'derives from carnal lust, which is in women insatiable': 'Prov. Penult.: "Drei Dinge sind unersättlich etc. und das vierte, das niemals sagt: genug!, nämlich der Schlund der Gebärmutter." Darum haben sie auch mit den Dämonen zu schaffen, um ihre Lust zu stillen' (Kramer and Sprenger 238). Sexual aberration also played a significant role in the interrogation of Catharina Schmid and her daughter Maria Dornhauser, executed for witchcraft in 1746 (Roper, 'A Witch').

[25] 'So bringen alte boshaftige Vetteln, oder auch andere Weibspersonen, welche böser Complexion seynd, und bei ihrem habenden Menstruo in den Mond sehen, und ihre gifftige Augengeister oder Strahlen gegen denselbigen ausfließen lassen, anderen gesunden Leuthen, welche eben zu derselbigen Zeit und in solchem Moment den Mond anschauen, dadurch böse Augen zu wege und fügen ihnen merklichen Schaden zu.' From an unattributed eighteenth-century treatise quoted by the ophthalmologist S. Seligmann (I 7–8).

eyes, droopy eyes, bushy eyebrows, cataracts, one-eyed or cross-eyed women,[26] or simply women who stared: 'There is general unanimity in the belief that the effect of the evil eye is brought about by staring at the victim. The direct, long-held, piercing stare is what people fear and recognise as the one, which carries malevolent power. ... Staring, then, is the physical method by which the evil passes from the eye to the victim.'[27] Strangely – and this connection will interest us later –, the evil eye was also linked with intuition, postulating that such 'in-sight', the ability to grasp the unknown with the mind's eye, is intrinsically related to the faculty of sight.[28]

The case of Anna Göldi, born in 1734 and beheaded in 1782, has much to teach us about the belief in witchcraft in the late Enlightenment. Göldi, a domestic servant accused of bewitching her employer's daughter, was simultaneously the last woman executed as a witch in Europe and the first 'witch' whose execution sparked any kind of public disagreement or debate. Described in several books, novels, articles and even a documentary film, Göldi's case is probably the best-documented witch trial of this or any age.[29] In the year that marked the 225th anniversary of her death, Göldi was showered with honours in recompense for her execution: Glarus now boasts an 'Anna Göldi Foundation';[30] the Anna Göldi Museum in Mollis opened on 22 September 2007; the Wiessstrasse in Mollis was renamed 'Anna-Göldi-Weg' in autumn 2007; and an Anna Göldi festival, on which the canton of Glarus is expected to spend as much as 120,000 Swiss francs, is planned for 2010.[31] Although the Glarus Parliament did not rehabilitate Göldi at its initial meeting on the question in September 2007, this was the first session of any European parliament concerning itself with the rehabilitation of a woman executed as a witch.[32] In August 2008, the Glarus Parliament unanimously decided in favour of Göldi's rehabilitation.[33] The

---

[26] Seligmann I 66–79.   [27] Louis C. Jones 156.   [28] Meerloo 119.

[29] Aside from several smaller works such as newspaper articles and websites, literature on Göldi now comprises the works by Hasler; Lehmann; Freuler (novel); Wimmer; Winteler; Pinkus (screenplay); 'Anna Göldin – letzte Hexe' (documentary film); and most recently Hauser's book, which includes transcriptions of archival documents and some new documentary evidence and offers a brief overview of the most important publications from 1865 to 1992 (44–9). See also Behringer's brief account of the story in *Witches and Witch-Hunts*, 190–1.

[30] Walter Hauser, the initiator of the foundation (www.anna-goeldi.ch, last accessed on 24 June 2008) and many efforts to rehabilitate Göldi, is also the author of the most recent study about her case.

[31] See Hauser 200; the announcement of the level of funding on the Göldi website www.anna-goeldi.ch.

[32] For local press coverage on these remedial initiatives and public debate, see the articles by Rohner. On the parliamentary session, see the article 'Anna Göldi bleibt Hexe'. See also Hauser on efforts at rehabilitation (176–83).

[33] 'Die letzte Hexe Europas wird voll rehabilitiert' (9).

only contemporary analysis of the case based on the trial records and contemporary witness accounts is the *Confidential Letters to a Friend* (*Freundschaftliche und vertrauliche Briefe*) authored by Heinrich Ludewig Lehmann (1754–1828) and published in two parts in 1783, the year after Göldi's execution. The first part is dedicated to Lehmann's interpretation of the case in letters to an unnamed friend and a Dr Schintz in Zurich, 'who very much doubted the truth of the matter and wished to obtain further clarification'.[34] The second part contains trial records as well as letters and depositions from persons directly connected with the case: witnesses, physicians, accusers and prosecutors (all, in fact, except for the accused).

The facts on which the various (sometimes fictitious and often biased) accounts from three centuries agree are these: from 1780 on, Anna Göldi, a woman in her forties, served as a housemaid in the Swiss canton of Glarus in the house of Dr Johann Jakob Tschudi, whose second eldest daughter, eight-year-old Anna Maria (known as Anna Migeli) accused Göldi of having put pins in her morning milk. The pins kept appearing in the milk, and Göldi was discharged. Shortly before her dismissal, Göldi officially accused her employer of sexual abuse. She left her (for a servant) substantial savings, sixteen doubloons, in the charge of her only friend in town, the metalworker Rudolf Steinmüller, with a request to send them after she established herself elsewhere. After Göldi's departure, Anna Migeli began to vomit pins and nails on a daily basis (whereas by all reports she always managed to get a good night's sleep). The town councillors had Göldi arrested and kept her in prison for seventeen weeks while they debated whether a witchcraft case should be heard before a Catholic or a Protestant council.[35] Meanwhile, all efforts to cure Anna Migeli had failed; one magic healer pronounced her incurable by all but the person who had harmed her. Accordingly, the town councillors, led by Dr Tschudi, asked Göldi to cure the child, promising her a reduced sentence if her cure was successful and threatening her with torture if she refused. Göldi hesitated, which may indicate that she was aware of the trap: refusal would result in torture; consent was tantamount to a confession. In the end, she agreed to help, all the while insisting on her innocence, and indeed managed to cure the afflicted child within days. Anna Migeli responded to Göldi's help by claiming that she (Anna Migeli) had been bewitched by a magic biscuit designed to make her vomit pins, baked by Steinmüller and administered by Göldi, and that Göldi had only put the pins in her milk to cover up her crime. Göldi

---

[34] '… der die Wahrheit der Sache sehr bezweifelte, und eine nähere Aufklärung zu haben wünschte' (Lehmann, part 1 'An den Leser', unpag.).
[35] On the consequences of confessional differences for the Göldi case, see Hauser 99–103.

initially refused to incriminate Steinmüller, but finally did so under torture, at times recanting her testimony against him and claiming that she had poisoned the child with the Devil's help.[36] Steinmüller was nevertheless arrested and hanged himself in prison. Göldi was beheaded and her body buried beneath the gallows; her savings and Steinmüller's estate were used to defray the substantial costs of the trial. Göldi's employer, Dr Tschudi, was officially cleared of all suspicion of inappropriate behaviour toward her.

Göldi's trial was highly publicised, not only throughout Switzerland but in Germany as well, and had two immediate consequences. One was a veritable epidemic of bewitched children spitting pins and needles (some of whom later admitted or were discovered to have simulated their affliction[37]), which resulted in another accusation of witchcraft.[38] The other was a minor, but nonetheless noticeable, surge of dissent, perhaps the first critical response to a specific witch trial.[39] In an article in the *Göttinger Staats-Anzeigen*, August Ludwig Schlözer coined the term 'Justizmord' (judicial murder, edition of 4 January 1783); and the satirist Wilhelm Ludwig Wekherlin published a highly sarcastic account of the case in the *Chronologen* of Nuremberg, for which the canton of Glarus declared him an outlaw.[40] In Switzerland itself there was no criticism of either the case or the sentence, perhaps understandably, given the following passage in Göldi's death sentence:

Whosoever dares to condemn, disparage or attempt to avenge the poor sinner's death, now or in the future, or vilify, hate or denigrate anyone for it, he or she will, according to the edict and decree of our Penal Code, follow in the poor sinner's footsteps, be treated in a like manner, and be subject to the same sentence.[41]

---

[36] See the transcript of six interrogations, three under torture, in Hauser 113–39.

[37] Simulation is also the obvious explanation for Anna Migeli Tschudi's condition. Eyewitnesses stated that whenever Anna Migeli was overcome by the urge to vomit pins and nails, her mother judiciously blocked the child from view and covered the child's mouth with a white cloth, which invariably, once withdrawn, contained a pin or a nail. All twenty witnesses to these scenes were related to, friends with or employed by the Tschudis (see Hauser 74–5).

[38] Elsbeth Bösch from Toggenburg was accused of having bewitched fourteen-year-old Heinrich Kubli, who was kept under observation and soon cured. Bösch, terrified of being tortured, jumped out of the window of the interrogation room and broke both feet. She was acquitted, but remained crippled for life. See Hasler 252; Hauser 76.

[39] As opposed to the great texts condemning witch trials in general, such as Friedrich von Spee's *Cautio Criminalis* (originally published in 1632).

[40] For responses to the case, see Hasler 251–2; Hauser 144–50.

[41] 'Ob dann jemand wäre, der jetzt oder hernach des armen Menschen Tod änzte, äferte oder zu rächen unterstände, und jemand darum bächte, hassete, oder schmähte, der oder die solches thäten, sollen laut unserer Malefiz-Gerichtsordnung in des armen Menschen Urthel und Fußstapfen erkannt seyn, und gleichergestalten über sie gerichtet werden' ('Malefiz-Process und Urtheil über die zum Schwerdt verurtheilte Anna Göldinn aus dem Sennwald verurtheilt den 17. Junii 1782', addendum no. 12, cited in Lehmann, part II 88–96). The original death sentence is in the Landesarchiv Glarus.

The threat to execute anyone who objected to the execution of a witch in the same manner, an integral part of the judicial system dealing with witch trials, had been one of the recommendations of the *Malleus* and effectively suppressed any kind of discussion of or objection to the persecution of witches for centuries. Without question, this passage is one aspect that marks this case as a traditional witch trial, as it might well have occurred in the 1580s rather than the 1780s, with little to mark the passage of 200 years or the advent of the Enlightenment. Another is the fact that Göldi's warrant lists, as one of her distinguishing features, her red eyes and her furtive stare, presumably intended to hide her inflamed eyes: 'Anna Göldi … has grey and somewhat unhealthy eyes that appear reddish most of the time, her gaze is downcast …'.[42] This and other aspects of the trial – among them the credence given to Göldi's repeated statement that she was in league with the Devil and the emphasis in the court records that Göldi did not weep, even under torture[43] – indicate that Göldi's persecutors not only adhered strictly to the judicial procedures advocated in the *Malleus*, but were also affected by the myth of the evil eye and other superstitions that seem to have no place in the Age of Enlightenment.

The single aspect that marks the case of Anna Göldi as an Enlightenment witch trial, oxymoronic as that may sound, is the defensive tone with which Lehmann tells the tale. Not only does he anticipate verbosely the scorn of the sceptics, philosophers and free spirits against whom he feels compelled to break a lance for the 'truth'.[44] He also seeks to distance himself from his own text and its twofold project of affirming that Göldi got no more than she deserved and defending her prosecutors and judges, 'the sage authorities of Glarus',[45] in Lehmann's deferential turn of the phrase, from criticism. Among these distancing techniques is the pretence that if he had not agreed to publish his letters, they would have appeared without his consent.[46] This fiction, while standard for eighteenth-century women authors,[47] is unusual

---

[42] 'Anna Göldin … hat graue etwas ungesunde Augen, welche meistens rothlecht aussehen, ihr Anschauen ist niedergeschlagen …'. Warrant on Anna Göldi published in *Neue Zürcher Zeitung*, 9 February 1782 (unpag.), reprinted in Hauser (61, facsimile on 62). Göldi's purported accomplice, Rudolf Steinmüller, is likewise described by Lehmann, who, writing months after Steinmüller's death, could not have known him in person, as 'a small, dark, wizened and bald sixty-year-old midget with bulging eyes' ('ein kleines, schwarzes, hageres, kahlköpfiges, 60 Jahr altes Männchen, mit hervorstechenden Augen', part 1 56).

[43] Witches were assumed to be incapable of shedding tears. For these facets of Göldi's trial, see Hauser 142.

[44] 'May the free spirits, philosophers and psychologists say what they will – for me it is enough to have told the truth' ('Meinetwegen mögen Schöngeister, Philosophen und Psychologen daraus machen, was ihnen beliebt – für mich ists genug, Wahrheit erzehlt zu haben', Lehmann, part 1, 'An den Leser', unpag.).

[45] Lehmann, part 1 43: '[d]ie wohlweise Obrigkeit von Glarus'.

[46] Lehmann, part 1, 'An den Leser', unpag.: 'mein Freund in Bünden bedrohete mich so gar: diese Briefe ohne meine Einwilligung drucken zu lassen'.

[47] See Kord, *Sich einen Namen machen*.

for male writers of the age and indicates the extent to which the author perceived his own premises as assailable. Lehmann's letters purport to be personal letters written to an unnamed friend, but numerous aspects define these epistles as a highly fictionalised apologia of the verdict, written with publication in mind, possibly even at the behest of the Glarus 'authorities', in the sheep's clothing of a private correspondence.[48] Suspiciously, the letters are stripped of all identifying characteristics (date, place, addressee); none of them ever refer to answering letters from the purported correspondent. Lehmann's introduction to the second volume points to the sensation his account caused and announces a third volume.[49] Although this third volume never appeared, the announcement reveals how Lehmann saw this venture: from the standpoint of a successful publication, a third volume would make more sense than from the standpoint of a factual, disinterested case history, which had moreover exhausted its store of original court documents and witness accounts in the second volume.[50]

Even more suspicious, because clearly designed to pre-empt the reader's scepticism, is Lehmann's self-stylisation as the 'doubting Thomas'[51] who initially scoffs at the superstitious fancies of the good people of Glarus but is finally convinced by the irrefutable facts of the case:

Now that I have studied the facts as closely as possible, all the objections that I had voiced as a declared enemy of demonology … have been utterly vanquished … Thus, in deference to the truth and for love of this divine virtue, I must needs confess: the story is true.[52]

---

[48] But see Hauser, who has read Lehmann's account as a criticism of Göldi's trial and verdict, going so far as to claim that 'Lehmann's treatise, originally intended to vindicate the Glarus authorities, turned out to be an invective against them' ('Lehmanns Schrift, gedacht zur Ehrenrettung der glarnerischen Obrigkeit, geriet zu einer Schmähschrift gegen dieselbe', 18). Hauser's theory is that Lehmann intended to criticise corrupt politics in Glarus (see 16–22 and 141; on the political background and possibilities of political opposition in eighteenth-century Switzerland, see particularly 151–63). While it is true that there was a falling-out between Lehmann and the Glarus officials shortly after publication of Lehmann's first volume (see note 61 below), I can find no sign of criticism of the trial and death sentence in Lehmann's work itself, or indeed an indication that Lehmann intended for the work to be anything but a justification of these proceedings and the authorities' handling of the case. Since Hauser does not cite exact sources for his quotations, it is often difficult to verify the documentary basis for his interpretations.

[49] Lehmann, part II, 'An den Leser', unpag.

[50] Hauser has read this announcement quite differently, namely as a direct threat to publish court records for the expressed purpose of indicting the Glarus proceedings (21).

[51] E.g. part I 14–48, the citation 'mich ungläubigen Thomas' on 15.

[52] 'Die Thatsache, die ich nun so genau untersucht habe, als es nur möglich gewesen ist, hat alle meine Einwürfe, die ich als ein Feind der Dämonologie … machte, gänzlich getödtet … so muß ich dennoch lediglich zur Ehre der Wahrheit und aus Liebe zu dieser göttlichen Tugend gestehen: die Geschichte ist wahr' (Lehmann, part I 37).

Despite Lehmann's ceaseless reiteration of this truth-claim, some features of his text are clearly defining characteristics of fiction, among them his gushy dramatisation of scenes that he did not witness[53] and his speculations regarding the innermost thoughts of people he never encountered in person. Where dramatisation and speculation occur in Lehmann's narrative, they are habitually presented as indisputable facts. Consider, for example, Lehmann's account of Steinmüller's last moments in prison:

Now, perhaps, he was beset by the most melancholy reflections; he saw himself forced to confess his terrible secret – for that is what it was, and will now remain so in all eternity – either voluntarily or under torture. The immensity of his crime, the terror of the shameful death that he would now have to suffer at the executioner's hands, the torments of an evil conscience – all these beset his heart; his nerves were shaken or strained beyond endurance; he succumbed to despair and died that death that many Turkish nobles are forced to die: he strangled himself, not with the help of a silk cord but with that of a length of linen torn off his bed sheet.[54]

---

[53] Lehmann arrived in Glarus two months after Göldi's execution (Hauser 15) and thus did not have first-hand knowledge of the events he described. Consider one scene in which he describes Frau Tschudi's maternal distress upon encountering her suffering child: 'The best of mothers, cast to the ground by the most distressing sentiments, her eyes shrouded by the veil of melancholy, the pallor of death on her face, her soul beset by the depths of anxious despair, wanted to weep but could not; deep sighs choked the anguished cry that grief forced from her; faltering, she sank into her husband's arms, seeking solace from one who was himself inconsolable. The poor child, who, on occasion, revived from her faint, her head thrown back, her back arched inward, held out her little arms towards her mother with a glance that demanded such utter compassion, that pleaded so earnestly for relief, and with such tears of helplessness, that everyone present – no matter with which beliefs, attitudes, knowledge or preparation they had come –, found here a scene that moved them to fury, horror and fear, that stirred them to rescue the child, if not, to weep' ('Die beste Mutter von den traurigsten Empfindungen zu Boden gedrückt, die Augen verhüllt mit dem Schleier der Wehmuth, Todesblässe auf dem Antlitz, die Seele versenkt in die Fülle einer bangen Verzweiflung, wollte weinen und konnte nicht, tiefe Seufzer erstickten den jammernden Ton, welche ihr der Schmerz auspreßte, taumelnd sank sie in die Arme des Gatten, und suchte Trost bey dem, der selbst untröstbar war. Das arme, sich zuweilen aus seiner Sinnlosigkeit erholende Kind streckte mit hinabwärts liegendem Kopfe und einwärts gekrümmten Rücken seine Aermlein mit so einem ihr ohnehin schon volles Mitleiden und Beistehen fodernden Blick, mit so vielem Weinen der Hülflosigkeit nach der Mutter aus, daß jeder, er mochte mit einem Herzen, einer Faßung, Kenntniß und Vorbereitung gekommen seyn, mit welcher er wollte, hier eine Scene antraf, die ihn rührte, bey der er zörnen, schaudern, erschrecken, retten und weinen wollte' (Lehmann, part 1 64–5). Considering that Lehmann did not witness this scene or meet anyone described in it until months after these events had taken place, the only thing that could account for such detail and sentimentality is a literary imagination run wild.

[54] 'Nun mochte er den traurigsten Betrachtungen nachhangen; er sahe sich genöthiget, sein schreckliches Geheimniß, denn das war es, und wird es nun auch in Ewigkeit bleiben, entweder gütlich, oder peinlich zu gestehen; die Größe seines Verbrechens, das Schreckliche eines entehrenden Todes, den er von der Hand des Nachrichters würde erdulden müßen, die Qualen eines bösen Gewissens – alles stürmte auf sein Herz los, sein Nervensystem ward erschüttert oder überspannt, er gerieth in Verzweiflung, und starb den Tod, den so mancher türkische Große gezwungen sterben muß, er erwürgte sich selbst, doch nicht mit einem seidenen Stricke, sondern mit einer vom Leintuch abgerißnen Binde' (Lehmann, part 1 92–3).

Even the most trusting of Lehmann's readers must have known that unless Lehmann – who had arrived in Glarus months after these events – had been present at Steinmüller's suicide and witness to his final exclamations of despair, he could not possibly have known any of the things he relates in this passage. But only a single word, 'perhaps' (in German the first verb 'mochte'), marks this passage as the pure fantasy that it is; in the same sentence, Lehmann quickly reclaims discursively the definition of his tale as an objective account of facts ('for that is what it was'). Both the tortuous detail of Steinmüller's thoughts and the mention of his means of suicide are meant to underscore the story's factuality. It is easy to see why: to justify the Glarus verdict in the near-total absence of actual evidence against either Steinmüller or Göldi, Lehmann attempts to 'prove' Steinmüller's guilt, as well as silence the plausible suspicion that Steinmüller might not so conveniently have done away with himself. 'This is included in my account because it was rumoured in Glarus that the unhappy man's accomplices had killed him in prison for fear of being betrayed by him.'[55] In two volumes, this is the only sentence that mentions Steinmüller's 'accomplices', possibly because this is the only passage where they have a part to play: to distract the reader's attention away from the possibility that Steinmüller was indeed murdered in prison, but not by accomplices, but by the 'wise and enlightened authorities'[56] of Glarus. Lehmann himself inadvertently brings up this possibility in his mention of the Turkish nobles who received the silk cord from their sultan (the Turkish 'authorities'), a gift that amounted to a direct order to commit immediate suicide.

Lehmann never answers the question that would most obviously occur to the reader: why he became involved in the case in the first place. He offers no explanation as to why he, a theology student engaged in recreational travel through Switzerland, should want to burden himself with the investigation of a case already closed, an investigation that he describes as onerously work-intensive:

Above all, I must study the character of every person involved in this case; I must examine innumerable minor circumstances that make up the whole, scrutinise the

---

[55] 'Dies wird abgedruckt, weil man zu Glarus ausgesprengt hat: es hätten Complices den Unglücklichen in der Gefangenschaft ums Leben gebracht, aus Furcht von ihm verrathen zu werden' (Lehmann, part II 87).

[56] Lehmann, part I 43: 'weise, erleuchtete Obrigkeit'. See also Hauser's comment on Steinmüller's death: 'Weil eine unabhängige Untersuchung des Todes von Steinmüller unterblieb, die den Selbstmord bestätigt hätte, entstand das Gerücht, Steinmüller sei ermordet worden. Es konnte nie widerlegt werden. Möglicherweise wusste Steinmüller zu viel über die wichtigsten Persönlichkeiten des Landes' (112).

personal characteristics of all witnesses, read the court records, weigh advantages and disadvantages that this or that person could have obtained from the case – then, and only then, will I be able to provide you with a trustworthy report.[57]

Lehmann states quite clearly in this passage that he had access to the trial records, without explaining how he obtained them or why, if acquired through regular channels, Glarus officials would offer him, a complete stranger and moreover a self-professed 'doubting Thomas', open access to them. Indeed, these records were considered sensitive material; so much so that they disappeared immediately after the trial, never to be seen again.[58] Hauser's discovery of recent documents pertaining to the case clears up the mystery: Lehmann's account is based on a heavily excerpted handwritten copy[59] of the original trial records, which was leaked to him by the court scribe, Johann Melchior Kubli (1750–1835), whom Hauser describes as critical of the trial and its outcome.[60] This adequately explains Lehmann's silence as to the provenance of his records, and shows that the Glarus officials' support for Lehmann's project was less than complete. Nevertheless, it is reasonable to suppose that the town officials must have initially cooperated with Lehmann to a considerable extent, for example by granting him licence to interview witnesses, among them – most implausibly – the plaintiff, then nine-year-old Anna Migeli Tschudi. Particularly in view of the officials' harsh response to Wekherlin's criticism of the case, their support for Lehmann's project indicates that they hoped for public vindication of their proceedings, which in turn makes it highly unlikely that they perceived him as the impartial sceptic he appears to be in his own account.[61]

The case of Anna Göldi and Lehmann's description of it are not antithetical to the Age of Reason; in fact, they can justifiably be considered

---

[57] Lehmann, part 1 27–8: 'Ich muß vor allen Dingen die Karaktere aller im Handel verwickelten Personen studiren, muß unzählige Nebenumstände, die zum Ganzen gehören, sondiren, die Eigenschaften der Zeugen untersuchen, die Acten des Processes lesen, Schaden oder Vortheile, den dieser oder jener dabey hätte haben können, abwiegen, und dann erst werde ich im Stande seyn, Ihnen zuverläßige Nachrichten mitzutheilen.'

[58] See, among others, Hauser 26; Hasler 252.

[59] The copy contains no records of Tschudi's alleged sexual misconduct, although these must have formed part of the original files (Hauser 26–7).

[60] Lehmann's source, the *Copia*, is in the Landesarchiv Glarus (see the following sources: Altes Evangelisches Archiv, Prozess Anne Göldi, Kriminalfälle 1782–1783 AE 15.1781:6; Evangelisches Landsgemeinde Protokoll AG I 92 I.; Evangelisches Ratsprotokoll AG I 145 I.; Vermischtes 5er Gerichts Protokoll AG II 40). Hauser describes his discovery of new documents and their significance as well as Kubli's attitude towards the trial on 28–40.

[61] The relationship between Lehmann and the Glarus officials became strained following his publication of letters and court records. In January 1783, an arrest warrant was issued for Lehmann, who had left Glarus in late September or early October 1782 (Hauser 16, 31).

narratives of the Enlightenment. Both Lehmann and Göldi's judges, for example, pay lip service to enlightened discourse by steering clear of all direct concessions of the existence of witches or witchcraft.[62] This is another way in which Lehmann's text, despite its clear bias, lays claim to objectivity: 'I am merely presenting facts whose veracity is not in doubt. In so doing, I wish neither to prove nor disprove the existence of sorcery.'[63] In Lehmann's account, the prosecutors, far from believing in witchcraft, appear themselves as learned sceptics who operate strictly on the basis of 'seeing is believing' and insist on the highest standards of evidence: 'Not that they themselves believed in witchcraft … – they merely did not think it entirely impossible, so long as not disproven beyond any doubt.'[64] In this, the intelligentsia of Glarus is distinguished from the commoners: 'Ideas of witchcraft … dominated the thoughts of the rabble … This opinion did not prevail until after the child was cured, although especially D. Marti [the physician examining the child] had spoken against it on several occasions. It is impossible to fault the authorities.'[65] Thus the author sets out to absolve the witch prosecutors of Glarus from *both* possible charges that an enlightened sceptic might bring against them: they cannot be faulted for a miscarriage of justice, but they also cannot be accused of believing in witchcraft. In the end, Lehmann claims the same defence for himself: 'In short, this entire affair remains very mysterious, and it is equally difficult and dangerous either to believe or to disbelieve.'[66] Time and again, Glarus officials, doctors, judges and witnesses are quoted as testifying to the inexplicability of the events; *nobody* connected with the case other than the plaintiff, an eight-year-old child, and the defendant herself, openly

---

[62] Several contemporaries commented on the strict avoidance of the terms 'witch', 'witchcraft' and 'magic' throughout the trial; see Hauser's discussion of responses to the trial in the press, 144–50, and his own interpretation on 94.

[63] Lehmann, part I, 'An die Leser', unpag.: 'Ich lege blos Thatsachen vor, an deren Gewißheit sich nicht zweifeln läßt. Ich will weder die Möglichkeit, noch die Unmöglichkeit der Zauberey damit beweisen.'

[64] Lehmann, part II, note to his second addendum [letter from Johann Rudolf Ulrich to Pfarrer Tschudi, Dr Tschudi's cousin, dated 19 April 1782], 5: 'Nicht daß Sie eben geradezu Zauberey geglaubt hätten, … aber sie hielten die Thatsache nicht für ganz unmöglich, so lange man nicht das Gegentheil zuverläßig darthun könnte.'

[65] Lehmann, part II, 'An den Leser', unpag.: 'Der Gedanke von Hexerey habe sich … der Köpfe des Pöbels bemeistert … Herrschend sey diese Meinung erst nach der Kur des Kindes geworden, obgleich immer hie und da und besonders vom D. Marti manches dawider sey gesagt worden. Der Obrigkeit könne man nichts zur Last legen.' Lehmann paraphrases in this passage a letter by Pfarrer Tschudi, without distancing himself from it in any way. Compare this with Hauser's assertion that Lehmann intended to embarrass the Glarus officials publicly for their belief in witchcraft: '[so] machte auch Lehmann den peinlichen Umstand publik dass führende Persönlichkeiten im Land Glarus noch Ende des 18. Jahrhunderts dem mittelalterlichen Aberglauben huldigten' (18).

[66] Lehmann, part II, 'An die Leser', unpag.: 'Kurz, noch immer bleibt dieser ganz besondere Handel im Ganzen ein verdecktes Essen, ubi credere et non credere difficile et periculosum.'

referred to the case as a witch trial; the trial records repeatedly emphasise that Göldi committed her crimes 'in an incomprehensible manner';[67] and the death sentence is ultimately handed down for poisoning, not witchcraft.[68]

Göldi's trial thus takes its place in a long line of eighteenth-century trials of poisoners, infanticides or murderesses which, upon perusal of the trial records, turn out to have been witch trials.[69] Cases that would have been openly conducted as witch trials a century earlier are now, as a concession to the enlightened discourse, cloaked as unsolved mysteries. The belief in witchcraft moves into the discursive underground, from where it nonetheless, as long as not *disproven*, controls trials and dictates judgments. Where sixteenth- and seventeenth-century superstitions encounter eighteenth-century scepticism and humanitarian justice – *in dubio pro reo* – , they are magically transformed into the discourse of indecision: *in dubio pro dubio*.

THE BLUE-EYED MONSTER: CASE STUDIES OF ANNA LOUISA KARSCH (1775–1858)

Johann Caspar Lavater's monumental *Physiognomic Fragments* (*Physiognomische Fragmente*, 1775–8), like Lehmann's *Freundschaftliche Briefe* authored by a Swiss theologian, provides us with an excellent case study of the belief in witchcraft gone underground. The text is characterised by a defensive tone and motivations quite comparable with Lehmann's. Like Lehmann, Lavater presents himself as defending the 'truth' against all doubters and taunters and spends considerable time rebutting their criticisms.[70] Just as Lehmann attempted to justify Göldi's trial by removing it from the realm of witchcraft, Lavater tried to rid physiognomy of its association with dubious magic arts such as astrology, chiromancy and divination,[71] to silence the sceptics, and to establish physiognomy as a serious science on a par with physics and mathematics. And just as is the

---

[67] 'auf eine unbegreifliche Weise'; see Lehmann's addendum no. 12: 'Malefiz-Process und Urtheil über die zum Schwerdt verurtheilte Anna Göldinn aus dem Sennwald verurtheilt den 17. Junii 1782' (Lehmann, part II 88–96, the quotation 89).

[68] Addendum no. 12: 'Malefiz-Process' (Lehmann, part II 88–96, the quotation 94).

[69] Hauser arrives at a similar conclusion: 'Obwohl auch das Urteil den Begriff "Hexe" nicht verwendete …, erfüllte der Göldi-Handel wesentliche Merkmale eines Hexenprozesses' (142). Similar examples are cited in Behringer, *Hexenverfolgung*, 355 and *Witches and Witch-Hunts*, 190.

[70] Lavater, *Physiognomische Fragmente*, I, 'Vorrede' (unpag.) and the following passages: I 17–20, 44–56; II 41–54; III 89–99; IV vii–viii, 3–38.

[71] See Rivers; Gray, *About Face*, xix–xxx. On Lavater's treatise, see also Graham and the anthologies by Shookman (*The Faces of Physiognomy*); Stadler and Pestalozzi; Pestalozzi and Weigelt.

case in Lehmann's text, the discourse discernible beneath the surface of Lavater's rhetoric transparently harks back to the very superstitions his text disclaims.

Two aspects of Lavater's writing show this most clearly: first, his theories of poetic genius; second, his physiognomy of the 'peasant poet' Anna Louisa Karsch, which inspired two further physiognomic analyses by her daughter Caroline von Klencke and her granddaughter Helmina von Chézy. In its emphasis on innateness and inspiration as opposed to book learning, Lavater's definition of poetic genius is indistinguishable from the natural genius theories of the age:[72] 'Where there is effect, power, drive, thought, and feeling that has not been taught by Man and cannot be learned by Man – there is genius.'[73] Physiognomically, Lavater saw genius as represented in the eye: 'In all persons who were judged by others to be endowed with genius, regardless of their field, I found the mark of genius in the eye – namely, in the gaze, fire, light or fluid of the eye.' Genius, then, is neither imagination, reason nor talent, but a *gaze*: Lavater was convinced 'that genius is the gaze – the soul concentrated in the gaze, lightning gaze of the effort-straining soul … There, if anywhere, is where genius reveals itself.'[74]

In physiognomic analyses of Anna Louisa Karsch, who served, for many theorists of the age, as the epitome of 'natural' or 'unlettered' genius,[75] two features recur that, while intended to corroborate her poetic genius, link these analyses with the belief in witchcraft. One is her piercing eye or penetrating gaze, a clearly recognisable descendant of the evil eye; the second is her fabled ugliness, which also, in many Karsch biographies, connotes poetic genius. It is this symbolic value that often results in depictions of the poet not merely as homely, but as shockingly, implausibly hideous. Klencke describes Karsch as so repulsive at birth that her mother spontaneously expressed a wish to have the child drowned in the river[76] and has this to say about Karsch's later physical development:

[72] See Kord, *Women Peasant Poets*, chapter 1.

[73] 'Wo Wirkung, Kraft, That, Gedanke, Empfindung ist, die von Menschen nicht gelernt und nicht gelehrt werden kann – da ist Genie' (Lavater, 'Zehntes Fragment: Genie', IV 80–93, the quotation 80).

[74] 'Bey allen, allen aber, die in irgend einem Fache nach aller Menschen Urtheil Genieen waren, fand ich den Ordensstern im Auge – und zwar einerseits im Blicke, im Feuer, Licht, oder Saft des Auges.' – 'daß Blick Genie ist – die Seele in den Blick konzentrirt, Blitzblick der schnellgespannten Seele … Hier zeigt sich das Genie, wenn es sich irgendwo zeigen muß' (Lavater, 'Zehntes Fragment: Genie', IV 80–93, both quotations 86).

[75] See Kord, *Women Peasant Poets*, 70–93.

[76] Klencke 12. The story is later repeated by Helmina von Chézy, who reports that Karsch's mother screamed in horror on first looking on her child (I 3–110, the citation 5).

Nonetheless, it must be noted that the poet later grew up nothing less than ugly, and if she had had any control over her body and her facial expression, she could almost have been considered beautiful, even to her dying day. She had a regular and fine figure of middle stature, a beautiful and lasting skin colour, light brown hair, the most beautiful forehead ever seen on a human being on which lay fully the light of her great spirit; the most brilliant, brightest and most expressive blue eyes, unchangingly red lips, and when in a good mood warm cheerfulness in her expression. But when she displayed that searching gaze that predominated in her face most of the time, she was difficult to tolerate, and one could not have borne to be in her company if her thoughts and occupations had not been easily distracted by diversions such as the moment often afforded. Her eyelids contracted in this gaze, her eye became smaller, and like the sun concentrated through a burning glass its rays shot towards the object of its contemplation. It was an all-consuming gaze ... The poet, who was not aware of her own facial expression, was subject to innumerable aggravations because of it, and at bottom, this gaze can be considered the source of all of her misfortunes.[77]

In Klencke's account, Karsch is only fearfully ugly at moments of intense concentration. As soon as she is distracted, she drops her penetrating gaze and reverts to 'Belloise',[78] her normal, 'almost beautiful' self. The dynamic aggressiveness attributed to Karsch's eye ('its rays shot towards ...') implies less penetrating thought than an attack on the object of contemplation, an aspect that eloquently evokes the witch's evil eye. That the intensity of Karsch's gaze, her all-consuming absorption, is related to her poetic activity would be obvious even if Klencke had not stated elsewhere that Karsch 'rarely, due to the poetic fire raging within her, looked straight with her eyes, but was nearly cross-eyed'.[79] Both an intense gaze or stare and a

---

[77] 'Indeß ist anzumerken: daß die Dichterin nachher nichts weniger als häßlich aufwuchs, und hätte sie ihren Körper und ihr Mienenspiel in der Gewalt gehabt, so würde sie bis zu ihrem Tod beinahe für schön haben gelten können. Sie hatte einen wohlgeordneten feinen Wuchs mittlerer Größe, schöne und daurende Gesichtsfarbe, hellbraunes Haar, die schönste menschliche Stirn, welche jemals gesehn worden ist, auf welcher ganz das Licht ihres großen Geistes ausgebreitet lag; die strahlenvollsten, hellsten, sprechendsten blauen Augen, beständig rothe Lippen, und bei guter Laune herzlichen Frohsinn in den Mienen. Allein, wenn sie ihren Forschblikk hatte, welcher die meiste Zeit in ihrem Gesichte herrschte, so war sie schwer auszuhalten, und man würde nicht mit ihr haben Umgang pflegen können, wenn ihre Gedanken und ihr Thun nicht leicht wären abzulenken gewesen, durch Zerstreuung, welche oft der Augenblick würkte. Die Augenlieder zogen sich bei solchem Blikk zusammen, das Auge wurde kleiner, und seine Strahlen schossen, gleichsam wie die Sonne in einem Brennpunkt, auf seinen Gegenstand, zusammen. Es war ein verzehrender Blick ... Die Dichterin, welche nichts von diesem Mienenspiele wußte, hat sich unzählige Verdrüßlichkeiten dadurch zugezogen, und eigentlich kann man es die Grundlage aller ihrer Unglücksfälle nennen' (Klencke 12–14). For an analysis of this passage, see Schaffers 163–4.

[78] 'Belloise' (= belle Louise) was Karsch's self-designation in her autobiographical poem 'Belloisens Lebenslauf', in *Gedichte und Lebenszeugnisse*, 69–70; analysis in Becker-Cantarino, '"Belloisens Lebenslauf"'.

[79] Klencke 36: 'damals, vermöge ihres in ihr wirkenden Dichterfeuers selten mit den Augen gerade sah, sondern beinahe schielte'.

convergent squint were commonly known as signs of the evil eye. Karsch's all-consuming gaze is defined in terms that point negatively to its intellectual component (*Forschblikk*); apparently this was a recurring subject in Klencke's interaction with Karsch, who more than once recorded her daughter's disapproval of her mental ability and its manifestation in writing.[80] Klencke's assessment of Karsch's poetic nature, distilled in her description of Karsch's frightful gaze, is highly pejorative – surprisingly so, given that it appears in the introductory biography to an edition of Karsch's poems –; but it also evokes the nature aesthetic in defining Karsch's poetic activity as involuntary: Karsch was not in control of her horrifying expression, she could not help it, and the implication is that had she been able to, she would have discarded her poetic gift to be able to live a normal life. For her poetic talent, condensed in the horrific gaze, disfigures the poet's usually congenial appearance, repels human companionship and is held responsible for every misfortune that later befell the poet.

This theme is later taken up by Klencke's daughter Helmina von Chézy in her description of her grandmother on her deathbed: in this episode, the dead Karsch appears as more beautiful than she had ever been in life.[81] Barely disguised in Chézy's physiognomy is a condemnation of Karsch's poetic activity. True to Lavater's theory that dead subjects are the best for physiognomic analysis because the physiognomy (the analysis of permanent features) of the dead is not hampered by pathognomy (the analysis of mien, movement and other aspects under the subject's control),[82] death is the ultimate revealer of Karsch's 'true' nature as beautiful and, by implication, unpoetic. Like Klencke's, Chézy's biography links the poet's ugliness with her poetic talent. Beauty can only be attained by relinquishing this gift, in Klencke's account momentarily through distractions, in Chézy's permanently in death. In both accounts, poetic inspiration comes at a cost: the 'innumerable aggravations' and 'misfortunes' that make up the poet's life reach their pinnacle in the portrayal of other humans recoiling from the poet whose image becomes bearable only in death.

Karsch's fabled hideousness was a recurring theme not only in posthumous biographical writing, but also during her lifetime partly because it

---

[80] Karsch in a letter to Gleim, 14 November 1788: 'meine Tochter bittet ich Sol weniger dennken, sol fast gar nicht mehr schreiben, daß heißt nicht mehr leben' ('*Mein Bruder in Apoll*', II 304). In my translation of Karsch's letters and poems, I have made no attempt to represent the author's erratic spelling.

[81] Chézy 96–7.

[82] Lavater, vol. II, 'Einige Beobachtungen über Neugeborne, Sterbende und Todte', 33–5, and vol. IV, 'Zweytes Fragment: Physiognomik und Pathognomik', 39. On the distinction between physiognomy and pathognomy, see Gray, 'Aufklärung und Anti-Aufklärung', 172; Rivers 83–5; and Boehm, particularly 24–6.

Fig. 1 Anna Louisa Karsch at her desk. Pencil drawing by Ernst Wilhelm Hempel (1764)

stood in crass contrast to that other authorial image of her, beautiful Sappho.[83] Her first letter to Gleim, written before they met in person, warns him not to expect a beautiful Sappho,[84] and she repeatedly had to contend with readers' conjectures of her beauty based on her pen name.[85] All portraits that we have of her portray her as intensely ugly; several, for instance Ernst Wilhelm Hempel's drawing of Karsch at her desk (fig. 1)

[83] For an analysis of Karsch's appearance in biographical writing and physiognomic analysis, see Schaffers 159–64.
[84] Letter to Gleim, 14 May 1761, *'Mein Bruder in Apoll'*, I 7.
[85] See Klencke 78; Nörtemann 81.

Fig. 2 Anna Louisa Karsch. Oil on canvas by Karl Christian Kehrer (1791). Courtesy of the Gleim-Haus, Halberstadt

and Karl Christian Kehrer's painting for Gleim (fig. 2), depict her as unmistakably witch-like. These renditions thus identify Karsch, the erst-while peasant, with the most quintessential image of the woman 'from the people'; simultaneously, they echo both Gleim's and Uz's appellation of Karsch as 'poetical witch'[86] and her own repeated statement that people were so astonished by the speed and spontaneity of her poetic production that 'everyone said that I must have produced these verses by magic'.[87]

---

[86] See Gleim's letter to Karsch, *'Mein Bruder in Apoll'*, II 461; Uz's letter is quoted in Barndt 174.

[87] Karsch in her third autobiographical letter to Sulzer, *'Mein Bruder in Apoll'*, I 357: 'alle sagten ich müste den Gesang gezaubert haben'. See also her second letter, in which she relates being called a 'Zauberinn' (sorceress) by her admiring listeners (I 352).

Fig. 3 Anna Louisa Karsch. Etching by Johann Heinrich Lips, based on a drawing by Daniel Chodowiecki. From Johann Kaspar Lavater, *Physiognomische Fragmente* (1777)

The iconic representation of Karsch as a witch and its exploitation as indicative of her poetic genius culminates in Johann Heinrich Lips's engraving (fig. 3) of 1777, based on a drawing by Daniel Chodowiecki, which Lavater, to both Gleim's and Karsch's dismay, included in his *Physiognomische Fragmente*. In Lavater's analysis, the link between her physical repulsiveness and her poetic talent is just as strong as it is in Hempel's and Kehrer's art or Klencke's and Chézy's writing: one, it appears, is the price for the other. "'Much better not to write verse than to look like this!' … But no! "better to look like this and to write verse" …'[88]

It is hardly profitable to speculate how close to life these portraits were, but it is nonetheless worth noting – without intending to present Karsch's self-image as more 'accurate' than Karsch iconography – that the author considered her ugliness in paintings greatly exaggerated. In 1761, she complained about the disfigurement of her image in Oeser's portrait;[89] in 1784,

---

[88] Lavater III 315: "'Lieber keine Verse machen, als so aussehen!" … Nein! "lieber so aussehen, und Verse machen" …' See Ortrun Niethammer 249 for a brief discussion of Lavater's physiognomic analysis of Karsch. For Lavater's physiognomy of women, see Schuller, particularly 112–14; Rivers 71.
[89] Letter to Gleim, 27 December 1761, *'Mein Bruder in Apoll'*, I 55–7, the reference 56.

she worried that children looking at Stubinitzki's sculpture of her would mistake her for a witch:

> And all the little boys and girls
> would quake in unnamed terror
> Even the babes in arms would scream
> And call me 'witch!' in error
> They'd see the wrinkles on my face
> and run as quick as they could chase
> through vale and glen and stream[90]

Six years earlier, she had this to say about the inclusion of Lips's portrait of her in Lavater's work:

I am indebted to Lavater for introducing me to him [Chodowiecki], although my botched portrait in his Physiognomics seems to frighten away visitors so that nobody calls on me or greets me anymore since the world is convinced that my face could scare off children.

I don't put much store in such honours, but nonetheless, I liked it when young men from foreign lands wanted to see me. You know that I don't have such a piercing, wild and fiery owl's eye as that given to me by Lips …

But what's the use, dear Gleim? In general, I don't think much of this deeply analytical Lavaterising, since I find it very untrustworthy.[91]

Karsch's critique encompasses not only Lavater's entire methodology, but also, applied specifically to Lips's portrait of her, singles out that one facet that was at the centre of Lavater's analysis of her poetic talent: the eye. For it is that same eye in Lips's portrait, an eye whose real-life existence Karsch emphatically denied, that Lavater's physiognomic analysis diagnosed as the abode of Karsch's poetic talent.

Karsch's objections, while understandable, cannot conceal the significant points of agreement between contemporary analysis and posthumous portrayal. Her 'natural' poetic genius was celebrated, but it was also demonised

---

[90] 'Da würden sich erschüttern / Die Knäblein und die Mägdellein / Getragen vonn den Müttern / Sie würden Eine Hexe mich / mit lautter stimme nennen / bey so viel Runnzeln fürchtterlich / Sie würden vor mir rennen / bergab inns Tal und übern bach' (in a letter to Gleim, 6 April 1784, *'Mein Bruder in Apoll'*, II 207–9, the quotation 209). Chézy, on the other hand, claimed that Karsch was commonly flattered in portraiture (110).

[91] 'ich danks dem Lavater, daß er mir zu seiner Bekanntschaft verhalf, obgleich mein mißlungenes Porträt in der Physiognomik die Fremden abzuschrecken scheint, daß keiner mich mehr aufsuchen und grüßen will, seitdem die Welt glauben muß, mein Kopf könnte Kinder scheuchen. / Ich mache mir endlich nicht viel aus dieser Ehre, dennoch war mirs lieb, wenn die Jünglinge aus fremden Ländern mich sehen wollten. Sie wissens, ich habe kein solches stieres wildflammendes Eulenauge, als mir Herr Lips gegeben hat … / Doch was kanns helfen, lieber Gleim? Ich halte überhaupt wenig von der tief forschenden Lavaterei, weil ich sie sehr unzuverlässig finde' (letter to Gleim, 24 February 1788, *Herzgedanken*, 181–2, the quotation 182).

by reference to two or three aspects of her physiognomy that recur obsessively in all texts. Both in Karsch's interpretation of Lips's portrait and Klencke's later biography, Karsch's eye is described as 'piercing' (Klencke: 'verzehrend'; Karsch: 'stierend') and associated with searing heat (Klencke: 'gleichsam wie die Sonne in einem Brennpunkt'; Karsch: 'wildflammend')[92]; both qualities are deemed intensely repellent by both writers. Both Lavater and Klencke identified the eye as the central and *exclusive* focal point expressing Karsch's poetic gift (Lavater analysed the remainder of her face as that of 'a coldly probing thinker' and claimed that while the eye clearly defined her as a poet, the rest of her face suggested predilections for philosophy rather than poetry).[93] And the vision of others recoiling in horror from Karsch's repugnant exterior appears in Karsch's reading of Lips's portrait in her letter to Gleim and in Klencke's later biography, which must have made at least some use of her mother's letters. In fact, we might speculate that Klencke's depiction of Karsch's repulsive gaze was less biographical than discursive, based less on personal observation than on Karsch's desperate denial of both the actual existence of this eye and the symbolic significance attributed to it by Lavater.

However one may read the relationship between these three texts, there is enough evidence to suggest that these visions of the poet's eye were direct descendants of the witch's evil eye. Physiognomically, as we have seen, a direct line can be drawn from one to the other. Both evil magic and natural genius manifest themselves in a piercing stare, shocking repulsiveness and searing, consuming heat. The convergent squint common to both the witch and the unlettered genius points to their abnormality and, moreover, their own *self-awareness* as aberrations, expressed in their inability to look ordinary humans straight in the eye. We might go so far as to suspect an affinity of purpose behind these analogous discourses: the desire to eradicate the exceptional, the extraordinary, the strangely incomprehensible and eerily unfamiliar – all that which, in different contexts, would have excited the enlightened scholar's thirst for knowledge – as soon as it manifested itself in female form. As the burning of the witch at the stake was thought to purify her and return her to a state of grace, so the hideous poetic witch is stripped,

---

[92] Compare the discussion of the evil eye as 'burning eyes' in the *Malleus* ('brennende Augen'; Sprenger and Institoris 22).

[93] Lavater III 315: 'Die Poesie als Poesie scheint ihren Sitz in den Augen dieses Gesichtes zu haben – Sonst ist die ganze Form des Kopfes, wenigstens in der Stirn und der Nase, mehr des kaltforschenden Denkers – und, wer weiß – vielleicht hätte sie, die Karschinn, noch mehr Philosophinn, als Dichterinn werden können.'

in death, of her genius and thereby returned to her most basic state of beautiful femininity.

The uncanny affinity between these ideas deserves further study, not as an insignificant aberration, but as an integral part of Enlightenment thought. Indeed, the repetitiveness of such discourses, their way of resurfacing in different guises, might make us reconsider the Enlightenment as an ongoing project rather than an eighteenth-century triumph, a journey fraught with as many delays and detours as advances and signs of progress – a journey that, it seems, we have yet to complete.

CHAPTER 3

The plague: vampires

OUTBREAK: SERBIAN VAMPIRES COME TO LIFE IN GERMANY
(LEIPZIG AND VIENNA, 1732–1755)

In January 1732, Duke Karl Alexander of Württemberg, then Imperial
Governor of Belgrade, received a report that was to throw the still relatively
young German Enlightenment into considerable disarray. The report was
written by Johannes Flückinger, field surgeon of the Infantry Regiment of
Baron Fürstenbusch, and countersigned by two other army physicians and
two additional witnesses.[1] Flückinger, under orders to investigate persistent
rumours of vampirism in the Serbian village Medvegya, began by interview-
ing the village *hajduci*,[2] who offered him the following unanimous testimony: that one Arnold Paole, also a *hajdúk*, had died in a fall five years
previously; that Paole had throughout his life complained of being haunted
by a vampire and taken counteractive measures; that twenty to thirty days
after Paole's death, several villagers stated that Paole had returned from the
grave to torture them, and that four of Paole's self-declared victims had died
within a matter of days. Forty days after Paole's death, the village elders
exhumed his body and found it to be free from decay, emitting fresh blood
from nose, ears and mouth, shedding its skin and nails, and growing new
ones in their place. The villagers then drove a stake through Paole's heart,

---

[1] Flückinger's report (*Visum et repertum*) has been reprinted in its entirety in many contemporary and
later publications, including *Acten-mäßige und Umständliche Relatio* (9–15), Ranft (168–75), Horst
(255–61), Harenberg (27–35) and Harmening (*Der Anfang*, 3–10); in English translation in Barber,
Vampires (16–18). Summers has retold the story (149–54) and closely paraphrased Flückinger's report
(154–6). Calmet also reports extensively on the Medvegya case (52–61). Modern editions of documents
related to the Medvegya vampires are in Hamberger's *Mortuus* and Aribert Schroeder's collection. The
following quotations from the report are taken from the transcription in Ranft's *Tractat*, 168–75. For a
discussion of the Medvegya event, see Kreuter.
[2] *Hajdúk* (plural *hajduci*) = originally Balkan shepherds and cattle-drovers who had formed a military
order, fighting as mercenaries against the Turks; later a police force in Hungary. In Balkan folklore, the
hajdúk was turned into a romanticised hero who fights against the Ottoman oppressors (Thorne,
Countess Dracula, 130).

43

causing him to groan audibly and bleed profusely, and burnt the corpse; the same procedure was used on all of his known victims.

But the matter did not rest there. Paole, apparently, had not confined his vampiric activities to people, but also attacked livestock, causing the vampiric contagion to spread to all who had eaten of the tainted cattle. Within a mere three months, seventeen persons, both young and old, had died, some without a trace of previous illness, and returned as vampires to plague the community. Faced with a vampire epidemic that threatened to decimate the entire village, the villagers had finally sent a request for help to the duke, who dispatched the physician Glaser, a specialist on contagious diseases, to investigate. Glaser found the villagers in a panic and threatening to abandon Medvegya, but his examinations of them revealed no trace of physical disease. Possibly in an attempt to disabuse the villagers of their superstition, Glaser seized upon the only means that might convince them: he agreed to exhume all bodies that had come under suspicion of vampirism, along with a control group of 'innocent' corpses. Much to his surprise, he found some of them without signs of decay, although they had been buried for a considerable time. His report, which refers to the inexplicably fresh corpses as 'vampires', may well be the first document in German employing the term. Glaser's tersely factual statement was immediately shelved and did not receive any further attention, but it was nevertheless deemed important enough to dispatch Flückinger to Medvegya, where he received, with what level of credence we do not know, the villagers' report of the outbreak in their midst.

Much of Flückinger's report is taken up by a second post-mortem examination of the bodies exhumed by Glaser, conducted by Flückinger himself and army physicians Johann Friedrich Baumgärtner and Johann Heinrich Siegel, in the presence of a lieutenant-colonel and a cadet from a different regiment who later witnessed his report. His description is not only more extensive and detailed than Glaser's, it also contextualises his findings to a far greater degree.[3] The corpse of twenty-year-old Stana, who died in childbirth and was buried two months before her disinterment, was found 'completely perfect and undecayed. After opening the body, there emerged a quantity of fresh blood from the chest cavity; the arteries, veins and the heart valves were not, as is normal, filled with coagulated blood.'[4]

---

[3] For a comparative reading of the reports by Glaser and Flückinger and on the 1725 autopsy of Peter Plogojovic, see Kreuter 114–21.

[4] 'Ein Weib, Nahmens Stana, 20. Jahr alt, so vor zwey Monathen nach dreitägiger Kranckheit seit ihrer Niederkunfft gestorben … war gantz vollkommen und unverweset. Bey Eröffnung des Cörpers zeigte sich in cavitate pectoris eine Quantität frisches extravasirtes Geblüthe; die arteriae und venae nebst denen ventriculis cordis waren nicht, wie sonst gewöhnlich, mit coagulirtem Geblüthe angefüllet' (Ranft 170–1).

Sixty-year-old Miliza, buried over ninety days previously, was found to have liquid blood in her chest cavity; her intestines – among the softest organs of the body and hence among the first to decay – were found to be in excellent condition. Incredibly, Miliza, malnourished and bony in life, had gained considerable weight in the grave; witnesses who had known her all her life testified that she looked better nourished than ever.[5] Ruscha, more than six weeks in her grave, had fresh blood in her chest and stomach, as did her eighteen-day-old baby buried one week after her and a ten-year-old girl buried two months prior to disinterment. Milosova, on the other had, buried mere days before and right next to the well-preserved Ruscha, was nearly completely decayed. The same rate of decay was observed in another woman who had been buried more than a week after Ruscha and over three weeks after the ten-year-old girl whose body came, fresh as a daisy, out of the same ground.[6]

Medvegya was not the only village in Serbia plagued by lively corpses. Georg Conrad Horst tells us that another female vampire, the returned corpse of Katharina Lerchin, 'set many quills in motion',[7] and in the same month in which Flückinger composed his report to the duke, Cadet Sigmund Alexander Friedrich von Kottwitz wrote to a physician in Leipzig, reporting further sightings in the village of Kucklina. Kottwitz stated dispassionately that vampires were capable of decimating an entire village in a very short time, adding that the local government received many complaints about them on a daily basis. Kottwitz's purpose was to ask his

---

[5] '2. Befand sich ein Weib, Nahmens Miliza, ohngefehr 60. Jahr alt, welche nach 3.monatl. Kranckheit gestorben und vor etlich und 90. Tagen begraben worden. In der Brust befand sich viel liquides Geblüthe, die übrigen Viscera waren gleich der vorgemeldeten in einem guten Stande. Es haben sich bey der Secirung die umstehenden Heyducken sämmtlich über ihre Fettigkeit und Vollkommenheit des Leibes sehr verwundert, einhellig aussagend, daß sie das Weib von ihrer Jugend auff wohl gekannt und Zeit ihres Lebens gantz mager und ausgedöret ausgesehen, mit Versicherung, daß sie in dem Grabe zu dieser Verwunderungs-würdigen Fettigkeit gelanget' (Ranft 171–2). See Kreuzer 120–1 on the differences between Glaser's and Flückinger's autopsy of Miliza and differences between witness testimonies on each occasion.

[6] 'Ein Weib, Namens Ruscha, welche nach 10.tägiger Krankheit gestorben und vor 6. Wochen begraben worden, bey welcher viel frisches Geblüte nicht alleine in der Brust, sondern auch im Magen gefunden worden: ihr Kind, das 18. Tage alt und vor 5. Wochen begraben worden, befand sich in gleichen Umständen. / 7. Nicht weniger befand sich ein Mägdgen von 10. Jahren, welche vor 2. Monathen gestorben, in obangezogenem Stande ganz vollkommen und unverweset, und hatte in der Brust viel frisches Geblüte. / Hat man des Hadnacks Eheweib, Milosova genannt, mit ihrem Kinde ausgegraben, welche vor 7. Wochen, ihr Kind aber, so 8. Wochen alt war, vor 3. Wochen gestorben, und gefunden, daß so wohl Mutter als Kind völlig verweset, ob sie gleich zunächst an denen vorgemeldten Gräbern derer Vampyrs gelegen. / 10. Des hiesigen Bariacters Weib, sammt dem kleinen Kinde, so vor 5. Wochen gestorben, ist gleichfalls gantz verweset gefunden worden' (Ranft 172–3).

[7] Horst 264 ('brachte eine Menge Federn in Bewegung').

addressee to confirm or deny the physiological possibility of an unusual level of posthumous vigour: he reports that a recently deceased *hajdúk* had returned to his wife the night after his burial to engage in posthumous intercourse, citing – without any sign of amusement – the wife's remark that her husband had performed as well dead as he had in life.[8]

To later interpreters, the Medvegya outbreak and the extensive scientific debate it sparked became 'the hour of the Vampire',[9] that is: the precise moment that the belief in vampires entered the Western European consciousness. Described in dozens of publications and buttressed by further sightings, Flückinger's report became *the* German media event of the 1730s. To hear contemporary observers tell it, Serbian vampires were the sole subject of conversation at social gatherings – even the ladies, Ranft tells us with unmistakable disapproval, began to 'contemplate' the matter[10] – and inspired a widespread scholarly debate that spanned decades. Of the many authors who sought to explain the matter – at least fifteen books, treatises and pamphlets appeared in the same year, followed by a further twenty-five over the next thirty years[11] – none has ever expressed even the slightest doubt regarding the exactness and veracity of Flückinger's report. The idea that three army surgeons – who had nothing to gain from this and, potentially, much to lose – might conspire in concocting a fabricated report to the Duke of Württemberg; that two witnesses – one a high-ranking officer, the other a cadet, neither under the direct command of these

---

[8] Letter from Sigmund Alexander Friedrich von Kottwitz, 26 January 1732: 'Es werden solche Aeser in der Türckischen Sprache Vampyren oder Menschen-Sauger genennet, welche capable seyn, in kurtzer Zeit ein gantzes Dorff an Menschen und Vieh zu ruiniren, deßwegen fast täglich häuffige Klagen bey hiesiger Regierung einlauffen … was noch abscheulicher, so ist ein gestern beerdigter Heyducke folgende Nacht zu seinem Weibe gekommen und solcher ordentlich beygewohnet, welche solches gleich Tages darauff dem Hadnack selbiges Orts angedeutet, mit Vermelden, daß er seine Sache so wohl, als bey Lebzeiten verrichtet' (quoted in Ranft 176–7). The letter is also cited in *Actenmäßige und Umständliche Relatio*, 16–18.

[9] Ruthner 17.

[10] 'Durch diese Nachrichten wurde iederman in die gröste Verwunderung gesetzet. In allen Zusammenkünfften hoher und niederer Stands-Personen wurde davon geredet. Auch die Dames fiengen an darüber zu raisonniren. Niemand wuste, was er daraus machen noch vor was er es ausgeben solte' (Ranft 178).

[11] I will limit my list to those books and treatises to which I have had access. Works that appeared in the same year and that explicitly refer to Flückinger's report include the anonymously published *Curieuse Relation*, *Acten-mäßige und Umständliche Relatio*, *Schreiben eines guten Freundes*, *Putoneus besondere Nachricht*, *Visus et repertus*, *Christliche Betrachtungen*, *Eines Weimarischen Medici Muthmaßliche Gedancken* and *Curieuse und sehr wunderbarliche Relation*, as well as the treatises by Demel, Vogt (*Kurtzes Bedencken*), Fritsch, Harenberg, Graben zum Stein, Pohl and Stock. Zopf took up the theme a year later; Ranft two years later; Calmet in 1751; the anonymous *Abhandlung des Daseyns der Gespenster und des Vampyrismus* followed in 1768 and Tallar's treatise in 1784. Some of these texts are collected in Hamberger (*Mortuus*) and Schroeder.

physicians – might falsely sign a declaration stating that '*all medical examinations on the vampires have been conducted in our presence and subject to our
visual inspection, and we confirm that the report issued by the army physician of
the Honourable Regiment of Fürstenbusch is true in every detail*'[12] was simply
unthinkable. More unthinkable, possibly, than the proposition that the
Medvegya dead had returned from the grave as un-dead to plague the living.

Clearly, however, the Medvegya vampires were an affront to enlightened
minds. Explanations for the events of 1732 ranged from the physiological
and geological to the psychological and theological, with a healthy dose of
proto-mesmerism thrown in for good measure. Physicians stated that the
composition of the soil, cold temperatures, the absence of air or the *vis
vegetans*, a lingering vegetative state characterised by the simultaneous
presence of life and death,[13] could delay physical decomposition considerably, even indefinitely. None of them, however, took on Flückinger's
statement that he had examined corpses in an advanced state of decay
who had been buried *more recently* than the fresh bodies, in the same
ground and under the same conditions, sometimes even in graves immediately adjacent to those containing his vampiric suspects.[14] Others explained
the difference between an unspoiled and a rotten corpse with their previous
owners' psychological state before death: if the victims had firmly *believed*
that they would return as vampires, this alone might be enough to prevent
putrefaction, just as the belief in vampires alone might be enough to kill
people.[15] Group hallucination of the three examining physicians and both

---

[12] '*Wir Endes Unterschriebene attestiren hiermit, wie daß alles dasjenige, so der Regiments-Feldscheer vom
löblichen Fürstenbuschischen Regimente, sammt beyden neben unterzeichneten Feldscheers-Gesellen hier-
oben, die Vampyrs betreffend, in Augenschein genommen, in allen und jeden der Wahrheit gemäß und in
unserer selbst eigenen Gegenwart vorgenommen, visitirt und examinirt worden. Zu Bekräfftigung dessen ist
unsere eigenhändige Unterschrifft und Fertigung.*' The declaration was signed by (L. S.) Büttner,
Obrist-Lieutenant des löbl. Alexandrinischen Regiments. (L. S.) J. H. von Lindenfelß, Fähndrich
des Alexandrinischen Regiments' (Ranft 175, italics original).

[13] Ranft was one of the first to propose this option. The theory proposes that life is not extinguished at
the moment of death but only once the body is decayed; complete decomposition marks the moment
of the body's detachment from Earth and the soul's ascent to Heaven (or descent into Hell). The same
idea is expressed in the common belief that the bodies of the excommunicated could not decay; their
inability to decompose served as proof that their souls could not enter into Heaven. For these theories,
see Arnold-de Simine 137.

[14] See, among others, *Eines Weimarischen Medici*, 53–61; van Swieten 13–16; Calmet 58. In 1988, Barber
offered a forensic explanation for the inconsistent rate of decay amongst Flückinger's corpses; see his
chapters '*Visum et Repertum*' (15–20) and 'The Body after Death' (102–19) in *Vampires*. His 'Staking
Claims' offers a brief summary of his scientific answer to the Medvegya mystery.

[15] Ranft 182: 'Da sie nun gehöret, daß Paole von einem Vampyr geplagt worden, so haben sichs dessen
Nachbarn und Verwandten so feste in die Gedancken gesetzt, daß es kein Wunder gewesen, wenn
ihre Phantasie und Einbildung durch des Verstorbenen sympathetische Operation so erhitzt worden,
daß sie darüber den Gebrauch ihrer Sinne verlohren, und endlich als wie vom Schlage für grosser

witnesses was a popular theory; and rare epidemics, poison, eating tainted meat, or smoking opium were all proposed as factors preventing decomposition.[16] Some were content to refer admonishingly to the Devil's power on earth; others directly accused the Serbian villagers of superstition and the examining doctors of an overactive imagination.[17] The Benedictine monk Augustine Calmet raised the possibility that the vampiric outbreak was due to the increasing number of people excommunicated and buried in unhallowed ground.[18] Another popular theory advanced was that of the tripartite division of humans into body, soul and spirit (Paracelsus's *corpus, anima* and *spiritus*), with the spirit, even after the departure of the soul, keeping dead bodies sufficiently animated to break out of their graves and bite the living.[19] And finally, those in favour of simple solutions surmised that the exhumed corpses had appeared alive because they in fact *were*. Opening the door to what would become one of the most persistent nineteenth-century obsessions, the fear of live burial, Calmet pronounced the Medvegya corpses 'not yet dead' at the time of disinterment. These unfortunates, he explained, having successfully survived in their coffins for weeks, even months,

have been killed by beheading them, piercing their heart, and burning them; in all of which people were very wrong, for the pretext on which they acted, of their pretended reappearance to disturb the living, causing their death, and maltreating them, is not a sufficient reason for treating them thus.[20]

Calmet's indignation notwithstanding, it is clear that none of Flückinger's contemporaries adequately explained his report,[21] and that some of their ideas stretch credulity to more or less the same extent. No explanation, however, regardless of where it fell on the scale between quite rational and patently absurd, and no amount of enlightened scepticism succeeded in burying vampires for good. Barely fifteen years after the Treaty of Požarevac (1718) had brought parts of Hungary, Serbia and Bosnia under the rule of

---

Angst und Gemüths-Beunruhigung gestorben. Ja da auch vielleicht gedachter Paole selbsten in der gewissen Einbildung gestorben, er werde ein Vampyr werden und die Leute heimlich erwürgen, so ist die Sympathie und magische Würckung zwischen seinem frischen und vegetanten Cörper und denen Personen, mit denen er in seinem Leben am meisten zu schaffen gehabt, desto hefftiger und stärcker gewesen.' A similar theory is advanced in *Eines Weimarischen Medici,* 65.

[16] See, among others, Vogt, *Kurtzes Bedencken* (tainted-meat theory; poison); Ranft 190–1 (group hallucination), Harenberg 6, 95–7 (epidemic and/or opium); Calmet 154 (rare disease).

[17] For example, Zopf; Harenberg 105; *Eines Weimarischen Medici,* 53–7; van Swieten 9, 16; Calmet 157.

[18] McNally 117.

[19] For example in *Acten-mäßige und Umständliche Relatio,* 25–7; Ranft 217–27; Demel. Vogt vehemently rebutted this theory in his *Der eingeschlichene, nun aber Wieder ausgemertzte Dritte Theil des Menschen*; see also Harenberg's objections to this theory, 65–70. For a brief discussion of this, see Hock 44–7.

[20] Calmet 179–80.

[21] See Barber, *Vampires,* 15–20, 102–19, for a modern explanation of Flückinger's findings.

the Habsburgs, indigenous belief in vampires stole across the redrawn border, never to leave again. How persistently and exasperatingly vampirism returned to haunt Germans is evidenced in the level of intellectual defences mounted to keep it at bay.[22] In the end, even crowned heads had to contend with vampires. The Prussian Royal Academy of Sciences issued a report to King Friedrich Wilhelm I, cautiously stating that while the question was a difficult one, there seemed to be no reason *yet*, barring further evidence to the contrary, to believe that the dead could return from the grave as vampires and infect others by sucking their blood.[23] And in 1755, Empress Maria Theresia of Austria was haunted by the spectre of a female revenant, Rosina Polakin of Hermersdorf, who, deceased in December 1754, was exhumed by municipal decision because the people of Hermersdorf claimed she had turned into a vampire, broken out of her grave and attacked them.[24] At disinterment, Polakin's body was found to be free from all signs of decomposition, with blood flowing in its veins; the corpse was beheaded and burned. As had Duke Karl Alexander, Maria Theresia sent two of her court physicians to investigate the matter, and following a report by her principal court physician Gerard van Swieten, she issued a *rescriptum* outlawing the disinterment of corpses and all traditional countermeasures to 'posthumous magic'.[25]

How to explain the outbreak of an vampire epidemic in the Age of Reason? Certainly, it is no coincidence that vampires entered the German imagination in the Age of Enlightenment, at the precise time, in other words, when the immortality of the soul was no longer accepted as a given and the processes of physical death became the subject of medical research.[26] On the other hand, vampirism not only related to the modern aspects of the enlightened age, but also to the ancient and eerily familiar. In

[22] The scientific debate never again reached the fever pitch of 1732, but neither did it completely abate. Numerous treatises on vampires dot the eighteenth-century landscape, for example Tallar's *Visum Repeterum* of 1784, which defines vampiric beliefs as hallucinations caused by a bad diet and alcohol abuse (Tallar; see discussion in Kreuter 123–7).

[23] 'Bey welcher der Sachen Bewandtniß denn wir davor halten, daß man bey dieser Quaestion behutsam zu verfahren, und noch zur Zeit nicht glauben kan, daß dergleichen Aussaugung von den todten Cörpern geschehe, auch selbige ihre Qualität durch die Aussaugung oder den Gebrauch ihres Bluts, und der Erde von den Gräbern, worinnen sie liegen, nicht fortpflantzen können.' The report is published in its entirety in Ranft 286–91 (citation 290) and in *Eines Weimarischen Medici*, 75ff.

[24] Her case followed closely upon an incident involving the bodies of two women, Anna Tonner and Dorothea Pihsin, who were blamed for the deaths of several miners in 1753. Both were exhumed; a postmortem examination found Pihsin's corpse free from decay and Tonner's completely decomposed, although Tonner had been buried twenty-four days after Pihsin. Pihsin's body was burnt and Tonner's reburied. For a discussion of these and other cases, see Kreuter 122–3.

[25] On Maria Theresia's edict and the story of Rosina Polakin, see Klaniczay, *The Uses*, 170–1.

[26] Pointed out by many, e.g. Ruthner 21.

the eighteenth century, beliefs that are today firmly banished to the realm of vampiric folklore were commonly accepted in other contexts. Until the late sixteenth century, female criminals were routinely buried alive, with a stake driven through their hearts immediately after interment;[27] as late as 1773, an executioner was ordered to drive a stake through the heart of Maria Egger following her beheading.[28] That executed criminals might come back to haunt the living or avenge their own deaths was also common coin; to forestall this eventuality, the condemned were forced to swear *Urfehde*, the Oath of Non-Retribution, before proceeding to the scaffold.[29] And drinking the blood of the executed was thought to be a sure-fire way of curing epilepsy: at an execution in 1820, six epileptics, drinking vessels in one hand and a medical certificate attesting to the beneficial effects of blood in the other, gathered around the scaffold.[30] In part, such behaviour was inspired by the belief that repentant sinners who went to their deaths in a state of grace attained the status of martyrs, their bodies acquiring the healing powers of relics.[31] But another part of the faith in these powers was probably quite down to earth: sudden death, it was believed, cut people off in their prime, lending extra potency to parts of their body – not just blood but fingers, toes, heads, pubic hair and genitalia – that could be used for anything from warding off lightning, fires, floods and witchcraft to increasing the likelihood of conception and fattening cattle. These parts, a pragmatic householder of the time might have reasoned, were still good: why let them go to waste?

Central aspects of what later became vampiric lore – revenantism, its prevention through decapitation, staking the heart and burning the body, and drinking blood for the purpose of either curing disease or rejuvenation – were already a part of common eighteenth-century 'knowledge', a part of what many people at the time were prepared to accept. That vampires kept returning to the eighteenth- and nineteenth-century German imagination can perhaps also be explained by the universal perception of vampirism as an *epidemic*. Worried villagers, postulating the exponential spread of the contagion from one vampire to the next, must have envisioned their entire community on the brink of extinction. Scholarly sceptics, as becomes clear in the Medvegya debate, saw in vampirism an attack on the values of the Enlightenment, an epidemic of superstition and folly that must have

---

[27] van Dülmen, *Theater des Schreckens*, 122.   [28] Evans, *Rituals*, 87.
[29] See Martschukat, *Inszeniertes Töten*, 125.
[30] On drinking the blood of the executed, see Evans, *Rituals*, 90–6, the story of the medical certificate 92.
[31] See the final chapter for a more extensive discussion.

seemed to them no less virulent. In both cases, the perception is that of a plague, a universal threat from which nobody is safe. To the silent majority who fell neither into the camp of the fervent believers nor that of the scornful detractors of vampirism, thinking of it as a plague may even have had its comforting aspects. It explained 'the spreading of evil as pure contagion' and 'naturally exculpated the living victims attacked by or related to vampires'.[32] Ultimately, even the criminal, the vampire, was merely a victim; the countermeasures of staking, beheading and burning were thought of as much in terms of a cure as in terms of preventing further contagion. As revenant monsters, vampires merely inspire terror; as the victims of a plague that could theoretically strike anyone, they become eligible as subjects of identification.

WHAT IS AT STAKE, OR WHY WE CANNOT LET IT (THEM) REST

Perhaps this explains that even as vampires were laid to rest in the physical world – although we are, apparently, still working on that[33] –, they acquired considerable meaning in the symbolic realm. Historians and psychoanalysts have seen them as emblematic of the human inability to accept death and mourn the dead – sometimes from a safe historical distance,[34] sometimes in the immediacy of the present.[35] Catholic theologians have been disturbed by the parallels between vampirism and the Eucharist: returning, body and all, from the grave, acquiring eternal life and passing it on through the drinking of blood – which for Catholics, through the detour of transubstantiation, is not meant to be symbolic, but *real* – feature prominently in both mythologies.[36] And vampires have attracted the attention of feminists, for they appear to offer what seems otherwise unattainable in patriarchy: a gender-free space.

When feminists claim, as they occasionally do, that 'vampires are female', they tend to point out that female vampires have survived in mythology

---

[32] Klaniczay, *The Uses*, 187.

[33] As late as 2006, physicists at the University of Central Florida scientifically disproved the vampire myth; see Efthimiou and Ghandi and the report on their work by Gardner. My thanks to Clare Griffin for pointing me to these sources.

[34] According to Barber, vampires tell us something about 'how people in preindustrial cultures look at the processes and phenomena associated with death and the dissolution of the body' (*Vampires*, 1).

[35] Rickels explains the phenomenon of vampires psychoanalytically: we wish death on our nearest and dearest who then, once finally dead, are transformed into the 'vengeful undead out to get the survivor' (23). And: 'vampirism, haunting, all these morbid manifestations are frequent analogies for mourning and aberrant mourning in psychoanalysis' (ix).

[36] Pointed out by Masters 4; Flocke 10; Klemens 11, among others.

since antiquity and dominated the literary landscape until Bram Stoker.[37] More importantly, female vampires link the two most primary sources of myth, sexuality and death, as no other subject could. Blood as a life-giving force (menstruation vs vampirism) and the corresponding view of women/ vampires as hallowed in some cultures and unclean in others[38] are central subjects here, as is the theme of the female vampire as the paradoxical parent. The female vampire is the antithesis of motherhood: she does not feed her offspring but feeds from it; she does not give life but un-death. At the same time, she offers an analogy to *fatherhood*: like a man, she can produce as many offspring as she wants, and for as long as she wants. Her parenthood is absolute, that is: independent of a partner; like the male vampire (but unlike men), she has gained reproductive omnipotence.[39] If women, in the history of Western philosophy and mythology, have been associated with the body, sexuality and the material, vampirism, the 'most material of all cosmologies', proclaims their predominance: vampirism represents the triumph of sexuality over death, of body over spirit, of the material over the invisible.[40] But although, in this sense, 'vampires are female', some feminists have seen the most liberating aspect of the vampire myth in its *neutralisation of gender*. In the world of vampires, gender makes no sense: bodies and gender are dissociated from procreation. Both male and female vampires have only one 'sex organ', the mouth. This is why literature that portrays the female vampire's body as if it were a female body misses the point of vampirism entirely.[41]

Vampire myths, in other words, are the ideal breeding ground for a feminist reinterpretation of psychoanalytic theories and social theories of sexuality. Vampires have been seen as the personification of Laqueur's single-sex model, prevalent from antiquity until the eighteenth century, which sees women as 'inverted' men and thus simultaneously insists on female inferiority and the essential sameness of man and woman. Once this model had become replaced, in the eighteenth century, with the two-sex model, which views men and women as fundamentally different, the single-sex model returned to 'haunt' modern society in the shape of the genderless

---

[37] Flocke 7: 'Vampire sind weiblich'; Volckmann 155: 'Die Vampire der vorchristlichen Jahrtausende sind weiblich. Nahezu alle Mythologien kennen die Vorstellung teils furchterregender, teils verführerischer Nachtdämoninnen, die sich vom Blut … ernähren.' (Flocke's work has been largely reiterated, although without attribution, by Elke Klemens.) See also Elke Liebs for an interpretation of female vampirism in male-authored literature.

[38] See Knight; Buckley and Gottlieb; Flocke 14.

[39] On vampirism and motherhood, see the discussion in Klemens 59–75 and Volckmann 155.

[40] The thought is David Pirie's, cited and discussed in Flocke 12.

[41] See Klemens 29–32.

vampire.[42] Psychoanalysis has taken the issue a step further by asking not only how gender identity is established socially, but also how we *know* what, and who, we are.[43] Post-Freudian psychoanalysis has viewed personal individuation as centrally influenced by social factors, a move that has deprived humans forever of the ability to view themselves as whole. Lacan's mirror stage, for example, is not only a central moment in the formation of individuality, it also establishes the 'dual relationship' between the Ego and the body, thus simultaneously setting in motion the process of individuation and that of alienation. The image in the mirror represents the forever unattainable idea of 'wholeness' and creates an irreparable rift between this ideal and the fragmented Self.[44] For women, the Lacanian 'mirror phase' is exacerbated by the fact that the mirror into which they gaze is 'the distortion mirror of patriarchy'. When women regard themselves in the mirror, 'they see *that* and *how* they *are* regarded; that is: their eyes see through male glasses'.[45] For women, individuation that is not entirely other-determined means developing a 'cross-eyed gaze': one that combines aware-ness of the male view with the capacity to develop a self-view beyond and outside of it, 'the Utopia of a liberated gaze, one that has taken off the glasses'.[46]

Since all of these theories posit that individuation, particularly sexual (Lacan) and gendered (Weigel), is a psychological as well as a social process, mirrors have become one of the central symbols for the socially formed part of the Self, the Other. Children looking into Lacan's mirror see an ideal, perfect wholeness that is incompatible with their experience of fragmenta-tion and strive forever, and vainly, to achieve the ideal represented by the

---

[42] For the theory of the single-sex and two-sex model and shift from one to the other in the eighteenth century, see Laqueur and Honegger, *Die Ordnung*; discussion of these theories, applied to female vampires, in Flocke 40–5 and Klemens 23–5.

[43] See Liebs for a contextualisation of vampirism in the theories of Freud and Jung (251–3).

[44] See Lacan; both Flocke (128–36) and Klemens (27) have interpreted female vampires in Lacanian terms. For a feminist interpretation of Lacan's ideas on the formation of subjectivity and particularly his ideas on the nature of feminine identity, see Grosz.

[45] 'Die Frau in der männlichen Ordnung ist zugleich *beteiligt und ausgegrenzt*. Für das Selbstverständnis der Frau bedeutet das, daß sie sich selbst betrachtet, indem sie sieht, *daß* und *wie* sie betrachtet *wird*; d.h. ihre Augen sehen durch die Brille des Mannes ... Ihr Selbstbildnis entsteht ihr so im Zerr-Spiegel des Patriarchats. Auf der Suche nach ihrem *eigenen Bild* muß sie den Spiegel von den durch männliche Hand aufgemalten *Frauenbildern* befreien' (Weigel, 'Der schielende Blick', 85, emphases original).

[46] 'Die Metapher "Brille" impliziert die Utopie eine befreiten, brillenlosen Blicks' (Weigel, 'Der schielende Blick', 85). See also her elaboration on 130: 'das Vermögen des *"schielenden Blicks"'* [enables a woman] 'sich mit einem (bebrillten) Auge im Alltag zurecht zu finden, um in dem anderen (freien) Auge ihre Träume und Wünsche zu entwerfen, damit sie selbst überleben konnte, ohne ihr Begehren zu töten'.

image. Women looking into Weigel's mirror see man's ideal of woman and either strive forever, and vainly, to achieve this ideal or develop a cross-eyed gaze that permits them to look at, but also beyond the male distortion mirror. But what does the vampire see when she looks in the mirror? In the vampire myth, she sees nothing. Psychoanalytically speaking, this means that her self-image is independent from the Other; she is freed from the obligation to be clearly male or female, clearly homo- or heterosexual,[47] or even, for that matter, clearly alive or dead. What is the purpose of a vampire's life? She lives forever and thus feels no need to procreate for the preservation of her species. She lives forever, and thus death does not force her to inject meaning into her finite existence.[48] In their embodiment of female-identified philosophical categories like earth, death, the body and the material, vampires may well be female, but they also offer all the freedom of an eternal life *independent of gender*. Vampires are not only un-dead, they are also un-sexed.

This is what is at stake for feminists: vampire myths, most clearly those focusing on vampires perceived as 'female', represent an unmatched potential alternative to the idea of gender. Conversely, 'engendering' the female vampire means to bring her back under cultural control. In the following two sections, we will have the opportunity to observe this process closely: in stories and histories of Elizabeth Báthory, the most famous female vampire of all time, and in literature about female vampires from Goethe to the Grimms.

BLOODBATHS: THE CASE OF ELIZABETH BÁTHORY (BORN 1560, SENTENCED 1611, DIED 1614, RETURNED FROM THE GRAVE FROM 1729 ON)

Báthory Erzsébet (1560–1614, fig. 4), or Elizabeth Báthory, stands unrivalled as history's busiest female vampire, or, as William Seabrook put it in 1940, as the 'World Champion Lady Vampire of All Time'. Legend tells us that Báthory, reportedly one of the most beautiful women of her age and relentless in her pursuit of eternal youth and beauty, murdered over 600 maidens to bathe in their blood, that she bled her victims dry in an 'Iron Maiden', a specifically designed 'blood press' installed immediately above her bath, and that it was she – not Prince Vlad III Dracula (1431–76), also known as 'Vlad Ţepeş', the 'Impaler' – who served as Stoker's historical

---

[47] On the female vampire in the mirror, see Flocke 7, 128–64.
[48] Idea and discussion in Klemens 96.

Fig. 4 Erzsébet Báthory. Late sixteenth-century copy of an original painting of 1585. Oil on canvas. By kind permission of Dennis Báthory-Kitsz

blueprint for his Count Dracula.[49] When Farin published his excellent collection of materials in 1989, his list of Báthory literature included five prose narratives, six novels, six poems or ballads, eight dramas or opera libretti, three feature films, more than thirty essays, thirteen independent publications and a magazine series spanning sixty issues and 1,440

---

[49] On the Dracula connection, see, among others, McNally xii, 99; Flocke 11; and Thorne. Stoker read about Báthory in the account offered by Baring-Gould, on which he took copious notes; one of the central ideas he took over from the Báthory legend is that Dracula looks noticeably younger after drinking blood (McNally 99). Thorne offers an explanation as to why Stoker clad Báthory's content into Vlad Dracul's form: 'the idea of choosing as a heroine a blood-obsessed lesbian mass-murderess would have been a short cut to literary obscurity' (*Countess Dracula*, 8).

pages,[50] a list that must now be amended to add numerous historical and fictitious accounts and nearly 200,000 websites and web citations.[51] To say that Báthory galvanised the imagination of her posterity would be a gross understatement. And as is perhaps characteristic of legends, hers rests on a very thin historical foundation.

Our sole source of historical knowledge about the infamous crimes of Elizabeth Báthory are the original trial records and written depositions accumulated by Báthory's accuser and judge, Count György Thurzó (1564–1616), then Palatine of Hungary.[52] Thurzó began to assemble evidence against her as early as March 1610, ordering two of his court notaries, András Keresztúry and Mózes Cziráky, to collect witness testimony to prove 'that this woman, Elisabeth Báthory, in disregard of the respect she owes to God and Man, has cruelly and by various means murdered or ordered killed we don't know how many girls and virgins and other women in her *gynaeceum*'.[53] Keresztúry responded in September, attaching thirty-four witness statements; Cziráky in October with a further eighteen.[54] That same September, Elizabeth Báthory made a testament in which she conferred all her current and future possessions on her children, leaving herself penniless.[55] On 12 December, her son-in-law, Count Nicolaus Zrinyi, wrote to Thurzó, confirming their agreement to imprison Elizabeth Báthory permanently in her castle and the planned distribution of her lands and assets.[56] On 30 December, Thurzó wrote to his wife, stating that he had visited

---

[50]   See his count on 179 and his extensive bibliography on 365–93.

[51]   Historians who have told Báthory's story include von Elsberg, Penrose, McNally and Thorne (see Thorne's introduction on the relative historical reliability of earlier literature on Báthory in *Countess Dracula*). Recent novels include those by Hohlbein and Varesi (both 2005). Websites on Báthory: 18,200 Google hits for 'Báthory Erzsébet'; 141,000 for 'Elizabeth Bathory'; 30,400 for 'Elisabeth Bathory' (Google search conducted on 7 September 2007). These include a site maintained by her descendant Dennis Báthory-Kitsz (http://bathory.org/) and a Wikipedia entry, http://en.wikipedia.org/wiki/Elizabeth_Báthory (last accessed 7 September 2007).

[52]   The trial records have been published in several sources, in both German and English: in their entirety in Farin 67–81 and Elsberg 179–90; both also append relevant correspondence by Thurzó, King Matthias II and others (Farin 263–350; Elsberg 198–204). English translations of the records are, sometimes in excerpted form, in Penrose 149–54 and McNally 204–12. Both German and English versions are translations, which at times differ considerably from each other. In the following, my discussion will rely on the German version published in Farin's collection; all translations into English are mine unless otherwise indicated.

[53]   György Thurzó to András Keresztúry, 5 March 1610: 'daß nämlich diese Frau Elisabeth Báthory unter Hintanstellung ihrer Ehrfurcht vor Gott und den Menschen man-weiß-nicht-wieviele Mädchen und Jungfrauen und andere Frauen ihres Gynaeceums grausam auf verschiedene Weisen ermordet hat und umbringen ließ' (Farin 265). On the same day, Thurzó sent the same letter to Mózes Cziráky; see Farin 277–8.

[54]   See Farin 267–74, 279–84 for their answers and transcriptions of the witness statements.

[55]   Báthory's testament is printed in Farin 286–8.   [56]   Farin 291.

Elizabeth Báthory's castle unannounced, had found one girl dead and another dying, and stated that he hoped to be able to return home as soon as 'the damned woman is brought into her prison and taken care of'.[57] The decision to imprison Báthory for life is also referred to in a local pastor's letter dated 1 January 1611.[58]

Báthory's sentence of life imprisonment, then, had not only already been decided when her trial began on 2 January 1611, but also announced to the community, as the pastor's letter confirms. She was not granted the right – or, as some historians have described it: she was spared the indignity[59] – of appearing in court to defend herself. Thurzó delayed the trial until Parliament was not in session, even though he had had the necessary depositions in hand for more than two months, presumably intending to present Parliament, once reconvened, with a *fait accompli*.[60] He conducted the trial not at Pressburg, the official Palatine's seat, but at his own residence Bicse, where he was, as several historians have pointed out, surrounded by people who owed him their positions and their allegiance.[61] His co-magistrates were Báthory's sons-in-law Nicolaus Zrinyi and György Drugeth Count Homonnay, as well as her son's guardian Imre Megyery, who not only stood to profit from her downfall in terms of money or status,[62] but were also thus put into an ideal position to influence the outcome in favour of Báthory's permanent imprisonment, avoiding a public trial, her possible execution, the resulting blot on the family name and – most importantly – confiscation of her assets by the crown.[63] In two court days, 2 and 7 January 1611, four servants, Báthory's suspected accomplices, were tortured, exhorted to confess and implicate Báthory; three of them were hastily executed immediately after the second session on 7 January. The allegations against Báthory were further substantiated by another 236 depositions, collected

---

[57] Farin 293: 'Ich warte nur, daß die verdammte Frau in die Festung gebracht und versorgt wird.'

[58] Pastor János Ponikenus to Elias Lányi, 1 Jan 1611, Farin 294–8, the reference 295: 'unsere Isebel (ich meine Elisabeth Báthory) empfängt die Strafen, die ihr nach ihren Verbrechen gebühren. Sie wird ins Verließ geführt und im ewigen Kerker, eingemauert, eingeschlossen.'

[59] Among others, Fessler in his massive history of Hungary, xv 492–4; Penrose 138.

[60] McNally 68, 73–4.   [61] Farin 244; Thorne, *Countess Dracula*, 51; McNally 76–7.

[62] Báthory's sons-in-law, or rather their wives, were already named in Báthory's testament; Megyery would have become regent at Báthory's abdication of power since her son Pál was still a minor at the time of her arrest (Thorne, *Countess Dracula*, 165).

[63] This possibility is mentioned by several family members, including Báthory's son Pál Nádasdy, in letters to Thurzó, begging him to avoid a public trial and execution of Báthory and preserve the family's reputation. See, for example, Pál Nádasdy to Thurzó, 23 February 1611 (Farin 306), Nicolaus Zrinyi to Thurzó, 12 February 1611 (Farin 303–4).

by Thurzó's investigators and sent to King Matthias II in July and December 1611.[64]

The interrogation of Báthory's four servants and supposed accomplices confirm the impression of a hastily conducted trial whose outcome had already been decided. János (John) Ujvári, nicknamed Ficzkó ('little fellow'); Dorottya (Dorothy) Szentes, a.k.a. Dorkó; the wetnurse Ilona (Helen) Jó and the washerwoman Katalin (Catherine) Benická, interrogated under severe torture, all confessed to having participated in burials of murder victims. None of them confessed to have taken part in murder, instead implicating each other, or Anna Darvulia, another servant who had already died and whom they all accused of the most bestial brutalities, or – as they were undoubtedly encouraged to do – Elizabeth Báthory herself. The number of victims in their statements vacillates between 37 in sixteen years (Ujvári), 51 in ten years (Jó), 36 in five years (Szentes) and 50 in ten years (Benická). Beyond the two 'Sittkey-girls', who appear in two depositions, none of the accused could state the victims' first or family names or any further details as to who they were. The way in which the questions were posed conforms to the structure of inquisitions of witches, as analysed by Topalović, in every detail: the questions are suggestive, phrased in terms of *how, when, where, who* and *how many*; the question *whether* – giving the accused the option for exculpation – never appears.[65] Other aspects reminiscent of witch trials emerge here as well, including the frequent incrimination of a person already deceased: we know from seventeenth-century inquisition records that many accused witches, knowing that their indictment of someone else would invariably lead to that person's torture and execution, tried to point the finger at people who were either dead or already under arrest for witchcraft.[66]

With only two exceptions so far,[67] historians have pronounced Báthory guilty, and the massive number of witness testimonies that Thurzó mobilised against her certainly appears to be irrefutable. But reading these witness statements only increases the doubts regarding these proceedings. Of the 289 witnesses interviewed by Thurzó's interrogators, 229 stated that they knew nothing but hearsay; twenty-nine stated that they knew nothing at all; two were guessing, and four claimed to have first-hand knowledge of Báthory's

---

[64] See Farin 317–47 for their reports and transcriptions of testimonies.

[65] See the trial records published by Farin 67–81. For a recent account of such procedures, see also Niehaus, *Mord, Geständnis, Widerruf*.

[66] See the trial records published in Kors and Peters; Behringer, *Hexen und Hexenprozesse*, and the discussion in Topalović and Henschel.

[67] One is Tony Thorne (in *Countess Dracula*, 1997), who bases his exculpation of Báthory on previously ignored archival material; the other is László Nagy, who has drawn much ridicule from subsequent historians for his portrayal of Báthory as the victim of political intrigue (1984).

crimes but did not say how (or the nature of their knowledge was not deemed worthy of being recorded). Twenty-five witnesses claimed to have seen corpses – without any knowledge of how they had died – or injured girls – without any knowledge of how they had come by their wounds. Three witnesses unhelpfully referred the interrogator to the (meanwhile executed) accomplices, who would be better able to answer these questions. One doctor testified that he had examined a girl with flesh ripped out of her shoulder and buttocks and cuts on her hands, but does not state whether she was employed by, or indeed had anything to do with, Elizabeth Báthory. Only two witnesses were willing to testify that they had themselves been present at a scene of torture and/or murder.[68]

What we 'know' of the life and crimes of the historical woman who later entered legend as 'Countess Dracula' is, in a word, not very much. What seems clear, however, is that Thurzó, the Habsburg-loyal King Matthias II, and the Habsburgs themselves had excellent reasons to get rid of her. Since the death of Franz Nádasdy, Elisabeth Báthory's husband, the court of Vienna had owed her the massive sum of 17,408 gulden, a debt that she had unsuccessfully tried to collect for six years,[69] and one that would instantly disappear if she were found guilty of a crime. A mere fourteen days after her husband's death, Báthory received a letter from her mother-in-law, Ursula Nádasdy, warning her that a law was being proposed that would strip all non-Catholics – Báthory had converted to Lutheranism, her husband's confession, at her marriage[70] – of their possessions.[71] And Báthory's possessions were vast indeed: owning three castles in today's Austria, seven in today's Czech Republic and Slovakia, three in today's Romania and eight in today's Hungary, she may well have been the richest woman of her country.[72] Previously disregarded archival material translated by Thorne shows clearly that Báthory was involved in anti-Habsburg politics.[73] Thorne

---

[68] See the four reports and transcriptions of testimonies by Keresztúry and Cziráky (Farin 267–74, 279–84, 317–47).

[69] Elsberg 134–5.

[70] The first text available in Germany on Báthory, Turóczi's *Tragica Historia* (1729), attributes her entire life of crime (which in his account consists of literal bloodbaths and the murders of 600 victims) to her conversion to Lutheranism: 'Elisabeth Báthory, Gemahlin des Grafen Franz Nádasdy, entsagte aus Liebe zu ihrem Mann dem katholischen Glauben und trat zum lutherischen über, dem ihr Gatte angehörte. Hierin liegen die Anfänge des Untergangs' (Turóczi, in Farin 23–4).

[71] Ursula Nádasdy to Elizabeth Báthory, 18 January 1604 (Farin 237–8).

[72] See Farin 241 for a list of her assets.

[73] Thorne, *Countess Dracula*, 202–22; see also McNally, who has read the accusation against Elizabeth Báthory in the context of Thurzó's plan to bring Gábor Báthory to heel. Gábor Báthory, Prince of Transylvania, was Elizabeth Báthory's cousin and involved in a plot to topple King Matthias and expand Transylvania to absorb Habsburg lands (72).

also describes the cases of other rich widows in seventeenth-century Hungary who were, immediately after their husband's deaths, accused of witchcraft and deposed, their lands and assets falling to their accusers.[74] Báthory herself forestalled this fate by making a will – in September 1610, in the month Thurzó received the first report and witness statements against her, and over three months *before* she was officially accused – in which she deprived herself of all present and *future* possessions, including the potential repayment of the large debt she was owed, keeping not a single penny that could be confiscated. Matthias II, in fact, only gave up his quest to have Báthory dragged before an official court once the Hungarian Parliament had convinced him that there was no financial benefit to the crown in doing so, since Báthory, at that point, owned nothing.[75]

The fact alone that the only written sources documenting Báthory's guilt were authored by those who had set out to destroy her and who stood to profit from her downfall[76] should make us more suspicious than historians have tended to be. In their works, Báthory appears as guilty beyond any reasonable doubt because, to cite one of them,

> one cannot explain away ... the hundreds of witnesses who testified at the investigations before and after the formal trial ... To doubt all this evidence one would be obliged to assume that the hundreds of witnesses were part of a vast conspiracy to entrap Countess Bathory; but such a huge plot, involving so many people, is not a likely prospect given the conditions of those times.[77]

In the end, though, these hundreds of witnesses did not, collectively, say very much, and the sheer quantity of witnesses Thurzó mobilised, undoubtedly impressive, should not blind us to the dubious quality of their testimony. Certainly, there is some damning evidence against Báthory,

---

[74] Thorne, *Countess Dracula*, 223–46.

[75] Parliamentary missive to Matthias II, 31 March 1611 (Farin 310–12): 'Und wenn auch der Staat gerade in diesem Fall zulassen würde, daß die Todesstrafe gegen sie verhängt würde, so kann dennoch kein größerer Vorteil zu hoffen sein, als nur der dritte Teil der Güter der zum Tode Verurteilten nach üblicher Schätzung, welcher genau genommen nach Abzug der Anteile der jeweiligen Söhne und Töchter übrigbleibt ... Ja, es scheint dem Fiskus Eurer Majestät nicht einmal dieser Vorteil zufallen zu können, weil die vorgenannte Frau Nádasdy schon vor einigen Jahren alle ihre Besitztümer abgetreten und diese ihren Söhnen überantwortet und ihre gesamten und völligen Ansprüche darauf ihnen übertragen haben soll, so daß die nun Gefangene und Eingekerkerte weder etwas besitzt noch sich etwas in ihrem Eigentum befindet. Daraus folgt, daß auch nichts, auch wenn sie verurteilt würde, eingezogen oder der Fiskus irgendetwas in Besitz nehmen kann. So blieben Mühe und Aufwand, welche dadurch entstehen, gänzlich vergeblich' (311). Matthias's mercenary motives in pursuing 'justice' against Báthory have been noted by Elsberg 159; McNally 84–7; and Thorne, *Countess Dracula*, 173–6, among many others. An English translation of this letter is in Thorne, *Countess Dracula*, 173–5.

[76] Discussion by Thorne, *Countess Dracula*, 213–32.   [77] McNally 92.

consisting in two eyewitness testimonies to torture, twenty-five testimonies as to its result, the trial testimonies of her four accomplices, and Thurzó's own claim that he stumbled over a corpse when entering her castle. If we discount Thurzó's statement due to his obvious bias, the crushing weight of 'hundreds of witnesses' has dwindled to thirty-one who can even be taken seriously. Based on their testimonies, we may well surmise that Báthory was guilty of multiple murder, or at least extreme cruelty to her servants (which, by all accounts, was nothing unusual in the noble houses of seventeenth-century Hungary[78]). Alternatively, we may assume that her suspected accomplices, crazed by the pain of torture, agreed to whatever confessions were put in their mouths: after all, we know of thousands of documented confessions elicited under very similar circumstances in which accused 'witches' testified that they saw Goody Müller, Maier or Schmidt fly off to the witches' sabbath.[79] In the absence of verifiable evidence either way, historians are faced with two unappetising options. Either we believe that Elizabeth Báthory murdered, over the course of anywhere between five and sixteen years, anywhere between thirty-six and 650 young girls, without anyone raising an objection until Thurzó began to scour the countryside for witnesses, at which point they obligingly poured fourth in their hundreds. Alternatively, we can read the confessions of Báthory's accomplices on the same level as we would read the confessions of accused witches, and further surmise that Thurzó, whose control over his subjects has been described as near-absolute,[80] 'instructed' twenty-seven witnesses successfully and 262 less successfully. Which of these options seems more likely is up to the individual to decide.

Without question, the two most titillating aspects of Báthory legend – and the two most relentlessly repeated in literary and 'historical' accounts – are the claims that she killed 650 girls and literally bathed in the blood of her victims. Both are almost certainly apocryphal. No bloodbaths, other than in the figurative sense, were mentioned at the trial or in any of the nearly 300 depositions. The story of the 650 victims appears only once in the trial

[78] For example, McNally 42–3: 'Such treatment of individual Slovak peasants by their Hungarian lords was perhaps a little extreme even for those days, but it would have aroused little comment even if it were well known. Peasants were in general treated quite harshly; servants were often recruited by force and usually subjected to bodily punishment by their Hungarian overlords. They were considered chattel and had no legal rights.' See also Elsberg, who comes dangerously close to claiming that work-hardened, primitive and entirely servile Slovak peasants, faced with the prospect of being tortured and murdered, would not have minded all that much (113).

[79] See the records published by Kors and Peters; Behringer, *Witches and Witch Hunts* and *Hexen und Hexenprozesse*; Schwerhoff, 'Strafjustiz', and the linguistic analysis by Topalović, among many others.

[80] For example, Farin 244; Thorne, *Countess Dracula*, 51; McNally 76.

records, in a deposition by a girl whose first name was Susanna and whose last name and connection with the case are not on record. Susanna claimed that she had heard from court official Jakab Szilvásy – who, for some reason, was not called in to confirm the story – that he had found a list of 650 names in a casket owned by Báthory, signed by Elizabeth Báthory herself. No explanation is offered for why Báthory would possibly want to incriminate herself in this fashion, and the incredible number 650, which later became a central part of Báthory lore, is not confirmed by anyone else. (Susanna herself later amended her estimated number of Báthory's victims to eighty.[81])

The complete absence of verifiable evidence for either the bloodbaths or the 650 fatalities has done nothing to dampen the enthusiasm with which later authors have seized upon these features. Both already appear as indisputable facts in the earliest sources available in Germany, László Turóczi's *Tragica Historia* (1729) and Matthias Bel's *The Castle and Town of Csejte* (*Burg und Stadt Csejte*, 1742).[82] In the flood of publications that followed, the number of victims varies between twelve and 650, although there is hardly an account, fictional or not, that does not refer to the bloodbaths. Bathing or washing in blood is a prominent motif in the anonymous tale 'Countess Nádasdy, or: On the Bad Advice of Old Crones' ('Die Gräfin Nádasdi, oder: was rathen alte Weiber nicht', 1795), Michael Wagner's *Contributions to a Philosophical Anthropology* (*Beyträge zur Philosophischen Anthropologie und den damit verwandten Wissenschaften*, 1794–6), Bornschein's novel *Isidore Countess Nádasdy, Vicereine of Hungary, a Twelvefold Murderess for Vanity* (*Isidore Gräfin von Nadasdi, Vicekönigin von Hungarn, zwölffache Mörderin aus Eitelkeit*, ca. 1805), Baron of M-y's *Elisabeth Báthory. A True Story* (*Elisabeth Báthory. Eine wahre Geschichte*, 1812), J. A. Fessler's *History of Hungary and Its People* (*Die Geschichte der Ungern und ihrer Landsassen*, 1815–25), Aloys Baron Mednyánszky's *Picturesque Travels on the River Vág in Hungary* (*Malerische Reise auf dem Waagflusse in Ungern*, 1826), Johann Nepomuk Vogl's poem 'The Lady of Castle Cseitha' ('Die Burgfrau zu Cseitha', 1836), A. Marienburg's 'Elisabeth Báthori. A Tale Based on Historical Sources' ('Elisabeth Báthori. Historischen Quellen entnommene Erzählung', 1838), Michael Dionys Doleschall's 'Addendum on Elisabeth Báthori' ('Noch etwas über

---

[81] For Susanna's testimony, see Farin 78; see also Thorne, *Countess Dracula*, 52–3.

[82] Bel, 'Burg und Stadt Csejte (1742)' and excerpts from Turóczi's *Tragica Historia* are reprinted in Farin 21–7. Fr László Turóczi's name is given, in many sources, as Turáczi; I will refer to him as Turóczi, following Farin, from whose version of the text I am quoting.

Elisabeth Báthori', 1838) and Moriz Gans's historical novel *Elisabeth Báthory – The Secrets of Castle Csejte* (*Elisabeth Bathory – Die Geheimnisse der Schachtizburg*, 1854).[83] The credit for the Iron Maiden or blood-press probably has to go to Leopold von Sacher-Masoch, in whose tale 'Eternal Youth. 1611' ('Ewige Jugend. 1611', 1874) it makes its first appearance.[84]

These sources vary considerably in genre, ranging from histories, anthropological treatises and travelogues to various literary genres, but hardly at all in their portrayal of the Báthory story. When the trial records were published in German in 1817, they did nothing to deflate the story of the bloodbaths and Báthory's 650 victims, which spread like an infection to virtually all texts – even those by historians like Fessler or Mednyánszky or historical fiction writers like Marienburg or Gans. Farin is quite right in claiming that these sources are 'redundant to a degree that cannot be surpassed'.[85] And yet, two recurrent motifs in this history of monotony deserve our momentary attention. The first is the way in which literature on Báthory has attempted to domesticate the horror of the Báthory myth, not, as we might assume, by revisiting the rather less garish and more ambiguous trial records, but by containing Elizabeth Báthory within the realm of feminine 'normality'. The second is the introduction of fairy-tale motifs in Báthory texts, even those that lay claim to the highest degree of historical accuracy.

The most obvious way of repressing the myth of Báthory as a *vampire*, which is strongly suggested in the tale of rejuvenation by means of the blood of hundreds of virgins, is to turn her back into a 'normal' woman. Wagner's *Anthropology* was the first to effect this transformation on a scientific basis:

The difference between the sexes with regard to feelings, affect and passions is too obvious not to be readily apparent to everyone. Women's delicate physique, the sensitivity of their nerves, and their very structure increases their susceptibility to all sensual impressions, and their lively imaginations and temperaments make them more extreme in their emotions and passions. Love is their main interest and occupation; vanity is their most frequent moral disease, which is most dangerous if founded on beauty and accompanied by the obsession to please the other sex or to

---

[83] All of these texts have been republished, in excerpts or in their entirety, in Farin 31–144, along with later nineteenth- and twentieth-century versions of the story (145–260).
[84] Reprinted in Farin 145–61.
[85] 'Alle diese Bücher und Schriften im Gefolge des Elsberg-Buches sind von einer kaum zu überbietenden Redundanz. Aus Mangel an Neuem wird das altbekannte Material, meist noch nicht einmal auf originelle Weise, gewendet und geknetet' (Farin 199).

attract attention. Often it is the source of the most revolting cruelties and inhumane actions.[86]

Since Wagner assumes these anthropological 'facts' to pertain to all women, their application to Báthory seems to explain the inexplicable: in his text, Elizabeth Báthory's revolting cruelties are not those of a vampiric monster, but fall well within the scope of feminine normality. Indeed, her main objective seems to have been at first to please her man ('Elisabetha *** preened herself, to please her husband, to an inordinate degree and spent half of her days at her *toilette*'[87]) and later other men ('She continued on her mission after the death of her husband in 1604 in order to gain new admirers and suitors'[88]). We have no indication that the historical Elizabeth Báthory showed any interest in men; she has even, although this may well also be apocryphal, occasionally been accused of lesbianism.[89] Yet Báthory's proposed desire to attract men seemed sufficient to most writers to explain her incredible cruelty: it made her understandable to the patriarchal imagination.

That a coquettish and vain woman would assiduously attempt to preserve her physical charms in a state of permanent loveliness is entirely natural. Cosmetics, after all, have been a science for untold ages. No means that even remotely promises the hoped-for success will be left untried in order to please men, to beguile them and to turn them into love-slaves.[90]

Báthory's crimes, in other words, were merely an augmentation of her 'entirely natural' wish to 'please men', in a word: her longing 'to be

---

86 'Der Unterschied welcher zwischen den beyden Geschlechtern in Ansehung der Gefühle, Affecte und Leidenschaften statt findet, ist zu auffallend, als daß er nicht jedermann in die Augen springen sollte. Der zarte Körperbau der Frauenzimmer, die Empfindsamkeit ihrer Nerven, und die Beschaffenheit ihrer gesammten Organisation erhöhet ihre Empfänglichkeit gegen alle sinnliche Eindrücke, und die Lebhaftigkeit ihrer Einbildungskraft und ihres Temperaments macht sie in den meisten Affecten und Leidenschaften heftiger. Die Liebe ist ihr Interesse und ihre vornehmste Beschäftigung; die Eitelkeit eine ihrer gewöhnlichsten moralischen Krankheiten, welche letztere am gefährlichsten wird, wenn sie sich auf die Schönheit gründet, und von der Sucht, dem andern Geschlechte zu gefallen, oder Aufsehen zu machen, begleitet wird. Nicht selten ist sie die Quelle der empörendsten Grausamkeiten und der unmenschlichsten Handlungen' (Michael Wagner ii 268–9).

87 'Elisabetha *** putzte sich ihrem Gemahle zu Gefallen in ungemeinem Grade, und brachte halbe Tage bey der Toilette zu' (Michael Wagner ii 269).

88 'Sie setzte daher dieses Handwerk auch nach dem Tode ihres Gemahls fort, welcher im Jahr 1604 starb, um neue Anbeter und Liebhaber zu gewinnen' (Michael Wagner ii 270).

89 See Thorne's overview of literature on Báthory, *Countess Dracula*, 1–12; see Farin 251–60 on Báthory and lesbian vampire movies.

90 'Daß eine gefallsüchtige, eitle Frau eifrig sich bemüht, den Reiz ihrer äußeren Erscheinung im Stadium unveränderlicher Anmuth zu erhalten, ist überaus natürlich. Die Kosmetik ist ja seit urdenklichen Zeiten schon eine Wissenschaft. Um den Männern zu gefallen, sie zu berücken und zu Sklaven der Liebe zu machen, wird ja kein Mittel unversucht gelassen, wenn es nur halbwegs den erwünschten Erfolg verspricht' (Elsberg 8).

loved'.[91] The idea is already expressed in the first source of Báthory lore available to Germans. In a scene later to be repeated *ad infinitum*, Turóczi shows us Elizabeth Báthory seated at her mirror, observing a tiny speck of blood on her skin and discovering, after wiping it off, the rejuvenating effects of human blood. This promptly inspires the following idea:

How now? if such a small amount of blood can increase my beauty to this extent, what effect will occur if I bathe in it completely? Above all, my desire is to be attractive to men; in order to attract attention, I must be the most beautiful …[92]

upon which she unhesitatingly slaughters all the girls in her *gynaeceum* and sinks, sighing langourously, into the first of many bloodbaths (fig. 5).

The woman in the vampire, the reasoning seems to be, is the only way to tame the vampire in the woman. Moriz Gans, for example, presented his heroine as a force of nature: 'Elizabeth was like the Plague: wherever she appeared she claimed her victims, but nobody knew the origin of the evil.'[93] But this force of nature is easily domesticated by her *feminine* nature: she is on the brink of murdering young Gyöngyike – for 'feminine' motives: 'I am Elizabeth Báthory – and you the bride of a man whom I have loved since yesterday! Do you understand now?'[94] Shortly thereafter, however, she discovers that her potential victim is her long-lost daughter, and her feminine nature once again asserts itself: 'This woman, who had plummeted to the depths of such unparalleled bestiality – she still had a sigh for the memories of the blissful hours of her first love, there was still in her heart a warm place nurturing a mother's sacred feelings!'[95] Motherhood, in this version, trumps love, and young Gyöngyike is spared. Similarly, Elsberg records appreciatively that Báthory was 'unquestionably a good housewife, economical, active, industrious, and seeing to everything', a woman who put great stock in her domestics' 'order and punctuality', even if he 'cannot approve

---

[91] 'Geliebt will sie sich sehen, schwärmerisch und zärtlich, triumphirend über die Zeit, welche ihrer Schönheit nichts anhaben kann' (Elsberg 50).

[92] 'Was? wenn so eine kleine Menge Blut die Schönheit so sehr zu steigern vermag, welche Wirkung wird erst eintreten, wenn ich mich ganz darin bade? Vor allem strebe ich danach, den Männern zu gefallen; um ins Auge zu fallen, muß ich die Schönste sein' (Turóczi, in Farin 24).

[93] 'Elisabeth war wie die Pest; wo sie erschien, forderte sie ihre Opfer, aber Niemand wußte, wo der Sitz des Uebels sei' (Moriz Gans, *Elisabeth Bathory – Die Geheimnisse der Schachtizburg* (1854), excerpts in Farin 103–43, the quotation 116).

[94] 'Ich bin Bathory Elisabeth – und Du die Braut eines Mannes, den ich seit gestern liebe! weißt Du nun genug?' (Gans 121).

[95] 'Das Weib, so tief gesunken, so beispiellos entmenscht, es hatte doch einen Seufzer für die Erinnerung an die seligen Stunden der ersten Liebe, es fand sich in seinem Herzen noch ein warmes Plätzchen für die heiligen Empfindungen der Mutter!' (Gans 125).

Fig. 5 Elizabeth Báthory in the popular imagination. From McFarlane's Monsters
series 3: 'The Six Faces of Madness'. Photo by Toni Tasić

of the means she usually employed' in her pursuit of perfect domesticity (by
which he means the torture and murder of neglectful servants).[96]

The idea that Báthory's crimes were, at bottom, inspired by the quintessentially feminine 'mission' to please men (and possibly tempered by other
feminine joys like motherhood and good housekeeping) is harshly attacked
by other authors who place the emphasis on Báthory's (unfeminine) cruelty

---

[96] 'Auf Ordnung und Pünktlichkeit sah die Herrin eben überaus streng, doch die Mittel, welche sie in
dieser Absicht anzuwenden pflegte, können wir nicht billigen … Unzweifelhaft war sie eine gute
Hausfrau, sparsam, thätig, rührig, sich um Alles kümmernd. Mit einer Consequenz, die unter
anderen Umständen rühmenswerth wäre, hielt sie ihre Dienstboten zur Arbeit, zur Pflicht an'
(Elsberg 99 and 100 respectively).

rather than her (more understandable) vanity. Their point may be the exact opposite of Turóczi's and Wagner's, but their argumentation is identical:

Endowed by the Creator with a more delicate organisation in order to soften the storms in the passionate souls of men, destined by physique, education and civic constitution to stem the wild destructive tendencies of the stronger sex, we see, all over the world, the more beautiful half of Mankind dedicate themselves faithfully to this delightful calling. Only the conjuncture of extraordinary circumstances could remove Woman from such a sweet destiny and plant the horrible impulse to torture, hate and murder humans into her soft heart, which was fashioned to feel only compassion, tenderness and love.[97]

Both texts describing Báthory as a 'natural' but perverted woman and those understanding her as the antithesis of femininity represent an attempt to interpret the female vampire within the framework of the female. This, of course, necessitates an explanation as to what 'extraordinary circumstances' might have estranged this particular woman from her 'sweet destiny' to such a radical degree. Those writers whose imaginations were unequal to the task found a way of partially exculpating their heroine by endowing her with accomplices whose unrestrained sadism and bloodthirst are only matched by their repulsive exterior. This is the tactic employed in the anonymously published tale 'Countess Nádasdy, or On the Bad Advice of Old Crones' (1795) and in Bornschein's novel *Isidore Countess Nádasdy, Vicereine of Hungary, Twelve-fold Murderess for Vanity* (1805). In both stories, an old crone leads the hapless countess from the path of virtue to that of butchery. The anonymous tale, ending horribly with the burning of both crone and countess, issues to young girls the twofold warning to avoid feminine vanity and old hags with equal alacrity.[98] Bornschein's Isidore falls even more squarely

---

[97] 'Sanfter vom Schöpfer organisiert, um die Stürme in der leidenschaftlichen Seele des Mannes zu mildern, durch körperliche Beschaffenheit, Erziehung und bürgerliche Verfassung bestimmt, dem wilden Zerstörungstriebe des stärkeren Geschlechtes Einhalt zu thun, sehen wir bei allen Nationen der Erde die schönere Hälfte der Menscheit [sic] auch treu sich diesem schöneren Berufe widmen. Nur das Zusammentreffen ausserordentlicher Umstände kann das Weib solch' einer süssen Bestimmung entrücken, und in das sanfte, nur zur Theilnahme, Zärtlichkeit und Liebe geschaffne Herz den gräßlichen Trieb pflanzen, Menschen zu quälen, zu hassen, zu morden' (Freyherr von M-y: 'Elisabeth Báthory, Eine wahre Geschichte' (1812), Farin 61–5, the quotation 61). See also A. Marienburg's 'Elisabeth Báthory. Historischen Quellen entnommene Erzählung' (1838), Farin 83–90, which copies liberally from the Baron's tale (this passage, near-verbatim, on 83).

[98] 'Lernet an diesem Beispiele, Mädchen und Weiber, daß euere unschuldig scheinende Putzsucht oft die einzige Quelle ist, aus welcher euer Lasterleben entsteht … Hütet euch, Mädchen und Weiber, für dem Umgange mit alten Weibern … Der Umgang mit alten Weibern, (pflegt ein junger Philosoph zu sagen) bringt jungen Mädchen und Weibern Unheil, und wäre ich Mann, so wäre dies die einzige Bedingung, die ich meiner Frau vorschreiben würde, daß sie den Umgang mit dieser Klasse der Menschen aufs strengste vermeiden sollte' (Anon., 'Die Gräfin Nádasdy', Farin 31–3, the quotations 31–2).

into Wagner's category of anthropologically determined femininity: his novel opens with Isidore lolling languorously on her sofa, wondering what means might gain her a young courtier's love who has so far resisted her advances.[99] Sibylle (!), 'an old, ugly hag with a hunchback and red, bleary eyes',[100] has the answer, of course. Overcoming Isidore's scruples, it is she who murders the virgins and draws Isidore's bloodbaths, degrading Isidore herself to a mere and frequently remorseful accomplice. This continues until both are discovered and burnt at the stake – Isidore with prayers and the unavoidable moral of the story,[101] Sibylle with curses and blasphemies on her lips. Clearly, this literature owes nothing to the history of Elizabeth Báthory, to the extent that we know it; and yet – and paradoxically – the old-crone motif, with its irresistible contrast of beauty and ugliness, was persistent enough to mutate into several Báthory 'histories':

The Countess, perfumed and beautiful, was constantly framed by Jó Ilona and Dorkó, each one smelling as bad as the other. Counting on their ugliness, trusting in their foulness and unbelievable cruelty, Erzsébet made accomplices of these two powers of stale blood, of squelched bones, and disembowelled beasts.[102]

We are now squarely in the realm of fairy tales. Here, outward beauty may deceive, but ugliness of appearance nearly always betrays an equally hideous core. Here, Báthory's wetnurse and washerwoman are turned into 'old crones' or witches; her servant Ujváry, whose nickname 'Ficzkó' may or may not have described his short stature, metamorphoses into a dwarf.[103] But the fairy tale of Elizabeth Báthory is not depleted in the story of Beauty

---

[99] 'Eines Nachmittags lag Isidore halbträumend auf dem Sofa, und dachte über die Mittel nach, um Seltings Gegenliebe zu erringen. Keins von allen schien ihren Beifall zu erhalten. "Ach! seufzte sie dann, gäb es doch noch wohlthätige Feen in der Welt, deren Zauberstabe es leicht war, die Runzeln des Alters mit der Lenzröthe des Lebens zu vertilgen. Selting sollte mir dann nicht entgehen"' (Ernst Johann Daniel Bornschein, *Isidore Gräfin von Nádasdy, Vicekönigin von Hungarn, zwölffache Mörderin aus Eitelkeit*, ca. 1805, excerpts in Farin 37–59, the quotation 37).

[100] 'Sybille war ein altes, häßliches Weib, mit einem Höcker und rothen triefigten Augen. Sie stand mitten in den siebzigen' (Bornschein, in Farin 37).

[101] 'Oh! that I could warn you, with all my heart, from the snake's bite of feminine seduction! How often did vanity become the downfall of the female sex! How many women have lost their honour and peace through vanity!' ('O! möcht' ich dich recht innig warnen können vor diesem Schlangenbiß der weiblichen Verführung. Wie oft ward die Eitelkeit der Fallstrick des weiblichen Geschlechts! Wie viele Frauenzimmer verlohren dadurch Ehre und Ruhe!', Bornschein, in Farin 56).

[102] Penrose 47.

[103] For example in Mednyánszky's *Malerische Reise*: 'Durch mehrere Jahre opferte Elisabeth, mit Beyhülfe zweyer alter Weiber und ihres Hofzwerges Fitzko, bey [sic] 300 Mädchen' (95–6); Elsberg: 'Geistig beschränkt und körperlich verunstaltet soll er [Ujváry] gewesen sein, ein zwerghafter Krüppel nach jeder Richtung hin', and: 'Sie soll von hoher Statur, hager, aber dabei doch sehr kräftig gewesen sein, zahnlos und abschreckend häßlich' (on Dorottya Szentes, 97–8); Ilona Jó is described by the same author as massively fat, ugly, small, stocky and missing one eye (78). Elsberg comments laconically on these descriptions: 'Der naiven Auffassung war es ein Bedürfniß, die

and her beasts: in several accounts, both literary and 'historical', Báthory is also endowed with a mirror.

This mirror leads the same double life as the more famous mirror belonging to Snow White's evil stepmother, serving both as a surface of reflection and as a means of magic divination. In fairness it has to be said that the story of the mirror did originate in the trial records. It constitutes one of the most incongruous parts of Ujváry's confession: 'There was something in a box, in the shape of a pretzel, with a mirror in the middle, she prayed in front of it for two hours.'[104] Whatever the actual meaning of Ujváry's rather mysterious statement, Wagner added the missing link in 1796: 'She was also devoted to putative magic and had her own magic mirror in the shape of a pretzel, praying in front of it for hours.'[105] In his text, ostentatiously not a fairy tale but an anthropological treatise, Báthory's pretzel-shaped device began its long discursive life as a magic mirror. Thirty years later, we find Báthory again in Mednyánszky's travelogue of Hungary, as 'a vain woman' seated – where else – 'in front of her mirror'.[106] Elsberg's *The Blood Countess*, long considered the most reliable historical account of Elizabeth Báthory, shows her to us 'seated for hours in front of a small "mirror shaped in the form of a pretzel, which she kept in a box", assidu-ously seeking to discern the future'.[107] But it is not until Penrose's surrealist adaptation of the Báthory myth that Báthory's mirror comes into its own:

In order to have confidence in herself, she had to have her beauty praised continually; five or six times a day she would change her dress, her adornment, her coiffure; she lived in front of her great gloomy mirror, the famous mirror for which she herself had drawn the model, and which was made in the form of a *pretzl* (a figure of eight), to allow her to slip her arms through it and remain leaning there without getting tired throughout the long hours, by day and by night, she spent in contemplating her own image. This was the only door she ever opened, the door into herself. And her taciturnity was such that in the mirror, where every woman

---

Dienerin der Gräfin möglichst abschreckend zu gestalten, weil ein Mensch mit einer schwarzen Seele den Stempel der Verworfenheit an der Stirne tragen muß' (78). This insight, however, did not transfer to his own analysis of Báthory's painting (8–9), which is hardly more sophisticated.

[104] 'In einer Schachtel ist etwas wie eine Bretzel eingefaßt, in der Mitte ein Spiegel, vor dem betet sie auch zwei Stunden lang' (Farin 70).

[105] 'Sie war auch der vermeynten Zauberei ergeben, hatte einen eigenen Zauberspiegel in Gestalt einer Bretze, bey dem sie stundenlang bethete' (Michael Wagner II 271).

[106] 'Eines Tages sass die Eitle am Spiegel, und aufgereizt durch ein geringes Versehen der Dienerinn, schlug sie dieselbe so gewaltig in das Gesicht, das alsobald das Blut hervor strömte.' Mednyánszky goes on to repeat Turóczi's original story of Báthory's recognition of the beneficial effects of the blood on her skin and her immediate decision to take a bloodbath (*Malerische Reise*, 95).

[107] 'Stundenlang saß sie daher vor einem kleinen, "nach Art einer Bretze gewundenen Spiegel, den sie in einer Schachtel aufbewahrte", eifrig bemüht, die Zukunft zu erforschen' (Elsberg 163; the double quotation marks indicate Elsberg's transcription of the relevant passage in Ujváry's confession).

smiles at her reflection, she struck at herself over and over again, hammering her own effigy at her dumb forge. No flame, no air. Clad in red velvet, adorned in white, in black or pearl, her face heavily made up beneath the large pale forehead. In the heart of her room, encircled by candelabras, nothing but herself; a self always unseizable, and whose many faces she was forever unable to assemble in a single look.[108]

Although this story starts innocuously enough – Báthory appears, at the outset, as nothing more than the typically 'female' paragon of vanity and insecurity –, there is more here than the mirror used for purposes of reflection or divination. This is, unmistakably, the mirror that is the source of both individuation and alienation. Grown to full height from the trinket once kept in a box, this mirror becomes simultaneously Lacan's nightmare and Weigel's dream. Báthory's mirror, unlike all others, does *not* reflect the Other: both the mirror itself and the image it produces are of Báthory's own devising. The door she opens leads only into herself. In this way, Penrose defines Elizabeth Báthory as a vampire in the feminist sense. Her Báthory has achieved what is forever beyond the reach of Lacan's children, what is attainable to Weigel's women only in the far reaches of Utopia. She has taken off the male glasses, she sees nothing but herself in the mirror: she has eliminated the Other. Independent of society, independent of the obligations of her gender, she fashions herself in her own image. If anyone can achieve 'wholeness', truly see *herself* and nothing but herself when she looks in the mirror, it is this Elizabeth Báthory. And yet, her own and exclusive authorship of her self-image does not solve the problem of alienation.

Penrose's Báthory book has often been criticised, and justly, for not being a reliable 'history'. Nevertheless, among all the stories and histories of Elizabeth Báthory – even those that indulge in the most lurid descriptions of maimings, murder, blood and guts – this is the only one that takes her seriously as a female *vampire* rather than reducing her to a (natural or antithetical) *female*. Penrose's story is not one of vanity but one of self-hatred; Penrose's mirror is not the place 'where every woman smiles at her reflection' but a place where Báthory strikes out angrily at herself, at her own creation. No Other intrudes on her process of formation, but wholeness still eludes her: her creation, her Self, remains 'unseizable', splintering into 'many faces' that she is 'forever unable to assemble in a single look'. And 'forever', in this case, has to be taken literally: the figure eight is the sign of infinity; the vampire lives forever, condemned to eternal hate-filled interaction with her own abhorred Self. The horror that unfolds here is

---

[108] Penrose 20, emphasis original.

one that goes to the very core of individuation: the fragmentation of the Self is not something imposed on it from the outside, it is in and of the Self. Wholeness is beyond reach even in a space free from gender roles, social strictures or outside pressure of any kind. Even the act of self-creation can produce no more than an 'effigy'. Penrose's story, while being the first to take Báthory's vampirism seriously on a meta-textual level, is simultaneously a dispiriting answer to the feminist celebration of the female vampire, as well as a serious repudiation of highly influential psychoanalytic and feminist theories. It refutes the idea that 'wholeness' can be attained in a space that contains no Other, and that once we have eliminated the Other, whatever remains must be the Self.

CONTAINMENT: FEMALE VAMPIRES IN LITERATURE FROM GOETHE TO THE GRIMMS (1797–1823)

Beyond the copious literature on Elizabeth Báthory, German literature is comparatively rarely haunted by vampires.[109] The few that do appear tend to be stripped of many of their vampiric credentials. Often their chief horror derives from one aspect alone, their revenantism. Since German literature focuses chiefly on the erotic aspects of vampiric lore, its vampires are no longer a threat to humanity but tend to focus their attentions on a single human, the either faithless, overly bashful, or lost lover. Male vampires in literature are endowed with an extraordinary sexual aggressiveness; female vampires with a – for a vampire – extraordinary degree of mortality. As this already indicates, vampires in literature have lost, in addition to the better part of their eeriness, that genderlessness that is a central attribute of their mythological counterparts. Gender, in fact, is what literary vampires are all about.

In its muted form as either a romantic story of love lost or a gruesome tale of thwarted sexual fulfilment, German vampire literature tends to cast male vampires as sexual predators.[110] Fifty years before Stoker 'created the archetypal image of the bloodsucking undead as a representative of a phallocentric and patriarchal sexuality',[111] Ossenfelder's vampire, in a poem that is

---

[109] Certainly compared to the English gothic tradition, which is the focus of most German studies of vampire literature.

[110] See Barber's description of this tradition, *Vampires*, 83: 'his attacks usually have a pronounced sexual component: he is magnetic, irresistible, and deliberate in his movements, as though he knows that the lady really wants it this way. This implicit sexuality is suggested by the fact that, while he attacks men as well, he seldom does so in close-up, and both location and pace are apt to differ: women are attacked in their boudoir, in a leisurely manner, men in some dark place where they know better than to be, and quickly.'

[111] Barkhoff 128.

barely more than a vicarious celebration of rape ('Der Vampir', 1748), overcame the reluctance of his 'Christianchen'.[112] In Bürger's poem 'Lenore' (1774), his eponymous heroine, who had refused to let go of her dead lover, is punished for her rejection of God's will: her paramour returns from the grave to take her to his 'wedding bed' six feet under. These texts, while disturbing enough in their portrayal of sexual aggression, already demonstrate the domestication of the mythological vampire. Literary vampires do not attack at random; they pose a danger only to their 'brides'. The universality of the threat is contained within the specificity of sexual attack. This type of the 'phallocentric and patriarchal', but at the same time reassuringly domestic and heterosexually attached, male vampire reappears in several early nineteenth-century texts, including Theodor Hildebrand's novel *The Vampyre, or Death's Bride* (*Der Vampyr oder die Totenbraut*, 1828), Johann Spindler's story 'The Vampyre and his Bride' ('Der Vampyr und seine Braut', 1826) and its dramatic adaptation by Alexander Cosmar (*Der Vampyr: Trauerspiel in fünf Abtheilungen*, 1828).[113]

The link in this literature between vampirism and sexuality (or rather: the reduction of vampirism to an *aspect* of sexuality) practically mandates the protagonists' conformity with contemporary gender ideology. In literature describing female vampires, this is even more pronounced. Vampiric transformation here often coincides with central stages of female sexual initiation: it occurs during the wedding night, as in Goethe's 'Bride of Corinth' ('Die Braut von Korinth', 1797),[114] or, as is hinted in Hoffmann's 'Tale of a Vampire' ('Eine Vampirgeschichte', from *The Serapion Brethren*, 1821), at the onset of pregnancy.[115] These 'virtuous vampires', as Volckmann has aptly named them,[116] retain more than a hint of 'femininity'; they are cast not only as blushing brides but also as obedient daughters. The mother plays a central part in both Goethe's ballad and Hoffmann's tale. Deference to feminine virtue coupled with the understanding of vampirism as awakening sexuality makes the usual means of transmitting the plague of

---

[112] A brief discussion of the poem is in Hock 66, who offers an excellent overview of vampire literature until 1900.

[113] For a brief discussion of this and other literature, see Hock.

[114] We might also think here of Kleist's Penthesilea, another domesticated vampire of contemporary literature, who, 'mistaking' bites ('Bisse') for kisses ('Küsse'), bites her lover Achill to death (Kleist, *Penthesilea*, 425).

[115] In the tale, a doctor explains Aurelie's extreme aversion to cooked food with her pregnancy and resulting strange appetites; this diagnosis is neither confirmed nor denied in the tale. One of symptoms of pregnancy the doctor lists, the desire to bite, kill and eat their own husbands, is enacted by the Countess at the end of the tale. See Arnold-de Simine 133–4.

[116] Volckmann 157.

vampirism – another vampire's bite – unworkable. Thus both authors hit upon an ingenious device: the *mother* causes her daughter's condition – either directly, through heredity (Aurelie), or indirectly, by forcing her daughter to renounce her love and languish in a convent, where she dies of a broken heart (the Corinthian Bride). Both Goethe's and Hoffmann's vampires are thus victims in a twofold sense: first denied a life as a 'normal woman' by their mothers, they are later 'driven' by what masquerades as vampirism,[117] but can easily be deciphered as frustrated feminine sexuality.

If female vampirism in literature is a matter of thwarted sexual development, it comes as no surprise that the activities of female vampires are, as all female activity was expected to be, confined to the house. Like male literary vampires, they attack only lovers, husbands and bridegrooms; unlike male vampires, they hardly appear threatening, even in the already muted context of an individual attack. Hoffmann's Aurelie does not drink the blood of the living but contents herself with the flesh of the dead; her single vampiric attack on her husband, in the final sentences of the story, is easily deflected: 'wailing loudly, the Countess hurled herself at him, and with a hyaena's rage bit him in the chest. The Count flung the frenzied woman away from him, down to the ground, and she expired in gruesome death throes.'[118] Even in this scene, at her most menacing, the Countess is not granted full vampiric status but remains what she has been throughout the tale, a hyaena, a parasite feeding from dead bodies, easily flung aside the moment she attacks something not entirely defenceless. In Goethe's ballad, there is a brief indication that the vampiric bride might pose a threat to others:

> From my grave to wander I am forc'd,
> Still to seek Desire's long-sever'd link,
> Still to love the bridegroom I have lost,
> And the life-blood of his heart to drink;
> When his race is run,
> I must hasten on,
> And the young must 'neath my vengeance sink.[119]

---

[117] See the different readings of the term 'getrieben' and its implications for female agency in Volckmann (162) and Ruthner (39).

[118] E. T. A. Hoffmann, 'Eine Vampir-Geschichte', *Kritische Ausgabe*, VIII 233: 'Doch sowie der Graf diese Worte ausstieß, stürzte die Gräfin laut heulend auf ihn zu und biß ihn mit der Wut der Hyäne in die Brust. Der Graf schleuderte die Rasende von sich zur Erde nieder, und sie gab den Geist auf unter grauenhaften Verzuckungen.'

[119] 'Aus dem Grabe werd' ich ausgetrieben, / Noch zu suchen das vermißte Gut, / Noch den schon verlornen Mann zu lieben / Und zu saugen seines Herzens Blut. / Ist's um den geschehn, / Muß nach andern gehn, / Und das junge Volk erliegt der Wut' (Goethe, 'Die Braut von Korinth', 273).

Here emerges, however fleetingly, the ancient understanding of vampirism as a *plague*, as a threat that combines the universality of an epidemic with the individuality of vengeance and evil intent. But since 'the woman in the vampire is always stronger than the vampire in the woman',[120] there is no real danger here. In what Ruthner has called 'pre-emptive obedience', the bride instructs her mother (!) to burn her body along with that of her soon-to-be-dead bridegroom, alluding simultaneously to the burial rites of antiquity, one of the three means of killing a vampire, and the traditional execution method for witches.[121] Given that Goethe's poem has often been read as representing the struggle between the sexual impulses of the individual and societal-ideological restrictions,[122] the role of the mother, the repressive element, is strangely validated. Initially the origin of the disease, she is finally charged to effect its cure; originally responsible for her daughter's death, she ultimately liberates her from an eternity of un-death. As Ruthner has pointed out, the daughter's own anticipation of continued vampirism/promiscuity might even be read as the text's confirmation of the mother's initial judgment that such unbridled sexuality might best be tamed in the convent.[123]

Of course there is more to Goethe's and Hoffmann's vampires than I have conveyed here. They can be, and have been, productively interpreted in a number of ways – as metaphors for female sexuality and reproduction,[124] as allegories of an aesthetic debate,[125] as the personified struggle between individual desire and social control,[126] between Greek and Christian culture,[127] and most recently in the context of contemporary ideas on metaphysics and mesmerism.[128] Certainly, these various cultural, social, historical and metaphysical meanings are central in these texts. To mobilise these meanings, however, it is necessary to pull the female vampire's teeth. Perhaps this point is best illustrated by a brief glance at the only female vampire in contemporary literature who poses a real physical threat. Ernst Raupach's 'Let the Dead Rest' ('Lasst die Toten ruhn', 1823) tells the horrifying story of Walter von Burgund, who, unable to accept the death of

---

[120]   The formulation is Gautier's, cited in Volckmann 164: 'In der Vampirin ist allemal, wie Gautier es sehr treffend ausgedrückt hat, "die Frau stärker als der Vampir".'

[121]   On this scene, see Ruthner 35–9, the citation 39, and Volckmann 163.

[122]   For example in Volckmann 157.   [123]   See Ruthner 39.

[124]   Volckmann on Goethe, Arnold-de Simine and Gustafson on Hoffmann.

[125]   Arnold-de Simine on Hoffmann, particularly 130–1.   [126]   Volckmann on Goethe.

[127]   Volckmann, Schemme, Hock 71 and others (this is one of the standard interpretations of Goethe's poem).

[128]   Barkhoff on Goethe and Hoffmann.

his beloved wife Brunhilde, reanimates her with the help of a magician. She returns as an undomesticated vampire, sucking the blood of others – including that of Walter's children from his second wife Swanhilde – and continues on her murderous rampage until only Walter remains. Horrified, Walter kills her with the help of the same magician. Walter then marries a mysterious 'black huntress', who confronts the reader with a confusing array of symbols: she resembles his second wife, virtuous Swanhilde, and hunts with the aid of a raven rather than a falcon. On Walter's wedding night, Brunhilde returns as a serpent, biting Walter to death as a thunderous voice calls out the moral of the story: 'Let the dead rest!'[129]

Raupach's tale is a straightforward gothic horror story, one that fails entirely to convey a deeper cultural or metaphysical significance, despite an over-abundance of symbols and metaphors (the magician, the black huntress, the raven, the serpent). Significantly, Raupach's text is also the only one in which the female vampire poses a grave danger to the *community*, as opposed to confining her activities to home and hearth, and the only text in which the vampire's attack on her victim succeeds. The link between the story's lack of metaphysical content and the reality of the vampire is rather direct: Raupach's character is a true vampire – a killer, and a plague – *because* his tale remains trapped in the realm of the *physical*. In literature containing a *metaphysical* dimension, true vampires, deprived of their literalness, of their *body*, cannot survive. As Arnold-de Simine has pointed out, the greatest fear expressed in such texts is that physiological processes might prevail, consigning that which is 'truly human', the soul, to irrelevancy.[130] It is a danger that can only be averted in two ways: by the death of the body (Goethe and Hoffmann) and the triumph of the spiritual over the physical (Goethe). The 'virtuous vampire' is not a vampire but a woman; she is plagued by all-too-human desires rather than being a plague on humanity herself. Consequently, the task of the text becomes not to safeguard the community but to tend to the individual, either by returning the virtuous vampire to true, 'unspoiled' femininity, or, failing that, to execute the monster she has become.[131]

If Goethe and Hoffmann's texts confront us with a vampire who has lost most of the mythological vampire's power and menace, other literature of the time 'contains' the vampiric plague – in both senses of the word – by

---

[129] 'Lasst die Toten ruhn!' (Raupach 88). The tale is briefly discussed in Hock 108–10.
[130] See Arnold-de Simine 134–5.
[131] It has become standard in feminist criticism to see these aspects not as alternatives but analogies, understanding the death of the heroine as a metaphor for the ideal state of femininity and thus also as a powerful aesthetic symbol (see above all Bronfen's seminal *Over Her Dead Body* as well as the anthology by Bronfen and Webster Goodwin). But see also Barkhoff, who has taken a different stance in reading Goethe's and Hoffmann's texts 'as part of the literary imaginary that counters and destabilizes the dominant gender discourses of their time' (141).

retaining vampiric motifs while deleting the vampire. A classic example is
the Grimms' tale 'Snow White' (1812), which scholars have yet to discover as
a vampiric tale,[132] but which shows considerable kinship with vampire lore,
including that of Elizabeth Báthory.[133] Vampiric motifs are thick on the
ground here: we have a queen obsessed with eternal youth and beauty; a girl
whose very name is derived partly from blood; the cutting out and eating of
a heart (or lungs and liver) as proof of death; a coffin that does not hold the
dead; a body that refuses to decay; a revenant, and, of course, a mirror. Snow
White's character simultaneously embodies her paleness/bloodlessness
(innocence) and the suppression of blackness/darkness (blood, lust, bloodlust). 'If only I had a child whose skin was as white as snow, whose cheek
and lips were as red as blood, and whose hair was as black as the ebony wood
of the window frame', sighs the Queen. 'Soon afterwards she gave birth to a
daughter whose skin was as white as snow, whose cheeks and lips were as red
as blood, and whose hair was as black as ebony wood, and thus she was
called Snow White.'[134] The 'thus' in this passage is rather incongruous:
Snow White's name no longer contains any hint (we might suspect: actively
denies) that blood is an essential part of her nature as well as physical
composition. Snow, on the other hand, is not.[135] Naturally, her name's
suppression (repression) of Snow White's darker colours (nature) only
serves to emphasise them even more.

As if this were not enough, Snow White is a revenant, although her
interpreters have determinedly misread her state after eating the poisoned
apple as *apparently* dead' or 'as *though she were* dead'.[136] The tale itself,

---

[132] The only critic so far to note the story's vampiric aspects is Walter Rankin (81–7), who identifies not
Snow White but her stepmother as the tale's vampire. Reading Snow White as a vampire is, however,
common coin in popular adaptations and visual culture. See, for example, Gaiman's tale 'Snow,
Glass, Apples' and Claire Beauchamp's Goth Princesses series (http://clairebeauchamp.deviantart.
com/, last accessed 11 September 2007). For scholarship on Snow White, see Bettelheim, Tatar,
Birkhäuser-Oeri, Hans Dieckmann and Kast.

[133] I do not wish to claim that Báthory inspired the Grimms' tale, but their note 'Nach einem Wiener
fliegenden Blatt' (1815) documents that they knew of her story. Their source was almost certainly
Bornschein's 1805 novel, since they take over many aspects that appear in the novel but not in
historical records (including the pairing of Báthory with an old-crone accomplice and the public
burning of both on the marketplace). Farin has republished the Grimms' note (60).

[134] I am using Boris Matthews's translation of the tale, which precedes his translation of Seifert's treatise
(Seifert 1–11, the quotations 2). '"Hätt' ich ein Kind so weiß wie Schnee, so rot wie Blut und so
schwarz wie das Holz an dem Rahmen." Bald darauf bekam sie ein Töchterlein, das war so weiß wie
Schnee, so rot wie Blut und so schwarzhaarig wie Ebenholz und ward darum das Sneewittchen
(Schneeweißchen) genannt' (Grimm and Grimm 301).

[135] In the Italian tradition, for example, the tale is called 'La ragazza di latte e sangue' ('The Girl Made of
Milk and Blood'; see Bettelheim 199): snow is replaced by other white matter in countries where it is
uncommon; blood, however, is non-negotiable.

[136] For example in Seifert 103, emphasis mine.

however, leaves us in no doubt: 'But scarcely did she have a bite of it in her mouth than she fell down dead on the ground.'[137] This is unequivocal: Snow White is not sick, not dying, but *dead*. The mirror, of whom the Queen knows that it 'spoke no falsehoods',[138] confirms it to the Queen in the joyous news that she is now the fairest in the land, and the text confirms it to us, too insistently not to be taken seriously:

When they got home at nightfall, the dwarfs found Snow White lying on the ground, and she was not breathing. She was dead. They lifted her up, looked to see if they could find anything poisoned, loosened her body laces, combed her hair, washed her with water and with wines, but nothing helped. The dear child was dead, and dead she remained.[139]

Like a vampire, Snow White does not decay; in death, she looks 'as fresh as a living person',[140] the comparison with 'as ... as' indicating rather directly that 'a living person' is precisely what Snow White is *not*. In case we missed it, the message is repeated: 'Snow White lay a long time in the coffin and did not rot, but rather *looked as though she were* sleeping, for she was still as white as snow, as red as blood, and as black as ebony wood.'[141] The common misreading of Snow White as alive and appearing 'as though she were dead', rather than dead and appearing 'as though she were sleeping', is one way of containing the horror of the tale; the same act of containment turns the potential vampire, 'red as blood', into the beautiful princess, 'white as snow'[142] (fig. 6).

This act of containment is also expressed in two further standard interpretations. One is the (exceedingly common) psychoanalytic reading of Snow White as a tale of female sexual initiation, which establishes the same link between vampirism and human sexuality that we have seen in other

[137] Trans. in Seifert 9: 'Kaum aber hatte es einen Bissen davon im Mund, so fiel es tot zur Erde nieder' (Grimm and Grimm 308).
[138] Trans. in Seifert 5: 'Da erschrak sie; denn sie wußte, daß der Spiegel keine Unwahrheit sprach' (Grimm and Grimm 305).
[139] Trans. in Seifert 9: 'Die Zwerglein, wie sie abends nach Haus kamen, fanden Sneewittchen auf der Erde liegen, und es ging kein Atem mehr aus seinem Mund, und es war tot. Sie hoben es auf, suchten, ob sie was Giftiges fänden, schnürten es auf, kämmten ihm die Haare, wuschen es mit Wasser und mit Wein, aber es half alles nichts; das liebe Kind war tot und blieb tot' (Grimm and Grimm 308–9).
[140] My translation. Matthews misleadingly translates 'fresh and alive' (Seifert 10); the original is a great deal more explicit: 'Da wollten sie es begraben, aber es sah noch so frisch aus wie ein lebender Mensch' (Grimm and Grimm 309).
[141] Trans. in Seifert 10 (my emphasis): 'Nun lag Sneewittchen lange lange Zeit in dem Sarg und verweste nicht, sondern sah aus, als wenn es schliefe; denn es war noch so weiß als Schnee, so rot als Blut und so schwarzhaarig wie Ebenholz' (Grimm and Grimm 309). On Snow White in her coffin, see Bronfen, *Over Her Dead Body*, 98–108.
[142] On the significance of these colours, see Seifert 53–7.

Fig. 6 Snow White as a vampire, red as blood, biting into a human heart with visible enjoyment. From Claire Beauchamp's Goth Princesses (August 2007). By kind permission of Laura Ambrós (http://clairebeauchamp.deviantart.com)

vampire literature of the time.[143] The other is the scholarly insertion of a male object of female love, lust and competition into a story that shows no trace of such a person, a tradition that we have encountered in much literature on Elizabeth Báthory. In the Grimms' tale, the King only appears twice, and only in a purely mechanical role necessary to engender the action: he inseminates Snow White's mother and marries her evil stepmother. These essential functions accomplished, he disappears from the story,

---

[143] Bettelheim's interpretation of Snow White as a maturing girl and the Queen as a narcissistic mother has become paradigmatic: he reads Snow White's existence in the coffin as a 'period of gestation which is her final period of preparing for maturity'. Snow White, he argues, needs this 'prolonged period of inertia [... to] recuperate fully from her premature and hence destructive experiences with sexuality' (213). Bettelheim is referring to her three sexual temptations through the Queen's gifts of comb, bodice lace and apple, presuming that sexual maturity, for women, entails an ability to resist such temptation (212).

neither playing a part as Snow White's father nor as the Queen's husband.[144] His absence, however, has not prevented Bruno Bettelheim, to this day the tale's most influential psychoanalytic reader, from casting him as a central character. What appears to be, in the text itself, a struggle between the two women is unmasked as a 'triadic existence': 'We are told nothing about her relation to her father, although it is reasonable to assume that it is the competition for him which sets (step)mother against daughter.'[145] Why, we might ask, is it reasonable to assume this? Because, we might suspect, the story of Snow White is not read literally but metaphorically, not 'physically' (a reading that would have to take seriously the repeated description of Snow White as dead) but metaphysically, not as a tale of the vampire but as a tale of *women*. And women, in the gender ideology of the time (Bettelheim's time as well as the Grimms') are creatures whose entire existence is presumed to exhaust itself in the competition for a man, even if, as Bettelheim reluctantly admitted, 'the person for whose love the two are in competition is not mentioned'.[146]

Strategies of containment are also represented in the critical distinction between 'high art' and 'trivial' literature, which has banished the vampire, seemingly irrevocably, to the nebulous kingdom of gothic horror and other unmentionable spheres. In a critical tradition that values metaphysical depth, intertextual allusions, cultural meanings and the intricacies of philosophical complexity, vampires are no longer presentable, or, to use an inimitable Germanism, no longer *salonfähig*. Whatever terror they once held is most effectively counteracted by ridicule and cultural arrogance. Goethe, whose literary judgment has prefigured modern canonical thinking in so many ways, can perhaps stand as the inspiration for this tradition in his sarcastic stage direction in the scene 'A Spacious Hall' of *Faust* II:

The poets of night and graves excuse themselves, because they are just engaged in a most interesting conversation with a newly arisen vampire, and from it a new school of poetry may perhaps arise; the Herald is obliged to accept their apologies and meanwhile he calls forth Greek mythology which even in modern masks loses neither its character nor its charm.[147]

---

[144] Pointed out repeatedly in Tatar's interpretation of the tale.   [145] Bettelheim 203.

[146] Bettelheim 201.

[147] Goethe, *Faust. Der Tragödie zweiter Teil*, 165: 'Die Nacht- und Grabdichter lassen sich entschuldigen, weil sie soeben im interessantesten Gespräch mit mit einem frisch entstandenen Vampyren begriffen seien, woraus eine neue Dichtart sich vielleicht entwickeln könnte; der Herold muß es gelten lassen und ruft indessen die griechische Mythologie hervor, die selbst in moderner Maske, weder Charakter noch Gefälliges verliert.'

It is a compelling image, showing us the modern literary consciousness at the crossroads between the ascent to Parnassus and the descent into the grave, between the genteel charm of Greek mythology and the confrontation ('conversation') with nameless physical and psychic horrors, either of which might furnish the basis for literary modernity. We know, of course, which path German literary history has taken. What is essential to understand is that it keeps itself at its lofty Olympian heights not by conversing with, but by looking down on, the alternative. The threat of vampires is finally contained once they are no longer perceived as dangerous but as *distasteful*. This is why the few literary critics who have bothered with vampires have usually explained the rare appearance of vampires in German literature by summarily judging the entire subject to be 'unpoetic'.[148] This is why Goethe's 'Bride of Corinth' became the centre of a storm of controversy between those at a loss to explain how the Great Master could possibly have sullied his reputation with such a distasteful subject and those who claimed that the theme, 'exalted by the powerful contrast between Greek culture and churchy Christianity, between free humanity and the strictures of a narrow-minded and stifling dogma', had turned into a Work of Art in the Great Master's hand.[149] Authors with less metaphysically transfigurative power at their disposal can only earn the critic's approval by avoiding such repulsive subjects altogether: 'Clemens Brentano, as well, has not left us a literary version of the vampire saga, and we thank him for it. For only the all-purifying poetic power of Goethe was able to raise this repugnant material to the loftiest heights of beauty.'[150]

What, then, is the meaning of the German vampire, who began her life in German writing as a medical mystery and kept returning in the different guises of feminine vanity, feminine virtue and antithesis of the aesthetic? Where she appears in literature and where she fails to appear in literary history, she exemplifies mechanisms of cultural control. In a literary tradition that values the male over the female, the female un-dead

---

[148] Paradigmatically in Hock 64.

[149] Both Hock (66–72) and Schemme have referred to this controversy; the quotation is taken from Hock 71 ('erhoben zu dem gewaltigen Gegensatz zwischen Griechentum und Pfaffenchristentum, zwischen freier Menschlichkeit und den Geboten eines engen und beengenden Dogmas'). See also Erich Trunz's annotations to the poem in Goethe, *Goethes Werke: Hamburger Ausgabe*, I 662–4, in which he cites many contributors to this debate.

[150] Hock 89: 'auch Clemens Brentano hat uns keine Bearbeitung der Vampyrsage geschenkt, und wir wissen ihm Dank dafür. Denn nur die alles läuternde poetische Kraft Goethes war imstande, diesen abstossenden Stoff zu höchster Schönheit zu verklären.'

of myth are turned into the dead women of literature. In a critical tradition that values the metaphysical over the physical and intertextual intricacies over literalness, vampires become the un-persons of literary history. Both are strategies of containment, assigning to vampires in literature a role they have long played in the metaphysical and psychological realms: to embody that which we do not wish to acknowledge. For this very reason, they keep coming back. Drawing most of their life's blood from our rejection of them, vampires – as a subject of art, literature, even science[151] – are forever young. Or, to adapt a statement by Abraham van Helsing: 'The strength of the vampire is that people will not believe in her.'[152]

---

[151] Cf. the recent attempts of physicists to refute the existence of vampires and other ghosts (see note 33 above).

[152] 'The strength of the vampire is that people will not believe in him.' The statement is attributed to the American screenwriter Garrett Fort (1900–45) and Tod Browning (1880–1962), the director of the famous 1931 *Dracula* with Bela Lugosi in the title role. The line is spoken by Abraham van Helsing, played by Edward van Sloan, in a scene in which he tries to convince Mina's father and fiancé that vampires do exist. Fort's screenplay is available online (www.horrorlair.com/scripts/draclugo.txt, last accessed 11 September 2007).

CHAPTER 4

Pride: husband-killers

MURDEROUS MARRIAGES AND MARRIAGE AS MURDER

Spousal murder appears to have been one of the rare violent crimes committed as often, or nearly as often, by women as men.[1] Many of these cases are described as lacklustre, even banal, as crimes of planning, not passion, committed by disenchanted wives who, typically, resorted to poison[2] at a time when divorce was not available.[3] But not all husband-killers dissolved their unions in this calm and tidy fashion. There is, for example, the case of Katharina Krävogel, who beat her husband to death with a wooden log, obliterated his genitalia, and stated at her trial that she had no regrets and would do it again, given another chance. And in 1715, a peasant woman took an axe to her husband and added insult to injury by hiding his dismembered body in the manure pile. She did this with the full support of her neighbours, most of whom knew or suspected that she had killed her husband, and who advised her to flee when pieces of his corpse were discovered. Given that both murders had been preceded by years of physical and emotional mistreatment, such community support may have

[1] Statistics for the eighteenth and early nineteenth centuries, where available, seem to indicate this. For example: of thirty-one cases recorded in Schleswig-Holstein between 1700 and 1810, sixteen were committed by women (Göttsch 331–2). While regional studies of spousal murder, such as those conducted by Göttsch and Thieser, are illuminating, it is difficult to generalise beyond regional specificities due to the sporadic nature of crime statistics at the time. Göttsch offers the following comment on these statistics: 'der Anteil von Frauen, die entweder des Gattenmordes überführt oder verdächtigt wurden, ist, gemessen an ihrem Gesamtanteil an Tötungsdelikten, wenn man den Kindsmord ausklammert, überproportional hoch. Über die Gründe für diese Ungleichgewichtigkeit kann aufgrund fehlender Untersuchungen nur spekuliert werden. Es läßt sich vermuten, daß Männer stärker als Frauen auch andere Formen der ehelichen Konfliktlösung, wie z.B. Prügel oder das Verlassen der Ehefrau nutzten' (332). Whereas Göttsch reads these statistics as documenting the disproportionately high number of husband-killings compared to the relatively low number of other violent crimes committed by women, they can obviously also be seen as showing the relatively *low* occurrence of wife-killings compared to the high number of other violent crimes committed by men.
[2] Fifteen of the sixteen Schleswig-Holstein husband-killers listed by Göttsch used poison, compared with only five of the fifteen wife-killers during the same time-frame (331; see also chapter 6 below).
[3] For other options of dissolving marriages and marital violence at the time, see Schörkhuber-Drysdale.

been inspired not only by sympathy for the abused, but also by a sense of populist justice. The very messiness of these killings made them believable as unplanned crimes of passion committed by someone at the end of her endurance, as one apocalyptic instance of tit for several years of tat.[4]

Even if it did not come to that, it was, and is, common to imagine the married state as a violent affair. Throughout the twentieth century and into the twenty-first, 'self-help' literature addressed to women, sporting titles such as *How to Murder Your Husband* or *How to Kill Your Husband (and Other Handy Household Hints)*,[5] offered tongue-in-cheek solutions to serious conjugal problems. In the eighteenth and early nineteenth centuries, treatises in praise of Holy Matrimony as a state of individual fulfilment, the foundation of the family and a pillar of society[6] were nearly evenly matched by works portraying marriage as murder. Matrimony, in these writings, becomes the battlefield of the sexes; sexual relations are seen as an act of cannibalism. Immanuel Kant, perhaps the age's most famous philosopher of marriage, outlined the progress in the cultural view of marriage, from the brutal subjection of wives in pre-bourgeois societies – 'Here, women are chattel'[7] – to the bourgeois marriage, in which the 'mutual usage of sexual organs and facilities'[8] is contractually regulated. 'As culture progresses',[9] the image of the wife also progresses from *Haustier* to *Hausfrau*, but this does not affect the principal understanding of marriage as the subjugation of one person by another. 'The coincidental coming together of two persons is not sufficient to render this union absolute and irresolvable', Kant wrote, 'one part must be *subjugated* by the other, one or the other must be superior in order to rule over and govern

---

[4] The case of Katharina Krävogel is related in Thieser 97–8, the case of the peasant woman by Schnabel-Schulte 196–7.

[5] John Kirkpatrick's *Lady-Killers, or 'How to Murder Your Husband'* is *A Farce in One Act for Six Women and an Offstage Man* (1949); Kathy Lette's *How to Kill Your Husband (and Other Handy Household Hints)* is part of the ironic advice literature, offering marital guidance such as 'Don't Get Mad, Get Bad' and 'If He Wants Breakfast in Bed, Tell Him to Sleep in the Kitchen' (2006).

[6] For example: Friedrich Nathaniel Volkmar, *Philosophie der Ehe* (1794); Adolph Freiherr von Knigge, 'Ueber den Umgang unter Eheleuten' (*Ueber den Umgang mit Menschen*, II 23–56); Carl Friedrich Pockels, *Versuch einer Charakteristik des weiblichen Geschlechts*, 5 vols., 1797–1802 (on marriage, see particularly the section 'Wie muss die Ehe geführt werden, wenn sie glücklich seyn und bleiben soll?', III 317–99); Theodor Gottlieb von Hippel, *Über die Ehe*; Joseph Unger, *Die Ehe in ihrer welthistorischen Entwicklung* (1850).

[7] 'Das Weib ist da ein Haustier' (Kant, *Anthropologie in pragmatischer Hinsicht*, Werkausgabe, XII 395–690, the quotation 649).

[8] Kant, *Metaphysik der Sitten*, Werkausgabe, VIII 389: 'usus membrorum et facultatum sexualitum alterius'.

[9] Kant, *Anthropologie*, 648: 'Im Fortgange der Kultur'.

the other.'[10] Sexuality, or to speak with Kant, the contractual regulation of the 'mutual usage of sexual organs and facilities', is described not merely as subjugation but annihilation:

Whether the woman is *used up* by the man through pregnancy and the resulting possibly fatal process of birth, or whether the man is used up by the woman through the woman's frequent demands of his sexual capacity and resulting exhaustion, whether mouth or teeth are used: the only difference is the mode of gratification, and one person is for the other, when it comes to this mutual use of sex organs, nothing but a thing to be *consumed*.[11]

Here and elsewhere, Kant's distinction between the figurative and the literal is disturbingly hazy: 'Sexual gratification', he continues, 'is *cannibalistic* in principle (if not always [!] in its effect).'[12] And he was not alone. The author of the anonymously published *Philosophy of Marriage* (1800) left even less to the imagination when he stated that 'sexual gratification is indeed akin to cannibalistic consumption, the sole difference between these two kinds of enjoyment being that the cannibal enjoys his dead enemy and the spouse his still [!] living spouse.'[13]

That perfectly healthy and functional marriages – or what these authors take to be such – are routinely described in terms of subjugation, annihilation and cannibalism seems puzzling and revealing in equal measure. Similarly, many treatises extolling the virtues of matrimony devote considerable space to a topic that seems more appropriate in the context of murder rather than marriage, namely the cruelty, vengefulness and sadism of women. 'That an ignoble woman's revenge is terrible, cruel, lasting and difficult to reconcile', wrote Knigge, 'has so often been said that I hardly

---

[10] Kant, *Anthropologie*, 648: 'Zur Einheit und Unauflöslichkeit einer Verbindung ist das beliebige Zusammentreten zweier Personen nicht hinreichend; ein Teil mußte dem andern *unterworfen* und wechselseitig einer dem andern irgendworin überlegen sein, um ihn beherrschen oder regieren zu können' (emphasis original).

[11] Kant, *Metaphysik* (1968), 484: 'Ob, mit Maul oder Zähnen, der weibliche Teil durch Schwängerung, und daraus vielleicht erfolgende, für ihn tödliche Niederkunft, der männliche aber durch, von öfteren Ansprüchen des Weibes an das Geschlechtsvermögen des Mannes herrührende Erschöpfungen *aufgezehrt* wird, ist bloß in der Manier zu genießen unterschieden, und ein Teil ist in Ansehung des anderen, bei diesem wechselseitigen Gebrauche der Geschlechtsorganen, wirklich eine *verbrauchbare* Sache' (emphases original). Kant wrote this at a time when women frequently died in childbirth (see Lindemann, *Health*, 237–43); conversely, I am not aware of a single instance in Kant's entire century of a man expiring due to his wife's undue sexual demands and 'resulting exhaustion'.

[12] Kant, *Metaphysik* (1968), 483–4: 'der fleischliche Genuß [ist] dem Grundsatz (wenn gleich nicht immer der Wirkung nach) *kannibalistisch*' (emphasis original). On this particular passage, see also Duden 129.

[13] 'Der Geschlechtsgenuss ist dann in der That dem kannibalischen Genusse ähnlich, und der Unterschied zwischen beyden Arten des Genusses besteht bloss darin, dass der Kannibale seinen getödteten Feind, der Gatte aber seinen noch lebenden Gatten geniesst' (*Philosophie der Ehe*, 43).

find it necessary to repeat. Indeed, it is hard to believe the means that these furies employ to torture and persecute an honest man they suspect of having insulted them; how inextinguishable their hatred, and how vile the means to which they resort.'[14] Such manifestations of female viciousness, according to the anonymous Philosopher of Marriage, find their expression in all spheres of feminine activity, from the scullery to the scaffold:

It is a daily experience in the kitchen that many women, in cold blood and without showing the slightest compassion, kill edible animals, especially fish, in such an excruciating manner that one might believe that they take immense pleasure in seeing such an animal die in agony. I have even heard a woman who was watching the execution of a criminal on the wheel, a woman who was by no means a member of the lower classes, laugh out loud in great delight every time another of the unfortunate man's bones was broken, every time the breaking of the bone on the hollow wooden scaffold made that awful sound, a sound that went right through the rest of us. And when some of the bystanders showed their disapproval, she answered quite coldly: 'The wretch deserves it, after all!'[15]

Both Knigge and the Philosopher interpret female cruelty as the vindictive desire of the powerless to exercise power.[16] Sadism, they conclude, is a quintessential feminine quality because it is an attribute of the weak. As an

---

[14] 'Daß die Rache eines unedeln Weibes fürchterlich, grausam, dauernd und nicht leicht zu versöhnen ist, das hat man schon so oft gesagt, daß ich es hier zu wiederholen fast nicht nöthig finde. Würklich wollte man es kaum glauben, welche Mittel solche Furien ausfindig zu machen wissen, einen ehrlichen Mann, von dem sie sich beleidigt glauben, zu martern, zu verfolgen; wie unauslöschlich ihr Haß ist; zu welchen niedrigen Mitteln sie ihre Zuflucht nehmen' (Knigge II 77).

[15] 'Auch kann man täglich die Erfahrung in den Küchen machen, dass viele Weiber, mit kaltem Blute und ohne die geringste Theilnahme zu beweisen, essbare Thiere, insonderheit Fische, umbringen und zwar auf eine so quaalvolle Art umbringen, dass man glauben sollte, sie fänden recht ihr Vergnügen daran, ein solches Thier unter Martern sterben zu sehn. Ja, ich habe ein Weib, das der Hinrichtung eines Verbrechers durchs Rad zusahe und keineswegs aus der gemeinen Klasse war, bey jedem Stosse, den der Unglückliche erhielt und der durch das Zerknicken der Knochen auf dem hohlen hölzernen Gerüste einen durch Mark und Bein dringenden Misslaut von sich gab, mit einer Art von Wonnegefühl auflachen, und, als Einige der Umstehenden ihr Missfallen darüber zu erkennen gaben, ganz kalt erwiedern hören: "Der Kerl hat es ja verdient!"' (*Philosophie der Ehe*, 178–9).

[16] Knigge, concisely: 'Es scheint übrigens in der Natur zu liegen, daß Schwächre immer grausamer in ihrer Rache sind, als Stärkre, vielleicht, weil das Gefühl dieser Schwäche die Empfindung des erlittnen Drucks verstärkt, und lüsterner nach der Gelegenheit macht, auch einmal Kraft zu üben' (II 78). The Philosopher, more verbosely: 'Allein dieser besondre Zug von Grausamkeit lässt sich aus dem allgemeinen Charakter des Geschlechts leicht erklären. Der Schwache und Furchtsame ist, wenn er gereizt wird und dann als Sieger den Gegenstand seines Zorns in seine Gewalt bekommt, allemal grausamer in seiner Rache, als der Starke und Beherzte, der auch im Siege eine gewisse Grossmuth beyzubehalten pflegt. Jener fürchtet sich immer noch, auch wenn er schon gesiegt hat, und will sich gleichsam seines Siegs recht versichern, dadurch, dass er nicht aufhört, den Besiegten sein Übergewicht fühlen zu lassen. Furchtsamkeit mit Gewalt bekleidet macht allemal grausam, wie alle Despoten und Usurpatoren beweisen. Die weibliche Grausamkeit unterscheidet sich aber in diesem Falle von der männlichen auch dadurch, dass sie in ihren Äusserungen oft ins Kleinliche fällt' (*Philosophie der Ehe*, 181–2).

integral part of the female character, such female cruelty – 'a daily experience' – is an unavoidable blight on even the happiest marriage.

THE CASE OF MARIA KATHARINA WÄCHTLER (HAMBURG, 1786–1788) AND THE DEBATE ON TORTURE

When Maria Katharina Wächtler (1750–88) took a hatchet to her husband,
killing, beheading and dismembering him in their marital bed, she was
enacting a radical version of marital normality as described in these and
other works.[17] Of course, this is not to say that she took her cue from them:
to infer this would be as naive and one-dimensional as to see the only
possible relationship between deed and discourse as being a causal one.
Certainly, however, word and deed do relate to one another, if in a more
complex and indirect fashion. In the case of the Wächtler murder, this
becomes particularly transparent when deed is turned into discourse, in the
myriad and ubiquitous pamphlets, biographies, stories and histories that
made her case one of the best documented in Germany and that continued
to appear until at least sixty years after Wächtler's death. Serialised broadsheets, published on a weekly or biweekly basis, describing known facts,
new evidence, witness testimonies, and Wächtler's own statements and
behaviour under interrogation and torture, kept Hamburg's population
up to date on every aspect of her case for the two and a half years that
passed between her arrest in March 1786 and her execution in November
1788.[18] Almost without exception, these pamphlets presuppose their readers'
intimate knowledge of the case; one even conjectured that every last one of
Hamburg's then 120,000 inhabitants was familiar with it.[19] The high

---

[17] The material in and excerpts from this section will be published, in German, in my article 'Der Fall
Wächtler: Die Hamburger Flugblattliteratur zur Folter (1788) und die Lust am Lesen', *Zeitschrift für
Germanistik* 2 (2009).

[18] These include: *Abermalige wahrhafte Aussagen der Inquisitin Wächtlern als Dieselbe den 10. October
wiederum zum Verhör in die Raths-Stube geführet wurde*; *Aussage der Inquisitinn Wächtlern in Hamburg
bey dem am 25ten Januar 1788 erhaltenen Ersten Grade der Tortur*; *Bekenntniß der Inquisitinn Wächtlern
in Hamburg. Nebst fortgesetzten Bemerkungen über die Tortur*; *Haupt-Auszüge aus der Defension der
Inquisitinn Maria Catharina Wächtlern*; Hofmann; *Inquisition gegen die berüchtige Wächtlern*; *Merc.
den 3 Sept. 1788*; 'Ueber die letzte Defension der Inquisitinn Wächtlern in Hamburg'; *Unverfälschte
Nachricht von dem Betragen der Wächtlern in der Frohnerei*; *Urtel in Sachen Fiscalis&c.c. Wächtlern*;
*Wahre Aussagen der in der Frohnerey zu Hamburg sitzenden Inquisitin Wächtler als dieselbe den 11ten
Julius 1788 nach dem Hamburgischen Niedergericht gebracht wurde*; *Wahrhafte Aussagen der Inquisitin
Wächtlern, als sie den 4ten März auf die Folter gebracht werden sollte*. These pamphlets are bound
together in the Staatsarchiv Hamburg in two volumes, Sigs. A427/0031 and 0032.

[19] A few examples: 'Die Sache der Inquisitinn Wächtlern ist zu bekannt, als daß man solche dem
Publicum wiederholen dürfte' (*Aussage der Inquisitinn Wächtlern*, 3); 'Da in dieser Sache schon so
vieles geschrieben und öffentlich verkauft worden, konnte ich kein Bedenken tragen, auch diesen

demand for literature on Wächtler is further documented by the publication of her biography[20] and the extensive resurrection of her case, fifty-six years after its conclusion, in the sixth volume of *Der neue Pitaval*.[21]

Part, not all, of this notoriety can certainly be attributed to the shock-value of the crime. In February 1786, the decapitated and dismembered body of her husband, the tobacconist and merchant Wächtler,[22] was found in two different packages by the side of the road from Hamburg to Lübeck. Suspicion quickly fell on his wife, who had undertaken a coach journey to Lübeck, with two heavy packages of wares she planned to sell there, the day before her husband's body was found. Twice along the way, she asked the coachman to stop and give her some privacy, saying that she felt unwell; in the end she ordered him to return to Hamburg because she was too ill to continue. The packages did not return with her and her husband's torso, head and hands were later found, neatly wrapped in similar parcels, at or near the locations where she had asked the coach to stop (fig. 7). Circumstantial evidence against her mounted: the coachman was unable to discern a trace of the illness that forced her to return to Hamburg, testifying that shortly after she had ordered him to turn around, she feasted merrily at an inn and treated other guests there to her entire life story. Her servants testified that she had borrowed a cleaver from a butcher the night before her husband's disappearance, that they had helped her strip extremely bloody sheets off the bed the following morning (which she explained with a miscarriage during the night), that her account of her husband's absence – a journey to Lübeck – seemed unconvincing since he had not mentioned travel plans the night before his purported departure, and that he could not have left on his own account since all of his shoes and boots were in the house.[23] Wächtler's cook added that the day after his

Aufsatz zur Publicität zu bringen' (*Bekenntniß der Inquisitinn Wächtlern*, 2); 'Der Kriminalprozeß dieser wegen Ermordung ihres Ehemanns berüchtigten Inquisitinn ist durch viele öffentliche Schriften zu bekannt geworden, um den Anfang dieses Prozesses hier zu wiederholen' ('Ueber die letzte Defension', 3); and: 'Die Geschichte selbst, worüber wir schreiben, ist Stadt-kündig. Bis in die entferntesten Winkel unserer großen Stadt, wissen es alle 120000 Menschen die Verstand haben, eine eine [sic] Erzählung zu hören oder zu lesen, daß der Körper eines Mannes, mit Namen *J. R. Wächteler*, nach dem er einige Tage abwesend gewesen war, auf der Hamburgischen und Lübecker Post-Straße, zerstümmelt gefunden wurde' (*Berichtigungen*, 3). This pamphlet takes the recurring formulation 'Everybody knows' – 'Alle wissen es:' – as its stylistic organising principle).

[20] *Ausführliche Lebensbeschreibung der Wächtlerin geborne Wunschin* (Staatsarchiv Hamburg, Sig. A427/0032).

[21] Hitzig and Häring, *Der neue Pitaval* VI (1844), 448–518. The correspondence of the *Pitaval* editors with the Hamburg Senate, asking permission to use the Wächtler files for their version, is appended to the case file ('Acta, Inquisition, Urtheil u. dessen Vollstreckung wider Maria Catharina Wächtler', in the Staatsarchiv Hamburg, Sig. Cl. VII. Lit Me no. 8 vol. 10).

[22] There is some confusion regarding the victim's first name, which is given variously as 'Julius Adolph' (*Aechte und vollständige Akten* 5, *Urtel in Sachen Fiscalis&c.c. Wächtlern* 1), 'Johann' (Lindemann, 'Narratives'), or 'Joseph Adolph' (Martschukat, *Inszeniertes Töten*, 94 and '*Düsterheit*', 332).

[23] Several contemporary broadsheets mention this aspect specifically. See, for example, Hofmann 25.

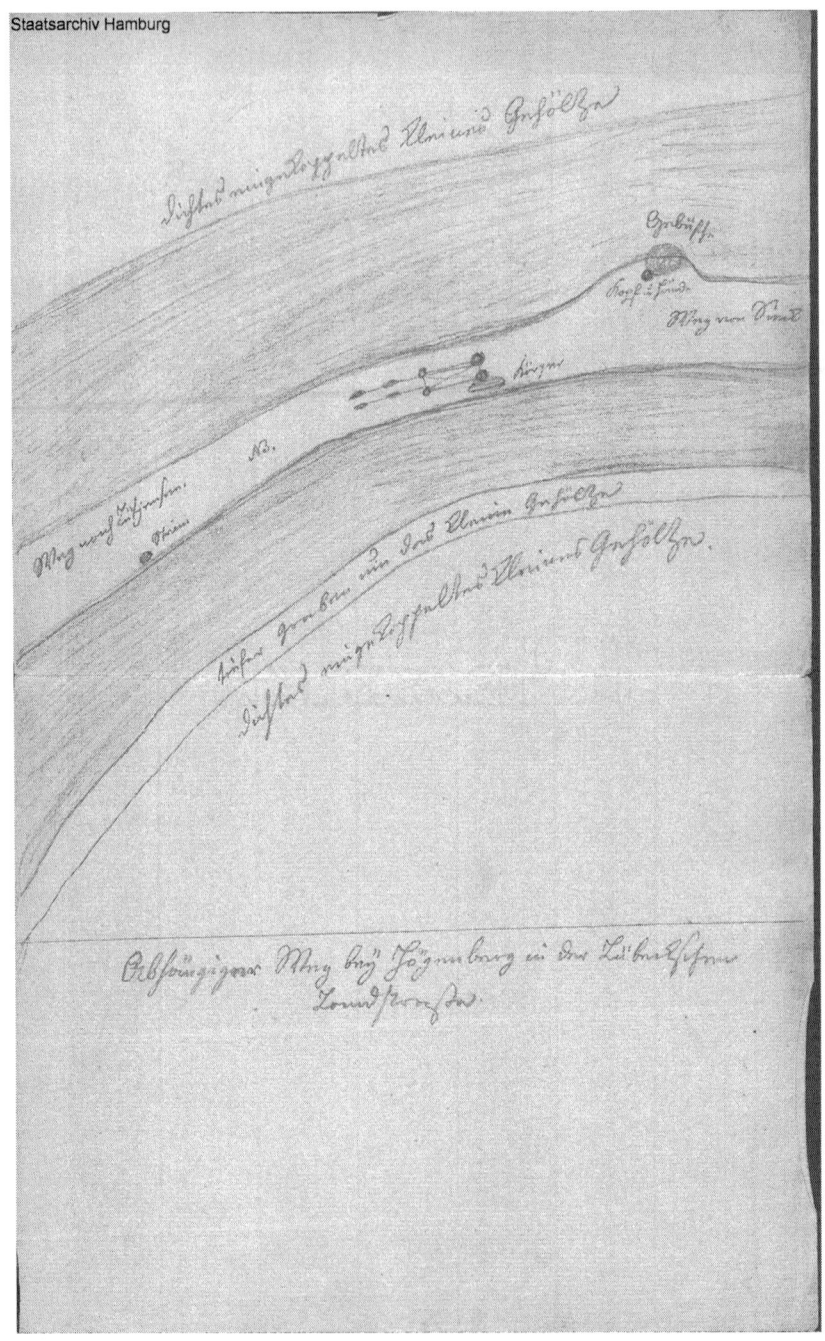

Fig. 7 'Abhängiger Weg beÿ Tögenberg in der Lübeckschen Landstraße'. Drawing of the place of discovery. In 'Acta, Inquisition, Urtheil u. dessen Vollstreckung wider Maria Catharina Wächtler geb. Wunsch pcto. Ermordung ihres Ehemannes. Nebst div. Nebenacten. 1786–1788'. Staatsarchiv Hamburg. Cl. vii. Lit Me no. 8 vol. 10

disappearance, she had touched a sack, assuming that it contained the washing, that she thought to have felt a human head inside, and that her hand came away bloodied. A workman testified that immediately before her departure for Lübeck, Wächtler had asked him to carry a package to the coach, which weighed about 100 pounds and smelt of rotten meat. Most damningly, her seven-year-old daughter, asleep in another bed in the same room during the night in question, stated that she had awoken between two and two-thirty in the morning to see her mother hit her father repeatedly on the head with a hammer, cut his throat, cover him with a blanket, and then call in a man standing at the door to help her dispose of the body.[24] These salacious details, published successively in local pamphlets, turned the Wächtler case into a major media event with a huge readership eagerly awaiting the next instalment.

Public interest in the case was further stimulated in its final year, when the decision of the Hamburg Senate to subject Wächtler to torture sparked a city-wide debate.[25] The Senate's decision was a response to Wächtler's steadfast refusal to confess, even in the face of persuasive circumstantial evidence and several damning witness statements. By law, however, neither was acceptable as the basis for a death sentence, which could only be administered on one of two grounds: either the culprit's confession or eyewitness testimony by two reliable witnesses. Thus Wächtler's obstinacy and the existence of only a single eyewitness testimony, which was moreover useless since the witness was still a minor, meant that the case was effectively stalled unless and until Wächtler could be forced to confess.[26] The Senate's controversial decision inspired a number of treatises that drew its significance not only from Wächtler's specific case, but also from a more theoretical but no less heated nationwide discussion on the permissibility and efficacy of torture.

Most eighteenth-century criminal codes, including the *Carolina* and the *Constitutio Criminalis Theresiana*, regulated the application of torture by limiting its use to crimes punishable by death and its extent to – usually – one

---

[24] All of these statements are collected in the handwritten court records of the Wächtler case ('Acta, Inquisition, Urtheil u. dessen Vollstreckung wider Maria Catharina Wächtler', see note 21 above); a published compendium of the interrogation records and witness depositions is available in *Aechte und vollständige Akten der berüchtigten Inquisitin Wächtler zu Hamburg* (Staatsarchiv Hamburg, Sig. A427/0032). The case has recently been interpreted by Martschukat ('*Düsterheit*' and *Inszeniertes Töten*, 89–112) and Lindemann ('Narratives').

[25] For a discussion of the Wächtler case in the context of the contemporary debate on torture, see Martschukat, '*Düsterheit*'; Wosnik; and Trummer 1 89–93, as well as numerous contemporary pamphlets (see note 18 above).

[26] On the legal dilemma, see especially Baldauf 207 and Schmoeckel 207–10, 237. Wächtler's contemporaries were well aware of the dilemma; see, among others, Hofmann 22 and *Haupt-Auszüge aus der Defension*: 'Wenn keine Augenzeugen dabey gewesen, und Inquisitin ihr eigenes Geständniß nicht da ist, so ist es keine Gewißheit, sondern nur bloße Muthmaßung' (8).

single occasion,[27] but left implementation entirely to the magistrates, who frequently skirted the one-session-only rule by defining repeated torture sessions as a 'continuation' of the first.[28] (Wächtler's own 'single' torture session was a case in point; it lasted for ten months, from January until October 1788.) The concurrence of these circumstances – the pre-eminent status of the culprit's confession as the 'queen of proofs',[29] the resulting pressure on the court to obtain it by any means necessary, and the fact that the public was excluded from all stages of the proceedings until the public execution – was grist to the mill of those who opposed torture as outdated and irrational, a group that included some of the greatest names in eighteenth-century jurisprudence and philosophy, such as Thomasius, Beccaria, Voltaire, Montesquieu and Sonnenfels.[30] But these thinkers did not necessarily represent the majority opinion. That confessions were the only admissible proof but also, if extracted under torture, profoundly unreliable is a dilemma described in juridical dissertations throughout the eighteenth century.[31] At least two of them focused on the thorny issues of the ban on repeated torture and confessions that were obtained under torture but later retracted.[32] The problem was commonly

---

[27] See Helbing II 163–78 on the *Constitutio Criminalis Theresiana* and 179–99 for its regulation of torture. Repeated torture was generally permitted only in cases where further evidence of guilt came to light after the first torture session had concluded. Death-penalty crimes, that is, crimes for which torture was permissible, included blasphemy, witchcraft and sorcery, crimes against majesty and high treason, counterfeiting of coins, forgery, abuse of an official position, bestiality and sodomy, rape, adultery and bigamy, homosexuality, fornication with non-Christians, abduction, manslaughter and murder, poisoning, theft, robbery, arson, escaping from gaol and slander (Helbing II 200–15; Baldauf 166).

[28] See Baldauf 164–6, 208.

[29] 'Confessio est regina probationum' (Art. 22 of the *Carolina*, quoted in Baldauf 207); and: 'confessus pro iudicato habetur' ('a confession can serve as a judgment', quoted in Schmoeckel 411). A confession was considered *probatio plena* ('complete proof'). It relieved the court of the obligation to collect further evidence and could not be contradicted by evidence to the contrary; it made good flawed proceedings, replaced a missing accusation, and excluded appeals and proofs of innocence. The only two conditions were that the confession seemed credible to the judges and that it was not obtained directly under torture (although confessions made under threat of or influenced by the memory of recent torture counted as 'voluntary' confessions). To satisfy this condition, most penal codes, including the *Carolina* and the *Theresiana*, required that a confession made under torture was later confirmed 'freely' in the presence of the court. See Schmoeckel 203–10, 237.

[30] See Martschukat, '*Düsterheit*', 335–6; Sven Kramer 60–6; Stöckle. Many less famous contemporaries took up the theme; see, among others, Wiederholdt's extensively argued case against torture as a truth-finder on the grounds that people's ability to withstand physical pain is unrelated to guilt or innocence (114–20).

[31] See, for example, Dondorf, *Dissertationem Inauguralem, de Confessione Tormentis Extorta* (1717); Schönitz, *Disputatio Juridica de Quaestionibus seu Tortvris* (1767); Günther, *Dissertatio Juridica de Convicto non-Confesso* (1715); Wiedemeyer, *Disputatio Juridica de Confesso Non Convicto* (1715).

[32] Hommel, *Q. D. B. V. de Revocatione Confessionis per Tormenta Extortae* (n.d.); Selpert, *de Repetitione Tormentorum confesso* (1714). Selpert states unequivocally that a confession obtained under torture is

recognised; the solutions advanced were various. Some of these writers advocate the abolition of torture; others propose other legal reforms; others still support a further increase of the magistrates' already extensive discretionary powers, and only one – Daniel Bernstein, writing more than seventy years before Wächtler entered the torture chamber – passionately called for the legal prosecution of judges who had overstepped their authority in the application of torture.[33] These treatises seem to me to offer little support for the often confidently advanced claim that they show evidence of either 'general' support for or 'overwhelming' opposition to torture.[34] Clearly, torture was widely debated throughout the eighteenth (and earlier[35]) centuries, with impassioned arguments being launched both in its defence and in opposition. In fact, the idea of abolishing torture *without* simultaneously de-throning confession as the 'queen of proofs' raised serious misgivings in the minds of lawmakers and magistrates, who protested that once they had been deprived of the only means to obtain what was, in effect, the sole basis for sentencing, it would become impossible to conclude any trial with a 'guilty' verdict.[36] The alternative – *poena extraordinaria*, that is: the option to impose lifelong imprisonment in the absence of an actual sentence[37] – sat uncomfortably both with the jurists' desire for a reliable procedure and with the civic sense of justice (to the extent that we can discern from contemporary writings what this was considered to be).

insufficient for sentencing and that torture cannot be repeated after intervals of non-torture: 'Confessio in tormentis facta ad condemnationem non sufficit, nisi tortus ex intervallo eam ratam habeat' (47).

[33] Bernstein, *Dissertatio Juridica de Judicum Circa Torturam Excedentium Emenda* (1716).

[34] See, for example, Sven Kramer: 'Während des gesamten Jahrhunderts wandte sich die überwiegende Zahl der Gelehrten entschieden gegen die Folter' (60) versus Schmoeckel's claim that throughout the century, most jurists and citizens remained convinced of the necessity and justifiability of torture, and that jurists everywhere rose in defence of torture wherever attempts were made to abolish it or limit its use (568). Kramer speaks of the intelligentsia, Schmoeckel of jurists and the populace. Neither of these scholars admits that there may have been severe disagreements on the issue amongst any of these groups, and neither contextualises one group's position (pro or contra torture) in that of any other, instead conveying the impression of a near-universal agreement on the issue, either in favour or opposed.

[35] See Schmoeckel's claim that eighteenth-century arguments in opposition to torture differed only slightly from those advanced in the Middle Ages: 'Es ist bereits sogar von einem Stillstand der Rechtsentwicklung gesprochen worden' (501). Sven Kramer states that most of the eighteenth-century arguments against torture had already been made in the fifteenth (53).

[36] See Baldauf 207; see also Niehaus on the inexperience of judges and interrogators immediately after the abolition of torture in a 1787 case in Konstanz (*Mord, Geständnis, Widerruf*).

[37] *Poena extraordinaria*, that is the imprisonment of suspects in the absence of a sentence until they either confessed or died, was almost universally imposed by those enlightened rulers who outlawed torture in their territories, including Frederick the Great (see Baldauf 182; Schmoeckel 575). See also the critique of this practice in *Bekenntniß der Inquisitinn Wächtlern*, 15.

The pamphlets commenting on Wächtler's case recast many of the arguments made in the context of the nationwide debate. Wächtler's frequent confessions under torture, invariably retracted as soon as the torture stopped, her incrimination of others who later turned out to be innocent, even her statement that she would never have confessed if she had not been tortured were cited by some as proof of the unreliability of confessions extracted by torture.[38] Others defended the decision of the Hamburg Senate, arguing that torture in this case was justified by the weight of the incriminating evidence, the necessity to discover Wächtler's accomplices since it was unfathomable that she could have committed a crime of this nature by herself, and the legal requirement for a confession, which could not be obtained by any other means.[39] Numerous observers took the Wächtler case as an occasion for more general remarks on legal procedure. The anonymous commentator on Wächtler's first torture session, for example, attacked the presumption of guilt inherent in the very idea of torture:

> Torture is inadmissible because a person who has not yet been proven guilty, that is, a human being who is innocent in the eyes of the public, is treated like a criminal and subjected to physical pain in order to determine whether he should be treated like and punished as a criminal. In an effort to catch the culprit, the as-yet innocent are presumed guilty.[40]

The notions implied here *ex negativo*, namely the presumption of innocence and the accountability of the law to the public, were not anchored in law at the time of writing but later became cornerstones of criminal law in Germany. The accountability issue is taken a radical step further in the author's demand that the Senate make Wächtler's trial records available to the public, a blow he softens by claiming diplomatically that 'many citizens of Hamburg' wished to understand the Senate's rather unusual decision to subject Wächtler to torture[41] at a time when

---

[38] See especially *Bekenntniß der Inquisitinn Wächtlern*, 8–9; *Aussage der Inquisitinn Wächtlern*, 12; 'Ueber die letzte Defension', 4–5.

[39] Among others: Hofmann 28–9; *Unverfälschte Nachricht*, 3; *Berichtigungen*, 3–4.

[40] 'Die Folter ist unzulässig, weil man einen unüberwiesenen, also für das Publicum unschuldigen Menschen, wie einen Schuldigen, mit körperlichen Schmerzen belegt, um zu erfahren, ob man ihn wie einen Schuldigen behandeln und bestrafen solle. Man bestrebt sich, einen Schuldigen zu erhaschen, deswegen nimmt man einen noch Unschuldigen indessen dafür an' (*Aussage der Inquisitinn Wächtlern*, 15). The author echoes Wiederholdt, who had already argued in 1739 that torture should not be regarded as part of the trial but as a sentence akin to the death penalty, and that in cases where there was not sufficient evidence to administer the one, the other should also be excluded (187–8).

[41] 'Unterdessen glauben doch Viele, ein Hochweiser Senat würde gewiß kein so hartes Urtheil gefället haben, wäre diese Inquisitinn nicht vielleicht in gewissen Stücken gravirt, welche aber dem Publicum unbekannt geblieben. Es ist daher der Wunsch vieler Hamburger dahin gegangen, man mögte

most had already considered torture effectively, if not legally, abolished.[42]

A further point of attack concerned the common procedure of asking leading questions in the context of an inquisitional trial, questions designed to elicit not the truth but confirmation of already existing witness depositions. This, reviewers of the Wächtler case argued, compelled the accused to confess not the truth, but whatever they thought their interrogators wanted to hear, knowing that the cessation of torture depended entirely on an accurate guess.[43] 'What, then, can the culprit do in such a desperate situation?' asked one critical observer of Wächtler's case, promptly answering his own question: 'The best advice for him is to conform to his judge's ideas, and after a few wrong guesses he won't have any trouble discerning what these ideas are, even if he is innocent.'[44] Wächtler's legal defender employed the same argument, claiming that Wächtler's answers represented not the truth, but her ability to read the judge's leading questions, enabling her to guess accurately what he would accept as a correct reply. Thus her replies, he added, demonstrated not her guilt, but merely her ardent desire 'to satisfy her judges and escape further torture'.[45]

---

erlauben, die Original-Akten abdrucken zu lassen, um jedermann zur richtigen Einsicht einer Sache zu verhelfen, die besonders in diesen Tagen so ausserordentliches Aufsehen erregt hat' (*Aussage der Inquisitinn Wächtlern*, 10).

[42] The point was made by both supporters and opponents of the use of torture in this case. Pro torture: 'Viel wollen es unserer weisen Obrigkeit verübeln, daß sie die, beinah schon für abgeschaft gehaltene Tortur, bey dieser Inquisitinn wieder hervorsucht: allein die Leute reden ohne Kenntniß der Sache' (*Unverfälschte Nachricht*, 3). Contra: 'So scharf auch diese Anklage war: so enthielt sie doch zugleich trefliche Bemerkungen über die Tortur und über ihre Unzulässigkeit. Sie wird darinn ein trügliches, fast in ganz Teutschland verworfenes, und selbst in Hamburg durch vieljährigen Nichtgebrauch stillschweigend abgeschaftes Mittel genannt' (*Aussage der Inquisitinn Wächtlern in Hamburg bey dem am 25ten Januar 1788 erhaltenen Ersten Grade der Tortur*, 3–4). Contra torture (but in favour of sentencing in the absence of a valid confession): 'Zwar müßte nach den Gesetzen, da ihr Eingeständniß nicht da ist, ihr die scharfe Frage vorgelegt werden; allein da jetzt in unsern aufgeklärten Zeiten sie beynahe gänzlich abgeschaft ist, und man Inquisitin ihrer Schandthat vollkommen überführt hat: so muß, meines Erachtens, ein solches schändliches Geschöpf, welches so sehr die Menschheit beschimpft, gänzlich aus der menschlichen Gesellschaft heraus gestossen, und nach dem 23sten Artikel der peinlichen Halsgerichtsordnung, welcher den Todtschlag zwischen Eheleuten mit dem Rade gebietet zu bestrafen, auch dieses Todesurtheil an ihr vollzogen werden' (*Aechte und vollständige Akten*, 107–8).

[43] See, for example, the following analysis: 'Des Gefolterten Aussage mitten unter der Marter ist nicht gültig, selbst nach Anweisung der Halsgerichtsordnung. Es wird darauf ankommen, ob ihm der gewaltige Schmerz allen Lebensmuth benommen, oder seine Glieder und Nerven noch auf die Zukunft brauchbar gelassen hat. Wenn dies, so wird er auf seinem Läugnen beharren; wenn jenes, so wird er bekennen, was die Richter wollen. Er wird Umstände hinzu dichten, um seine Aussage ja recht glaubhaft zu machen, und seinen Erlöser, den Tod, näher zu locken' (*Aussage der Inquisitinn Wächtlern*, 16).

[44] 'Und was soll dann der Inquisit in so mislicher Lage thun? Das Rathsamste für ihn ist, sich nach der Idee seines Richters zu bequemen, und nach einigem Fehlrathen wird es ihm nicht schwer werden, solche zu treffen, auch wenn er unschuldig ist' (*Bekenntniß der Inquisitinn Wächtlern*, 14).

[45] 'Wenn man übrigens (sagt Defensor) die ganze Aussage der Inquisitinn betrachte, so wäre darinne auch gar nichts neues, sondern alles gerade so enthalten, wie es bereits in dem summarischen Verhöre befindlich gewesen. Das wären Fragen, die man ihr vorgelegt, und folglich wären nur die beyden Fälle

The disease many contemporaries diagnosed based on the symptom of leading questions was, once again, the presumption of guilt, a presumption very often derived from incriminating witness statements obtained before the interrogation of the suspect even began. There is good evidence that this was precisely the procedure used on Wächtler, who was arrested in early March 1786 but not interrogated until July.[46] The following excerpt from the trial records may indicate the extent to which Wächtler was able to influence the course of the trial. In question number 182 (out of a total of 340), she was asked to identify the hammer with which, according to her daughter's statement, she had killed her husband. She said she had never seen the hammer before. The following exchange ensued:

[Question] 183. Whether she had also hidden this same hammer with the wooden handle for protection in her bed, or fetched it in the course of the night?

A.) She said she had never laid eyes on this hammer, she now saw it for the very first time.

184. Whether she had hidden a different hammer for protection in her bed, or fetched it during the night?

A.) She had never laid eyes on any hammer whatsoever.

185. Whether she had not hit her husband several times on the side of his head with this hammer as he lay peacefully in bed?

A.) No, this was not the case! She had done no such thing.

186. Whether she had done this perchance using a different hammer?

A.) She had not hit her husband on the head with any instrument: she had not hit him at all.

187. Whether the blood caused by these wounds had not flowed immediately upon the bed?

A.) No, she knew nothing of this.

188. Whether her husband had not moved a little, as if to defend himself?

A.) No, she did not know anything about this.

---

möglich, entweder, es sey ein Ohngefähirt, daß die ihr im ehemaligen Verhöre vorgelegten Fragen gerade so mit dem Bekenntnisse der Inquisitinn übereinkämen, (welches aber nicht wahrscheinlich, daß die Nebenumstände bey der Ermordung, die man ihr als Fragen vorgelegt, so genau mit den bey Vollziehung der That vorgefallenen Umständen übereinstimmen sollten), oder es ist von Seiten der Inquisitinn ein durch Zwang, Drohung und wirkliche Marter herausgepreßtes Geständniß, welches sie bloß nach dem ihr bewußten summarischen Verhör eingerichtet, um die Richter zu befriedigen und der fernern Marter überhoben zu seyn' ('Ueber die letzte Defension', 6–7).

[46] See the initial interrogations described in 'Examen der Inquisitin Maria Katharina, gebohrne Wunschen, des ermordeten Julius Adolph Wächtlers Ehefrau, wegen vieler äusserst gravirenden Umständen in Ansehung der von ihr geschehenen Ermordung, Verstümmelung und Transportirung ihres Ehemanns, den 10. Julii et sequentibus 1786' (in *Aechte und vollständige Akten*, 4–102). This initial round of interrogations, during which Wächtler was constantly confronted with witness statements obtained previously, concluded on 9 August 1786.

189. Whether she had not thereafter cut his throat with a knife?[47]

A.) No.

190. What had moved her to such a murderous decision?

A.) She had not harboured any murderous thoughts against her husband.

191. Whether she had carried out her decision by herself or had help from others?

A.) She had neither had help from another nor done it by herself.

192. In which way and with whose aid had she removed the murdered corpse from the bed?

A.) She had not removed her husband's murdered corpse at all since no murder had been committed in her house.

193. Who was the man standing on the landing, whom she had called into the bedroom at night, during or immediately after the murder of her husband?

A.) There had been no man in the house during that night, other than her husband, consequently she could not have called any man into the room.[48]

---

[47] Questions 183–9 were clearly written to confirm her daughter's testimony, which was inadmissible due to the witness's age: 'My mother took me from my father's bed while I was sleeping and put me into another bed; this woke me up, and I saw that she hit my father on the head with a hammer, a few times, and immediately thereafter cut his throat with a knife so that the blood gushed in a great spurt over the blanket, upon which he violently thrashed his arms around' ('Meine Mutter hat mich schlafend aus dem Bette meines Vaters herausgenommen, und in ein anderes geleget; darüber bin ich aufgewachet, und habe gesehen: daß sie meinen Vater ein Paarmale, mit einem Hammer, auf den Kopf geschlagen, und gleich darauf mit einem Messer über den Hals geschnitten hat, daß das Blut gewaltig über die Bettdecke hingestürzt ist, worauf derselbe heftig mit den Armen um sich geschlagen hat', quoted in Hofmann 28). Hofmann quotes this passage in direct speech, making its provenance questionable: court depositions were usually recorded in third-person indirect speech, and the vocabulary and diction of this passage make it unlikely that this was verbatim speech by a seven-year-old child.

[48] Interrogation on 19 July 1786: '183. Ob sie diesen gegenwärtigen Hammer mit hölzernen Stiel ebenfalls zu ihrer Sicherheit im Bette versteckt, oder erst in der Nacht hergeholet habe? / A.) Ihre Augen hätten diesen Hammer niemals gesehen, sie sähe solchen zum erstenmale. / 184. Ob sie etwan einen andern Hammer zu ihrer Sicherheit im Bette versteckt oder wohl in der Nacht hergeholet habe? / A.) Sie habe gar keinen Hammer mit Augen gesehen. / 185. Ob Sie nicht mit diesem Hammer ihren im Bette ruhig liegenden Mann etlichemal vor den Kopf in die Schläfe geschlagen? / A.) Nein, dieses wäre nicht andem! sie habe solches nicht gethan./ 186. Ob sie solches etwan mit einen andern Hammer gethan? / A.) Sie hätte überhaupt mit keinem Instrumente ihren Mann vor den Kopf geschlagen, sie hätte ihm gar keinen Schlag gegeben. / 187. Ob nicht gleich darauf das Blut aus dem durch diese Schläge verursachten Wunden, aufs Bette geflossen? / A.) Nein, sie wisse nichts davon. / 188. Ob ihr Mann sich dabey nicht noch ein wenig bewegt, als wenn er sich wehren wollen? / A.) Nein, von der ganzen Sache wäre ihr nichts bekannt. / 189. Ob sie ihn nicht hierauf mit dem Messer über den Hals geschnitten? / A.) Nein. / 190. Was sie zu diesen mörderischen Entschluß bewogen? / A.) Sie habe gar keine mördrische Gedanken gegen ihren Mann gehabt. / 191. Ob sie solchen Entschluß allein ausgeführt, oder Hülfe von fremden dabey gehabt? / A.) Sie hätte so wenig einen fremden dazu gebraucht, als daß sie es selbst gethan. / 192. Auf welche Weise und mit wessen Hülfe sie den ermordeten Körper aus dem Bette genommen? / A.) Sie habe den ermordeten Körper ihres Mannes gar nicht aus den Bette genommen, denn es wäre diese Mordthat in ihrem Hause gar nicht begangen worden. / 193. Wer diejenige Mannsperson gewesen, welche sie in der Nacht bey und gleich nach der geschehenen Ermordung ihres Mannes von dem Vorplatz ins Schlafzimmer herein gerufen? / A.) Es wäre in dieser Nacht, ausser ihrem Manne, sonst gar keine Mannsperson im Hause gewesen, folglich hätte sie auch keine hereinrufen können' (*Aechte und vollständige Akten*, 52–5).

The modus operandi here corresponds precisely to seventeenth-century inquisitional trials of women accused of witchcraft.[49] A catalogue of predetermined questions is read out, and both questions and answers are duly recorded in the subjunctive of indirect speech. But there is no assumption that follow-up questions should take answers to previous questions into account or relate to them in any way. That the interrogators simply ignored Wächtler's answers, continuing straight on to the next predetermined question, shows clearly that the goal of the interrogation was not to obtain information. Whatever its true purpose, its effect would have been twofold: it would have provided the interrogators with a series of disconnected statements, which could later be used to catch the accused in a contradiction and which would have been difficult for the accused to remember because none of them were ever acknowledged or discussed. And it would have thoroughly demoralised the accused by conveying the impression that none of her statements, protestations or denials made the slightest impression on her judges.[50]

What makes Wächtler's case so unusual is that the public debate cast her, albeit very indirectly, as a symbol for individual rights, and occasionally even as the victim of a capricious judicial system, *even though she was generally presumed guilty.*[51] The entire debate never concerned itself with her guilt or innocence but with the juridical and ethical legitimacy of her treatment, and, by extension, the potential conflict between civic rights and state power (including positively perceived state powers such as the protection of citizens' lives and property[52]). In the pamphlets, Wächtler played a contradictory part: she was guilty but also an injured party. Not so in her biography, or in the court documents. As these sources never tire of

---

[49] See Topalovic's analysis of the trial records of accused witches, as well as Schwerhoff, 'Strafjustiz'; Zelle, 'Autorität'; and Henschel on eighteenth-century inquisitional trials.

[50] See the recent study by Michael Niehaus, who has described precisely this process, using the 1787 interrogation records of Jakob Sauter (*Mord, Geständnis, Widerruf*).

[51] For the few dissenting voices, see Lindemann, 'Narratives', and Heckscher 351.

[52] Valentin Hofmann, for example, suggested several breaches of existing law, which included accepting the inadmissible testimony of Wächtler's daughter and the recognition of confessions made under torture without later confirmation, arguing that her harsh punishment was the only guarantee of 'internal security' (see the general passage on the mild punishment of crime on 4–5 and its application to Wächtler's case on 28–9: 'daß, da sonst in gewissen andern peinlichen Fällen untüchtige Zeugen zugelassen werden, nicht einzusehen sey, warum solches nicht auch hier, bey einem so abscheulichen Verbrechen, geschehen solle, *wo kein anderer Augenzeuge vorhanden, und die Wahrheit auf andere Art zu erfahren, nicht möglich ist,* an deren Erörterung und Bestrafung der Urheberin einer solchen verruchten That dem Staate, der häuslichen Sicherheit wegen, gleichwol nicht viel weniger, als an der Bestrafung eines Verbrechens gelegen ist', emphases original).

pointing out, she had been an adulteress, a 'loose woman' and a thief even before she turned to murder;[53] several writers unfussily concluded from this that she was a woman 'well capable' of the deed of which she stood accused.[54] Unquestionably, her previous conduct was a decisive factor at her trial: the official accusation lists as the first point of proof that she was guilty of murder (out of a total of five) the fact that 'she has been a debauched person from the very beginning';[55] and her defender weakly protested that 'the prosecution can hardly pronounce her guilty because of the sins of her youth'.[56] And yet, this stereotypical view of Wächtler as a depraved tramp whose life as a fornicator, vagabond, adulteress, thief and embezzler predestined her for axe-murder did not become the dominant discourse in the pamphlet literature. Instead of her life, most writings focused on her behaviour, particularly her behaviour under torture. Whereas her accusers and judges took the long view, linking Wächtler's crime to her biography, the pamphlets offer momentary snapshots of her. The difference in outlook translates into a significant disparity in the view of Wächtler and her crime. Whereas the court literature assumes a congruence between Wächtler's life and crime that can only express itself in terms of continuity and intensification, the pamphlet literature, its sole focus on 'Wächtler this week', allowed for change, discrepancies and contradictions. In fact, these were the aspects that kept the pot boiling: readers' fascination with her and corresponding sales naturally depended on the assumption that one never knew what she would do next.

Accordingly, the pamphlets made as much hay of Wächtler's unpredictability as they could. One moment she proudly faced down her accusers, the next moment she burst into tears.[57] Faced with another round of torture,

---

[53] See especially *Ausführliche Lebensbeschreibung* and Wächtler's reincarnation in *Der neue Pitaval.* Wächtler's sexual lapses, vagabondism, wastefulness, shamelessness and sloppiness as a housewife also play a prominent role in *Berichtigungen und Anmerkungen*, Hofmann and other sources.

[54] See, for example, Hofmann 23: 'Sie war eine Person, zu welcher man sich, wie die vorerwehnte peinliche Halsgerichtsordnung erfordert und sich ausdrücket, einer solchen Missethat wohl versehen konnte, welche eine dergleichen zu begehen, wohl im Stande war, und auf welche der Verdacht derselben, mit dem vollkommensten Rechte fiel.' The passage is later copied near-verbatim in *Der neue Pitaval*: 'Ein Weib, das nach solchen Anschuldigungen eine solche Lebensweise unter den Auspicien des Rabensteins fortsetzen kann, durfte man, auch ohne die ermittelten Präcedentien für eine Person halten, zu der man sich der angeschuldigten That versehen kann' (Hitzig and Häring VI 492).

[55] '… vielmehr sind folgende Beweise da, daß sie diese Mordthat begangen: / 1. Weil sie von Anfang an eine ausschweifende Person gewesen' (from: 'Fiskalische Anklage im Niedergericht gegen die Wächtlern', *Aechte und vollständige Akten*, 103–8, the citation 105).

[56] '… überdem kann Fiscal gar nicht verlangen, daß Inquisitin darum strafbar wäre, daß sie in ihrer Jugend ausgeschweift' (*Haupt-Auszüge aus der Defension*, 2).

[57] See, for example, the description of her behaviour in 'Ueber die letzte Defension', 7–8.

Wächtler's mood changes from terror, self-control, pride, affronted inno-cence, patience and composure to depression and lachrymose plaintiveness in the space of a single paragraph.[58] Invited to descend into the cellar to be tortured, she flatly refused, but after a beating 'she changed the role she had played so far at once', begging for mercy and promising to confess all.[59] In another account, she 'courageously' refuses to confess even when threatened with torture, but her long and severe imprisonment and repeated torture 'wear her down' and 'break her will' to the point of driving her to attempt suicide.[60] Obviously, these passages not only describe Wächtler's behav-iour, but also the conditions of captivity and physical pain that elicited it, and the authors' doubts regarding the legitimacy of Wächtler's treatment may well express themselves in occasional and seemingly inappropriate descriptions of her as 'courageous' and 'serene'.[61] But Wächtler's ability to surprise her readers was far more marketable than social controversy. In the entire criminal history of Hamburg, one pamphlet stated, nobody had ever subjected the authorities to such a merry-go-round of confessions offered and confessions retracted.[62] And the longer she could hang on, the more

---

[58] One fairly typical passage: 'Wir haben schon neulich erwähnt, daß besagte Inquisitinn anfänglich, da sie dies Urtheil erhielt, ganz ausser sich gewesen, auch den Anblick der Frohnerei nicht ohne Entsetzen ertragen können; daß sie sich aber nachher ziemlich wieder gefaßt habe. Denn als sie in der Frohnerey ankam, nahm sie sogleich ihr freies Wesen wieder an, und stellte sich als die höchst beleidigte Unschuld. Allein der Frohnknecht bewog sie bald durch gar fühlbare Hülfsmittel sich geduldig darein zu ergeben. Nach der Zeit betrug sie sich wieder ganz ruhig, wozu vermuthlich das etwas beytragen mochte, daß sie nun in ihrem neuen Logis bessern Tisch und Bette, als auf der Hauptwacht hatte. Doch als ein Prediger sie besuchte, und sie zum gutwilligen Bekentniß [sic] ermahnte, auch sie versicherte, daß sie ohne daßelbe, der Marterbank nicht entgehen könnte, so sank ihr Muth wieder etwas. Nichts desto weniger blieb sie immer bey der Behauptung, daß sie unschuldig und sehr zu beklagen sey' (*Unverfälschte Nachricht von dem Betragen der Wächtlern*, unpag.).

[59] 'Als man ihr andeutete, daß sie nach dem Keller, worinnen sie gefoltert werden sollte, gehen müßte; so weigerte sie sich, solches zu thun. Man brauchte Gewalt und Prügel, und augenblicklich änderte sie ihre bishieher gespielte Rolle. Sie bat um Gnade; sie wollte alles freywillig gestehen, man möchte sie nur nicht nach der Folter bringen' (*Wahrhafte Aussagen*, unpag.).

[60] 'Hierauf ward sie aufs ernstlichste von den Herren des Raths ermahnt, die Wahrheit zu bekennen, und widrigenfalls mit Anlegung der fernern Grade der Tortur bedroht. Sie blieb muthig beym Läugnen, und mußte mit Gewalt zur Marterkammer hinuntergeführt werden. Angethan mit dem Marterkittel, sahe sie die fernere Peinigung unausbleiblich vor Augen. Ohnedies hatte sie ihren vormaligen Muth durch die Härte des Gefängnisses verloren: denn weil die Inquisitinn geschworen, sie wolle sich selbst das Leben nehmen, war sie des Nachts an Händen und Füßen, und des Tags über mit den Füßen am Tisch geschlossen worden. Entmuthet durch die Härte des Gefängnisses, und mürbe gemacht durch die Quaalen der Folter, erlag ihre Natur, und sie gestand nun ohne weitern Rückhalt' (*Bekenntniß der Inquisitinn Wächtlern*, 3–4).

[61] For example: 'Sie blieb muthig beym Läugnen' (*Bekenntniß der Inquisitinn Wächtlern*, 3–4); or: 'Inquisitinn schien anfangs gesetzt und ruhiger, als jemals zu seyn' ('Ueber die letzte Defension', 7).

[62] 'Solch eine frevelhafte, boshafte und verstockte Mörderin weiß sich wol keiner hier in unserm Staate zu erinnern, welche auf ihre begangene Mordthat eingestanden und so oft geläugnet, wie diese Inquisitin *Wächtlern*' (*Abermalige wahrhafte Aussagen*, unpag., emphasis original).

grist to the mill of local pamphleteers, and the more nail-biting pleasure for their readers:

Everyone believed that the defendant Wächtler, after her last interrogation, would remain in a humble and remorseful attitude. But when questioned again and asked to reconfess freely, confirming her previous statements, she became very brazen and angry. Her exact words were: 'What I said is what I said, once and for all.' When she was again instructed clearly that she had to confirm her previous deposition explicitly, she answered again: 'What I said is what I said.' … This shows that if possible, she intends to draw out the trial for the murder of her husband, although [her guilt] is obvious and known through her own confession.[63]

Or, to paraphrase briefly: 'To Be Continued'. Wächtler's famous unpredictability coupled with the rather direct assurance of a long, drawn-out trial serves as the pamphleteer's promise of many intriguing future issues. Wächtler buffs must have been delighted.

Beyond her volatility, the one constant that emerges from these writings is Wächtler's pride, although the word itself is rarely used. She is described as 'recalcitrant',[64] possessed of a 'fiery temperament' and 'quick to anger',[65] 'brazen and contemptuous',[66] 'very cheeky and angry', 'obstinate', 'brazen', full of 'malice and bitterness' and as 'stomping her feet' in anger.[67] This is in some contrast to her trial records, in which the defiant Wächtler only makes a very occasional appearance.[68] In illustration of Wächtler's famous temper, one pamphleteer relates that she struck a soldier in the face because he had dared criticise her sexual conduct. Torn between censoring her morals and

---

[63] The passage refers to a confession made under torture, which by law had to be confirmed 'freely', that is: not directly under torture: 'Ein jeder hat geglaubt, daß die Inquisitin Wächtler, nach ihrem letzten Verhör, demüthig und voll Reue in dieser Gemüthsfassung würde verblieben seyn; allein bey diesem abermaligen Verhör war sie, auf die bisher schon eingestandnen Aussagen, die ihr aufs Neue zum abermaligen freyen Geständniß vorgelesen wurden, sehr frech und böse. Ihre wahren Worte waren: "Was ich gesagt habe, das habe ich ein für allemal gesagt." Als ihr hierauf deutlich angezeigt wurde: Sie müßte die vorigen Aussagen nochmal bestimmt bekräftigen, so antwortete sie abermal: "Was ich gesagt habe, das habe ich gesagt." … Man siehet hieraus, daß sie, wenns möglich wäre, noch gerne ihre so offenbar durch eigenes Geständniß bekannte Mordthat an ihren Mann, in die Länge ziehen möchte' (*Wahre Aussagen*, unpag.).
[64] 'widerspenstig' (*Unverfälschte Nachricht*, unpag.).
[65] 'Ihr Temperament war schon damals überaus feurig und wie sie auch selbst bekannte, war sie leicht zum Zorn zu reizen' (*Ausführliche Lebensbeschreibung*, 11).
[66] 'frech und höhnisch' (Hitzig and Häring VI 497, describing Wächtler's interrogation under torture on 25 January 1788).
[67] 'sehr frech und böse'; 'im hartnäckigen Stillschweigen'; 'so bewies sie in ihrem frechen Herzen noch herrschende Bosheit und Bitterkeit dadurch, daß sie sogar mit den Füssen trampelte' (all in *Wahre Aussagen*, unpag.).
[68] For example in the session of 3 August 1786, during which she flatly refused to answer a question, '(Wobey Inquisitin sich ziemlich trotzig bezeigte)' (*Aechte und vollständige Akten*, 57).

admiring her courage, he finally inclines toward the latter: 'but still this can be taken as evidence of her fiery temper and her courage, since few women would dare to strike a Prussian musketeer'.[69] Another author tells us that Wächtler, emerging from yet another torture session, 'put on a brazen face, used scornful language, regarded everyone with contempt and did not act at all as if she had murdered her husband'[70] (fig. 8). And in the final words of Wächtler's biographer, her pride (or, in his parlance, her 'brazenness'), unbroken even after her long imprisonment, is described as the most remarkable aspect of her personality – more significant, in fact, than her entire life.[71] Years later, the 'dogged tenacity, even brazenness, with which Wächtler defended herself' was presented merely as an impertinence that had cost the judicial system of Hamburg a lot of money.[72] But contemporaries were less sure how to judge Wächtler's sangfroid under torture, even in the face of death. On the one hand, such behaviour was acceptable only when read as an indication of innocence; coupled with Wächtler's guilt, which was nearly universally assumed, it became an expression of insubordination that should have been condemned unequivocally and harshly. What makes the Hamburg pamphlets so intriguing is that it was not.

One such monument to ambivalence is Valentin Hofmann's elaborately titled treatise *Is a delinquent's confession, according to the Carolingian Penal Code and our Legal Statutes, absolutely necessary for the delinquent's execution? An Attempt at an Answer occasioned by the Case of the Infamous Husband-Murderess Wächtler* (1788; *Ist das eigene Geständniß eines Delinquenten, zu seiner Hinrichtung, nach der carolinischen peinlichen Halsgerichtsordnung, und nach unsern Statuten, durchaus erforderlich? Bey Gelegenheit der Sache der berüchtigten*

---

[69] '… aber doch immer ist es ein Beweiß ihres feurigen Temperaments und ihrer Herzhaftigkeit, weil einen preußischen Musquetier zu schlagen, sich wenige Frauenzimmer unterfangen werden' (*Ausführliche Lebensbeschreibung*, 11).

[70] 'Als die Inquisitin *Wächtlern* am Freitage des Morgens um 9½ Uhr, unter eine Menge von Zuschauern aus der Froneri geführt ward, machte sie eine freche Miene, bediente sich unterschiedene spöttische Reden, sah jedermann mit Verachtung an und that gar nicht, als wenn sie die Mörderin ihres Mannes wäre' (*Abermalige wahrhafte Aussagen der Inquisitin Wächtlern*, unpag., emphasis original).

[71] 'Ihre Lebensgeschichte ist weniger bemerkenswerth, als ihre Frechheit, die immer ein Hauptzug ihres Karakters gewesen, und die sich auch durch das langwierige Gefängniß nicht vermindert hat' (*Ausführliche Lebensbeschreibung*, 24).

[72] 'So einfach die Thatsache in diesem Processe scheint, so ausgedehnt, ja verwickelt wurde derselbe durch die zähe Ausdauer, ja die Frechheit, mit welcher die Wächtler sich vertheidigte'. Later, the authors refer rather judgmentally to 'die unendliche Mühe, welche der freche Trotz und die Ränke dieses Weibes den hamburger [sic] Gerichten vor sechzig Jahren gemacht haben müssen' (Hitzig and Häring VI 458).

Staatsarchiv Hamburg

*Transport der Wächtlerin
von der Wache am Großneumarkt nach dem Stadthause.*

Fig. 8 Maria Katharina Wächtler, surrounded by city soldiers, on her way to torture. In keeping with contemporary descriptions, she shows no sign of terror, gazing directly at the viewer and calmly adjusting her clothing. Contemporary lithograph, artist unknown.
Courtesy of the Staatsarchiv Hamburg

Mannsmörderin, Wächtlern, zu beantworten versucht). Compared to most contemporary commentators on the case, Hofmann has an unequivocal position: he entertains no doubts as to Wächtler's guilt; he defends the Senate's decision to torture her; he asserts that for a criminal like her, no punishment can possibly be harsh enough.[73] Given the penalties for mariticides in the *Carolina*, which he lists as tearing off the culprit's flesh with hot pincers followed by breaking on the wheel, beheading, drowning or live burial, he considers Wächtler's death sentence – execution on the wheel – undeservedly mild.[74] Himself an attorney, Hofmann was the sole commentator who proposed that the incriminating testimony of Wächtler's seven-year-old daughter should be included, dismissing the child's age and her close relationship with the accused as irrelevant compared with 'the truth of her testimony'.[75] He did his level best to portray Wächtler as a monster bare of all human feeling, as 'a cannibal, born in the middle of Christendom, who used the knife, still dripping with his [her husband's] blood, to eat a meal in excellent appetite next to his still-warm corpse, as if glorying in his murder'.[76] Sparing no effort in his hatchet job on Wächtler's image, Hofmann even contested the common depiction of Wächtler's defiance and bravery under torture. He gleefully relates that Wächtler broke down during the first minutes of mild physical pain and confessed all, although – in his theory – women are better able to withstand torture since their bodies, fashioned for childbirth, are less pain-sensitive than men's. This leads to his definition of Wächtler as both unfeminine (because of her intolerance to pain) and inhumane (because of her insensitivity to the pain of others): 'we must assume', he wrote, 'that Nature made a mistake when forming her, endowing her with an otherwise female body, but also with the

---

[73] In her case, Hofmann states, 'wäre Mitleid selbst Verbrechen; so empört sich die ganze Menschheit gegen einen solchen Auswurf der Natur, der zur Begehung einer solchen abscheulichen That fähig war; so ist keine Strafe hart genug' (13–14).

[74] 'Der 23ste Artikel des lediglich von peinlichen Fällen handelnden 4ten Theils unsrer Statuten, bestimmt die Strafe derjenigen, die ihre Eltern, Kinder, Schwestern, Brüder, oder nahe verwandte Freunde ermorden, – worunter bekanntlich Ehegatten und Dienstherrschaften mitgerechnet werden – oder die Leibesfrucht abtreiben, dahin: "daß sie mit glühenden Zangen angegriffen, und darauf lebendig mit dem Rade getödtet, mit dem Rade am Leben gestraft, mit dem Schwerdte hingerichtet, oder im Wasser ertränkt, oder lebendig begraben werden sollen"; und nach diesem statutarischen Criminalgesetze ist also der Wächtlern nicht nur nicht zu viel, sondern nicht einmal genug geschehen' (14–15).

[75] 'Wollte man ein Gericht, was so erkannt hätte, einer Ungerechtigkeit beschuldigen und einwenden, daß der, nach peinlichen Gesetzen erforderliche Zeuge, welcher die Missethat *mit seinen eigenen Augen gesehen habe*, das eigene und noch dazu unmündige Kind der Wächtlern gewesen, und mithin unzulässig sey; so liesse sich hierauf erwiedern: daß es nicht sowohl auf die Beschaffenheit des Zeugen selbst, als vielmehr auf die Wahrheit seines Zeugnisses ankomme' (Hofmann 28, emphasis original).

[76] 'Denn, mit nur sehr weniger weiblicher Weichheit, mit einer ganz kleinen Portion blos natürlicher Fühlbarkeit, hätte sie ihren Mann nicht umbringen – nicht, als eine, mitten in der Christenheit gebohrne Cannibalin, mit dem, noch von seinem Blute rauchenden Messer, neben seinem noch nicht kalten todten Körper, gleichsam im Triumphe über seine Ermordung, mit dem besten Appetite, ihre Mahlzeit verzehren können' (Hofmann 33). There is no mention in the court records of such a repast.

more sensitive nerve system of our sex, and the inhumanity of the heart of Nero'.[77]

And yet: even Hofmann's appalling images of Wächtler as a cannibal in the conjugal bed, as a cruel-hearted coward and a freak of nature, are tempered by his obvious, if grudging, admiration for her pride. His description of Wächtler's execution injects a note of ambivalence into his treatise that compromises all of his previous certainties:

Afterwards she embarked on foot, quite cheerfully, on her way to the scaffold. At the convent in Steinstraße, she drank a glass of wine; on the scaffold itself – and presumably no delinquent before her has ever done this – she not only carefully examined the edifice on which she was to be broken but also picked up the wheel itself. Even as she lay on the scaffold, she asked: 'Am I in the correct position?'

In all, this woman, always unfortunate and thus to be pitied for her misfortune, was endowed by Nature with such gifts so as to become unique, either in great goodness or in great evil. To the last moment of her execution, she displayed a mental composure for which our language evidently has no other word than 'steadfastness'. But only suffering innocence can lay claim to this word and this admiration; only true virtue can show greatness of the soul.[78]

What was to be done, discursively, with a gifted and unique and yet debauched woman, an adulteress, thief and finally axe-murderess, who – steadfast without being innocent, great without being virtuous – resisted torture like a martyr and went to her death like a hero? How to resolve the dilemma that Wächtler was both guilty and the victim of a procedure that many opposed as unjust and nearly everyone considered harsh? By virtue of the fact that Wächtler was tortured, at a time when torture was no longer universally accepted as part of the 'justice' meted out by the authorities, she became a symbol for the

---

[77] 'Da die Ursache hievon allerdings in ihrer Leibesbeschaffenheit zu suchen ist; so muß man annehmen, daß die Natur bey ihrer Formung einen Irrthum begangen, und ihr, bey ihrem sonstigen weiblichen Körperbau, das angestrengtere Nervensystem unsers Geschlechtes, und die Unmenschlichkeit eines neronischen Herzens zugetheilt haben müsse' (Hofmann 33). On Wächtler's cowardice under torture and Hofmann's theory of male vs female bodies' ability to tolerate pain, see 32–9.

[78] 'Hiernächst hat sie ihren Weg nach dem Richtplatze, zu Fuße, ganz munter angetreten; in der Steinstraße, vor dem Convent, noch einen Römer mit Wein ausgetrunken; auf dem Richtplatze selbst – welches wohl noch nie von einem Delinquenten geschehen ist – nicht nur das Gerüste, auf welchem sie gerädert werden sollte, in genauen Augenschein genommen, sondern auch das Rad selbst in die Höhe gehoben, und, wie sie schon auf dem Gerüste gelegen hat, noch gefragt: "ob sie so recht läge?" – / Ueberhaupt war diese immer unglückliche, und mithin in dieser Rücksicht, zu bedauernde Frau, von der Natur mit solchen Gaben ausgestattet, um ein recht gutes, oder auch ein recht böses Original zu werden. Sie hat bis zum letzten Augenblicke ihrer Hinrichtung eine Gemüthsfassung gezeigt, zu welcher unsere Sprache freylich kein anderes Wort, als "Standhaftigkeit" hat; die aber nur bey der leidenden Unschuld diese Benennung und Bewundrung verdienet – nur da Größe der Seele – wahre Tugend ist' (Hofmann 40).

individual at the mercy of the State. The fact that many writers portrayed her in this role *while* assuming her guilt indicates that they exercised an ability that Hofmann acknowledged briefly in the final sentences of his treatise and immediately tried to take back: the ability to distinguish between the specific and the general, between cause and potential effect, between the case and its possible consequences. It is, simply put, the capacity to think in terms of 'and-and' rather than 'either-or'. Wächtler's guilt did not erase the fact that she was also unjustly treated; it did not cancel out the knowledge that had she been innocent, she might still have been caught in the net woven of leading questions, repeated torture and the presumption of guilt.

The 'and-and' attitude that was apparent in the debate on the Wächtler case stood in stark contrast to the 'either-or' expressed in the official position. The first is clearly communicated in the pamphlets' emphasis on the eternal changeability of Wächtler's behaviour, the second in the State-sponsored portrayal of the eternal sameness of Wächtler's character. For mercenary, perhaps also psychological reasons, the pamphlets created a chameleon character whose bewildering unpredictability was its greatest appeal to readers. The authorised version of the story in the court records, on the other hand, 'explained' Wächtler; it drew a direct line from her life to her crime, defining the second as a mere escalation of the first. Wächtler's ability to entertain, the Horatian *delectare*, depended on the ultimate inexplicability of her character; her ability to instruct (*prodesse*) on the ultimate explicability of her crime in light of her life. If Wächtler's crime of murder followed logically and inevitably from her previous sins of fornication, adultery and theft, just as her execution followed logically and inevitably upon her crime, safety for the citizens observing this execution lay in leading a virtuous life. Avoidance of sin equals the prevention of crime; subjection to the authorities of both God and the State means to avert punishment.

Wächtler's pride, her refusal to embody this moral, demonstrated once more her unwillingness to acknowledge the authority of the State and the justness of her sentence. Those who expected Wächtler to play the part of the penitent sinner on the scaffold – praying loudly, thanking the authorities for her 'mild sentence', admonishing her audience to take example from her wicked life and horrible end[79] – were bitterly disappointed. 'For the good and salvation of her soul, and for the defendant's own sake, we wish that she would turn her eyes inward and confess',[80] one last

---

[79] For a more extensive discussion of these conventions, see the final chapter.
[80] 'Zum Besten und Heil ihrer Seelen, wäre es der Inquisitinn wohl zu wünschen, daß sie in sich ginge, und gestände' (*Unverfälschte Nachricht*, unpag.).

commentator reflected after her death sentence had already been confirmed by the Higher Court. It was a vain hope. Instead of inward, she turned her eyes to the instruments of death, not in panic but with a nearly scientific curiosity. Her inspection of the apparatus about to kill her seemed to indicate that nothing was further from her final thoughts than what was expected of her: fear of Hell, or, at the very least, terror of death. And in deviating so drastically from the predetermined script of the Penitent Sinner, she not only managed to salvage her pride, but also presented her spellbound audience with a final surprise.

THE CASE OF CHRISTIANE RUTHARDT (STUTTGART, 1844–1845) AND THE DEATH-PENALTY DEBATE

In 1844, the year in which *Der neue Pitaval* published its account of the Wächtler case, Christiane (Nanette) Ruthardt (1804?-45) administered arsenic to her husband, the goldsmith Eduard Ruthardt. Her case can be read as a mirror image of Wächtler's, its likeness reversed. Wächtler resisted for years; Ruthardt, on the other hand, cooperated fully and immediately. In Wächtler's case, all the court lacked to sentence her to death was a confession. In Ruthardt's case, all they *had* was a confession: postmortem examinations by several doctors could not establish beyond doubt that Eduard Ruthardt had died of the poison administered by his wife.[81] In the absence of all other evidence, Ruthardt's confession, still the 'queen of proofs', became the exclusive basis for her condemnation and execution.

As was the case for Wächtler, Ruthardt's life was assigned a significant role in understanding her crime. But whereas Wächtler's life of 'debauchery' was seen in direct and unambiguous relation to her crime, Ruthardt was endowed with alternate biographies. The one her defence favoured was the heartbreaking story of a young girl abandoned by her family, constantly and deliberately thwarted in her fortunes by a jealous aunt, and finally forced to marry not the man she loved but a good-for-nothing who plunged her and her child into economic misery and ultimately drove her to her act of despair.[82] This touching story was harshly rebutted in an article in the *Schwäbischer Merkur* on 27 June 1845, the day of Ruthardt's execution. According to this article, Ruthardt led a debauched life à la Wächtler that

---

[81] The court records, writs of prosecution and defence, witness depositions, and newspaper coverage of the case as well as Ruthardt's biography in *Der neue Pitaval* have been published in the extensive article by Linder and Schönert, who also contextualise these materials and offer an interpretation of the case. On the Ruthardt case, see also Kohut 119–22 and Moser 164–70.

[82] Cited in Linder and Schönert 262–9.

began, in early childhood, with lying, stealing and ingratitude, continued on to fornication and affairs with married men, and ended in murder.[83] The argument here is the same as that applied to Wächtler, namely that Ruthardt's sinful life led predictably and inexorably to her crime: the writing had been on the wall, clearly legible for those who knew her even as a child. Thus her well-meaning aunt capitulated in the face of her 'deep-rooted vices', and the director of the 'institute' where she was subsequently educated predicted as early as 1820, when Ruthardt was sixteen, that she would 'abandon herself to her passions without restraint and plummet down to join the most miserable wretches'.[84]

Ruthardt's case further mirrored Wächtler's in the sense that it led to a widespread debate on an aspect of juridical procedure that was viewed with considerable misgivings: in her case, the death penalty. The controversy surrounding her case, one of the *Pitaval* editors mused, led to the public articulation of people's 'natural or artificially created distaste for the application of the death penalty'. Were it not for its significance for this debate, he added, Ruthardt's case, a garden-variety poison murder, would not even have been included in the collection.[85] Ruthardt was executed only three years before executions were abolished all over Germany, albeit only temporarily,[86] in the course of the 1848 Revolution. Whereas the death penalty had already come under attack, during the eighteenth century, from thinkers such as Voltaire and Beccaria, several treatises appeared throughout the 1840s in defence of the death penalty – a sure sign that it was no longer taken for granted. Flourishes like the tearing of flesh with hot pincers or colourful and drawn-out methods of execution were eliminated in the mid nineteenth century because they were thought to arouse public sympathy for the victim. The penalty Wächtler had suffered, breaking on the wheel, was removed in Prussia six years after Ruthardt's execution.[87] Perhaps most

---

[83] Gustav Pfaff, 'Berichtigung zu den Veröffentlichungen in dem Kriminalprozeß gegen die Giftmischerin Christiane Ruthardt in Stuttgart', cited in Linder and Schönert 276–84.

[84] Her aunt admitted 'daß sie außer Stand sei, den tief eingewurzelten Untugenden der Angeklagten kräftig genug entgegenzutreten'; the director surmised '*daß sie sich ohne Rückhalt ihren Neigungen hingeben und in die Zahl der elendesten Geschöpfe hinabsinken werde*'. Pfaff, 'Berichtigung zu den Veröffentlichungen' (Linder and Schönert 279 and 284 respectively, emphasis original).

[85] Häring: 'der natürliche oder künstliche Widerwille gegen die Anwendung der Todesstrafe', quoted in Linder and Schönert 304. Ruthardt's case appeared in *Der neue Pitaval* XVI (1850), 325–60 and was reprinted in full in Linder and Schönert 304–18.

[86] The Basic Rights draft of 1848 included the abolition of the death penalty. Most German states abolished the death penalty in 1848–9. Post-revolutionary governments rushed to reverse this legislation; ironically, many revolutionaries were executed for treason in the following years. See Evans, *Rituals*, 267–85.

[87] On changing attitudes toward the death penalty and legal reform in the 1840s, see Evans, *Rituals*, 238–50.

significantly, some states responded to the public 'distaste' for executions by moving them indoors. From 1847 on, Prussian crowds who arrived to witness an execution found themselves listening to the moral exhortations of a priest at the prison wall while the execution took place inside, hidden from the public eye.[88]

In the mid nineteenth century, when executions moved indoors, criminal trials became a public affair, an exact reversal of the eighteenth-century procedure of secret trials followed by public executions. Ruthardt's case was one of several transitional cases that allowed for a maximum of public involvement: both the final part of her trial[89] and her execution were open to the public, well-attended and extensively discussed. *Der Beobachter* of 23–24 December 1844 reported that there were at least 2,000 demands for about 100 tickets for her trial, that tickets went for exorbitant prices on the black market, and that in the mad rush for tickets, one person was nearly trampled to death. The courtroom was so full, with people crushing each other and several spectators standing on chairs, that the bailiff had severe trouble getting the defendant into the room.[90]

The public debate of the Ruthardt case followed the same parallel trajectories we have already encountered in the Wächtler case, with the death-penalty debate flaunting the public conscience and descriptions of Ruthardt's behaviour satisfying public curiosity. Ruthardt's pride, the same characteristic that had so fascinated Wächtler's audience, soon became the centrepiece of the debate. Judge Bechter, her prosecutor, already defined 'pride' and 'pride's very common underling, haughtiness' as the central aspects of Ruthardt's character.[91] Trial reporters frequently criticised the lack of 'remorse and shame' in her behaviour;[92] even stating that the way she answered questions – 'without the slightest sign of fear or inner remorse, in

[88] Evans, *Rituals*, 262–6.
[89] In many ways, Ruthardt's trial still followed the inquisitional procedures under which Wächtler had been sentenced: *after* the investigation had been concluded, a defence counsel was appointed, provided with the court records and asked to write a defence brief. This part of the trial, which included all interrogations of accused and witnesses, was held in secret. The public trial then consisted merely of a public reading of both the indictment and defence statement, followed by deliberations and sentencing (Linder and Schönert 250).
[90] The article is reprinted in Linder and Schönert 295–304, the citations 295–6.
[91] Kriminalrichter Bechter in 'Protokoll über Verhaftung': 'Stolz [und] seiner sehr gemeinen Unterart, dem Hochmuthe' (quoted in Linder and Schönert 252).
[92] *Der Beobachter*, 23–24 December 1844: 'Doch machte ihr Wesen weniger den Eindruck der Reue oder Zerknirschung, als vielmehr jener stumpfen Ergebung in das Unvermeidliche, welcher die Gedanken ausgegangen sind' (quoted in Linder and Schönert 296–7). The passage was later quoted near-verbatim in *Der neue Pitaval*: 'Eine schwankende Bewegung des Oberleibs schien nur körperliche Schwäche zu verrathen, ihr ganzer Ausdruck deutete mehr auf stumpfe Ergebung als auf Reue und Zerknirschung' (Linder and Schönert 311).

well-phrased language and a loud voice, and in a bold, almost brazen manner' – cost her the sympathies of the audience.[93]

Ruthardt's execution in June 1845 became the most significant moment in the public discussion of both the death penalty in general and her demeanour as a death-penalty candidate in particular. Like Wächtler, Ruthardt not only showed unusual composure on the scaffold but also refused to play the part of the penitent sinner. By their own testimony, the two clergymen in charge of inducing this attitude experienced 'extraordinary difficulty in bringing her to a true self-judgment and self-knowledge, to purity and humility, and from there to entrusting herself entirely to Divine mercy'.[94] One of them finally wrote to her in despair:

You still take your blood-red guilt and the depths to which you have sunk rather too lightly, not at all like you will undoubtedly feel on Judgment Day, standing in the light of Him who has eyes like the flames of Fire. The more broken we are in spirit, the more battered our soul, the lower we bow beneath the weight of our sins, the closer to us is Merciful God … but we will not obtain him if we do not despair of ourselves, if we do not become as the poorest and most miserable of wretches, happy even to be allowed to touch the hem of his garment.[95]

That Ruthardt refused this role gained her the admiration of some of her contemporaries and the censure of others, and because her detractors and defenders were more or less divided along the same lines as defenders and opponents of the death penalty, her death – and particularly the way in which she faced it – became practically emblematic of the death-penalty debate itself.

---

[93] *Der Beobachter*, 23–24 December 1844: 'ohne irgend ein Zeichen von Erschrockenheit oder innerer Reue in fertiger wohlgesetzter Sprache mit lauter Stimme und in einer kecken, fast frechen Weise, welche augenblicklich beim ganzen Publikum wieder alle Sympathie erlöschte, die durch ihren Lebenslauf so rege für sie geworden war' (quoted in Linder and Schönert 298). Later in *Der neue Pitaval*: 'Auf verschiedene Anfragen des Präsidenten, welche die nähern Umstände der Vergiftung betrafen, antwortete die Angeschuldigte ohne irgend ein Zeichen von Befangenheit, innerer Aufregung oder Zerknirschung, in fertiger, wohlgesetzter Sprache, mit lauter Stimme und in einer kecken, fast frechen Weise … Von Rührung bei keiner Gelegenheit eine Spur' (Linder and Schönert 312–13).

[94] '… große Mühe, sie zu einer richtigen Selbstprüfung und Selbsterkenntniß, zur Lauterkeit und Demuth und dann zum alleinigen Vertrauen auf die göttliche Barmherzigkeit zu führen. Immer wieder suchte sie sich selbst zu rechtfertigen …, dann hoffte sie immer auf Begnadigung, wodurch eine wahre Bekehrung ungemein erschwert wird' (Moser 166).

[95] 'Sie nehmen Ihre blutrothe Schuld und den ganzen tiefen Fall, in den Sie gerathen sind, immer noch etwas zu oberflächlich, immer noch nicht so, wie Sie sich selbst am Tage des Gerichts im Licht dessen, der Augen hat, wie Feuerflammen, gewiß einst noch vorkommen werden. Je zerbrochener im Geist, je zerschlagener im Gemüth wir uns unter unsre Sündenschuld beugen, desto näher ist uns der erbarmungsreiche GOtt … aber er kann uns nicht zu Theil werden, wenn wir nicht an uns selber verzagen und als die Aermsten und Elendesten froh werden, nur den Saum Seines Kleides fassen zu können' (Moser 168).

'You will see, I will die with courage and dignity',[96] she announced when her death sentence was read to her, and she was as good as her word. By all accounts, she went through her final three days in prison, the public show trial on the marketplace, and the execution itself with unassailable composure. A rather sympathetic observer described her final moments as follows:

Her movements were still full of strength, if a broken strength. Death throes already coursed through her limbs. She kept her body under control. Standing before the cutty stool, she folded her hands and sent a final long gaze heavenward. It was an accusation of Mankind. I did not feel accused, but I have never seen anything more painful than this gaze. Then she sat down, firmly, on the stool, and as she gave instructions for all that was necessary with a clear voice, she put her hands into the fetters, as it seemed with some indignation. – A moment passed. – The executioner's aide grabbed her head, which had been covered with a cap – 'Stop!' screamed a loud voice from the crowd. And again: 'Stop!' – It was the call of a compassionate human being, it was the people's cry of fear. – The stroke had already happened. A clean stroke, and not the worst that she had endured. – Her body remained seated, then tilted. Two bright red fountains of blood sprayed up in the air, merrily, as if they rejoiced in their deliverance. If only we could understand what they said. To me it sounded like an interpretation of Article 237 of the Penal Code.[97]

This is the stage at which the personal, a description of Ruthardt's individual behaviour, becomes dangerously political: for this observer, Ruthardt's extraordinary composure became an expression of the injustice she had suffered in life and death, 'an accusation of Mankind'. Or, in a succinct formulation by the same observer: 'Observing such a death can cause one to doubt the crime, or justice.'[98] Such doubt is not only contained in the final sentence's direct attack on the death-penalty article, but also,

---

[96] '"Sie werden sehen", sprach sie, "ich werde mit Muth und Würde sterben!"' Her statement is quoted in several sources, among others in *Der Beobachter*, 28 June 1845 (quoted in Linder and Schönert 300) and *Der neue Pitaval* (quoted in Linder and Schönert 313).

[97] 'In ihrer Bewegung war noch immer Kraft, wenn auch eine gebrochene. Die Todesschauer rieselten ja bereits durch ihre Glieder. Sie behielt den Körper in ihrer Gewalt. Als sie vor dem Schemel stand, faltete sie die Hände und that einen langen und letzten Blick in den Himmel. Es war eine Klage gegen die Menschheit. Mich traf sie nicht, aber ich habe lange nichts Schmerzlicheres gesehen, als diesen Blick. Dann setzte sie sich nieder, rückte fest hinein in den Schemel und während sie mit klarer Stimme das Nöthige anordnete, steckte sie die Hände, wie es schien mit einigem Unwillen, in die Bande. – Ein Augenblick. – Der Gehülfe faßte den mit einer Kappe bedeckten Kopf – "Halt!" schrie eine laute Stimme aus der Menge. "Halt!" wiederholte es. – Es war der Ruf eines mitleidigen Menschen, der Angstschrei des Volks. – Schon war der Streich geschehen. Ein geschickter Streich und nicht der schlechteste, den man ihr gespielt. – Noch blieb der Leib fest sitzen, neigte sich dann und zwei helle rothe Blutsquellen sprudelten in die Luft hinauf, lustig, als freuten sie sich der Erlösung. Wer es verstanden hätte, was sie sangen. Mir klang es wie eine Interpretation des Artikels 237 des Strafgesetzbuches' (*Der Beobachter*, 28 June 1845, quoted in Linder and Schönert 301).

[98] 'Der Anblick solchen Todes kann irre machen am Verbrechen oder an der Gerechtigkeit' (quoted in Linder and Schönert 300).

and more disturbingly, in the author's statement that this criticism was shared and expressed in public sympathy for Ruthardt. It is this sympathy, then, that had to be denied in order to defuse the potential political bomb contained in Ruthardt's execution. This explains why two witnesses of the same event – Ruthardt's final moments – saw two entirely different scenes, depending on their stance on the death penalty, and why particularly the audience response, while noted in both cases, is interpreted differently. One commentator's compassionate populace witnessing an outrage against humanity are another's gullible dupes taken in by an accomplished performance:

All of a sudden, the city of Stuttgart is full of admiration for this criminal's courage in facing death. For my part, I confess that of all criminals that I have had occasion to see thus far, she alone managed to arouse not even a spark of sympathy, even in her final misfortune. I was merely moved by the fact that the law took its just revenge on a woman's frail body. Unquestionably, it was astonishing to see the composure with which this woman endured the public reading of the description of her guilty life, the solemn proclamation of her death sentence, the staff broken and thrown at her feet with the terrible words: 'You have forfeited your life, may God have mercy on your soul' and finally being conveyed to the executioner. 'Thank God,' she said blithely as she entered the cell for the condemned, 'this too has passed.' … Even more astonishing was the composure with which she left the place where her death sentence had just been publicly proclaimed, the carefree manner with which she mounted … the scaffold which would soon be red with her blood. But not only the witnesses of Truth know how to die with serenity: a deceitful spirit also knows how to play its part to the end. Such composure, refusing even a final sigh, a last tear, is not within the realm of true humanity, much less femininity. Sitting in the cart, she did not even forget etiquette … and smiled …. Yes, she smiled, taking a carriage ride to Death, all the way to the scaffold, where she raised her hands and eyes with a picturesque gesture. Of course we are right to admire the steadfastness of this performance: but let us not forget to account to ourselves for the nature of this admiration. With her heartlessness, with the soullessness which lay hidden beneath the surface of her superficial education, with her steadfastness which was indeed rooted in an extraordinary spirit, she would have been, had she been born in different circumstances, predestined to occupy one of the 'social positions' in which women of loose morals and a predilection for intrigue exercise their influence on the most important affairs of state. She was something similar in a lower sphere. She gave me the impression that she looked upon the boards of the scaffold as theatrical scenery, and she took pleasure in flirting even with her ultimate fate, just as she had flirted with everything in life. As she had been throughout her life, a loose woman, she made loose at the end even with Death. But this I would never deny: that it takes an extraordinary degree of inner elasticity and mental ability to play such a role to the end, to enact a lie that dissembles spirit underneath the make-up of heroism, a role that, of course in a broader sense, is a symbol for modern society. She has done it, and for this reason, she will always mark a new epoch in the history of crime.[99]

The author's main project is to remove Ruthardt's execution from the realm of social controversy and to transfer it to the realm of gender roles, where her astonishing composure can be interpreted more safely. His analysis of Ruthardt's disturbing lack of humanity and femininity echoes precisely Hofmann's definition of Wächtler as simultaneously unfeminine and inhumane. Conversely, seen as an *act* and moreover an act of coquettishness, Ruthardt's bravery becomes an aspect of stereotypical femininity. His attempt at gendering Ruthardt expresses itself in other ways as well, for example in his statement that it was her gender, rather than her nerve, that elicited the single momentary spark of sympathy he is willing to grant her, and in the imaginative exposé of Ruthardt's alternative career as royal concubine and evil influence behind the throne. And finally, he echoes

---

[99] 'Die Stadt Stuttgart ist auf einmal von Bewunderung über den Todesmuth der Verbrecherin voll. Ich meines Orts gestehe, von den verschiedenen Verbrechern, die ich bis jetzt zu sehen Gelegenheit hatte, hat sie allein in diesem ihrem letzten Unglück auch nicht einen Funken von Sympathie in mir erweckt. Was mich ergriff, war allein, daß es eines Weibes zerbrechliche Gestalt war, an dem das Gesetz seine Sühne nahm. Es ist keine Frage, es war erstaunenswerth, mit welcher Ruhe dieses Weib die vorgelesene Beschreibung eines schuldvollen Lebens, die feierliche Verkündung des Todesurtheils, den ihr mit den fürchterlichen Worten zu Füßen geworfenen Stab: "Ihr habt Euer Leben verwirkt, Gott sey Eurer Seele gnädig" und die Uebergabe an den Nachrichter endlich ertrug. "Gottlob," sagte sie mit leichter Stimme, als sie in das Armensünderstübchen trat, "so ist auch dieses vorbei." ... Erstaunenswerth ferner ist es in der That, mit welcher Gelassenheit sie den Ort verließ, wo ihr so eben das Todesurtheil öffentl. verkündet worden, mit welcher Leichtigkeit sie die Treppen des Wagens hinanstieg, um sofort mit dem ersten und letzten Tritt daraus auf das bald von ihrem Blut geröthete Schaffot zu steigen. Aber es sind nicht allein die Zeugen der erkannten Wahrheit, welche mit Ruhe zu sterben wissen: seine Rolle bis zum Ende auszuspielen, das versteht auch der lügnerische Geist. Eine solche Ruhe, der selbst der letzte Seufzer, die letzte Thräne versiegt ist, liegt nicht in dem Bereiche wahrhafter Menschlichkeit, geschweige denn der Weiblichkeit. Als sie in den Wagen saß, vergaß sie selbst die Etikette nicht ... Ja, sie lächelte ... Ja, sie lächelte, zum Tode spazierenfahrend, bis zum Richtplatz, und hub da noch mit malerischer Bewegung Augen und Hände in die Höhe. Man hat allerdings ein Recht, die Consequenz eines solchen Spieles zu bewundern: aber nur versäume man nicht, über die Natur dieser Bewunderung sich die gehörige Rechenschaft zu geben. Bei ihrer Herzlosigkeit, ihrer durch die Oberfläche äußerlicher Bildung versteckten Seelenlosigkeit, bei ihrer Consequenz, die in der That ihren Grund in einem außergewöhnlichen Geiste hat, – wäre sie, in andern Verhältnissen geboren, berufen gewesen, eine jener "sozialen Stellungen" einzunehmen, in welchen Weiber von loser Sitte und intriguantem Geiste Einfluß auf die wichtigsten Staatsangelegenheiten zu erringen wissen. Sie war etwas Aehnliches in niederer Sphäre. Dem Eindrucke nach, den sie auf mich gemacht, betrachtete sie die Bretter des Schaffottes noch als Coulissen, und gefiel sich darin, wie mit Allem im Leben, so selbst mit ihrem letzten Schicksal zu kokettiren. Eine Buhlerin, wie sie durch ihr Leben war, buhlte sie am Ende selber mit dem Tode. Das aber will ich nimmer in Abrede stellen, welch außerordentlicher Grad von innerer Spannkraft und geistiger Fähigkeit dazu gehört, um eine solche Rolle auszuspielen, die Rolle der mit Heroismus übertünchten, geistgleissenden Lüge, welche im Großen freilich das Symbol der modernen Gesellschaft ist. Sie hat es gethan, und wird darum in der Geschichte der Verbrechen Epoche machend bleiben' (*Der Beobachter*, 28 June 1845, quoted in Linder and Schönert 299–300).

Hofmann's portrayal of Wächtler again in stating that Ruthardt's composure does not indicate her innocence. His point here, however, is not merely that a 'deceitful spirit' is perfectly capable of imitating the noble death of wronged virtue. His point – and this is possibly the sole point of agreement with the sympathetic observer of Ruthardt's execution – is that her act of courage on the scaffold marked, as he put it, 'a new epoch in the history of crime'. 'New' in this context is not only the dangerous defiance of authority, which Ruthardt's attitude exemplified, but also the fact that this defiance was now enacted in front of an audience. As another observer of her trial remarked, 'the blessing of the highly praised public trial would turn into a curse if a criminal could abuse it unhindered to gloss over his crimes, vindicate himself with the martyr's crown, and trample underfoot the good name of others'.[100] In the view of the public, Ruthardt's act came to stand for something much 'broader' than an individual act of defiance: it became 'a symbol for modern society'. The same point was made by Ruthardt's defender, although his argument is the exact reverse:

When we criticise the truly stoic courage of this woman, then we rightly doubt that it could originate from evil. This was not a superficial spirit: this was the spirit of humanity that proudly rises up against inexorable fate and conquers it. You may love to see a sinner broken and whimpering, I am glad to see him die with courage. Courage is virtue.[101]

'Only suffering innocence can lay claim to this … admiration', Hofmann had written in 1788, 'only true virtue can show greatness of the soul'. In so doing, he drew a line between ethical and stoic virtues that was hotly contested by some witnesses to Ruthardt's execution. It was precisely this admission that stoic virtues can be exercised by the guilty, the ability to think in terms of 'and-and' rather than 'either-or', that Ruthardt's detractors understood as 'modern'.

And it was precisely Ruthardt's ability to encapsulate this simultaneity that cast her as a symbol of humanity for one side and a symbol of modernity for the other. Perilously so, as becomes apparent in the attempts at damage control that set in immediately and endured for several years. On

---

[100] 'Der gehoffte Segen des hoch gepriesenen öffentlichen Verfahrens müßte zum Fluch werden, wenn der Verbrecher solches ungehindert dazu mißbrauchen dürfte, seine Missethat zu beschönigen, sich die Märtyrerkrone zu vindiciren und den Ruf Anderer mit Füßen zu treten' (*Schwäbischer Merkur*, 27 June 1845, quoted in Linder and Schönert 277).

[101] 'Wenn wir den wahrhaft stoischen Muth dieser Frau kritisiren, so zweifeln wir billig, daß er das Produkt eines Uebels sey. Das war kein äußerer Geist, das war der Menschengeist, der an dem unerbittlichen Geschick sich stolz erhebt, es überwindet. Mögt ihr den Sünder lieben, geknickt und winselnd, mich freut es, wenn er muthig stirbt. Muth ist Tugend' (Linder and Schönert 302).

29 June 1845, two days after Ruthardt's beheading, an article appeared that may have been designed to strip Ruthardt posthumously of her dignity in death. It relates that the coachman charged with conveying her body to the cemetery opened it out of curiosity, exposing her body to the 'inquisitiveness and the indelicate inspection and remarks of the crowd rushing to the scene'. Her head was passed from one hand to the next and showed 'deep scars the next day, from being tossed about'.[102] And in 1850, *Der neue Pitaval* portrayed Ruthardt as a thoroughly unremarkable person, a cheap tramp with 'a maidservant's mentality' who was propelled to undeserved martyrdom by the unruly spirit of modern times.[103] 'Smouldering discontent reached for anything at hand to wage a war against the old order, a war that was to break out all the more horribly on a later occasion [the Revolution of 1848/9]. It did not even scorn the option of raising a cold-hearted and dastardly poisoner to the status of a martyr.'[104] Thus deprived of her significance as a symbol of either humanity or modernity, Ruthardt is described as a mere pawn of social troublemakers and death-penalty opponents who used her to advance their cause: 'The murderess was to be saved in order to launch an accusation against the entire society in which we live, in order to prove that society is the true source of all crimes, and in order to move, initially, toward the abolition of the death penalty.'[105] And Ruthardt gladly accepted the part she was offered:

Long denials, a drawn-out trial, combatting the judge from the walls of her prison hold no attractions for her. She much prefers to envision a different drama: the walk to the scaffold, to die a hero and thus cause a sensation. Then her defender comes to her aid, himself, like her, only an emblem of an oppressed society's sickly

[102] 'Der Sarg wurde nämlich in Dettenhausen vom Fuhrmann geöffnet, und der Leichnam der Neugierde und den unfeinen Untersuchungen und Bemerkungen der herbeiströmenden Menge preisgegeben. Damit war aber sein unglückliches Schicksal noch nicht erfüllt, denn in Tübingen angekommen blieb er mehrere Stunden im Hofe der Anatomie stehen, wo eine ungeheure Menschenmenge zusammenströmte. Der Kopf wurde von Mägden und Medizinern an den Haaren in die Höhe gehalten und umhergezeigt; an manchen Händen klebte das noch rinnende Blut, und seiner Haare, die man ihm schon unterwegs, ich weiß nicht, um sie als Reliquie oder als Zaubermittel aufzubewahren, theilweise abgeschnitten hatte, wurde er vollends beraubt. Der Kopf zeigte am andern Tage vom Umherwerfen mehrere tiefe Narben' ('Schicksale der Ruthardt nach der Hinrichtung', *Der Beobachter*, 29 June 1845, quoted in Linder and Schönert 303).
[103] See *Der neue Pitaval*, quoted in Linder and Schönert 317 ('Kammermädchennatur').
[104] 'Das gährende Misvergnügen griff nach Allem, was sich ihm an die Hand gab, um gegen die alte Ordnung einen Krieg zu führen, der endlich desto furchtbarer bei anderer Gelegenheit ausbrechen sollte. Sie verschmähte es selbst nicht eine kaltherzige, ruchlose Giftmörderin zu einer Märtyrerin zu erheben' (*Der neue Pitaval*, quoted in Linder and Schönert 313).
[105] 'Die Mörderin sollte gerettet werden, um durch eine Anklage der ganzen socialen Verhältnisse, in denen wir leben, den Beweis zu führen, daß sie es seien, welche die wahre Quelle der Verbrechen wären, und zunächst damit auf Abschaffung der Todesstrafe hinzuarbeiten' (*Der neue Pitaval*, quoted in Linder and Schönert 305).

aura. The unnaturalness of social conditions, the injustice she had suffered at the hands of her family had turned her into a criminal; the fault was to be thrown entirely onto them. What could be better for her? A new role was offered to her, one that, as her common sense could tell her, would hardly save her life, but it would secure for her the people's sentimental sympathies, and it promised to endow her exit with a new and vainglorious lustre. To lie herself into this part was not her doing; the lie came from the outside: the role was lied onto her.

How do we know this? ... The ultimate proof for us (and the same seems to have applied to the public) was Ruthardt's deportment at her trial and her final walk to the scaffold.[106]

This, then, is the third way in which Ruthardt's behaviour at her execution can be perceived: not as courage but as a final act of female vanity, simultaneously transforming the viewer's laudable compassion or legitimate anger into pathetic gullibility. But whereas the contemporary observer who reinterpreted Ruthardt's stoicism as an act at least credited her with the authorship of her own performance, this critic relegates Ruthardt to the status of a mere puppet in someone else's play: in his interpretation, it was not even her own lie. Here, Ruthardt is not a symbol but a pawn; it is not she who poses a danger but antisocial malcontents who, for sinister purposes, endow her with a dignity in death she never possessed.

In the fifty-eight years that separate Wächtler's case from Ruthardt's, public attitudes changed and laws were reformed. Both shifts are clearly reflected in these cases. They were conducted differently: Wächtler's case as an inquisitional interrogation behind the closed doors of the torture chamber, Ruthardt's, at least in its final stages, as a public trial by jury. They ended differently: Wächtler suffered the late medieval punishment of 'breaking on the wheel', Ruthardt the cleaner and more efficient execution by beheading, in deference to 'modern' sensibilities. Interestingly enough, both cases clearly struggled with the outmoded legal basis on which they were tried: when Wächtler went to trial in 1786, confession was still the

---

[106] 'Auch hat ein langes Leugnen, ein langwieriger Prozeß, der Krieg mit dem Richter aus den Kerkermauern heraus für sie nichts Lockendes. Sie bildet sich viel lieber ein anderes Schauspiel aus: den Gang zum Schaffot, heroisch zu sterben, dadurch Aufsehen zu erregen. Da kommt ihr der Defensor zu Hülfe, auch er nur das Symbol eines krankhaften Fluidums in der gedrückten Gesellschaft. Die Unnatur der socialen Verhältnisse, das an ihr von ihrer Familie begangene Unrecht hat sie zur Verbrecherin gemacht, auf diese soll sie die Schuld zurückwerfen. Was konnte ihr lieber sein, es bot sich ihr eine neue Rolle dar, die ihr wol schwerlich das Leben retten würde, konnte ihr Verstand ihr sagen, ihr aber die sentimentale Theilnahme sicherte und ihrem Ausgang einen neuen eitlen Glanz versprach. In diese Rolle sich hineinzulügen, kam nicht von ihr, die Lüge kam von außen, sie ward ihr angelogen./ Woher wir das wissen? ... Der letzte Beweis für uns (auch scheint er es für das Publicum gewesen zu sein) ist aber die Aufführung der Ruthardt vor dem Gericht, ihr letzter Todesgang' (*Der neue Pitaval*, quoted in Linder and Schönert 317–18).

'queen of proofs', and yet, she was – in effect, illegally – executed without a final confession. Fifty-eight years later, Ruthardt was executed based solely on her confession, despite the modern propensity toward substantiating evidence, which was woefully inadequate in her case.

The discursive constants that link these cases seem as expressive as the historical shifts that separate them. Both husband-killers inspired a highly visible and volatile debate on a socially controversial aspect of law – torture in the first case, the death penalty in the second – not because they were innocent but because they were defiant. Both stood accused not only in a court of law, but also in the court of public opinion. And the public voiced this opinion in previously unprecedented numbers, actively – as writers and public debaters of the issues of torture and the death penalty – and passively, as voracious readers and recipients of this debate. As a writing and judging public, Wächtler's and Ruthardt's contemporaries documented the shift from the inquisitional process of the early modern ages to the criminal trial of modern times. As a reading public, they eagerly devoured every single detail made available on these cases in the mass media of their day – pamphlets in one case, newspaper articles in the other – thus fomenting the process by which these case histories were turned into stories.

THE ETHICAL MANDATE AND THE AESTHETICS OF HORROR

The unprecedented level of public interest in the cases of Maria Katharina Wächtler and Christiane Ruthardt can be read in (at least) two ways. One reading might focus not on the cases themselves, but on the debates on torture and the death penalty that they inspired and ultimately symbolised. This interpretation would take the broad readership of literature on Wächtler and Ruthardt to signify an awakening social consciousness that questioned the State's near-total power over the individual. The other would, with Jürgen Martschukat, interpret the contemporary reading public as scavengers in search of salacious details, enabling them to 'saturate themselves with cruelties [and] sexual debaucheries ... while simultaneously holding aloft the banner of Enlightenment and righteous indignation'.[107] It seems, then, that the meaning of the public debate surrounding Wächtler

---

[107] 'Die mediale Aufbereitung stieß in neue Dimensionen vor, denn die Biographien der Wächtlers machten es möglich, sich in Grausamkeiten, in sexuellen Ausschweifungen und insbesondere in einem weiblichen Leben abseits der Norm zu ergehen, und dabei zugleich das Banner der Aufklärung und Entrüstung aufrecht zu halten' (Martschukat, '*Düsterheit*', 344).

and Ruthardt can be formulated succinctly, as a simple alternative: either greater democratisation or the 'pornography of violence and pain'.[108]

Such a stark alternative between a social development to be lauded and a literary one to be censured seems somewhat out of synch with the parameters of the debate as they were set in the eighteenth century. Aristotelian fear and Horatian didacticism of literature linked legal and literary discourses far more closely than they would appear today, as indicated by Lessing's famous designation of the theatre as the 'supplement of laws' or Schiller's reference to the 'jurisdiction of the stage'.[109] By the time Schiller discovered, next to the Agreeable, the Good and the Beautiful, a fourth 'source of enjoyment', namely suffering, fear and horror,[110] eighteenth-century thinkers were already engaged in a lively debate on the question what conditions might justify abandoning oneself to pleasures of this nature.[111] The verdict was near-unanimous: in validation of the aesthetic of horror, literature was given an ethical mandate. Sulzer, for example, distinguished between 'empty', 'sublime' and 'beneficial' horror, instructing authors as to its use in tragedy:

It would be utterly indecent to employ horror as a mere pastime, in order to afford the mind pleasure … This, then, should instruct the tragic poet not to entertain his audience with such empty horrors. Whenever he incites this passion in us, it must happen so that its memory be an emphatic warning to deter us from evil.[112]

If the unmitigated enjoyment of horror is, for Sulzer, a sign of moral corruption, Karl Philipp Moritz is more amenable to its appeal: 'We are all', he admitted, 'at the bottom of our hearts little Neros, who would be not at all displeased by the sight of a burning Rome, the screams of the fleeing populace, the whimpering of babies, if it presented itself to our eyes as a *spectacle*.'[113] Simultaneously, though, he saw horror as the driving force of

---

[108] Martschukat, applying Karen Halttunen's term, in '*Düsterheit*', 344.

[109] Lessing: 'Supplement der Gesetze'; Schiller: 'Gerichtsbarkeit der Bühne', to which he also referred as a 'schrecklichen Richterstuhl'; both quoted in Zelle, 'Strafen und Schrecken', 78.

[110] Schiller, 'Zerstreute Beobachtungen', 228.

[111] On this debate, see particularly the work of Carsten Zelle.

[112] 'Ganz unschiklich wäre es, sich desselben blos zum Zeitvertreib zu bedienen, um durch vorhergegangenen Schreken das Gemüth blos in den Genuß der angenehmen Empfindung zu setzen … Dieses dienet also dem tragischen Dichter zur Lehre, daß er seine Zuschauer nicht mit solchen leeren Schreken unterhalten soll. So oft er uns in diese Leidenschaft setzet, muß es so geschehen, daß das Andenken derselben uns eine nachdrükliche Warnung sey, uns vom Bösen abzuhalten' (Sulzer IV 344).

[113] 'Wir alle sind im Grunde unseres Herzens kleine Neronen, denen der Anblick eines brennenden Roms, das Geschrei der Fliehenden, das Gewimmer der Säuglinge gar nicht übel behagen würde, wenn es so, als ein *Schauspiel*, vor unsern Blicken sich darstellte' (Moritz, 'Fragmente', 302, emphasis original). 'Schauspiel' in this passage could also be rendered as 'drama' or 'play'; Moritz's point here is obviously that the pleasure of the spectacle is derived, in considerable measure, from the vantage point of the spectator's own safety.

human culture, claiming that without the horrors of war, the *Iliad*, *Odyssey* and *Aeneid* would never have been written. '… *if all humans had herded sheep*, they might, as such, well have been happy. But what, then, would have happened to our history?'[114] Few eighteenth-century thinkers argued in favour of the permissibility of unmitigated gratification;[115] for most, the ethical mandate retained its place of pride as the sole justification of the pleasure derived from horror. The difference between those who enjoy horror for its own sake and those who need socially redeeming values to afford themselves the pleasure is defined in unmistakably judgmental terms: it is the distinction between 'the more sensitive and well-bred minds' and 'brutish people'.[116] This juxtaposition of 'well-bred' and 'brutish' readers is also applied to the texts they consume, resulting in the division of literature into 'art' and 'trivial literature' and corresponding scholarly divisions that have endured to this day.[117]

Zelle, who has worked extensively on the aesthetics of horror, makes two important points in his work: first, that the problematisation of pleasurable horror was the first sign of the rift between ethics and aesthetics in the eighteenth century, and second, that the enjoyment of horror only becomes possible once the ethical dimension is neutralised.[118] It is an intriguing point, but one that – in its unequivocal commitment to an 'either-or' – strikes me as not entirely applicable to these cases. Those who read and wrote about Wächtler and Ruthardt made no bones about their enjoyment of the salacious details, but neither did they surrender their claim to being participants in a public debate on one of the most important issues of their day. And they did not distinguish, as Mendelssohn did, between real life and literature: Mendelssohn's claim that murder 'can please on the stage but be abhorrent in real life'[119] enacts a difference (*either* it is literature, in which

---

[114] 'Aber freilich, *wenn alle Menschen Schafe gehütet hätten*, so wären sie zwar an sich wohl glücklich gewesen. Aber was wäre denn aus unsrer Geschichte geworden?' (Moritz, 'Fragmente', 301, emphasis original).

[115] See, for example, Ernst Friedrich Ockel's *Ueber die Sittlichkeit der Wollust* (1772) and Martin Ehlers's *Betrachtungen über die Sittlichkeit der Vergnügungen* (1779); both briefly discussed in Zelle, 'Angenehmes Grauen', 313.

[116] The distinction between 'empfindsamern und wohlerzogenen Gemüthern' and 'rohen Menschen' is Mendelssohn's, cited in Zelle, 'Angenehmes Grauen', 300.

[117] Zelle sees this distinction expressed in the rift between 'ideologiekritischer Werk- und hermeneutisch orientierter Rezeptionsästhetik' ('Angenehmes Grauen', 306).

[118] Zelle, 'Angenehmes Grauen', xxiii: 'Erst die von moralischen Bedenken freie ästhetische Einstellung garantierte das schauervolle Ergötzen.' On this subject, see particularly his chapter 'Die Trennung von Ethik und Ästhetik – Der angenehme Schrecken' (295–412).

[119] '[dass Mord] auf der Schaubühne gefallen, aber im gemeinen Leben abscheulich seyn kann' (Mendelssohn, 'Anweisung, wie junge Leute die alten und neuen Dichter lesen müssen', quoted in Zelle, 'Angenehmes Grauen' 322).

case it pleases, *or* it is real life, in which case it horrifies) that the literature on Wächtler and Ruthardt blithely ignored. These murders had happened *and* they were being re-enacted, *ad infinitum*, in print; they were simultaneously horrible *and* pleasurable (which is not entirely the same thing as to say that they were pleasurable *because* they were horrible).

My suggestion, then, would be to read the literature on Wächtler and Ruthardt not in terms of 'either-or' (*either* the pure enjoyment of horror *or* ethically and socially redeeming), but in terms of 'and-and': they simultaneously embodied the nobility of social protest and the base craving for smut. That the aesthetics of horror was a factor is clearly apparent in the texts' obsessive attention to detail; unabashedly, they subject (or treat) readers to a complete catalogue of Wächtler's denials, screams, curses and weeping fits under torture, or detailed descriptions of the wounds on Ruthardt's head after it had been mauled by the crowd. Obviously such passages border on the 'pornographic', but there is no good reason why we might not also read them as the oblique expressions of anger by a public excluded from the proceedings. Writing about Wächtler's torture sessions, in microscopic detail, implies that the writer was *there*, and that he could take his readers there as well: the presence of active observation is all the more grating and intrusive because it is, of necessity, vicarious. While these texts do not flaunt the ethical mandate that, according to aesthetic theorists, can alone justify their enjoyment of horror, they can be read as asking, not-so-subtly, *why* the public are excluded from criminal trials when there is such obvious and broad interest in them – be this interest social, political, ethical or simply salacious.

Clearly, Wächtler's and Ruthardt's cases did have considerable social and ethical significance in that they ignited widespread discussion of important legal issues. Clearly, on both occasions, a war was being waged between individual rights and State sovereignty, and it was waged in print. And equally clearly, the considerable fascination these cases exerted on their contemporaries was due less to social or ethical than to literary factors. Wächtler and Ruthardt captured the imagination not as culprits or victims but as literary characters who, quite possibly, bore little relation to their historical originals: we would do well to remember, for example, that Wächtler appears far more defiant in the pamphlets than in the court records.

That both Wächtler and Ruthardt could not be described in the traditional terminology of 'either-or' made them excellent dramatic characters. On the 'ethical' side, these characters' pride, their refusal of their prescribed roles first as obedient wives, then as penitent sinners, spurred on the social controversy about torture and the death penalty. More importantly, their unexpected behaviour made interesting reading, thus gaining the torture and death-penalty debate an audience it might otherwise not have had. Reading their case files today, aware that Ruthardt was convicted on her confession and otherwise flimsy evidence, aware too that Wächtler was, in the absence of a valid confession, executed illegally, we may be tempted to interpret these characters as victims of or heroic resisters against an oppressive juridical system. That is not, however, how they were seen by their contemporaries, and neither were they, as we might expect, unilaterally condemned as man-eating monsters. The most common interpretation of the Wächtler and Ruthardt characters effortlessly fused the most glaring contradictions: they were unfortunates *and* killers, guilty *and* unjustly treated, perpetrators *and* victims, equally deserving of punishment *and* admiration.

The 'and-and' stance taken by contemporary literature on Wächtler and Ruthardt is perhaps worth considering in our interpretation of their cases and in our assessment of what they mean. To frame the debate in terms of 'and-and' would enable us to bypass 'either-ors' whose function it is to systematise, but ultimately also to limit our thinking. Such alternatives might include, but not necessarily be limited to, that between ethics and aesthetics, between a contemptible sensationalism and laudable social engagement, between well-bred and brutish readers, and between the art or trash they consume. To frame the debate in terms of 'and-and' is also an important step in acknowledging the literary character not only of the case descriptions of Wächtler and Ruthardt, but also of the contemporary debates on torture and the death penalty that today's critics, to the extent that they are beholden to the 'either-or' school of thought, might be more likely to interpret as social and political.[120]

No matter how lowbrow or pornographic we may consider them to be, the pamphlets, articles, biographies and narratives on Wächtler's and Ruthardt's cases constituted the literary manifestations of two of the century's most important public debates. Had the authors of these works distinguished, like Mendelssohn, between literature and real life, had they not laid confident claim to social, legal and political significance *while* understanding their works as profoundly literary – in the sense of being free to embellish, directed at a broad readership, and willing and able to provide that readership with the scandalous revelations it craved –, their

---

[120] On the links between literary and philosophical discourses on the issue of torture and the death penalty, see most recently the contributions in Helmut Jacobs's anthology.

writings could never have fulfilled that role. And had the readers of these works not been able to enjoy the blood and gore of the case *while* engaging with its ethical dimensions, the social and political debates that ultimately led to the abolition of torture and the death penalty might never have taken place. Before Wächtler's thumbs were put into the screws, the permissibility of torture was discussed within the specialist circles of students of jurisprudence, who wrote learned Latin dissertations on the subject that were read exclusively by other jurists. Before Ruthardt's head was chopped off, the death penalty was hotly denounced by Beccaria, Voltaire and other philosophers who addressed their works and concerns to lawmakers, heads of state and other intellectuals. In brief: throughout much of the century, this important discussion involved a minuscule percentage of the reading public. Arguably, then, it was *literature*, most importantly the riveting, suspense-packed and unabashedly horrific literature on murderesses like Wächtler and Ruthardt, that earned the burning issues of torture and the death penalty the broad and critical audience they deserved.

CHAPTER 5

Shame: child-killers

WOMEN AS CHILDREN, WOMEN AS CHILD-KILLERS: POETIC IMAGES (1770–1790)

Seduction and, during the second half of the century, infanticide[1] can fairly be called *the* most popular themes in eighteenth-century German literature authored by men. Lessing's Sara Sampson (1755) and Emilia Galotti (1772), Schiller's Luise Millerin in *Kabale und Liebe* (1784), Goethe's Marie Beaumarchais in *Clavigo* (1774) and other bourgeois heroines die as a direct result of a man's – more often than not a nobleman's – sexual desire. Goethe's Gretchen in *Faust* (1790/1808/1832), Heinrich Leopold Wagner's Evchen in *Die Kindermörderin* (1776), Johann Michael Reinhold Lenz's Marie in *Zerbin* (1776) and many others are put to death for the crime of infanticide. This tragic view of the subject is relatively new in the eighteenth century: the literature of earlier ages frequently treated seduction and its possible consequences as a humorous theme. In this tradition, which ranges from the thirteenth all the way to the eighteenth century, the seduced girl loses her virginity through sheer naiveté, and the story ends either in a celebration of the seducer's wit and cunning, or the girl's parents give in to the lovers' wishes and permit the couple to marry.[2] Unwanted pregnancies are rare in this tradition but do not change the humorous tone of the story

---

[1] On infanticide as a topic in literature of the period, see, among many others, Becker-Cantarino, '"Meine Mutter"' and 'Witch and Infanticide'; Breithaupt; Fronius; Goetzinger; Jürgen Jacobs; Luserke-Jaqui; Mabee; Madland; Peters; Rameckers; Michael Schmidt; Rüdiger Scholz, 'Die Gewalt'; Weber; Werner; and Wittrock. – The first section of this chapter is indebted to the structure and argumentation of my earlier article 'Women as Children, Women as Childkillers'.

[2] Examples can be found in the collections by Hagen, Keller, Frey, Montanus and Schumann. Further pre-eighteenth-century literature treating the subject with similar levity includes Boccaccio's 'Novella of Alibech' (from *Decamerone*); Jean de la Fontaine's 'Comment l'esprit vient aux filles' (from *Nouveaux Contes*, 1674), a story that later reappears in folksongs; Cervantes's novella *La dos doncellas*, 1613; and Tirso de Molina's *Esto sí que es negociar*, 1635, *Don Gil de las calzas verdes*, 1617, *La villana de Vallecas*, 1627, *A Moreto y Cabaña*, and *El valiente justiciero*, 1657 (see Frenzel).

where they occur.[3] The conceptual shift that occurs in the eighteenth century, then, is a significant one: the girl's inexperience that results in her loss of virginity, heretofore ridiculed as stupidity or gullibility, is now reinterpreted as 'virtue', that alluring mélange of sexual innocence and becoming artlessness that is an indispensable trait of the bourgeois heroine. And her consent to premarital sex, which was, until the eighteenth century, easily repaired through marriage, metamorphoses, in the eighteenth century, into a loss of 'honour' and attending sense of shame that inevitably results in death.

The change from comedy to tragedy in the literary perception of unwanted pregnancies has often been attributed to the influence of the German Enlightenment with its emphasis on morals and virtue, and the new values placed on the middle classes and individual rights. The topic of infanticide attracted the attention of philosophers and legal reformers as well as literary authors. Treatises by renowned thinkers such as Beccaria, Pestalozzi, Voltaire and Kant called for the abolition of the death penalty for infanticide, and poetic treatments of the theme by the writers of the *Sturm und Drang* depicted the plight of the guilty mothers in heartrending terms. Among others, the subject was treated by Marianne Ehrmann,[4] Bürger, Seybold, Wucherer, Sprickmann, Buchholz, Meißner, Schubart, Maler Müller, Otto von Gemmingen, Goethe, Schiller, Lenz, Stäudlin, Schink and Wagner, many of whom, perhaps not coincidentally, were also or had been students of law.[5]

For the eighteenth-century dramatic heroine, then, premarital seduction leads to the grave rather than the altar,[6] although in most of these plays seduction does not result in unwanted pregnancy and the worst-case scenario, the birth and killing of an infant. Lessing's Sara Sampson, a 'fallen virtuous maiden' (*gefallene Tugend*), tries to rectify her mistake by persuading her seducer to marry her, and dies at the end of the play – ostentatiously because she is murdered by a rival for her seducer's affections, but in Sara's

---

[3] See, for example, the following stories: 'Wie ein junger Gesell einer im Schlaf ein Kind machte' (in Montanus, *Wegkürzer*, 22); 'Von eines Bauern Sohn, der zwei Beginen schwanger machte' (in Frey 93); Jean de la Fontaine, 'Comment l'esprit vient aux filles'.

[4] See Madland, 'Gender and the German Literary Canon' on Ehrmann's infanticide tale 'Die unglückliche Hanne' and thematic and structural differences distinguishing it from the copious infanticide literature by male writers of the age.

[5] Goethe, Heinrich Leopold Wagner, Klinger, Sprickmann and Gemmingen had studied law; Lenz had enrolled twice as a student of law in Straßburg. See Rameckers 103–4. Many literary contributions have been republished in both Rameckers's and Luserke-Jaqui's volumes; Luserke-Jaqui has also included some contributions to the reform debate.

[6] See Kord, 'Unmöglichkeiten', on tragic necessity and the interaction between father and daughter in relation to the death of the bourgeois heroine.

own view because her virtue has weakened and thus cannot serve as an example for others:

God must leave proven virtue on this earth for a long time, to serve as an example, and only feeble virtue, which might succumb to too many trials, he lifts suddenly from the dangerous field of battle –[7]

Emilia Galotti, a later variation on the same theme by the same author, successfully pleads with her father to kill her for very similar reasons; faced with the prince's attempts to seduce her, she feels unable to answer for her own virtue: 'I have blood, my father, as youthful and as warm as any other girl. My senses too are senses. I will answer for nothing. I will guarantee nothing.'[8] Schiller's Luise Millerin is killed by her lover/seducer because a court intrigue convinces him that she has 'lost her honour' to another man. Goethe's Marie dies when abandoned by her lover/seducer Clavigo.

What is striking about all of these characters is their childlike quality, which can perhaps be seen as an inversion of the female naiveté that caused so much merriment in pre-eighteenth-century literature. Sara, Emilia, Luise, Marie, Evchen and Gretchen (whose diminutive names speak volumes) are young and innocent, daughters first and foremost, and their role as a daughter, as a child, brings them into severe conflict with their role as a woman. Their naiveté is presented as a positive trait and frequently contrasted with the sophistication and sexual experience of an older woman, usually a rival, who is either condemned unilaterally as wicked or portrayed as sexually and morally damaged. This rival character (Marwood, Orsina and Milford, to name just a few) functions as a negative role model for the child-woman of the play, showing her her own future after the loss of her 'virtue', showing her also that the only conceivable alternative to death is a life in shame, a life without honour. It is partly this negative example that shows the extent to which innocence is a prerequisite for the child-woman's survival, in the sense of both sexual innocence and childlike innocence. Sexual innocence has already been, or is about to be, abandoned in the contact with the lover/seducer, which amounts, in the teleology of the play, to the child-woman's death sentence. Perhaps by way of compensation, childlike innocence is heavily emphasised, apparently for two reasons: to evoke pity at her sorry fate and to make the 'woman-as-child' a model of

---

[7] 'Die bewährte Tugend muß Gott der Welt lange zum Beispiele lassen, und nur die schwache Tugend, die allzu vielen Prüfungen vielleicht unterliegen würde, hebt er plötzlich aus den gefährlichen Schranken – ' (Lessing, *Miß Sara Sampson*, 245).

[8] 'Ich habe Blut, mein Vater; so jugendliches, so warmes Blut, als eine. Auch meine Sinne, sind Sinne. Ich stehe für nichts. Ich bin für nichts gut' (Lessing, *Emilia Galotti*, 464).

identification, a vehicle for the teaching of the sexual moral that is at the heart of so many of these plays.

The literary portrayal of infanticide can easily be read as a variation on this theme. In infanticide literature, the element that constitutes the main theme of the bourgeois tragedy, seduction, sets in motion a disastrous chain of events: illegitimate pregnancy follows on the heels of seduction; infanticide follows on the heels of illegitimate pregnancy. The characterisation of the woman as child-killer in infanticide literature is virtually indistinguishable from that of the woman as child in bourgeois tragedy. Both characters are defined by a childlike naiveté that is the source of both her fall (her vulnerability to seduction) and her death (from an overwhelming sense of shame and remorse after the deed has been done, a shame that simultaneously deprives her of her will to live and secures her the audience's sympathies). Most of these texts link shame and death directly, as does Goethe's Gretchen in her desperate plea to the Virgin-yet-Mother Mary: 'Help! Rescue me from shame and death!'[9] Shame *causes* death, first of the child, later of the mother. This is why women as child-killers invariably, as do Sara, Emilia and other literary child-women, accept death as just punishment for their sins, and why they so often bring about their own punishment. Goethe's Gretchen and Wagner's Evchen, both infanticides, refuse to be rescued and insist on being punished for their crimes; Lenz's Marie fails to report her pregnancy, gives birth to a stillborn child, and is executed as an infanticide, heroically refusing to reveal the father's identity.

Particularly interesting are the cases where the simultaneous treatment of women as children and women as child-killers takes the form of the poetic monologue, that is: the female child-killer's monologue of confession and contrition, always delivered at death's door, written by male poets. Poetry is the only genre in which the male author clearly assumes a female voice. The monologue delivered by his heroine often takes up the entire poem. In treatments of the theme in plays, novellas or novels, there are conflicting viewpoints, differing perspectives and other characters that supplement, but also detract from the infanticide's tragedy. In poetry, the emphasis is on her and her alone; she is not only the protagonist but also very often the narrator of her own tragic tale. Examples are Schiller's ballad 'The Infanticide' ('Die Kindsmörderin', 1782), the death scene in Anton Matthias Sprickmann's poem 'Ida' (1777), Gotthold Friedrich Stäudlin's fragmentary poem 'Seltha, the Infanticide' ('Seltha, die Kindermörderin', 1776), Johann Friedrich Schink's poem 'Sentiments of an Unhappy Seduced Woman While

---

[9] 'Hilf! Rette mich von Schmach und Tod!' Goethe, *Faust. Der Tragödie erster Teil*, 145.

Murdering Her Child' (Empfindungen einer unglücklich Verführten bey der Ermordung ihres Kindes', 1777), August Gottlieb Meißner's poem 'Song of a Fallen Woman' ('Lied einer Gefallenen', 1779) and its sequel, 'The Murderess' ('Die Mörderin', 1779), Sprickmann's dramatic fragment 'What Marie Said at Her Wedding' ('Mariens Reden bei ihrer Trauung', 1778) and David Christoph Seybold's fictitious sermon 'Address to the People at the Execution of an Infanticide' ('Anrede an das Volk bey der Hinrichtung einer Kindesmörderinn', 1777).[10] All were written in the 1770s or early 1780s, and all are informed by an identical concern: to return the fallen maiden, at least in fiction, to her childlike state. As does the death of the woman in plays that portray her as a child, the death and remorse of the child-killer in poetry enables the poet simultaneously to depict and transfigure feminine innocence and to deliver a warning directed at women tempted to stray from the path of virtue.[11]

As their titles at times indicate, these poems express the feelings of the murderess immediately after the murder, which is, without exception, committed almost unconsciously. Stäudlin's Seltha ('Seltha, die Kindermörderin') regains her senses after the murder – 'Oh, I stand as if struck by lightning!'[12] – to realise what she has done. Expecting God's avenging anger to strike her down immediately, she is comforted by the fact that her faithless lover will also fall victim to it. She spends the remainder of the poem cursing him, briefly wishes she could return life to her child, and addresses first her worldly and then her heavenly judges, expressing her willingness to die to the former and praying for mercy to the latter. Schink's poem 'Sentiments of an Unhappy Seduced Woman While Murdering Her Child' shows us the mother preparing to kill her child, doing the deed, immediately wishing she could undo it, and addressing a similar prayer to God as does Seltha, simultaneously asking him to kill and to damn her. She then perceives this act as sacrilege and ends, as does Seltha, with a prayer for mercy:

> Oh God, with torture without end,
> Crushed by a thousand pains of hell,
> May black remorse plague me forever!

[10] See Luserke-Jaqui for an interpretation of many of these texts (Sprickmann in his chapter 8; Schink in chapter 9; Schiller in chapter 13).

[11] In Helga Madland's straightforward formulation: 'Infanticide fiction is really not about morality, the reform of the criminal law, sexual emancipation, or an expression of the heightened social consciousness of the *Stürmer und Dränger*. It is about the intimidation of women' ('Infanticide as Fiction', 34).

[12] Gotthold Friedrich Stäudlin, 'Seltha, die Kindermörderin': 'Ha! Wie getroffen steh ich hier!', quoted in Rameckers 242–4, this citation 242 (also published in Luserke-Jaqui 273–4).

What have I done? – I cursed myself!
Oh God, forgive! do not avenge,
By Jesus' blood I beg: forgive![13]

Meißner's 'Song of a Fallen Woman' ('Lied einer Gefallenen') is set before the infanticide. His nameless protagonist reflects upon the doomed future of her illegitimate child: if it is a boy, he will become a seducer like his father, if a girl, she will incur shame like her mother. She ends on an ominous note, warning the child that she might kill it if it resembles the father.[14] In the sequel to the poem, 'The Murderess' ('Die Mörderin'), she carries out her threat: like Stäudlin's ' Seltha', the poem records her feelings immediately after the deed. Like Seltha, Meißner's murderess curses the father, whom she blames for the deed, upon which she loses herself in visions of hell and divine retribution. Her only hope is to escape eternal damnation by atoning in death:

I willingly bleed, I'll gladly atone
Upon the scaffold!
How would I kiss – how kiss the blade,
If it reconciled God![15]

Some vengeful thoughts surface: she promises her lover that if God does not forgive her, she will drag him down to hell with her. Nevertheless, she ends on a conciliatory note: 'End, oh end, ye powers of heaven, / These blazes of torment!'[16]

Schiller's ballad 'The Child-Murderess' ('Die Kindsmörderin')[17] combines many of these motifs. Luise remembers deed and motive on her way to the scaffold. After elaborately cursing her faithless lover, she relates how she killed her child in a fit of insanity, partly because it resembled him, and then 'hurried gladly to extinguish / in cold death my burning pain'.[18] In

---

[13] Johann Friedrich Schink, 'Empfindungen einer unglücklich Verführten bey der Ermordung ihres Kindes': 'O Gott mit Martern ohne Zahl / Zermalmt mit tausend Höllenqual, / Tref ewig mich die schwarze Reue! / Was that ich? – fluchte ich mir nicht? – / O Gott vergieb! nicht in's Gericht, / Im Blute deines Sohns – verzeihe.' Quoted in Rameckers 244–6, this quotation 246 (also published in Luserke-Jaqui 274–5).

[14] August Gottlieb Meißner, 'Lied einer Gefallenen', quoted in Rameckers 246–7, this citation 247 (also published in Luserke-Jaqui 282–3).

[15] Meißner, 'Die Mörderin': 'Gern will ich ja bluten, gern will ich ja büssen / auf hohem Schafot! / Wie wolt' ich das Eisen – wie wolt ich es küssen / versöhnt es nur Gott! – ', quoted in Rameckers 247–9, this citation 249 (also published in Luserke-Jaqui 283–5).

[16] Meißner, 'Die Mörderin': 'O Mächte des Himmels, endet o endet / die folternde Glut!' (in Rameckers 249).

[17] For an interpretation of the poem in the context of contemporary infanticide literature, see Madland, 'Infanticide as Fiction'.

[18] Friedrich Schiller, 'Die Kindsmörderin': 'Freudig eilt' ich, in dem kalten Tode / Auszulöschen meinen Flammenschmerz' (20).

part, her monologue is a plea for understanding: 'Alas! what my heart felt was all too human! / And thus my sentiment shall be my grave!';[19] partly, it is a warning directed at 'those who never fell, / Those for whom lilies of innocence yet bloom':[20] at the foot of the scaffold, Luise delivers a father's moral and warning. 'Never trust the roses of your youth, / Never trust the oaths of men, oh sisters!'[21] As do most of her fictional predecessors, Luise ends by pleading for her death with worldly justice, in this poem personified in the figure of her executioner.

The similarities linking these poetic monologues are striking. Schiller's Luise, Sprickmann's Ida and Meißner's nameless murderess kill their child because it resembles the father,[22] so that the act of infanticide is presented here, in part, as an act of revenge upon the father. Such extreme hatred, it is implied, can only be induced by betrayed love, a deep emotional commitment that led to the loss of the women's 'honour', which in turn inspires the sense of shame that results in murder. This is why all three, as well as Stäudlin's Seltha, curse their seducers at length and/or hold them responsible for the deed; Ida, finally, acts out her revenge on both by killing the father as well as the child.[23] If this Medea-like rage seems a far cry from the childlike innocence that defines the woman as child of contemporary drama, it is counterbalanced by its portrayal as a state of temporary insanity. In this state, the women's hatred of, or rather their love for, their seducers coupled with an extremity of shame causes the death of their children: Luise and Ida, for example, recognise their lover's features in those of the child, take leave of their senses, and, as does Seltha, 'wake up' when the deed is done. Luise's description of the murder reads as follows: 'here the Hydra throttled me, / And the murder was committed';[24] Sprickmann's Ida, as well, 'awakens from her fury'.[25] Without exception, these

---

[19] Schiller, 'Die Kindsmörderin': 'Wehe! – menschlich hat dies Herz empfunden! – / Und Empfindung soll mein Richtschwert sein! – ' (18).

[20] Schiller, 'Die Kindsmörderin': 'Weinet um mich, die ihr nie gefallen, / Denen noch der Unschuld Lilien blühn …' (18).

[21] Schiller, 'Die Kindsmörderin': 'Trauet nicht den Rosen eurer Jugend, / Trauet, Schwestern, Männerschwüren nie!' (21).

[22] On this motif in infanticide literature, see Košenina, 'Ratlose Schwestern', 54.

[23] Anton Matthias Sprickmann, 'Ida', quoted in Rameckers 235–42.

[24] Schiller, 'Die Kindsmörderin': 'hier umstrickte mich die Hyder – / Und vollendet war der Mord' (20). The Hydra, a mythical nine-headed creature whom Hercules was ordered to kill as one of his nine labours, was virtually invincible because one of its heads was immortal while the others grew two heads for each one that was chopped off (Hamilton 164). Luise evokes this image to indicate that it would have required true heroism to resist the temptation (and initially, the seduction) to which she, a mere mortal, was exposed, a valiant resistance that could be offered only by 'those whom Nature has endowed with a hero's strength' ('Denen zu dem weichen Busenwallen / Heldenstärke die Natur verliehn', 18).

[25] Sprickmann, 'Ida': 'Deß erwacht die Mutter aus ihrer Wut', quoted in Rameckers 240.

unhappy women welcome death, a death closely associated with the death experienced, yearned for, or even brought about, by the woman as child in drama. The woman as child sees pre-emptive death as the only way to avoid the shame of seduction; for the woman as child-killer, retributive death constitutes simultaneously obliteration of the shame of seduction and restitution for the crime of infanticide, its direct result. For women as child-killers in poetry, this voluntary death constitutes a return to female innocence, just as it functions as preservation of female innocence for the women as children in plays of the period. Plagued by shame and remorse, unable to go on living, they beg for death, express their terror of hell, pray to God for forgiveness, and issue the requisite warning to other – as yet innocent – young women.

A glance at the contemporary social context reveals this to be a male fantasy, to cite Klaus Theweleit's inimitable term: the emphasis here being on both *male* and *fantasy*. *Male* because women's participation in the infanticide debate thoughout the eighteenth century was minimal to non-existent.[26] *Fantasy* because these infanticide poems bear no relation at all to contemporary reality as it has meanwhile been described in numerous sociological, historical, sociohistorical and legal studies on the subject.[27] Whereas literature juxtaposes a noble seducer with an innocent bourgeois maiden, in reality seducer and seduced were usually of the same social rank. By far the majority of women accused of infanticide were servants,[28] with their impregnators, in those cases in which the women were not sexually abused by their employers, also usually hailing from the class of servants or rural labourers.[29] In fiction, the woman as child-killer is also a woman as child, a girl of eighteen, like Wagner's Evchen, or just over

---

[26] The one fictional contribution consists of Marianne Ehrmann's tale 'Die unglückliche Hanne' (from her journal *Amaliens Erholungsstunden*, 1790; see Madland's 'Gender and the German Literary Canon'). Of the nearly 400 answers to Lamezan's prize question, three were authored by women, one of which was printed (see Ulbricht, *Kindsmord*, 224 n. 38). Overall, it is fair to say that infanticide is a non-subject in women's writing. See the following extensive studies on women's writings of the age: on drama, see Kord, *Ein Blick hinter die Kulissen*; on novels the studies by Touaillon, Schieth, Meise, and Gallas and Runge; on letters the study by French. Encyclopaedic works on women's literature (see, among others, Brinker-Gabler, Frederiksen, Eigler and Kord, and Loster-Schneider and Pailer) also do not list infanticide as a subject in the works of eighteenth-century women writers.

[27] Among them are the document collections published by Wahl and Rüdiger Scholz (*Das kurze Leben*) respectively as well as Birkner; Dudeck; van Dülmen, *Frauen vor Gericht*; Felber; Finkelnburg; Flach; Frede; Grütter; Habermas and Hommen; Hammer; Jackson; Klar; Luserke-Jaqui (chapters 3.6 and 3.7); Michalik; Neumeyer; Rodegra, Lindemann and Ewald; Schulte; Ulbricht, and Wächtershäuser.

[28] See Ulbricht's statistics and argumentation, *Kindsmord*, 31–47; van Dülmen, *Frauen vor Gericht*; Schulte, 'Strafrechtlicher Entwurf', 382–6 (on nineteenth-century infanticides).

[29] Ulbricht, *Kindsmord*, 45; see also statistics on 77 and discussion on 78–84; Evans, *Rituals*, 46.

fourteen, like Goethe's Gretchen.[30] Conversely, both Ulbricht's statistics for Schleswig-Holstein and Wächtershäuser's for Prussia have shown that nearly all real-life infanticides were between twenty and thirty years old, with the majority committing the crime at the same age at which married women in the eighteenth century also produced, on average, their first child: in their mid twenties.[31] A twenty-five to thirty-year-old may have been considered young by some contemporaries, middle-aged by others, but undeniably an adult capable of informed consent or, for that matter, refusal. Sentimental thoughts of the innocently seduced teen-aged girls of literature might not have occurred to contemporary magistrates confronted with a scullery maid twice Gretchen's age who had, to their way of thinking, compounded the crime of fornication by that of child-murder. Even more striking is the difference in attitudes between fictional heroines and what we know, from contemporary court records, of real-life culprits: the confessions, the remorse, the despair, the prayers, the death wish that are universal in fiction are nowhere to be found in court records. Few real-life women ever confessed to infanticide; the majority, in fact, tried to convince the court that they had experienced a stillbirth. Far from begging for execution, they pleaded social and financial hardship, fear of their parents, temporary insanity and other mitigating circumstances, no doubt in the hope that the death sentence would be commuted to life imprisonment. Of the very few defendants who did confess, many later retracted, claiming that they had been coerced into confession or confessed in fear of torture.[32] All of them, in other words, did their level best to survive. Until they were literally about to put their heads on the block,[33] real-life infanticides rarely stated, as their poetic counterparts inevitably did, that they deserved death as just retribution, or suggested that their sorry fate could serve as an example to

---

[30] Faust states that Gretchen is 'over fourteen years' and thus no longer a sexual minor (Goethe, *Faust. Der Tragödie erster Teil*, 85). While there is no indication as to Gretchen's actual age, several aspects of the play indicate that Gretchen is intended to be not much older than fourteen, certainly still in her teens. Among these aspects I would include the childlike flower petals game – 'Er liebt mich, er liebt mich nicht' – and Gretchen's absolute dependence on her mother, both of which would seem slightly ridiculous in the portrayal of a woman in her twenties. (That there is no talk, throughout the Gretchen plot, of finding a suitable husband for Gretchen also seems a good indication of Gretchen's youth.)

[31] See comparison and discussion by Ulbricht, *Kindsmord*, 30–3.

[32] See the cases related by Wächtershäuser, Ulbricht and others (see note 27 above) and the documents published by Wahl and Rüdiger Scholz respectively relating to infanticide cases in late eighteenth-century Weimar.

[33] On the dying declarations of real-life infanticides and other women condemned to die, see the final chapter.

others.[34] And even their confessions at death's door were usually the result of days, sometimes months, of browbeating by the clergy, as we shall see in the final chapter.

The single point at which both poems and non-fictional depictions of infanticide appear to converge is the stated *motive* for the crime: shame. In the poems, shame hurls the unhappy woman into a temporary frenzy from which she emerges unaware of what she has done, standing over her child's dead body with blood on her hands. Shame is the cause of the retributive death of the woman as child-killer in poetry, just as fear of shame leads to the pre-emptive death of the woman as child in drama. And fear of shame is also the single most frequently assumed motivation of real-life infanticides throughout the eighteenth century.[35] Aside from *belles lettres*, this assumption appears in non-fictional works by contemporary philosophers, reformists, jurists, physicians and other professional or lay writers: participants in what was certainly one of the century's most far-reaching and impassioned debates. When Ferdinand von Lamezan published his famous prize question, 'Which are the best achievable means to prevent infanticide?' in various newspapers in 1780,[36] he received 400 responses, ten times as many as even the most sensational public debates had ever attracted up to that time.[37]

Scholarship on the public infanticide debate of the 1780s has traditionally read it in the context of contemporary 'reality', that is: scholars have assumed a distinct relationship linking this debate to real-life infanticide cases and a distinct rift separating it from fiction.[38] However, it is also possible to find evidence for the exact opposite: some of the best-known

---

[34] Ulbricht cites one single case in his extensive study based on dozens of cases in Schleswig-Holstein. In 1741, Dorothea Niebuhr stated when asked why she had killed her child that the devil had instigated the act and that she wanted to pay for her crime: 'Der Teufel hätte ihr solches eingeblasen … Sie hätte Blut vergossen und wolle wieder dafür leiden.' Ulbricht emphasises that this statement was made at the outset of the investigation, that is: not after lengthy 'instruction' by the clergy (*Kindsmord*, 330). See also his 'Kindsmörderinnen vor Gericht'.

[35] Ulbricht's statement, based on court records of the time: '"Scham" oder "Furcht vor Schande" wird am häufigsten als der einzige Beweggrund oder als einer von mehreren genannt' (*Kindsmord*, 163); 'Schande wurde weit vor allen anderen Motiven als das häufigste genannt' (173). Shame also provides the primary motive for keeping the pregnancy secret (116–20).

[36] See Lamezan, 'Welches sind die besten ausführbaren Mittel, dem Kindermorde Einhalt zu thun?', which appeared simultaneously in *Rheinische Beiträge zur Gelehrsamkeit*, *Schlözer's Briefwechsel*, and *Ephemeriden der Menschheit*. On the 'Preisfrage', see especially Luserke-Jaqui's chapter 12 and Ulbricht, *Kindsmord*, 217–328. The original text has been republished in Luserke-Jaqui 287–8.

[37] Ulbricht lists among these Friedrich II's provocative question to the Berliner Akademie whether it was defensible for a ruler to deceive his people, which received 42 responses (*Kindsmord*, 217–18).

[38] Baerlocher, a lawyer, confidently claims that literary sources can be discounted in the discussion of real-life infanticide: 'Was den Einfluß "schöner Literatur" anbelangt, so kann dieser … ohnehin unberücksichtigt bleiben' ('Nachwort', 396) since 'Es ist evident, daß viele literarische Behandlungen

texts written as part of the public philosophical and legal debate seem more closely related to infanticide literature than to actual cases. The issue of 'shame' and its discursive incarnations demonstrate this most clearly. Most participants in the reformist debate assume as a motive for infanticide the guilty woman's fear of shame, demonstrated concretely in her desperate attempts to escape public penitence (*Kirchenbuße*)[39] or the penalties for fornication (*Hurenstrafen*) which could range, in different parts of the country, from fines to public flogging, branding and shaming in the pillory.[40] These penalties are a major point of attack in the responses to the 1780 prize question,[41] and the second half of the century saw abolition of both kinds of 'shaming' penalties throughout Germany, for the expressed reason that they contributed to infanticide.[42] Yet in the court records as analysed by Ulbricht, fear of either public penitence or *Hurenstrafen* very rarely appears as a motive,[43] and contemporaries in areas where these penalties had already been revoked noted that their abolition had not diminished the occurrence of infanticide in their region.[44] What this shows, rather unsurprisingly, is that reformist writings on infanticide by educated middle-class men did not necessarily describe contemporary reality as it was experienced by much less educated lower-class women.

Based on this and other divergences between reformist arguments and actual cases, there is good reason to believe that the link between the theories of reformers and the practice of infanticide is less robust than has

des Themas Kindsmord den Verhältnissen, wie sie sich den Behörden und der Gesellschaft darboten, wenig oder gar nicht entsprechen' (501). Wächtershäuser has also linked the public reform debate to real-life cases and distinguished it from fictional representation.

[39] Public penitence was a penalty imposed by the church, which involved public confession of the sin and repentance before obtaining forgiveness and readmission into the fold. *Kirchenbußen* were heavily criticised during the eighteenth century since they amounted to public shaming and were considered by many as the ecclesiastical version of the pillory; another source of criticism was that the well-off usually escaped with fines. See Frede.

[40] Whether fear of these punishments constituted the actual motivation for infanticide is still under debate: Wächtershäuser, for example, assumes this to be the case, a conclusion that Ulbricht has contested based on court records from Schleswig-Holstein (*Kindsmord*).

[41] Ulbricht has compiled some statistics using the 80 printed answers to the prize question that are still extant: of the 21 who mention church penalties, 16 plead for their abolition; of the 39 who mention state-imposed *Hurenstrafen*, 26 plead for their abolition (*Kindsmord*, 274); 27 published answers assume that fear of shame was a major contributor to infanticide. Not a single respondent supported the retention of church penalties (*Kindsmord*, 279).

[42] Prussia abolished church penalties in 1746 and penalties for extramarital sex (*Hurenstrafen*) in 1765 and did away with the requirement to report illegitimate pregnancies to the authorities (Ulbricht, *Kindsmord*, 242–3); Hanover abolished church penalties around 1769; Schleswig-Holstein in the 1760s (Ulbricht, *Kindsmord*, 214–15); *Hurenstrafen* were rescinded in Hessen/Waldeck in 1780, Sachsen-Weimar in 1786, Anhalt-Bernburg in 1799, Bavaria (for unmarried persons only) in 1780 and Baden in 1803 (Ulbricht, *Kindsmord*, 319–20).

[43] See his discussion of court records, *Kindsmord*, 281, 284–6.

[44] Ulbricht, *Kindsmord*, 281; see also Cyrus.

been assumed.[45] Conversely, we may also suspect a stronger relationship between reformist and literary writings than previously imagined. The discursive evidence for this is both apparent and plentiful. Many participants in the contemporary reform debate, who claim to draw their inspiration from real-life social and political conditions rather than literature, nevertheless present their arguments in ways that can only be described as literary, replicating the focal points of infanticide literature – virtue, 'feminine' honour and female shame – in nearly identical formulations.

How, then, can we interpret the link among the three distinct areas: literary texts, reformist debate and real-life cases? To claim either that life imitated art or that art influenced life would amount, in my opinion, to an act of overreading. It is impossible to prove that literary discourses, either in reformist or fictional texts, produced behaviours or ideas among those involved with infanticide – lawmakers, judges, or sovereigns, let alone perpetrators – across Germany and throughout the century, although there may be good individual evidence in support of such an influence. Conversely, infanticide literature and, to a considerable extent also the reformist debate, more or less ignored the circumstances leading to the actual crime as it occurred in eighteenth-century fields, barns, kitchens, or the often windowless sleeping quarters of female servants. These are reasonable objections which do not, however, justify the flat declaration, as issued by Baerlocher,[46] that no link exists between fictional or theoretical writing and reality. To follow his logic would be to declare the only possible link between two things to be a *causal* one, somewhat akin to those contemporaries of Darwin who misread his assertion that Man and ape have a common ancestor as the claim that Man had *descended* from the ape. In what follows, I would like to advance (and document) five theses regarding the links between these three distinct spheres:

1. In their attempts to uncover the motivation for infanticide, both literary and reformist writings focus on feminine virtue, lost honour and female shame.

2. The link between both kinds of texts cannot be assumed to be a 'causal' one (that is: it cannot be documented either that infanticide literature 'influenced' the reformist debate or that the reformist debate 'influenced' literary depictions of infanticide). What can, however, be assumed is that

---

[45] Among others, in Wächtershäuser's 1973 study of court cases and the contemporary infanticide debate.
[46] See discussion and citation in note 38 above.

both kinds of texts are indebted to a 'common ancestor': ideas regarding gender, particularly femininity, as they were conceived and formulated in the second half of the eighteenth century.[47]

3. 'Gender' is defined in reformist texts in precisely the same way as in literary texts, namely through the juxtaposition of feminine 'virtue' and 'vice' (innocent victims of 'seduction' versus 'whores'[48]). The most central motives for infanticide, a sense of 'honour' and 'shame', are also seen in gendered terms (as exemplified in the common idea of *Geschlechtsehre*).

4. Both kinds of texts tend to frame the debate *exclusively* in terms of gender, ignoring the issue of class completely – this is true even of texts that portray inability to raise the child due to poverty as a motive for infanticide. This should surprise us, given that infanticide literature describes a (historically inaccurate) class difference between seducer and seduced.

5. Real-life infanticide cases, as documented in court records, death sentences, council votes and other legal documents, were demonstrably affected by contemporary gender ideas, that 'common ancestor' that also shaped literature and reformist essays on infanticide. Conversely, real-life infanticide cases are the *only* area where class issues materialise to complicate ideas of gender. In these documents, class issues invariably *conflict with* ideas of gender.

'PUBLIC WHORES' AND 'HONOURABLE WOMEN': PHILOSOPHICAL AND LEGAL ISSUES (1760–1800)

In the second half of the century, infanticide became the subject of a nearly inescapable philosophical and legal debate and one of the most popular topics in fiction. As a subject of discussion, infanticide was practically ubiquitous; as a crime, it was not.[49] Contrary to the common assumption

---

[47] For an overview of the gender discussion in the second half of the eighteenth century, see Hausen; Dotzler; Duden; Gössmann; Volker Hoffmann; Lange; Lenk; Dietrick; and Cocalis.

[48] The term 'whore' is used throughout to translate German 'Dirne' or 'Hure', which, much like our present-day invective 'whore', were in the eighteenth century indiscriminately applied either to paid prostitutes or to women whose sexual morals were presumed to be loose (see Hull, *Sexuality*, 116; Schwerhoff, 'Geschlechtsspezifische Kriminalität', 106).

[49] Ulbricht's findings regarding the frequency of infanticide are clearly in dispute with Wächtershäuser's. Unlike Wächtershäuser, Ulbricht argues, in my view convincingly, that it would have been exceedingly difficult to conceal a pregnancy and birth among servants, who usually shared sleeping quarters. Schlözer's contemporary statistics only indicate approximately 11–12 infanticides per year in Sweden; Ulbricht's comparative statistics of prosecuted crimes would mean about 200–220 infanticides per year in Germany (in a population of about 29 million). See his statistics and

of an astronomical rise in the rate of infanticide in the eighteenth century, available statistics indicate that occurrences of the crime actually diminished in the eighteenth century compared with the seventeenth.[50] The heightened interest among lawmakers and philosophers in the theme, then, can hardly be ascribed to a real-life infanticide 'epidemic'.[51] The inspiration for the debate lay elsewhere: infanticide forced contemporaries to rethink a host of thorny issues, some of them legal, others social, many of them gendered. Among the legal ones was the death penalty, which indicates changing ideas about the retributive versus deterrent functions of the law; among the social ones was the status of children born out of wedlock and the issue of prevention, since many contemporaries saw infanticide as a result of insufficient anticipatory measures by the state. Gender was at the heart of the debate (rather than class, which might have been one of its focal points but, surprisingly, was not). Legal and social gender issues brought to the fore included the status of unwed mothers and the regulation of sexuality out of wedlock (*Unzucht, Unzuchtsstrafen*).[52] Philosophically, the reform debate asked no less of society than to reconsider the idea that women could be divided into two classes: 'honourable women', that is, virgins and wives, on the one hand and whores on the other. Many participants in the debate were clearly torn between warring ideas of gender: infanticide seemed both to *negate* femininity (exemplified in maternal love) and *express* it (exemplified in its prime motive, shame).

The transition from infanticide as a negation of femininity to infanticide as an expression of femininity, however perverted, is, in fact, the most significant change that occurs in the course of the contemporary debate. The *Carolina*, the penal code established by Emperor Charles V in 1532 under which infanticide was still judged in the late eighteenth century, took for granted that infanticide was committed by loose women attempting to 'conceal their depravity'.[53] Early eighteenth-century treatises often assumed the same motive, such as the elaborately titled *Astorgia Meretricia: Or: Natural Maternal Love Extinguished in Depraved Whores/Who, in Order to*

---

discussion, *Kindsmord*, 176–82. On the other hand, sexual offences (adultery, fornication, sodomy, abortion and infanticide) were among those for which women were most frequently prosecuted (see Hull, *Sexuality*, 72–3; Schwerhoff, 'Geschlechtsspezifische Kriminalität', 102).

[50] See Ulbricht's evidence and statistics, *Kindsmord*, 188–208.

[51] We might, speculatively to be sure, actually assume the reverse, namely that the intensity of the debate and the wealth of infanticide fiction helped create the impression that infanticide was a practically ubiquitous crime.

[52] On the legal regulation of women's sexuality, see Hull, *Sexuality* and 'Sexualstrafrecht'; Harms-Ziegler; Schulte; Schnabel-Schulte; Koch; Dilcher; and Vogel.

[53] Radbruch (ed.), Art. 131 II of *Peinliche Gerichtsordnung Kaiser Karls V. von 1532*: 'umb jre geübte Leichtuertigkeit zu verbergen'.

Conceal Their Fornication and Whoring/Abort or Slay the Fruit of Their Womb.[54] But already around mid-century, Mirabeau the elder defined the infanticide's shame as 'the final sigh of innocence'; once innocence was abandoned, he maintained, the woman's descent into the abyss was inevitable.[55]

Shortly thereafter, Cesare Beccaria proposed that illegitimately pregnant women, confronted with a choice between shame and the death of their newborn, would *understandably* and *necessarily* choose the latter: 'How should she who is forced to choose between shame and the death of a being unable to feel its miseries *not* prefer the latter to the inevitable suffering to which she and the unfortunate offspring would be exposed?'[56] In what was almost certainly the century's most influential treatise on the subject, Beccaria introduced the notion of shame as a *compulsory* force, and many writers after him took up the theme. Among them were Pestalozzi, who, like the poets of the age, speculated that infanticides killed their babies because they resembled the seducer,[57] and Schlosser, who followed Beccaria's train of thought exactly in his portrayal of a mother who considers the shame that awaits her if discovered far greater than the shame of public execution.[58] When the prize question was posed in 1780, its very wording identified infanticide as one of those crimes 'related to virtues; virtues which are perverted into vices'.[59] Contemporary discourse consistently defined this perverted virtue as specifically feminine. Many argued that women were practically predisposed towards infanticide because they were innately vulnerable to shame, its prime motivator. Consider the following argumentation, advanced by Franz Heinrich Birnstiel in his *Attempt to Discover the True Causes of Infanticide from Natural and Populist History*:

Due to the physical nature of both sexes, the female sex ... is *more sensitive* than the male; it follows that this inherent and immutable aspect makes it less perfect than

[54] *Astorgia Meretricia: Oder: Ausgelöschte natürliche Mutter-Liebe Der Leichtsinnigen Huren/Welche Ihre getriebene Unzucht und Hurerey zu verbergen/ihre eigene Leibesfrucht abtreiben oder entleiben.* The treatise was originally published as a sermon by Pancratius Caprez in 1683 and republished in 1716.

[55] Mirabeau 63.

[56] 'Chi trovasi tra l'infamia e la morte di un essere incapace di sentirne i mali, come non preferirà questa alla miseria infallibile a cui sarebbero esposti ella e l'infelice frutto?' (Beccaria, *Dei delitti*, 78–9; see also discussion in Ulbricht, *Kindsmord*, 308).

[57] Pestalozzi, quoted in Baerlocher, 'Nachwort', 417: 'die Stunde der lezten Verzweiflung; – die stähelte den Arm der Mutter! zu würgen das Kind ... Ihr wars, ... sie würgte mit der Hand den Verbrecher.'

[58] 'Die Schande so zu sterben wie das Gesetz will, ist weniger fürchterlich, als die, in die ich falle, wenn meine Unzucht entdeckt wird' (Schlosser 24).

[59] Lamezan in *Rheinische Beiträge*, 1780, 84: 'die mit Tugenden verwandt sind; Tugenden, die in Laster ausarten'.

ours. In this situation [illegitimate birth], it [the female sex] has … neither time, much less a complete freedom to reason, distinguish, or choose; as a result, this sex will, influenced by the confused sensations accompanying this situation, be more or less, but often not at all, capable of distinguishing between them and their cause and thus very often be compelled to impulsive actions.[60]

In nuce: women's predilection to commit infanticide is rooted in a permanent state, their 'natural' inability to reason logically or differentiate. The 'situation' of illegitimate birth further exacerbates this general state (although it does not cause it). Since the crime is a direct result of women's more sensitive nature, it is committed by compulsion, not choice. What is striking in Birnstiel's argumentation is the *normality* that he attributes to the event: if woman's weaker nature is, as he describes it, both 'inherent and immutable' *and* the ultimate cause of infanticide, it follows that infanticide is not, for women, an abnormal act. Throughout his treatise, Birnstiel speaks of *it* (the female sex) rather than *them* (women), thus deleting discursively the possibility of individual distinction, disparity, or choice. Infanticide, then, does not *negate* 'natural' femininity, it *expresses* it.

Birnstiel's argumentation recurs in an essay by Pfeil, one of the three prize-winning respondents to Lamezan's question, who saw infanticide as

rooted mainly in the uncontrolled predilection of these people [women] towards sensuality, feebleness and a false sentimentality, combined with flawed ideas of honour and shame. The latter alone, even without the influence of the former, would easily compel a tender creature, such as women actually should be, to a considerable degree of cruelty.[61]

Pfeil's idea that infanticides are merely women as they 'actually should be' echoes throughout the age in contributions to the debate, not only by philosophers but also by physicians and lawmakers. The Austrian official and jurist Joseph von Sonnenfels, for example, saw the origin of infanticide

---

[60] 'Vermöge der körperlichen Anlage unter beiden Geschlechtern ist das weibliche … *empfindsamer*, als das männliche; diese originelle und unabänderliche Eigenschaft macht es folglich unvollkommener, als wir sind, denn in dieser Lage hat es wegen der Menge, der Stärke und der Geschwindigkeit aller, oder wenigstens der meisten, sich in einem Brennpunct versammelnden Vorstellungen, weder Zeit, viel weniger die gänzliche Freyheit des Zerlegens, des Unterscheidens, oder Wählens; folglich muß sich dieses Geschlecht, nach Masgab der hier abfließenden Verworrenheit ihrer Empfindungen, oft mehr, oft weniger, oft aber gar nicht von der Ursache derselben unterscheiden können, somit sehr oft zu unwillkürlichen Handlungen hingerissen werden' (Birnstiel, 'Vorrede' to *Versuch*, unpag., emphasis original).

[61] '[daß die Gründe für den Kindermord…] hauptsächlich in dem ungemäßigten Hang dieses Volkes [des Weibervolkes] zur Sinnlichkeit, zur Weichlichkeit und zur falschen Empfindsamkeit, verbunden mit falschen Begriffen von Ehre und Schande bestehen. Letztere allein ohne den erstern, würden ein weiches Geschöpf, wie eigentlich jedes Weib seyn soll, leicht zu einem hohen Grad von Grausamkeit hinreissen können' (Pfeil's response in *Drei Preisschriften*, 1–77, the citation 23).

'in the shame of fallen maidens and in poverty',[62] and some magistrates judged cases based on the same hypothesis, even if there was no actual evidence that the 'fallen maiden' in question had been motivated by shame.[63] In *On Legislation and Infanticide* (*Über Gesetzgebung und Kindesmord*), Pestalozzi went so far as to claim that infanticide was the inevitable result of maternal feeling, that it was 'fundamentally necessary' for the 'female nature' to protect the child against 'indecency and shame'.[64] In the realm of medicine, infanticide was at times considered a psychological female ailment exacerbated by the physical pain of childbirth.[65] Johann Valentin Müller, writing for a specialist audience of physicians, surgeons and apothecaries, called infanticide a 'spiritual disease' and described its symptoms as follows:

> [Shame is] sufficient to fill the heart with despair, which grows stronger with each moment approaching birth. Add the pains of labour to this and the already insensitised spirit will be completely deadened, the strain will push the blood into the head, the tender fibres will be crushed and circulation inhibited – horrific images will originate in the soul; every human bond will be a burden to her [the woman], her despair will reach its highest pitch – and thus such an unfortunate has no choice but to remove the cause of this suffering – and of this great shame; and this cause is the poor creature who dies, and must die, given the circumstances, by her hands.[66]

Not unlike Birnstiel, Müller describes psychological effects exacerbated, but not caused by, physical pain. His rather pedantic listing of physical symptoms (inhibited circulation) and mental states (despair) float on a generous cushion of pure speculation (horrific images originating in the mother's

---

[62] Sonnenfels 213: 'Wenn man die Quellen untersuchet, aus denen die Kindsmorde entspringen, so sind es hauptsächlich, die Schande gefallener Mädchen, und die Armuth.'

[63] From the magistrate's ruling in an infanticide case in Husum in 1793: 'Die Schande, womit sich die geschwängerten Personen herumtragen müssen, haben [so] schon manchem Kinde das Leben gekostet. Es ist die Ehrliebe eine Eigenschaft, die in der Welt viel Gutes gestiftet hat, aber gar zu leicht, wenn die Grenzen überschritten werden, auf unglückliche Abwege führt' (cited in Ulbricht, *Kindsmord*, 364).

[64] Quoted in Breithaupt 172; see also his discussion of Pestalozzi's writings on infanticide on 172–6.

[65] For a medical/forensic consideration of infanticide that offers a different conclusion, see Lammel.

[66] Müller 89: '[Schande ist] hinlänglich, das Herz mit Verzweiflung zu erfüllen, die mit jedem Augenblick, wie die Stunde der Geburt herannahet, größer und stärker wird. Kommen nun die Geburtsschmerzen hinzu, so wird das schon fühllose Gemüth gänzlich betäubt, durch die starke Anstrengung das Geblüt nach dem Kopf getrieben, die zarten Fasern gedrückt, die Circulation gehemmt – schauderhafte Bilder in der Seele erreget; jedes äußere Verhältnis wird ihr zur Last, die Verzweiflung erreicht ihren höchsten Grad – und so bleibt einer solchen unglücklichen Person nichts anderes übrig, als die Ursache aufzuheben, welche dieses Leiden verursacht – und diese große Schande auflegt; und diese ist das arme Geschöpf, das unter ihren Händen stirbt, und unter diesen Umständen sterben muß.'

soul). Even from this confusing mélange, shame emerges as the solitary cause of the disease. As did previous writers, Müller portrays the guilty mother as bereft of all control and decision-making powers and infanticide as the *inevitable* result of female shame. Müller may be writing from a medical viewpoint and for a more restricted readership, but his diagnosis matches that of his more philosophically minded contemporaries in every detail.

In the legal debate surrounding the question of adequate punishment for infanticide, this gendered understanding of shame assumes a new meaning. The point that the death penalty was not an effective deterrent was made both by writers sympathetic to the women's plight, such as Beccaria and Pestalozzi, and by those less understanding. Both sides argued that the guilty women would feel their shame, their lost honour, more acutely than the fear of death. From this argument emerged a wide spectrum of proposed punishments, from no punishment at all (Pestalozzi)[67] to 'never-ending punishment through ceaseless shame' (Schlosser).[68] 'May the child-murderess dread not the executioner's axe, not the concealment of imprisonment, but the very thing she sought to escape: shame, tenfold, public, everlasting shame!'[69] Forms of punishment inspired by such sentiments included whipping, branding and other forms of 'marking' (such as the cutting off of hair), pillorying, publishing the names of women who had given birth in public birthing houses, exhibiting the offender in front of pictorial illustrations of her crime, naked exposure of the culprit, or parading her publicly with the dead child in her arms.[70] The range of punishments suggested here clearly mirrors the spectrum of contemporary visions of infanticides, from the 'fallen innocence' of contemporary fiction at one end of the spectrum to the depraved fornicators of the *Carolina* at the other. At one end, defenders of 'fallen maidens' suggested not only leaving infanticide unpunished, but also exterminating its root cause, the shame of premarital sexuality, through state-sponsored marriages for unwed mothers. Critical voices at the other extreme commented acerbically on such ideas, claiming that 'whores' and their children would receive better state support than 'honest' married

---

[67] See Baerlocher, 'Nachwort', 420–1.

[68] Schlosser suggested 'Einschliessung in ein Pönitenzhaus, wo eine lange Schande unaufhörlich straft' (65–6).

[69] 'Nicht das Beil des Henkers, nicht die Verborgenheit des Zuchthauses schröcke die Kindsmörderin, sondern eben das, dem sie zu entfliehen sucht, Schande, zehenfache, öffentliche, ewige Schande!' (*Fragmente*, 42).

[70] See Ulbricht, *Kindsmord*, 312–22.

women.[71] The interpretation of the infanticide as a 'fallen maiden' or 'depraved whore' could play a decisive role in determining punishments or recommendations for clemency: some participants in the debate actually suggested abolishing penalties for promiscuity (*Unzuchtsstrafen*) *only* for seduced 'virtuous girls',[72] and the Bavarian Penal Code (*Bayerisches Gesetzbuch*) of 1813 distinguished, in its infanticide legislation, between 'public whores' and 'honourable women'.[73] Clemency recommendations for women jailed for infanticide almost invariably hinged on the same distinction, as expressed in comments by prison wardens on the women's sexual conduct in prison.[74]

In the midst of this heated debate surrounding feminine virtue and vice, honour and shame, Immanuel Kant's treatise stands out as similar yet different: it is similar in its portrayal of infanticide as caused by shame, yet different in the conclusions he draws from this. Infanticide, Kant maintains, is one of only two kinds of killings (along with killing in a duel) that should not be considered murder and hence not be punishable by death:

Both are motivated by a sense of honour. One is *sexual honour*, the other the *soldier's honour*, each a genuine sense of honour which spells obligation and duty to these respective classes of people. One crime is *infanticide* committed by the mother (infanticidium maternale), the other the *murder of a fellow soldier* (commilitonicidium), a *duel*. – Since the shame of an illegitimate birth cannot be erased by legislation, it appears that human beings in this situation find themselves in a natural state, and the act of *killing* (homicidium), which can, in this case, not even be considered *murder* (homicidium dolosum), is indeed in both cases punishable, but no sovereignty can punish it by death. An illegitimately born child is born outside the law (for this would mean within marriage), and hence born outside the protection of the law. In a manner of speaking, it stole its way into society (like illegal wares), so that society is justified in ignoring its existence (since it should by rights not have come into existence in this manner) and hence also its destruction. If the illegitimate birth becomes known, no law can mitigate the mother's shame …

---

[71] See the following outburst by Justus Möser: 'Sie haben wohl recht in ihren letzten Schreiben zu fragen: Ob denn der Hurkinder so viel wären und Ehestand so wenig Beförderung verdiene, daß anderer ehrlicher Leute echte und rechte Kinder ihnen zu gefallen die Werkstätten räumen müssen? Denn seit zehn oder zwanzig Jahren ist in manchen Ländern für die Huren und ihre Kinder mehr geschehen als in tausend Jahren für alle Ehegemahlinnen, Ehegattinnen und Ehegenossinnen' (Möser 113 and discussion in Ulbricht, *Kindsmord*, 260).

[72] See Ulbricht, *Kindsmord*, 290.

[73] 'öffentliche Huren' versus 'ehrbare Frauen'; Ulbricht, *Kindsmord*, 355.

[74] Ulbricht, *Kindsmord*, 388. The Weimar infanticide Dorothea Altwein, for example, was pardoned after serving seventeen years following a reference from her warden which describes her as 'eine der fleisigsten und ordentlichsten Dirnen' in his prison (letter from Koppenfels to Carl August, 3 August 1798, cited in Rüdiger Scholz, *Das kurze Leben*, 134).

What, then, would constitute justice in these cases? – Here our penal system is indeed hard pressed: it must either declare the sense of honour (which is, in this case, no chimera) null and void by law and thus punish it by death, or it must remove the death penalty, which would otherwise be appropriate, from this crime.[75]

Kant does not argue morally but legally, and hence the touching descriptions of fallen maidens or the disparaging comments on whores find no place in his treatise.[76] Shame and honour once again emerge as the prime motivations for infanticide. In Kant's treatise, however, these qualities are divested of their gendered nature. Previous writers distinguish clearly between 'public whores' and 'honourable women', a juxtaposition that could affect sentences, commutations and pardons. Kant makes no such distinction but assumes the sense of shame that motivates infanticide to be a universal factor affecting *all* women, regardless of morality or individual sexual conduct. Other essayists consider shame a weakness attributable to gender: we need only remind ourselves of Birnstiel's claim that the female sex 'is *more sensitive* than the male', or Pfeil's rather contemptuous assessment of the 'uncontrolled predilection of these people [women] towards sensuality, feebleness and a false sentimentality, combined with flawed ideas of honour and shame'. In Kant's treatise, honour and shame are inescapable facts affecting *both sexes*, and their effect is both real and insurmountable. The sense of shame that inspires the crime of infanticide cannot be legislated away, it can only be denied post-facto – declared 'null and void by law' – to justify the death penalty. Other writers, even when suggesting changes to the law, tend to understand it as absolute and authoritative: the fact that infanticide is motivated by shame can, at most, serve as an argument for

---

[75] 'Zu beyden verleitet das Ehrgefühl. Das eine ist das der *Geschlechtsehre*, das andere, der *Kriegsehre*, und zwar der wahren Ehre, welche jeder dieser zwey Menschenclassen als Pflicht obliegt. Das eine Verbrechen ist der mütterliche *Kindesmord* (infanticidium maternale), das andere der *Kriegsgesellenmord* (commilitonicidium), der *Duell*. – Da die Gesetzgebung die Schmach einer unehelichen Geburt nicht wegnehmen … kann: so scheint es, daß Menschen in diesen Fällen sich im Naturzustande befinden und *Tödtung* (homicidium), die alsdann nicht einmal *Mord* (homocidium dolosum) heißen müßte, in beyden zwar allerdings strafbar sey, von der obersten Macht aber mit dem Tode nicht könne bestraft werden. Das unehelich auf die Welt gekommene Kind ist außer dem Gesetz (denn das heißt Ehe), mithin auch außer dem Schutz desselben, gebohren. Es ist in das gemeine Wesen gleichsam eingeschlichen (wie verbotene Waare), so daß dieses seine Existenz (weil es billig auf diese Art nicht hätte existiren sollen), mithin auch seine Vernichtung ignoriren kann, und die Schande der Mutter, wenn ihre uneheliche Niederkunft bekannt wird, kann keine Verordnung heben. … Was ist nun in beyden … Fällen Rechtens? – Hier kommt die Strafgerechtigkeit gar sehr ins Gedränge: entweder den Ehrbegrif (der hier kein Wahn ist) durchs Gesetz für nichtig zu erklären, und so mit dem Tode zu strafen, oder von dem Verbrechen die angemessene Todesstrafe wegzunehmen' (Kant, *Metaphysik*, 204–6, emphases original).

[76] This also accounts for his reduction of the illegitimately newborn to a non-entity, which is obviously morally problematic.

mitigating circumstances (if the guilty woman is presented as a 'fallen woman') or, conversely, as an exacerbation of the punishment (the public and repeated shaming of the whore). Kant is the first to attack the ability, even the *right*, of the law to judge infanticide, given its inability to 'legislate away' the shame that causes the crime. In making this last point, Kant argues implicitly that there can be no such thing as preventing infanticide, dealing a fatal blow to the basic idea behind the original prize question and hundreds of responses focusing on deterrence. And whereas infanticides in the public debate appear as either piteous or disgraceful, Kant's argument that they were acting out of a sense of 'sexual honour', which he likens moreover to military honour, endows them with an aura of thwarted decency, social doom and tragic inevitability. Kant's criticism that criminals are made by circumstances that the law then ignores in order to mete out punishment is not new: it is an argument well known to readers of Schiller's 'The Criminal of Lost Honour' ('Der Verbrecher aus verlorener Ehre', 1785), written at the height of the infanticide debate. What is new in Kant's argument is his application of this idea to *women*: specifically, to a group of women whose crime characterised them, in the minds of contemporaries, as either the classic exemplification or the utter repudiation of femininity and thus raised the issue of gender in new and unprecedented ways.

CRIMINALS OF LOST HONOUR? THE CASES OF DOROTHEA ALTWEIN AND JOHANNA CATHARINA HÖHN (WEIMAR, 1781 AND 1783)

In 1781, Dorothea Altwein stood trial for infanticide in the Duchy of Weimar. Hers was one of four infanticide cases judged by the court in Jena and, eventually, acted on by Weimar's sovereign, Duke Carl August, within only three years.[77] Altwein's death sentence of 31 March 1781[78] provides us with the following details: Margarethe Dorothea Altwein, a

---

[77] Those court records and official correspondence relating to these cases that are still extant have been republished by Rüdiger Scholz (*Das kurze Leben*) and Wahl respectively. Wahl's edition offers additional related material, Rüdiger Scholz the more reliable and accurate transcription, in which he also includes relevant details that Wahl omits, such as crossed-out passages and emphases indicated by underlining. In the following, citations of documents published in both will refer to Rüdiger Scholz's edition. Square brackets and other editorial interpolations are reproduced as in the original. For a discussion of the issue of infanticide in Weimar, see Wilson, 'Goethe, His Duke and Infanticide'.

[78] Cited in Rüdiger Scholz's transcription in *Das kurze Leben*, 116–23, and my translation. See also Scholz's brief summary of the case on 32–5. For a good overview of legal procedure and criminal trials in the eighteenth century, see Härter.

servant of unstated age,[79] bore a child out of wedlock on 11 February 1781. She testified that the father was one Abraham Eißmann, with whom she had slept twice. She was alone in the kitchen at the time of the birth, bore the child in a standing position, without help, and cut the umbilical cord herself. The child dropped to the stone floor. Afterwards she took it by both feet and smashed its head against the sharp corner of the kitchen wall, once the head and once the mouth, after which she threw the child into a washbasin filled with water. She had planned for months to kill the child by drowning it in the Ilm, and would have carried out this plan had she not been discovered immediately after the deed. Her stated reason for the murder was that her mother had threatened to disown her if she got pregnant.

For the Jena court, the case was open and shut. The fact that the child had made a sound akin to meowing indicated that it had been alive at birth, a suspicion confirmed by floating the child's lung, which indicated that it had drawn breath. By the defendant's own admission, she had intended to kill the child for a considerable period before it was born. The brutal manner of the killing may have had an influence at sentencing: the court recommended the ancient penalty of 'sacking',[80] adding that Carl August could, if he so desired, commute this sentence to a simple beheading.

Altwein's defence counsel mounted several counterarguments, all of which were rejected by the court. He denied intention to kill by stating that Altwein had been in such a state of stress and confusion immediately following the birth that she could not judge the consequences of her actions and so should not be held responsible.[81] This argument obviously echoes the discourse of the infanticide debate, which habitually portrayed women as unable to reason, confused, crazed with pain and unable to project into the future. The second part of the defence relies on an old wives' tale: Altwein's defender raised the possibility that the child was not viable since it

---

[79] Altwein's age is not mentioned in her death sentence. Rüdiger Scholz, so far the only researcher who has tried to locate biographical information about the Weimar infanticides, has found no record of her birth in the church records of her home town, which are extant in complete sequence from 1751 onward. If Altwein was born before 1751, this would have made her thirty years or older at the time of her trial (see Rüdiger Scholz, *Das kurze Leben*, 34, particularly n. 37).

[80] Sacking, being drowned in a sack, was the penalty for infanticide recommended in the *Carolina*, but had fallen out of use by the eighteenth century. In Roman antiquity, it was used primarily as a punishment for the murder of blood relatives. Often sacking involved being sewn into the sack with live animals (in ancient Rome usually a monkey, snake, cat and rooster, in Germany a dog, snake, cat and rooster). The symbolic meaning attributed to these animals is no longer known. See Gorgoni, van Dülmen, *Theater*, 123–4, and Evans, *Rituals*, 213–25, on the reduction of the variety of punishments between 1794 and 1839.

[81] 'Todesurteil gegen Dorothea Altwein', Rüdiger Scholz, *Das kurze Leben*, 118.

must have been premature. He based this claim on the defendant's testimony that she had slept with Eißmann twice, first when she had lost her virginity to him (and therefore could not have conceived) and the second time a mere thirty-three weeks before the birth.[82] This objection was countered by the court by the simple statement that they had no evidence that Altwein had not engaged in sexual activity prior to her affair with Eißmann.[83] The defence counsel's third argument was possibly the most serious: Altwein had confessed in fear of torture and had, for this reason, not only admitted killing her child, but also wildly exaggerated the manner of the killing. He pointed out that no blood had been found on the kitchen wall where Altwein had supposedly twice smashed her child's head, neither in the course of the official investigation nor, more importantly, by Altwein's employer, who entered the kitchen moments after the deed.[84] Altwein's defender concluded that the child's head wounds might very well have been caused by its fall onto the stone floor at birth. The fact that there was no blood on the wall moments after the killing took place was not disputed by the court and does indeed point to a grave discrepancy between Altwein's confession and the physical evidence available. The court, however, unilaterally dismissed this argument, merely stating, without further elaboration, that 'there are several possible reasons why no blood was visible on this spot',[85] and further argued 'that it makes no difference whether the child was killed by falling to the floor, or by being smashed against the wall, or by the water in the washbasin, since all three kinds of killing prove the defendant's intent to kill the child, as can be gleaned from the defendant's own confession …'.[86] This line of reasoning certainly documents a grave bias. Altwein's judges were quite content to leave the question of the missing blood unexplored, and to state that the manner in which the child had died *did not matter*. In a legal ruling, this is an astonishing conclusion. Not only does it sweep aside, without counterargument, the defence's objections that the baby's fall to the stone floor could have killed the child accidentally, it may very well indicate that the death sentence was handed down because Altwein had confessed 'intent to kill', regardless of whether or not she had actually carried out her plans.

---

[82] 'Todesurteil', 119.   [83] 'Todesurteil', 122.   [84] 'Todesurteil', 119.

[85] 'da mancherley Ursachen sich denken laßen, warum an diesem Orte vom Blute nichts wahrzunehmen gewesen' ('Todesurteil', 122).

[86] 'darauf aber, ob das Kind durch den Sturz auf die Erde, oder durch das Schlagen an die Wand, oder durch das Waßer im Keßel getödtet worden, nichts ankommt, da alle drey Arten der Tödtung von der Inquisitin in der Absicht, das Kind zu ermorden, [*eingefügt:*] ihrem Ge eigenen Geständnis … entnommen worden sind' ('Todesurteil', 122). On the role of the confession in eighteenth-century criminal trials, see chapter 4.

Altwein's judges also did not hesitate to cherry-pick which aspects of Altwein's testimony they chose to believe, and their decision in this regard was clearly not influenced by actual evidence. For example: they believed her confession that she had smashed the child's head against the wall, even though the physical evidence clearly contradicted this statement, and even though, in the final analysis, they claimed that the manner in which the child had died was beside the point. On the other hand, they disbelieved her testimony that she had lost her virginity to Eißmann, that she had only slept with him twice, and that the child must have been conceived the second time (since she believed it impossible for a virgin to conceive at first sexual contact). The court, clearly influenced by the same superstition, did not point out that the child might have been conceived at first intercourse. Instead, they simply presumed that there must have been a man before Eißmann, discounting Altwein's statement that he was the only man with whom she had ever been intimate.[87] This not only further damaged Altwein's reputation, it also, and crucially, dismissed the possibility that the child was premature and therefore might have died of natural causes. The two most sound foundations for a death-penalty ruling – that the child had lived and that Altwein had actually killed it, rather than merely intending to do so – were, in the end, based largely on the court's decision to disbelieve one part of Altwein's confession and believe another, which was, moreover, contradicted by available evidence.[88]

Perhaps it was this rather spurious manner of proceeding that led Carl August to commute the sentence,[89] not merely to beheading, which was the usual option that he had been suggestively offered in the ruling, but to life imprisonment and permanent banishment.[90] Altwein spent the next seventeen years imprisoned at hard labour in Bayreuth and was pardoned, although not permitted to return, in 1798.[91]

---

[87] 'daher die ~~Behauptung~~ Meinung des Defensors, daß aus dem erstern ... gepflogenen Beyschlaf keine Schwangerschaft entstehen können, um so weniger Aufmerksamkeit verdienet, als der Umstand, daß dieser Beyschlaf der ~~erstern~~ Inquisitin ersterer gewesen, nicht erwiesen ist' ('Todesurteil', 122).

[88] To avoid misunderstandings: my point here is not that Altwein was innocent, but that the court's standards of evidence and correctness of procedure must have been rather low. The only documentary evidence we have of this case is her death sentence, which supports this conclusion but not binding statements about other circumstances of the case, including Altwein's actual guilt or innocence.

[89] Carl August's reasons for commutation remain as unstated as the reasons for the court's decision why they considered the manner of the baby's death irrelevant: he merely cites 'verschiedene, auf die Beschafenheit des vorliegenden Falls und die dabey eintretende Umstände' ('Schreiben von Herzog Carl August an seine Regierung', Rüdiger Scholz, *Das kurze Leben*, 126–7, the quotation 126). Wahl reaches the conclusion that Carl August's decision was influenced by Voigt's essay (87, see below for further discussion).

[90] 'Schreiben von Herzog Carl August an seine Regierung', Rüdiger Scholz, *Das kurze Leben*, 126–7.

[91] See the correspondence between Chancellor Koppenfels and Duke Carl August in Rüdiger Scholz, *Das kurze Leben*, 134–6.

Two years after Altwein, Johanna Catharina Höhn, a twenty-four-year-old servant, went to trial for murdering her newborn. Shortly before the birth, she had openly displayed her belly to her employer, sufficient indication to the court that she had not concealed her pregnancy. This was a significant point in her favour since concealment of an illegitimate pregnancy was commonly considered an indication of 'intent to kill'. Minutes after giving birth on 11 April 1783, Höhn administered three stab wounds to the baby's throat. Unsure whether it was actually dead, she pushed its head into the bed straw. She confessed to the killing despite severe memory lapses. Unlike the Altwein case, in which the court had assumed premeditation, Höhn's judges ruled that she had committed her deed in a moment of panic. Possibly for this reason, they called for the milder form of death penalty, beheading.[92] This ruling was upheld by Carl August after consultation with his personal advisers, his 'Privy Council' (*Geheimes Consilium*), consisting of Jacob Friedrich Freiherr von Fritsch, Christian Friedrich Schnauss and Johann Wolfgang Goethe. Höhn was beheaded on 28 November 1783.[93]

The Höhn case once again shows up some irregularities of procedure: in her death sentence, which is simultaneously the presentation of the case to Carl August, her defence counsel is openly ridiculed.[94] The case also raises the question why Carl August upheld Höhn's death sentence whereas he had commuted Altwein's. Judging from the court's presentation of both cases to the duke – and ignoring, for the moment, its obvious bias –, Altwein's case was the more severe of the two. In the court's view, Höhn had killed her child in a moment of distress whereas Altwein had planned the murder for months; arguably, too, Altwein's method as described in her death sentence – smashing her child's head repeatedly against a stone wall – would have been considered the more gruesome of the two. And yet,

---

[92] See Rüdiger Scholz's summary of the case in *Das kurze Leben*, 10–17, and the documents published on 62–95.

[93] For the votes of the three councillors, see Rüdiger Scholz, *Das kurze Leben*, 81–7; Carl August's confirmation of the death sentence on 88.

[94] 'in general, an astute and conscientious judge will decide based on the testimony of expert physicians rather than the insinuations of [cut:] ~~chimeras of bold audacious assumption of garrulous~~ loquacious smooth-talking defence counsels' ('wie denn hierbey überhaupt ein kluger u. gewissenhafter Richter mehr / auf das Gutachten sachverständiger Ärzte, als auf die Vorbildungen [aus:] ~~Erscheinungen kühner verwegener vermuthung schwazhafter~~ wort- u. wisselreicher Defensoren anzusehen hat'; 'Todesurteil gegen Johanna Höhn', Rüdiger Scholz, *Das kurze Leben*, 72–9, the quotation 77). Wahl's edition of the same document does not include the crossed-out passages but instead edits the document to present a 'finished version', which amounts to a falsification of the original in that it conceals the court's obvious contempt for Höhn's defender (see 'Urteil des Jenaer Schöppenstuhls vom 25. September 1783', Wahl 98–101).

Altwein got away with her life and was later pardoned whereas Höhn was executed. Scholz has attributed this fact to political rather than judicial circumstances, explaining that Carl August's commutation of Altwein's sentence made it politically difficult for him to repeat this act of mercy in Höhn's case.[95] Instead, the duke presented his councillors with a suggestion to abolish the death penalty in *all* infanticide cases, which was voted down. The joint vote of Fritsch, Schnauss and Goethe to uphold the death penalty in general naturally resulted in the confirmation of Höhn's death sentence in particular.[96] There is a certain measure of support for Scholz's view that Carl August was cornered: both Fritsch and Schnauss mention Carl August's repeated commutation of sentences in previous infanticide cases in their votes,[97] and Schnauss does so in unmistakably critical, even sarcastic language.[98] It stands to reason that this may have resulted in a certain amount of pressure on the duke, whose motivation must ultimately remain

---

[95] Rüdiger Scholz, *Das kurze Leben*, 15, 38.

[96] Carl August's 'Reskript' of 13 May 1783 and the resulting votes, or rather Goethe's vote, have been hotly debated. Goethe's defenders such as Wahl, Baerlocher and Wittkowski, among others, attempt to shield Goethe from the charge of having supported a death sentence for an infanticide, in rather radical disparity with his touching depiction of Gretchen's plight in *Faust*. To do this, they insist that Fritsch, Schnauss and Goethe were not asked to pass sentence on Höhn directly, but merely to declare their opinions on the death penalty for infanticide *in general* (Baerlocher mentions this distinction obsessively in his description of the relevant documents on 341–55 and in his discussion of previous scholars' work; see 453–501 of his 'Nachwort'). Yet both Carl August in his 'Reskript' and Schnauss in his vote refer to Höhn directly (see the documents as published in Rüdiger Scholz, *Das kurze Leben*, 64–7 and 83–6 respectively, or in Wahl 93–5 and 104–6 respectively), making it impossible to argue that either Carl August or his advisers saw the Höhn case as unrelated to the general question. Everyone involved – Carl August as well as Fritsch, Schnauss and Goethe – was perfectly aware that a vote to retain the death penalty in general would result directly in a confirmation of the death sentence in Höhn's particular case. To claim that Goethe 'merely' voted to retain the death penalty in general, given that he could not possibly be unaware of the consequences of his vote for Höhn, is disingenuous: a difference that makes no difference is no difference. Even more surprising than the duration of this fairly insignificant debate is the fact that attempts to absolve Goethe have, at times, resulted in highly unprofessional work ranging from misrepresentations of the archival documents to *ad hominem* attacks. Baerlocher discredits his own work by heaping scorn upon scholars who have interpreted Goethe's involvement in the case differently (see Baerlocher, 'Anmerkungen', 'Goethes Schuld' and 'Nachwort'), and Wittkowski's venomous attack on some of these scholars disqualifies itself from serious discussion because of its vituperative language alone. For a more extensive discussion of this controversy, see Wilson, 'Goethe, His Duke and Infanticide'.

[97] 'Votum von Fritsch', Rüdiger Scholz, *Das kurze Leben*, 81–3: 'daß ja allemahl bey sich ergebenden Gründen zur Milderung des Schicksals der dadurch betroffenen Personen das Landes Herrliche Begnadigungs Recht eintreten können, auch mehrmahlen [*eingefügt:*] würcklich] eingetreten, folget, daß ich eigentlich keinen hinreichenden Veranlaßungs Grund zu einer anderweitigen Gesezgebung über diesen Punckt abzusehen vermag' (quotation 82).

[98] 'Votum von Schnauss', Rüdiger Scholz, *Das kurze Leben*, 83–6: after mentioning several 'vorhergegangenen Exempeln, daß die Kinder Mörderinnen nicht am Leben gestrafft worden', he continues: 'Nach den Gesetzen ist bekanntlich die Todes Strafe darauf verordnet, und solche ist auch bis in die neuern Zeiten der mehrern Aufklärung oder Empfindsamkeit, an dergl. Mißethätern vollstrecket,

a matter of speculation. Nevertheless, it is clear that both Fritsch and Schnauss judged the Höhn case in the context of other recent infanticide cases, Altwein's certainly among them, and that the passages in their votes referring to earlier cases served as rather blatant – if not, in Schnauss's case, outright disapproving – reminders of Carl August's inclination toward leniency. Thus these passages can reasonably be read as lending some credibility to Scholz's suspicion that Höhn was executed because Altwein was not.

Be that as it may: available archival documents in both cases show that judgments in actual infanticide cases in Carl August's Weimar can hardly be considered dispassionate.[99] Actual evidence, such as the presence or absence of blood, seems to have mattered little or not at all compared to the court's negative impression of 'loquacious and smooth-talking' defence counsels, whose arguments were dismissed out of hand in both cases. Most decisive, of course, would have been the court's impression of the defendant. Had she acted in a moment of panic or planned the crime? Was she a distraught woman frenzied by pain or a coldly scheming murderess? Most importantly: was she an honourable, if 'fallen', woman or a 'whore'? The debate about the degree of Altwein's sexual experience documents the importance of determining her *sexual character*, which was seen as directly related to motive. The criminal of lost honour, the woman motivated largely by shame, could only be a 'seduced' woman, not someone like Altwein, who stood accused not only of infanticide, but of repeated sexual experience with more than one man, a sure sign of depravity.

Commentators on both cases experienced considerable difficulty in deciding between these two alternatives, or even in applying the gender codes as they emerged from the contemporary infanticide debate to actual defendants. The reason for this is not the inevitably assumed rift between 'literature' and 'reality': there is good reason to assume that some writers describing real-life culprits owed much to the contemporary infanticide debate and its ideas on gender. Rather, these writers were directly confronted with an additional aspect that plays no part in either the contemporary infanticide debate or infanticide literature: the defendants' *class*. The ways in which, in their texts, class issues complicate the application of gender codes to Altwein and Höhn make extremely interesting reading.

---

vielfältig aber, wenn nur ein kleiner Umstand der Verbrecherin zustatten gekommen, sind solche begnadiget worden. Heut zu Tage, da man mit der Todes Strafe so sparsam umgehen will und zu hart findet, ein menschliches Geschöpf um eines einzeln Mords willen zu zernichten …' (quotation 84–5).

[99] The larger context of the understanding of legal and human rights in late eighteenth-century Weimar is extensively described, based on archival evidence, in Wilson, *Das Goethe-Tabu*.

One of those who read the Altwein case in the context of contemporary gender codes was Christian Gottlob Voigt, whose essay 'On the Prize Question: Which Are the Best Achievable Means to Prevent Infanticide?'[100] supposedly led to Carl August's commutation of Altwein's sentence and also later inspired his 1783 'Reskript' suggesting the abolition of the death penalty for infanticide. Voigt states at the outset that his essay was inspired by Altwein's murder, which he describes as follows:

How tranquil was this Sunday morning! how the sun of the heavens mirrored the ocean of serene reflection! – Shock and disgust abruptly blighted its purity.

Gossip at first, then confirmation told of a servant girl who gave birth today, but grasped her newborn at the first sign of life by his feet, smashing him against the wall

> so that his tender brains gushed down the bloody stones
> and whimpering softly, his innocent soul took wing.

Verily, the captured woman did not even deny having murdered for fear of shame.[101]

Voigt's essay, although describing an actual event that took place that very day, is obviously shaped by literary discourse. For one thing, the two stanzas describing the manner of the murder ('so that his tender brains gushed down the bloody stones ...') are a direct quotation from Klopstock's *Messias*.[102] For another, Voigt's statement that Altwein 'murdered for fear of shame' is factually incorrect – Altwein herself never cited such a motive, unless we count her statement that she feared being thrown out by her mother – ; it does, however, correlate in rather obvious ways with the motivation generally assumed by other contributors to the infanticide debate. As they did, Voigt sees shame as 'related to virtue', a clear sign of 'a most sincere chastity'. And chastity, he continues, is

a divine light shining even on the deed just committed, that penetrates posterity from paradise, and on whom ... would it have the most devastating effect if not on

---

[100] Voigt, 'Ueber die Preisfrage: Welches sind die besten ausführbaren Mittel, dem Kindermorde Einhalt zu thun?' Unpublished manuscript, 11 February 1781, printed in Wahl 56–60, in the following quoted as 'Manuskript'. The published version, entitled 'Ueber die Preisaufgabe: Welches sind die besten ausführbaren Mittel, dem Kindermord Einhalt zu thun? Den Chronologen mitgetheilt den 29. März 1781' (Wahl 60–8) is cited in the following as 'Preisaufgabe'.

[101] Voigt, 'Manuskript', 56: 'Wie ruhig war mir dieser Sonntagsmorgen! wie spiegelte sich Himmelssonne auf dem stillen Gedankenmeere! – Staunen und Abscheu trübte auf einmal seine Lauterkeit. / Erst Ruf, und bald Bestätigung erzälet von einer Dienstmagd, die heute gebar, aber ihren Neugebohrnen bei den ersten Zeichen des Lebens an den Füßen erfaßte, schleuderte wider die Mauern, / daß sein zartes Gehirn an blutigen Steinen herabrann, / und mit leisem Röcheln entflog die Seele der Unschuld. / Ja die Ergriffene läugnete gar nicht, aus Furcht der Schande gemordet zu haben.'

[102] Pointed out by Voigt himself in his annotation to the verses, note a, Wahl 56.

the creature defined entirely by weakness and imperfect virtue, and a creature utterly crushed now that Nature forces her to present the world with living proof of this imperfection?'[103]

This is more than a little reminiscent of Sara Sampson's distinction between 'proven virtue' and 'feeble virtue', and identical to many previous essays in its conclusion that 'feeble virtue', overwhelmed by 'shame', leads inevitably to what Voigt calls the 'tragedy' of infanticide.[104] In the published version he maintains this argument, claiming that 'fear of shame ... was once virtue, and chastity its origin ... A feeling of dishonour can often, in female creatures, escalate to the point of insanity ... – all these are precursors to the tragedy that is performed all too often!'[105] To Voigt, shame is the *sole* motivation for infanticide: 'The judicial documents relating to infanticide of an entire province, a considerable number, did not yield a single case that was not wholly founded on fear of shame.'[106] His line of reasoning corresponds precisely to that advanced in literary texts because he sees infanticide as *internally* motivated, entirely discounting external motivations such as fear of discovery, fear of punishment, even inability to raise the child.[107] Shame is a personal issue, an expression of humiliated virtue: it is the reason why Sara Sampson accepts her death, and the reason why Emilia Galotti pleads for hers. An unwed mother, Voigt argues, 'would not find anything in disgrace and shame than what she believes to be certain in any event [i.e. death], even if she does not commit the deed'.[108] In this, Voigt confirms the conclusion reached in infanticide poetry and bourgeois tragedies of compromised virtue: death is

---

[103] Voigt, 'Manuskript', 56–7: 'Ja wohl ist sie [die Schande] mit Tugend verwandt, wie die Ankündigung der Preisfrage sagt. Desto schwerer ists, mit dem wuchernden Unkraut nicht auch das edlere Kräutchen zu jäten. So wenig der Auswuchs am Stamme die Stammwurzel verlängern kann, so gewiß entquoll diese Frucht [*sic*; *recte*: Furcht?] der Schande, obschon in Richtung und Auffangung gefälscht, zuerst der ächtesten Schamhaftigkeit. Schamhaftigkeit, Übergang und Gränze zwischen Gut und Böse, sowohl wenn man abweicht, als wenn man wiederkommt, Gottesanker in unsrer Natur, hat nur an ihren Rechten verloren. Und ist sie, der Strahl Gottes auch auf frischer That, vom Paradies aus irgend auf Nachwelt durchdrungen, auf wen, bei welchem Erfolg soll sie wohl verzehrender wirken? Nicht erst Creatur, die ihrer ganzen Anlage nach schwach war bei reizbarer Tugend, und nun ganz darnieder liegt, wenn die Natur sie zwingt, einen lebenden Beweis davon selbst an die Welt auszuliefern?'
[104] Voigt, 'Manuskript', 57: 'welche Vorbereitung zum Trauerspiel!'
[105] Voigt, 'Preisaufgabe', 60: 'Furcht der Schande ... war Tugend im Anbegin. Schamhaftigkeit, aus der sie entsproß ... Gefül von Unehre wächst da oft in der weiblichen Kreatur bis zum Wahnsinn an ... – lauter Vorbereitung des Trauerspiels, das nur allzuoft gegeben wird!'
[106] Voigt, 'Preisaufgabe', 61: 'Kindermordsakten einer ganzen Provinz, in beträchtlicher Menge, ließen keinen Fall wahrnehmen, der sich nicht ganz auf Furcht der Schande gegründet habe.'
[107] If poverty were a main motive for infanticide, Voigt argues, married couples would be killing their newborns in inestimable numbers ('Manuskript', 57).
[108] Voigt, 'Preisaufgabe', 63: 'so fände sie in Schmach und Schande nichts anders, als was ihrer Meinung nach ohnehin gewiß ist, wenn sie auch die That unterläßt'.

the inevitable consequence of seduction for the 'fallen woman' *regardless of whether she kills the child*. From the moment her virtue is compromised, in thought or deed, she is lost.

Voigt's depiction of Altwein in his manuscript confronts us with an irreconcilable discrepancy of images: one the coldly scheming killer smashing her child's head against the wall, the other a blushingly demure innocent driven to her crime by dishonoured virtue. The latter idea surfaces briefly, probably under the influence of Voigt's essay and other contributions to the infanticide debate,[109] in the legal correspondence surrounding the cases of Altwein and Höhn. It may explain, in part, Carl August's commutation of Altwein's sentence, despite the violence of the crime, and it is discernible in his 'Reskript' of 13 May 1783 in which he suggested abolishing the death penalty for infanticide in general:

Consider the conditions leading to the deed, and how easily it may happen that the mind of a woman pregnant out of wedlock can be overwhelmed, during or shortly after birth, in a moment of weakness and stupor, overcome by fear of the inevitable shame that awaits her if her pregnancy becomes known, overcome also by the complexity of the difficulties arising from raising a child, compelled to the point where she first resolves and then abruptly carries out the unnatural decision to dispose of the unfortunate creature from whose existence all these miseries originate. Such considerations can hardly fail to add to the disgust that we feel for the crime itself a certain measure of compassion for the criminal, and provide us with a motivation to diminish her penalty.[110]

This view of the guilty woman as motivated by shame and 'compelled' to her deed, familiar from the infanticide debate, eventually clashed severely with opposing views of Altwein and Höhn as wanton women determined entirely by their sexual drives and utterly incapable of either rational thought or noble impulses, expressed – paradoxically – by Carl August

---

[109] Both Wahl, 'Einführung', 24–5 and commentary 87, and Baerlocher, 'Nachwort', 382, have claimed a direct influence of Voigt's essay on both Carl August and Goethe; see also Wilson, 'Goethe, His Duke and Infanticide'.

[110] 'Wenn man erwägt, unter was für Umständen die That verübt wird, und wie leicht es geschehen kann, daß das Gemüth einer [*eingefügt*:] unehelich schwangern] Weibes=Person, [*eingefügt*:] bey oder kurz nach ihrer Entbindung,] in einem Augenblicke der Schwäche und Betäubung, durch den Eindruck der Furcht [*eingefügt*:] vor] der sie, wenn ihre uneheliche Schwangerschaft bekannt würde, unausbleiblich erwartenden Schande und denen dabey aus der Belästigung mit einem Kinde für sie erwachsenden Beschwerlichkeiten übermeistert und zu Faßung, auch jählinger Ausführung des unnatürlichen Entschlußes, das unglückliche Geschöpf, von deßen Daseyn sie alle diese Übel zu besorgen hat, aus dem Wege zu reumen, hingerißen wird: So kann es nicht fehlen, daß diese Betrachtung nicht unter der Abscheu, den das Verbrechen selbst erweckt, einiges Mitleiden gegen die Verbrecherin mit mischen, und einen Bewegungs=Grund zu Milderung der Strafe an die Hand geben sollte' ('Reskript von Herzog Carl August an die Mitglieder seiner Regierung', Rüdiger Scholz, *Das kurze Leben*, 64–7, the quotation 65–6).

himself and members of his government. In brief: Voigt's *gendered* vision of Altwein as a 'fallen woman' collided with Carl August's and his councillors' image of Altwein's *class*. The topic under debate that demonstrates this discrepancy most clearly is the death penalty, and the reasons for this are, once again, both legal and literary. On the one hand, the death penalty was debated as a deterrent; on the other, this debate was clearly influenced by Voigt's idea – which also determines the outcome of contemporary bourgeois tragedies and contemporary infanticide poems – that death was inevitable because a 'fallen woman' would be unable to survive her own shame.

The death-penalty debate, as it now ensued between Carl August, his ministers and his advisers, was, to a considerable extent, driven by this clash between ideas of class and gender, by the presumed similarity or dissimilarity between characters like Altwein and Höhn on the one hand and characters like Lessing's Emilia and Stäudlin's Seltha on the other. The death sentence for Altwein, submitted to Carl August on 31 March 1781, suggests to him not only the *extent* to which he could show mercy – by commuting the sentence of sacking to a simple beheading – but also the *reasons* why he might do so. The defendant's fear of shame, for example, was deemed ineligible as a reason for clemency; on the other hand, the duke might consider her 'biological drives' and the fact that she belonged to a class of 'people of feeble insights', people 'whom nature had endowed in far greater measure with animal drives than with the power of reflection' and who were, for this reason, singularly unimpressed by 'the threat of harsh punishments'.[111] Carl August himself employed the class argument, whether diplomatically or not, in his 'Reskript': infanticides, he wrote, commonly belonged to what he called 'the lowest class of the rabble'; they were people whose minds were 'unused to reflection' and who were consequently unable to think beyond the moment or project into the future. On such people, he concluded, the death penalty would make little or no impression, leading him to doubt its efficacy as a deterrent[112] and to advocate, like some participants in the infanticide debate, methods of public shaming, such as

---

[111] 'Todesurteil gegen Dorothea Altwein': 'mithin bey Personen, denen die natur den thierischen Triebe weit stärker als die Überlegungs Kraft zugetheilet hat'; 'so wenig als die Furcht vor ~~frem~~der verdienten Hurenstrafe, nach Strenge der Rechte, eine Milderungs Ursach abgeben könne, wofür aber die gnädigste Landesherrschaft, in Betracht die Triebe der Natur und die eingewurzelten Vorurtheile durch Androhung ~~durch hartes Strafen~~ harter Strafen, ~~sich~~ bey Menschen von schwachen Einsichten sich nicht ausrotten laßen …' (Rüdiger Scholz, *Das kurze Leben*, 120, 123).

[112] Carl August's argumentation here is rather convoluted, but revealing enough to deserve a full quotation. 'Wir glauben, Uns nicht zu irren, wenn Wir die Ursache davon, daß die an denen Kinder=Mörderinnen vollstreckte Todes=Strafen den sich davon versprochenen Effect, in Ansehung

'branding' and public exposure of the culprit.[113] His councillor Fritsch employed the same reasons to argue the exact opposite, namely that 'nothing but the fear of retribution [i.e. the death penalty] would deter the class of people among whom this crime occurs the most frequently, and for whom even a life full of misery and shame always remains a desirable life'.[114] The efficacy of the death penalty as a deterrent – on its face a legal issue – thus occurred before a canvas that displays ideas of gender, as expressed in literature, at war with the social concept of class. The culprit's gender, her 'femininity', was defined by the extent to which she was able to embrace death *willingly*; her class was seen as the reason why she would not. Support of or opposition to the death penalty for infanticide hinged upon the all-important question whether the real-life infanticide was capable of experiencing the noble impulses of the women as child-killers in poetry who 'willingly bleed' and 'gladly atone / Upon the scaffold'. It hinged upon the question whether the guilty mother was a 'criminal of lost honour', that is, a woman capable of being motivated by shame: a shame that, in Voigt's argument, *inevitably* results in the death of the seduced woman, regardless of whether or not she is guilty of child-murder. This pre-emptive death of shame is also a literary motif: it is the noble suicide of a vulnerable virtuous girl to *avoid* seduction; it is Sara Sampson attributing her death to her own 'feeble virtue' rather than Marwood's poison; it is Emilia Galotti pleading for the dagger in order to escape her otherwise inevitable seduction by the prince. These were the images complicating life-and-death decisions in real-life infanticide cases, in Weimar and, most likely, elsewhere. Only the infanticide's class could offset her gender, as defined in poetry, drama and the unintentionally literary essays of the reformist infanticide debate. Only her redefinition as practically subhuman – ruled by her sexuality, incapable

---

der Abhaltung anderer von ähnlichen Übelthaten, nicht hervorgebracht, darinne suchen, daß, da die eines Kinder=Mordes sich schuldig machende Weibes=Personen gemeiniglich zur niedrigsten Claße des Pöbels gehören, der Eindruck, welchen das Beyspiel einer Hinrichtung auf die zum Nachdenken nicht gewöhnte Gemüther dieser Art von Menschen macht, mit so viel Schrecknißen derselbe auch anfänglich begleitet seyn mag, dennoch nur so lange, als die fürchterliche Scene selbst ihnen in die Sinne fällt, oder doch nicht viel länger, dauert, und in kurzer Zeit bey ihnen die unglückliche Stunde der Versuchung zu einem ähnlichen Verbrechen kommt, die als dann in ihrer vollen Kraft auf sie würckende Furcht vor der Schande und andern Beschwerlichkeiten nicht mehr überwiegen kan, Hofnung, diesen Übeln zu entgehen, gereizt fühlen, fast immer eher vollbracht ist, ehe sich das entferntere Bild der allenfalß zu befürchten habenden Todes=Strafe ihrem Gemüthe darstellt' ('Reskript von Carl August', Rüdiger Scholz, *Das kurze Leben*, 66).

[113] 'Reskript', Rüdiger Scholz, *Das kurze Leben*, 67.

[114] 'Votum von Fritsch': 'daß nichts als die Furcht vor der WiederVergeltung diejenige Classe von Menschen, in welcher dieses Verbrechen am häufigsten vorkömmt, welchen auch ein schmachvolles elendes Leben gemeiniglich ein immer wünschenswerthes Leben bleibt, von deßen Begehung abzuhalten vermögend sey' (Rüdiger Scholz, *Das kurze Leben*, 81).

of shame or the most basic reflection, too simple-minded to fear death (Carl August) or, conversely, desperately clinging to her dirty life at all costs (Fritsch) – could expunge the image of the woman as child-killer of poetry, who 'hurried gladly to extinguish' her shame in death, and the woman as child of drama, who wilts away, a plucked flower,[115] at the mere thought of seduction.

---

[115] The image of the plucked flower – particularly roses, signifying love, and lilies, signifying innocence, recurs frequently in both domestic tragedies and infanticide poetry. Two examples of many are Emilia Galotti's final words to her father, referring to his killing of her: 'Eine Rose gebrochen, ehe der Sturm sie entblättert' (Lessing, *Emilia Galotti*, 465) and Luise's final words to her executioner: 'Henker! Kannst Du keine Lilie knicken?' (Schiller, 'Die Kindsmörderin', 21).

CHAPTER 6

The female self: poisoners

THE SELF-EVIDENT AND EVIDENCE: CRIMINOLOGISTS
AND PSYCHOLOGISTS ON POISON AND GENDER

Women and poison have long been thought of as elective affinities: poison
is presumed to be the quintessential woman's weapon, and a predilection
for murder by poison an integral part of a female gender identity. The
chorus of consent on this issue has included voices from so many fields –
criminology, sexology, psychology, philosophy and literature – and
resounded, although not unopposed, for so long – from Suetonius and
Tacitus to the late twentieth century[1] – that most writers as of the late
nineteenth century have taken the link between poison and femininity to be
self-evident. In his *Criminal Psychology* (1898), Hans Gross claimed that

it is well known that poison murder is predominantly committed by women ... All
kinds of murder require courage, willpower and physical strength, poison murder
alone does not necessitate any of these characteristics, and since women possess
none of them, they automatically murder by poison. There is nothing strange or
remarkable about this, it follows logically from female characteristics familiar to us
all. Thus it makes sense, when in doubt regarding a murder by poison, to suspect a
woman in the first instance and a weakly, effeminate man in the second.[2]

Ten years later, Gross was echoed by the jurist Erich Wulffen in his
monumental *Psychology of the Criminal* (1908):

All criminologists agree that murder by poison is predominantly committed by
women. Its secrecy, combined with the cunning employed to entice the victim to

---

[1] See the literature and discussion in Weiler 1–3.
[2] 'Dass der Giftmord vorwiegend von Frauen begangen wird, ist bekannt ... Zu jedem Morde gehört
aber Muth, Thatkraft und physische Stärke, nur beim Giftmord ist keines dieser Momente nothwen-
dig, und da das Weib keines der drei besitzt, so kommt sie ganz von selbst zum Giftmord – daran ist
weder etwas Absonderliches, noch etwas Auffallendes, es gibt sich von selbst aus den Jedermann
bekannten Eigenschaften der Frau. Deshalb wird man auch hier im Zweifel bei einem vorliegenden
Giftmord vorerst nach einer Frau und dann nach einem schwächlichen, weibischen Mann fragen'
(Gross 479–80). See also Hallissy's discussion of these ideas throughout literature, 6 and 11.

154

swallow the poisoned drink, in and of themselves correspond to the female character,[3]

which he further defines as follows:

It is true that women tend more towards dishonesty, deceit, lies and hypocrisy than men. These are their strongest weapons, just as men's strongest weapons are their logic, their physical strength and their willpower. Women love cunning and intrigue, which indicates clearly their awareness of their own frailty. Nature has bred these characteristics in women in the course of millennia of social subordination.[4]

Two basic ideas emerge: first, that most poison murders are committed by women – which is statistically untrue – and second, that women's preference for poison murder is rooted in feminine 'nature', that it is, in other words, an integral part of the female self. Both ideas are presented as too self-evident to require any kind of substantiation, and both have turned out to be astonishingly resilient. As late as 1964, Robert Stemmle blamed women for 80 per cent of all poison murders and explained this with a female partiality for the 'most perfidious and basest' of all crimes.[5] Five years later, Hildegard Damrow implicitly echoed Gross's distinction between valiant masculine and furtive feminine criminality in stating that 'only in very rare exceptions do women appear as robbers. On the other hand, hardly ever does a man commit murder by poison, whereas women have mixed poisons since the days of Lucrezia Borgia and the Marquise de Brinvilliers.'[6] And as recently as the year 2000, Bolte and Dimmler defined poison murder as a 'feminine art form' and proclaimed that 'to commit murder, women predominantly reach for poison'.[7]

---

[3] 'Dass der Giftmord vorwiegend von Frauen begangen wird, darüber sind alle Kriminalisten einig. Seine Heimlichkeit, verbunden mit Anwendung von List, um das Opfer zum Trinken des vergifteten Trankes zu bringen, entsprechen schon an und für sich dem weiblichen Charakter' (Wulffen, *Psychologie des Verbrechers*, II 266).

[4] 'Richtig ist, dass das Weib zur Unaufrichtigkeit, zur Verstellung, Lüge und Heuchelei mehr neigt als der Mann. Es sind dies ihre starken Waffen, wie dem Manne seine Logik, seine physischen Kräfte, seine Tatkraft. Das Weib liebt die List, die Intrige, alles Anzeichen ihres Schwächegefühls. Die Natur hat ihnen im Laufe der Jahrtausende durch ihre soziale Stellung diese Eigenschaften angezüchtet' (Wulffen, *Psychologie des Verbrechers*, II 263).

[5] Robert Stemmle, *Der neue Pitaval* (1964), cited in Linder and Schönert 243: 'Ihm ist der Giftmord das "heimtückischste und gemeinste" Verbrechen, das kaum im Affekt, sondern "fast stets" mit kaltblütiger Vorbereitung und Überlegung verübt werde.' Stemmle may have based his estimate on that of the criminologist Robert Heindl, who also calculated the ratio of women amongst poison murderers to be 80 per cent (in 1926); Georg Buschan claimed in 1928 that two-thirds of all poisonings were committed by women. For sources and discussion, see Weiler 2–3.

[6] 'Als Räuberinnen treten Frauen nur in ganz seltenen Ausnahmen auf. Auf der anderen Seite gibt es kaum einen Mann, der einen Giftmord begehen würde, dafür aber seit den Tagen der Lukrezia Borgia und der Marquise von Brinvilliers immer wieder Giftmischerinnen' (Damrow 16).

[7] Bolte and Dimmler 316: 'Um zu morden, greifen Frauen mehrheitlich zu Gift.' Their chapter on Gesche Gottfried is entitled: 'Gesche Gottfried and Murder by Poison as a Feminine Art Form' ('Gesche Gottfried und der Giftmord als weibliche Kunstform'), 19–91.

Objections can clearly be made, and have been made, to some of these ideas, not least amongst them the valorisation of 'masculine' kinds of murder as ennobled by courage, willpower and physical strength. Monika Frommel has rightly pointed out that the glorification of open attack is part of a warlike culture that considers it normal to solve problems violently,[8] to which Inge Weiler has added that murder, by definition a cowardly act, can never constitute a heroic deed, no matter how it is committed.[9] Criminal statistics throughout three centuries, in direct contradiction to the wide-spread claim that most poison murders are committed by women, attribute only half or fewer than half of all poison murders to female perpetrators. Even *Der neue Pitaval*, the very publication that helped define poisoning as a 'woman's crime', documents no female majority amongst perpetrators: of the fifty poison murders related, twenty-four were committed by men, twenty by women, and six by teams of accomplices involving at least one person of each gender.[10] The assumed female majority amongst poisoners may simply be due to a gross misreading of proportionality. The percentage of poisonings committed by women, assumed to range between 40 and 50 per cent, is significantly higher than women's historical participation in violent crime overall, which is assumed to fall between 10 and 20 per cent.[11] Thus it may be, paradoxically, women's predominant *innocence* of violent crime, coupled with a poison murder statistic that outstrips their other violent activity by comparison (but that is still lower than that of men), that has saddled them with a reputation as 'natural poisoners'. And while there is no objective substantiation of the 'self-evident' link between poison and female 'nature', there is much evidence to indicate that women have historically committed poison murder more often than other kinds of murder simply because they had a practical monopoly on food preparation until deep into the twentieth century.[12]

To explain the female 'predilection' for poison with opportunity rather than sexual character, to set evidence against what appears to be self-evident, is to contest one of the most tenacious myths about female criminals in particular and about women in general. The link between the two has been established by criminologists and psychologists throughout the nineteenth and early twentieth

---

[8] Monika Frommel, 'Tötungsdelikte', citation and discussion in Weiler 109.

[9] Weiler 108: 'Der Mord als solcher ist, ganz gleich welchen Mittels sich der Täter bedient, kaum je eine heroische Handlung, sondern in aller Regel eine feige Tat.'

[10] See the statistics offered in Linder and Schönert, 321.

[11] On crime statistics, see Wetzell and the report 'Gewalthandlungen und Gewaltbetroffenheit von Frauen und Männern' published by the Bundesministerium für Familie; see also Weiler 1–109; Herx; Niehaus, 'Die Figur', 155.

[12] Presented and discussed by Schnabel-Schulte, particularly 196.

centuries, who have attributed the same 'gender characteristics'[13] to female criminals and women in general, among them cruelty, immorality, vanity, dishonesty, greed, malice, self-indulgence, nefariousness, affectability, guile and an excess of emotionality which is often equated with a lack of moral inhibition.[14] This equation of criminal and 'normal' (by which most criminologists mean: law-abiding) women also explains the blatant disregard of available statistics on women and crime. Statistical evidence of women's low criminality is swept aside by the philosophical conviction that criminal behaviour, for women, is normal. A similar logic as that dominating the discussion of women's criminality in general can be applied to murder in particular: the perception of the female self as quintessentially murderous may well account for the otherwise puzzling discrepancy between women's historically rare appearance as murderesses and their widespread discursive representation as natural-born killers.[15]

Given the tenacity of this image, it may be worth reiterating the conclusions that Liselotte Herx had already reached in 1937:

1. At no point in history was there a clear majority of female poisoners over male.
2. Characteristics that are commonly considered 'typical' for both poisoners and women (hypocrisy, cunning, secretiveness, intrigue etc.) do not apply to female poisoners to a greater degree than male, or to women to a greater degree than men. Poisoners are also not more cowardly, deceitful, or hypocritical than other murderers. Frequently, other murderers also do not confront their victims directly, but attack them unawares.
3. Poisoners are not made by gender but by opportunity: women, who were, until recently, nearly exclusively responsible for food preparation, constituted one historical group with increased opportunity for this crime; physicians and apothecaries constituted another.[16]

To follow Herx's lead means to acknowledge that the criminological and psychological discussion of female criminality and female 'normality' has been deeply infiltrated by ideas that are more at home in the realm of gendered myths than that of science. Nowhere is this more apparent than in the literature on female poisoners. The history of writing on 'venomous women' is, as Hallissy already notes in her title, a history of fear of the female.[17] The fear of 'female' deceitfulness as an integral part of poison

---

[13] For a discussion of contemporary 'gender characteristics' as conceptualised for 'normal' women, see Cocalis; Dietrick; Hausen; Duden; Dotzler; Volker Hoffmann.

[14] For a more extensive discussion of these ideas, see chapter 1.

[15] See the discussion and literature in Weiler 27, 84–7.

[16] Herx; see also discussion of her text and conclusions in Weiler 106–9.

[17] Hallissy, *Venomous Woman: Fear of the Female in Literature.*

murder is motivated not only by the secrecy of the method, but also by the presumed intimacy between poisoner and victim. Poison is rarely or never administered to strangers, but to parents, children, lovers, husbands, or friends, and this group of nearest and dearest also constitutes the classic victims of murderesses in general, whereas men tend to kill more strangers.[18] More visceral fears of the female emerge in the common association between poison and witchcraft;[19] poisoning wells, as will be remembered, was a specialty of witches. That poisoning comes naturally to women seems indicated even in biblical lore: the very first recorded interaction between female and male involved 'a woman giving a man something dangerous to eat'.[20] Thus writings about poisoners and poison murder are subject to a strange kind of metonymic slippage; they focus more on the 'character' of *woman* than that of the female poisoner, they try to solve the mystery of femininity rather than that of motive, and their investigation of the crime involves, more often than not, the study of the female self.

SELF-DELUSION: LITERATI, LAWYERS AND PHYSICIANS ON POISON AND CLASS

Der neue Pitaval, which appeared between 1842 and 1890, has made a lasting contribution to the history of writing about poison murder in Germany and its interpretation as a quintessentially female crime.[21] Not only does *Pitaval* commit fifty poison murder cases to public memory (which represent nearly 10 per cent of the 524 cases recorded in its sixty volumes), it was also the first to classify them, both by historical importance and by social class. None of the many infamous female poisoners assembled here – including Anna Maria Günther, Helene Jegado, Marie Jeanneret[22] and Christiane

[18] Pointed out by many, including Hallissy xii; Niehaus, 'Die Figur', 156.
[19] A decree of King Louis XIV of France in July 1682 defined poisoning as 'magic by natural means'; citation and discussion in Niehaus, 'Die Figur', 158.
[20] Hallissy 15; see also her chapter 'Mother Eve and Other Death-Dealers', 15–58.
[21] The nineteenth-century *Pitaval* collection capitalised on the success of *Causes célèbres et intéressantes* (22 vols., 1735–45), the original collection of criminal case studies by the French attorney François Gayot de Pitaval (1673–1743), translated into German by François Richer in 1772–88, edited by Friedrich Niethammer and preceded by Friedrich Schiller's much-cited foreword. *Pitaval* stories were written by jurists, based on actual court records, with the intention of allowing non-jurists insight into legal practice; they offered legal facts and psychological insights into the mind of the criminal and provided a public which was at that point excluded from the trial with details of the case. For an excellent overview of the *Pitaval* tradition, see Weiler 14–21; Schönert has offered a genre analysis of *Pitaval* stories in his essay 'Zur Ausdifferenzierung des Genres "Kriminalgeschichten'"; see also Linder's article 'Deutsche Pitavalgeschichten in der Mitte des 19. Jahrhunderts'.
[22] For a brief description of her case (Geneva 1868), see Kohut 162–71.

Ruthardt,[23] among many others – can hold a vial to the four undisputed Queens of Poison Murder: the French aristocrat Marie-Madeleine Marquise de Brinvilliers (1630–76),[24] the patrician privy councillor's widow Charlotte Ursinus (1760–1836),[25] the domestic servant Anna Margaretha Zwanziger (1760–1811)[26] and the lower-middle-class housewife Gesche Margarethe Gottfried. This 'quadriga of poisoners',[27] already isolated from all others, are further subdivided in two ways that are related yet distinct: they are grouped by class, with the 'aristocratic' poisoners Brinvilliers and Ursinus juxtaposed with the 'democratic' poisoners Zwanziger and Gottfried, and they are assigned a class-based *self*. Character, in this argumentation, is inescapably linked with class; nobility of birth is synonymous with nobility of motive:

Brinvillier [sic] and Ursinus were diabolical characters, one might say: the aristocrats among poisoners; whereas she [Zwanziger] is the democrat … Brinvillier … destroyed and annihilated the lives of others from on high, with scornful pride; similarly Ursinus … Her [Ursinus's] ghastly deeds, however, contain a trace of greatness for this very reason. She flouted all that is most sacred and dearest to humankind. Zwanziger exacted revenge, but it was the revenge of a vulgar and deeply slighted nature, that of an embittered soul. There was nothing diabolical in her nature, her crime was merely the product of a failed life, of a worm that is stepped on, which, in the agony of being squelched, accumulates and spurts poison in order to torment others in turn. She had neither the courage nor the suppleness of soul to bellow out the scornful laughter

---

[23] For a more extensive discussion of her case, see chapter 4. By far the most important source on this case is the lengthy description, analysis and transcription of court records and press accounts in Linder and Schönert. See also Kohut 119–22; Moser (1861) 164–70.

[24] On the Marquise de Brinvilliers, see, among others: Friedrich Niethammer III 3–102; Naso; Kohut 54–65; Hitzig and Häring II 104–60; Naish 72–5. The lengthy Wikipedia entry on her is the clearest sign of the extent to which she has entered the popular imagination; see http://de.wikipedia.org/wiki/Brinvilliers (last accessed 15 August 2007).

[25] For the Ursinus case, see Hitzig and Häring II 161–217; Kohut 94–104; and Stephany. Famous fictionalisations of the case include the anonymously published and purportedly autobiographical *Bekenntnisse einer Giftmischerin, von ihr selbst geschrieben,* which appeared in the year of Ursinus's arrest and has been variously attributed to Paul Ferdinand Friedrich Buchholz and Friederike Helene Unger (see Spokiene). Häring, one of the *Pitaval* editors, turned Geheimrätin Ursinus into 'Geheimrätin Lupinus' ins 1852 novel *Ruhe ist die erste Bürgerpflicht*, published under his pen name Willibald Alexis.

[26] See Hitzig and Häring II 218–55; Kohut 104–13; Feuerbach, *Aktenmäßige Darstellung*, I 1–53. Gribble retells the story without citing his sources and with many details omitted and others of unknown provenance added (257–88). Like Brinvilliers, Zwanziger has reached sufficient fame to be granted a Wikipedia entry; see http://de.wikipedia.org/wiki/Anna_Margaretha_Zwanziger (last accessed 15 August 2007).

[27] 'Viergespann der Giftmischerinnen', Hitzig and Häring II 243 (the term is Häring's).

of Hell; she was a crawler, one who only ever laughed hoarsely, inwardly, secretly.[28]

Thus the Great Four were turned into an opposition of pairs: the aristocrats Brinvilliers and Ursinus as great, demonic and fearsome she-devils, the low-born Zwanziger and Gottfried as vulgar, base and malicious worms. Type 1 is further characterised as well-born and -bred, beautiful, endowed with passion, *esprit* and demonic powers, surrounded by mystery, and inspired to murder by a great passion; Type 2 as low, ugly, repulsive, badly educated, jealous, hypocritical, egotistical, petty, cringingly obeisant and murdering for contemptible motives.[29] This twofold classification became the proto- and archetype of the female poisoner for over a hundred years; there is almost no murder case by poison described in subsequent legal, literary, medical, criminological or psychological writing that does not refer to these four cases or even treat them at length.[30] The psychology of the female poisoner, as developed by criminologists, criminal psychologists and legal writers between 1890 and 1930, is based almost entirely on the *Pitaval*'s juxtaposition.[31] And it has endured well beyond: Hans-Joachim Schiche apparently credited the *Pitaval* model with sufficient scientific substance to accept it as the foundation of his medical dissertation 'On the Psychopathology of Four Famous Poison Murderesses from the Pitaval', which he submitted to the University of Munich in 1954.[32]

The pervasiveness of the class-as-character argument that pits the 'aristocrats' against the 'democrats', the 'great' against the 'base' criminal is not only documented by its survival into subsequent psychological, legal and

[28] 'Die Brinvillier und die Ursinus waren diabolische Naturen, gleichsam die Aristokratinnen unter den Giftmischerinnen, diese ist die Demokratin … Die Brinvillier … zerstörte und vernichtete das Leben der Andern von ihrer Höhe herab, mit dem Hohn des Stolzes; ähnlich … die Ursinus … Ihre gräßlichen Thaten haben aber eben deshalb eine großartige Beimischung. Sie setzte sich über Alles hinweg, was dem Menschen am heiligsten und theuersten ist. Die Zwanziger übte das Werk der Rache, aber die Rache einer gemeinen, tief gekränkten Natur, einer durchaus erbitterten Seele. Das Diabolische war nicht in ihrer Natur, es war nur das Product eines verfehlten Lebens, der getretene Wurm, der, unter den Qualen des Zertretenwerdens, Gifte in sich sammelt und ausspritzt, um Andern wieder Qualen zu bereiten. Zum Hohngelächter der Hölle hat sie nicht Muth, nicht Elasticität der Seele genug; eine Schleicherin, die nur heiser, innerlich, bei sich lachte' (Hitzig and Häring II 249–50).
[29] See the discussion in Weiler 4, 9, 31–3; Niehaus, 'Die Figur', 157–64.
[30] For further literature, see Weiler 21–2, 95–7.
[31] See the discussion of Krauss's and Wulffen's work and much other literature in Weiler; the reference to Krauss and Wulffen 95.
[32] Hans-Joachim Schiche, 'Zur Psychopathologie vier berühmter Giftmörderinnen aus dem Pitaval' (discussion in Niehaus, 'Die Figur', 159; Linder and Schönert 247). Schiche explains the crimes of all four women with a mixture of character defects and sexual frustration: 'Das Gemeinsame des Mordantriebs liegt in dem Konflikt, der in allen vier Fällen durch die ungünstigen Eheverhältnisse heraufbeschworen wurde. Dieses sexuelle Unbefriedigtsein führte zu sexuellen Ersatzhandlungen' (37).

medical literature, but also in the fact that relatively few scholars on the Famous Four have written about anything *else*. Other intriguing commonalities linking these cases have remained virtually unexplored. Both Ursinus and Zwanziger have been accused, for example, of an exaggerated and unhealthy sentimentality that is attributed, in both cases, to their reading of maudlin literature (Goethe's *Werther* figures prominently in both cases).[33] The destructive role assigned to sentimental reading, which functions here as a contributing factor to murder, has never been followed up, although the obvious parallels with the contemporary discourse on the education of 'normal' women would certainly suggest this to be a fruitful line of inquiry. Another interesting but so far largely ignored aspect is the theme of diminished responsibility, which appears in all of the German cases.[34] The theory advanced in this context was that the culprits may have been subject to an uncontrollable impulse to poison,[35] a diagnosis based on the latest psychological research available at the time. However, both the courts and contemporary commentators rejected this argument out of hand as setting a dangerous precedent, fearing, as was clearly expressed at Gottfried's trial, that judges would have to 'call in the doctor for help at *every* crime'.[36] And yet, it has occurred to few scholars to reread these trials as early test-cases for the (still ongoing) struggle between medical/psychiatric and legal/retributive arguments.[37] Finally, the mere existence of

---

[33] Ursinus read Goethe's *Werther* and purportedly over-identified with Lotte because she shared her first name (Hitzig and Häring II 199). Zwanziger read Goethe's *Werther*, Lessing's *Emilia Galotti* and Richardson's *Pamela*; these books are blamed for stifling her true feelings by smothering them with assumed and fake sentiments (see Feuerbach, *Aktenmäßige Darstellung*, I 35–6; Hitzig and Häring II 228). Reading novels is also amongst Gesche Gottfried's self-confessed sins (Hitzig and Häring II 330).

[34] Zwanziger, presented with poison in the course of her interrogation, trembled violently with desire to touch it and reportedly stated shortly before execution that her death was a blessing for humanity because she would not have been able to leave off poisoning (related in Feuerbach, *Aktenmäßige Darstellung*, I 51; Hitzig and Häring II 253–4). See also Voget's diagnosis of his client with 'giftmordsüchtige Monomanie', on the basis of which he claimed diminished responsibility (*Die Giftmörderin*, 90–2). Fourteen years after this case, the defender of Christiane Ruthardt, executed for poisoning her husband in 1845, advanced the same defence on her behalf (Linder and Schönert 312).

[35] For example, in Hitzig and Häring II 253 (Zwanziger) and 351 (Gottfried).

[36] 'Wenigstens wird der Richter, wofern er nicht etwa bei *jedem* Verbrechen den Arzt zu Hülfe rufen will, doch nur dann Veranlassung haben, wenn die Handlung des Inquisiten … als so psychisch unerklärlich erscheint, daß er fast nothgedrungen annehmen muß (f.24), der Mensch habe nicht bloß unter somatischen *Einwirkungen* gehandelt …, sondern nach *absolut* physischen Gesetzen.' Voget not only published his own defence brief of Gottfried, in which he pleaded diminished responsibility based on addiction to the act of poisoning, but also the court's rejection and grounds for rejection of this defence; the quotation is taken from this document, published in Voget, *Die Giftmörderin*, 124 (emphases original).

[37] A notable exception is Christian Marzahn's article, which has splendidly accomplished this for the case of Gesche Gottfried.

diminished responsibility claims, at a time when they were still highly unusual, indicates that the motive, in at least three of these cases, was considered inadequate to explain the crimes. Had it not been simply swept aside by the class-as-character argument, we might suspect that finding a credible motive would have become a virtual quest in the lore of the Famous Four. Intriguingly, all of them offered their own views on the matter: Brinvilliers wrote a 'Confession';[38] Ursinus a document in her own defence, for which she underwent legal training;[39] Zwanziger a lengthy autobiography, from which all accounts of her case quote liberally,[40] and Gesche Gottfried extensive letters about her life and crimes, which later served as the basis for her defence counsel's two-volume biography.[41] These are all texts that might well be read as early examples of what later came to be called *Täterliteratur* (literature authored by perpetrators). And despite all these intriguing possibilities, the *Pitaval*'s original contention that class is character and that only character can 'explain' these crimes has, at least so far, proven virtually insurmountable to later interpreters of these cases.

The class-as-character argument, which has seemed to answer, or at least suppress, all other questions, is established in the *Pitaval*'s analysis of pre-crime biography. Three of the 'quadriga of poisoners', what we might call the 'German triumvirate', are presented as guilty of a social crime long before they reach for the poison vial: they stand accused of wanting to rise 'above their stations'. Even the well-heeled Charlotte Ursinus supposedly planned a suicide for no reason beyond 'appearing interesting, more elevated, more educated, more transfigured than the masses surrounding her'.[42] Anna Margaretha Zwanziger's series of poisonings, which mostly targeted wives of men she wished to marry, are easily explained by her loss of

---

[38] Friedrich Niethammer III 50–1; Hitzig and Häring II 145.   [39] Hitzig and Häring II 210.

[40] On Zwanziger's autobiography, see above all Feuerbach, *Aktenmäßige Darstellung*, I 32; Hitzig and Häring II 227: 'Zum Ueberfluß, und allerdings eine Curiosität bei Verbrecherinnen aus ihrem Munde, schrieb sie noch eine *Autobiographie*, in der Zwischenzeit vom Schluß der Untersuchung bis zur Publication des Urtheils. Sie ist 18 enggeschriebene Bogen stark, keine Beichte wie die der Brinvillier, sondern ein Versuch, die Greuel ihres lüderlichen und lasterhaften Wandels zu beschönigen und sich, nicht zu rechtfertigen, aber interessant zu machen' (emphasis original).

[41] Voget claims to have transcribed many of her letters and her autobiographical statements to him verbatim.

[42] 'Es war nichts als die Lust interessant zu erscheinen, höher, gebildeter, verklärter dazustehen, als die große Masse, die sie umgab' (Hitzig and Häring II 198). See also the motives attributed to Gesche Gottfried for writing her autobiography: 'Zu Hülfe kam ihm hierbei [Voget, in the process of writing his book on his client] eine Autobiographie, welche die Gottfried, wol vorzüglich aus dem Motiv der Eitelkeit, in ihrem Gefängnisse zu schreiben bewogen wurde. Sie selbst wünschte, daß ihre Geschichte geschrieben und dem Publicum bekannt gemacht würde, sie selbst trug dies ihrem Defensor auf ... so gab sie daneben doch auch der schmeichelnden Hoffnung Raum, daß man sie etwas besser und interessanter darstellen werde, als wofür die Menge sie hielt' (Hitzig und Häring II 268).

bourgeois respectability, her descent into demeaning service, and her fervent desire to sleep her way back to the top.[43] And Gesche Gottfried, raised early by adoring parents to despise her lowly station, is finally driven to a series of murders by selfishness, ambition, vanity and the desire to mingle with her betters as an equal.[44] The logic in this reasoning is obvious: if class determines character, then anyone attempting to raise herself above her class also destabilises her own character, leading from minor misdemeanours (Gottfried's love of theatre, Ursinus's and Zwanziger's reading of *Werther*) to severe trespasses (extramarital affairs in all cases) all the way to serial murder. Contemporary literature tends to agree with the *Pitaval* authors that this rather crude instrument is sufficient to dissect these crimes, and that no further investigation is needed. Only very occasionally, the depiction of the culprits' arrogant and stubborn refusal to content themselves with their lot assumes a tone that is not exclusively moralising. Feuerbach's description of Zwanziger's motives, for example, comes dangerously close to suggesting that her acts were not merely inspired by ambition or vanity but part of a struggle against social repression:

Chased from one place to the next for almost twenty years, nearly 50 years old and still a stranger on this earth; without home or fatherland; dishonoured by the world, only tolerated among humans due to a deceiving name change: she finally, fearfully, sought rest, an enduring haven, a reliable provider. And she wanted to be a lady, as she once had been, not a despised maid, as she was now! – Always to belong to others and never to oneself; never to issue orders but only to receive or dread them from others; to grovel and flatter only to please as a servant; forever condemned to sweet-talk, with a strained affable expression, to people whom she could nevertheless only hate; to be dependent, subservient, in the vivid memory of one's own past power; full of long-standing claims to the accommodating courtesies and the evident respect of others, but nevertheless so often teased, ridiculed, despised, given the cold shoulder: this was more than such a soul could continue to bear. She sought *redemption* from this miserable situation, or, if not redemption, then at least *compensation!*[45]

---

[43] Hitzig and Häring: 'Das Herabsinken von einer Herrin zur Magd, von einer Gebieterin nach Laune über ihre Liebhaber zu einem Dienstboten, den man wegen Unreinlichkeit fortjagt, war zu rasch' (II 231–2). And: 'Die diabolische Absicht der Zwanziger ist kein Geheimniß. Die häßliche, alte, wie uns noch zum Ueberfluß gesagt wird, mit einem ekelhaften Schaden behaftete Witwe hatte nichts Geringeres zur Absicht, als Justizamtmännin in Kasendorf zu werden' (239).

[44] 'es war der *Ehrgeiz*, in jener errungenen vornehmen, ausgezeichneten Sphäre, in die sie der Zufall und die Gunst der Menschen versetzt, sich zu erhalten, es war die *Eitelkeit*, welche ihr besseres Selbst mehr und mehr aufzehrte, und damit einer furchtbaren *Sebstsucht* [sic] Nahrung gab, welche sie endlich kaltblütig zu den gräßlichsten Mordthaten schreiten ließen' (Hitzig and Häring II 274, emphases original).

[45] 'Fast zwanzig Jahre lang von Ort zu Ort umhergejagt, beinahe schon 50 Jahre alt und noch immer ein Fremdling auf dieser Erde; ohne Vaterland und Heimath; von der Welt entehrt, blos durch einen

Feuerbach's theory – that Zwanziger's series of murders constituted compensatory killings in retribution for twenty years of misery in servitude – would probably have been enough to strike fear in the hearts of Zwanziger's contemporaries, particularly her 'betters'. Certainly, his passionate and seemingly empathetic portrayal of Zwanziger's sufferings appears to evoke a horrible spectre, the rise of the repressed. Ultimately, however, his point is not social, but psychological. Desires to transcend one's class are shown as not only deceiving others, they also, and equally fatally, deceive the self. The central problem, as diagnosed by Feuerbach and after him in *Der neue Pitaval*, is not Zwanziger's social ambition, but her 'self-delusion, sentimental flattery interspersed with religious feeling, a terrible aberration of the soul'.[46] Zwanziger's ultimate act of self-delusion lies not in aspiring to a social power to which she has no right, but in deceiving herself that she actually has acquired it:

But lo! she discovered the mystery of a clandestine and secret power, which she only had to subject to her will in order to traverse, fleet of foot, every mountain and every abyss, and to act as she saw fit, endowed with invisible power, transcending the irksome restraints of confining circumstances, the laws of civic life, even humanity itself: to *rule freely*. This mysterious power was – *poison*.[47]

What poison meant to Zwanziger is further recited in Feuerbach's ornate prose: it was her 'irresistible power', her 'magic sceptre', her 'magic wand', the 'golden gate of her last hopes', her 'consciousness of a terrible

---

Namenstrug unter den Menschen geduldet: suchte sie endlich angstvoll nach Ruhe, nach einer bleibenden Stätte, nach einer sicheren Versorgung. Und als Herrin, wie ehemals; nicht mehr als verachtete Magd, wie jezt! – Immer nur Andern, nie sich selbst angehören; nie befehlen, immer nur von Andern Befehle empfangen oder befürchten; immer kriechen und schmeicheln, blos um als Magd zu gefallen; fortwährend dazu verdammt, mit freundlich erzwungener Miene, den Menschen schön zu thun, welche sie gleichwohl nur hassen konnte; abhängig, unterthänig, bei dem erzürnten Gefühle lebhafter Erinnerung an die vergangenen Zeiten eigner Herrschaft; voll alter Ansprüche auf das gefällige Zuvorkommen und die äussere Achtung Anderer, und doch so oft geneckt, verspottet, verachtet, über die Achseln angesehen: – dieses war mehr, als eine solche Seele länger zu ertragen vermochte. *Rettung* muste ihr werden aus einer solchen Lage; oder, wenn nicht Rettung, wenigstens *Ersatz* dafür!' (Feuerbach, *Aktenmäßige Darstellung*, I 47).

[46] 'Der Selbstbetrug, das sentimentale Schönthun, das Hineinspielen religiöser Gefühle, diese furchtbare Seelenverirrung, welche bei der Gottfried eine noch nie dagewesene Höhe erreicht, spukt schon bei der Zwanziger' (Hitzig and Häring II 254).

[47] 'Doch, sieh! da entdeckt sich ihr das Geheimniß einer still verborgenen Macht, welche sie nur sich dienstbar zu machen braucht, um über alle Berge und Abgründe leichten Fußes hinüber zu schreiten, und, jenseits der lästigen Schranken beengender Verhältnisse, den Gesetzen des bürgerlichen Lebens entrückt, sogar über die Menschheit selbst hinausgehoben, mit unsichtbarer Gewalt nach eigener Willkühr *frei zu herrschen*. Diese geheimnißvolle Macht war – *Gift*' (Feuerbach, *Aktenmäßige Darstellung*, I 48, emphases original).

grandeur', 'her last true friend', 'her constant companion', her 'long lost lover'.[48] But of course, these are self-delusions: her actual situation has not changed. All her attempts to poison her way into an advantageous marriage are in vain, and when she is finally captured, she is in exactly the state in which Feuerbach originally described her: exploited, ridiculed, despised, disliked, dishonoured, homeless, friendless, fearful and alone. Tenaciously self-deluded to the end, she goes to her execution with a lie on her conscience: 'In lying to the judge she also lied to herself, and even in death she did not relinquish the role she had assigned to herself: always to appear interesting, at least to herself.'[49] The story of Anna Margaretha Zwanziger, which comes within a hair's breadth of containing a highly explosive social dimension, is thus reduced to the story of an individual ensnared between a harsh reality that she cannot endure and a pleasing appearance that she cannot uphold.

In his account of Zwanziger's life, Feuerbach does not belittle her sufferings and he does not portray them as imagined. Nevertheless, his account of her struggle for what he himself calls 'redemption' is devoid of all sympathy, despite Zwanziger's obvious despair, and despite the fact that her ambitions were in line with those permitted to women of her time – a husband, a home, security in old age. Instead, he makes an example of her. Zwanziger's rather modest aspirations to home, hearth and husband are recast as a manic will to power, the desire to exempt herself from all ties and responsibilities in order 'to *rule freely*'. Such desires, of course, can never be fulfilled for one of her class: presupposing the possibility of a life beyond community, humanity and beyond the rules of law, they represent both a delusion of grandeur and a delusion of self. Zwanziger is portrayed as forever caught within the confines of her class and her character; her attempt to transcend them is unmasked as a dreadful self-deception, to which she sacrifices not only numerous victims, but ultimately also her deluded self.

[48] Feuerbach, *Aktenmäßige Darstellung*, I 48–52: 'das *frohe Gefühl unwiderstehlicher Macht*'; 'Gift war ihr magisches Szepter'; 'Gift vertrat ihr die Stelle eines Zauberstaabs, womit sie das goldene Thor ihrer letzten Hoffnungen sich öffnete'; 'gewährte es das Bewußtseyn furchtbarer Erhabenheit'; 'Gift erschien ihr als ihr letzter treuer Freund'; 'Gift war ihr beständiger Gefährte'; 'erschien ihr einst der lang entbehrte Anblick des Arseniks, wie das frohe tröstende Wiedersehen eines lang entfernten Geliebten' (emphasis original).

[49] 'Im Lügen vor dem Richter log sie auch vor sich selbst, und fiel selbst mit dem Tode nicht aus der Rolle, die sie sich aufgegeben: immer, wenigstens in ihren eigenen Augen, interessant zu sein' (Hitzig and Häring II 254).

SELFISHNESS AND SELFLESSNESS: THE CASE OF GESCHE
GOTTFRIED (BREMEN, 1815–1831)

No murderess of the age has inspired as much literature,[50] or invited as much hatred, as the serial poisoner Gesche Margarethe Gottfried (1785–1831). To this day, she is the highlight of every city tour of Bremen, whose citizens and tourists are invited to express their disgust and contempt for her by spitting on the *Spuckstein* ('spitting stone', fig. 9) erected two weeks after her execution on 21 April 1831 on the very spot where her scaffold had stood.[51] Gottfried was convicted of murdering fifteen people between 1813 and 1827, including her parents, her twin brother, her three children, two husbands, one fiancé and her best friend. Besides this, she stood accused of a further fifteen poisonings without lethal result, as well as repeated adultery, repeated perjury, repeated theft, embezzlement and one count of attempted abortion.[52] However, Gottfried's enduring infamy is not entirely due to the unprecedented number or severity of her crimes, but also to the fact that they have remained unexplained to this day. By most accounts, not least her own, Gesche Gottfried had no motive for her murders.

The court records of her interrogations,[53] which span the two and a half years between her arrest on 6 March 1828 and her death sentence on 17 September 1830, reveal no purpose to her crimes. For each act of poisoning,

---

[50] Aside from her court records, available at the State Archive in Bremen (*Protokolle*; *Vorläufiger Bericht*; *Hauptbericht*) and numerous contemporary broadsheets (see, e.g., *Die Giftmischerin Gesina Timm*), contemporary sources include the two-volume biography of her written by her defence counsel Friedrich Leopold Voget, as well as more or less fictitious accounts by Weißenburg der ältere (pseud.), Feilner, Jöntzen and the entry *Die Giftmörderin Wittwe Gottfried* in Hitzig's *Amtliche Mittheilungen* of 1831. Her story is retold, based largely on Voget's account, in Hitzig and Häring II 256–359; Kohut 113–19. Secondary sources include (but are by no means limited to) the works by Hellwig, Heuser, Schwarzwälder and Ludwig Scholz. Bolte and Dimmler's lengthy chapter on her (19–89) and Gribble's account (99–128) purport to be historical accounts, but take considerable liberties with the available facts. The works by Marzahn, Meter, Seling-Biehusen and Seling-Biehusen and Feest are based on her court records, from which they all cite at length. Fictionalisations of her life include Rainer Werner Fassbinder's famous drama *Bremer Freiheit* (1971) and Peer Meter's play *Die Verhöre der Gesche Gottfried* (1996); three films have been made about her (*Bremer Freiheit*, dir. Rainer Werner Fassbinder, 1972; *Gesche Gottfried*, 1978; and *Gesches Gift*, 1996). There is even a local women's magazine named after her (*Gesche*, circulated in Bremen and Bremerhaven; see Marzahn 196), with an online version: www.gesche.bremen.de. A Wikipedia entry, divided into various subheadings and adorned with two portraits, is at http://de.wikipedia.org/wiki/Gesche_Gottfried (last accessed 15 August 2007).

[51] See Marzahn 196 and Meter 159.

[52] Her crimes are listed, with names and exact dates, in the defence writ (*Verteidigungsschrift*) of her defender Friedrich Leopold Voget, which is quoted in its entirety in his *Die Giftmörderin*, 17–99.

[53] Gottfried's statements are taken from her interrogation records (*Protokolle*). Voget quotes many of these instances verbatim, see, for example, his *Lebensbeschreibung*, 274 and *Giftmörderin*, 12, 73–8, 81–9, 217–18, 221, 223–5, 241–2, 267–8, 281–9, 313–14, 421–2, among others.

Fig. 9 Bremer Spuckstein, cemented into the ground where Gesche Gottfried's scaffold had stood in May 1831 and to this day a tourist attraction of Bremen. Photo by Jürgen Howaldt

she could provide the time, date, place, the dish used to administer the poison and the exact dosage – but no motive. She remembered, for example, that she had used zwieback and home-made meat soup to poison her first husband, Johann Miltenberg. Asked for a reason, she answered: 'I don't know. Your Honour probably believes that my actual motivation was to be able to marry Gottfried, but that was not the reason.'[54] Pushed on the question of motive, she requested a day's grace to think it over. When her request was denied, she suddenly claimed that she had not killed him at all, and could only be moved to reconfess to his murder after being reassured that the interrogation was over for the day.[55] Similarly, she claimed not to know why she had poisoned her mother, but promised her interrogators to think about it.[56] She poisoned her daughter Johanna on the day of her mother's funeral, between one o'clock and one-thirty in the afternoon, immediately

---

[54] 'Dies weiß ich nicht. Das Gericht glaubt wohl, daß der eigenthliche Grund gewesen sey, um Gottfried heirathen zu können, dies ist aber nicht der Grund gewesen' (*Protokolle*, I 421–2).
[55] See interrogation record in *Protokolle*, I 145–6. [56] Meter III.

after lunch, with cake served at her mother's funeral. Why? 'I acted without thinking. I don't know. I cannot tell you. I have to have a good think about that.'[57] Three or four days later, she administered poisoned leftover funeral cake to her daughter Adeline, in the living room; although Gottfried strained to remember the exact time of day,[58] she recalled clearly Adeline's symptoms, where she vomited, the room in which she died. But why did she poison her? 'I've already told you the reason why I gave something to Adeline, recently, when I told you about Johanna: it's the same reason.'[59] Her father was poisoned at a Sunday lunch with home-made veal soup. Why? 'I don't know how it happened that I gave poison to my father. If I ask myself why I did it, I really cannot come up with a reason.'[60] Pressed for a more satisfying explanation, she replied: 'I've never been able to come up with a precise reason, even to myself.' And: 'Why I did this God only knows.'[61] There is evidence that the unmotivated murder of her father bothered her interrogators more than any other crime she committed, because they returned to it several times. Her final answer, clearly intended to satisfy her questioners, is tentatively phrased, as if she could not quite persuade herself to believe it: 'I cannot give you a better reason for poisoning my father than this: maybe I was afraid that Father would not permit my marriage to Gottfried.'[62]

Virtually all of Gesche Gottfried's confessions follow this pattern. Her son Heinrich: Monday morning, 8 a.m., before school, buttered bread and zwieback, precise amount of poison. Asked for a motive, she deflected the question: 'I took the decision to give Heinrich poison on the same morning that I poisoned him and immediately carried it out.'[63] Her brother Johann Christoph Timm: Sunday lunch, meat soup, she remembered that he cleaned his plate. Or was it the shellfish or the potatoes?[64] Her husband Michael Christoph Gottfried: Saturday, vegetables; her fiancé Paul Thomas

---

[57] 'Ich habe unüberlegt gehandelt. Das weiß ich nicht. Ich kann es nicht angeben. Das muß ich erst ordentlich bei mir überlegen' (*Protokolle*, I 122).

[58] 'Die Tageszeit kann ich nicht mehr angeben. Wie ich glaube, war der Kuchen auch noch von dem Begräbniß übriggeblieben' (*Protokolle*, I 431–2).

[59] 'Den Grund weshalb ich Adelinen etwas gab, habe ich neulich schon bey Johanna angegeben, denn er ist derselbe' (*Protokolle*, I 431–2).

[60] 'Wie ich dazu gekommen bin meinem Vater Gift zu geben, weiß ich nicht. Wenn ich mich so darum frage warum ich es gethan habe, so kann ich mir den Grund gar nicht angeben' (*Protokolle*, I 439).

[61] 'Einen bestimmten Grund habe ich mir nie angeben können.' – 'warum mag Gott wissen' (*Protokolle*, I 439).

[62] 'Den Beweggrund, weshalb ich meinen Vater vergiftete, kann ich nicht genauer angeben, als daß ich wohl fürchtete, daß Vater die Heirath mit Gottfried nicht gestatten würde' (*Protokolle*, I 452).

[63] 'Den Entschluß Heinrichen Gift zu geben faßte ich am Morgen wie ich das Gift gab und führte ihn sofort aus' (*Protokolle*, I 452–3).

[64] 'Was außer der Suppe gegessen und getrunken ist, weiß ich nicht mehr. Ob er mehr als den einen Teller voll aß, weiß ich auch nicht … Über meines Bruders Tod habe ich mich auch näher bedacht,

Zimmermann: Saturday between 6 and 7 p.m., wine, beer, buttered bread and sausage (she even remembered on which side his bread was poisoned, although she was unsure which side he ate first). Later, she administered further dosages in a chicken and plum dish, about half a pound of poisoned plums in an oblong crockery dish. Why? 'I cannot say how the thought came to me to poison Zimmermann … […] It simply occurred to me, all at once, and I thought I'd give it a try.'[65] Her lodger Johann Mosees: summer, at a round table, apples and mashed potatoes, vegetables and beer, precise dosage. Why? 'I did not really have a particular reason.'[66] Wilhelmine Rumpff, to whose husband Gottfried had just sold her house: Wednesday, 7 p.m., porridge soup, exact dosage. Why? 'I really cannot say. That I really cannot say.'[67] At her interrogators' insistence, she pondered the question and then said: 'I suppose I wanted my house back.' Immediately thereafter, to the court scribe: 'Don't write that down, I don't think that was the reason.'[68] Her best friend Anne Lucie Meyerholz: Thursday, 10 a.m., breakfast of zwieback and wine. Why? 'I don't know what my intention was in doing this. Really, I cannot give you an actual reason. You may say, oh God, how is it possible to poison someone without cause? But I really did not have a cause. I don't know of a reason.'[69] Beta Schmidt and her child, Thursday morning, cherry soup. Why? 'Well, Senator, why don't *you* tell *me*. Why I did this, again. No particular reason.'[70] And so on.[71]

kann aber nichts weiter sagen als ich gesagt habe. Ich bin ungewiß, ob ich an Schellfisch oder Kartoffeln oder an der Suppe ihm gegeben habe, allein ich glaube doch an der Suppe' (*Protokolle*, 1 459ff.).

[65] 'Ich kann nicht angeben, wie mir zuerst der Gedanke kam, Zimmermann zu vergiften … […] Er kam mir so auf einmal, ich dachte, ich wollte diesen Versuch mal machen' (*Protokolle*, 1 494–5).

[66] 'Eine Hauptursache habe ich nicht dazu gehabt' (*Protokolle*, 1 510–11).

[67] 'Das kann ich gar nicht sagen. Ich kann es wirklich nicht sagen' (*Protokolle*, 1 516).

[68] 'Befragt wann der Entschluß gekommen und wie sie dazu gekommen, blieb sie eine lange Weile still und seufzte verschiedentlich laut auf, dann sagte sie. "Ich wollte ja wohl mein Haus wieder haben", doch fiel sie gleich darauf ein: "Schreiben Sie das noch nicht, das ist wohl nicht der Grund."' Quoted in Meter 91.

[69] 'Den Vorsatz, der Meyerholz Gift zu geben, faßte ich denselben Morgen, wie ich das Gift gab. Des Morgens, wie ich aufstand, beym Caffee, kam der Gedanke. Wie er eigentlich kam, weiß ich selbst nicht mehr. Eine eigenthliche Absicht weiß ich gar nicht, warum ich es that. Wirklich, ich kann keinen eigenthlichen Grund angeben. Ach Gott, Sie mögen wohl sagen, wie es möglich ist, ohne Grund jemand zu vergiften, allein, ich hatte keinen Grund. Ich weiß keinen … Ich wußte wohl, daß sie sterben würde, aber ich gab ihr das Gift ohne einen Grund warum. Die Meyerholz hat mir nie etwas zu Leide gethan. Ich war ihr nichts schuldig, hatte auch keinen Haß gegen sie. Ich kann mir gar kein Grund nennen, ich weiß keinen. Ich kam am Morgen der That zu dem Entschluß dazu. Ich dachte bloß, daß ich es thun wolle und nichts weiter' (*Protokolle*, 1 503–4).

[70] 'Ja, Herr Senator, das sagen Sie nur. Warum habe ich es auch hier gethan. Um wenig' (*Protokolle*, 1 518–19).

[71] Further poisonings for which she claimed to have no motive are those of Friedrich Kleine, her friend Marie Heckendorff, Antoinette Luchting, the child of teacher Specht as well as his child-minder,

The court records give us no indication that she withheld her motives deliberately. On the contrary, she seems to have tried to come up with the answers, possibly in an attempt to end the interminable succession of questions. The two-and-a-half-year-long merry-go-round of who, what, when, how and, above all, *why*, found her occasionally out of sorts: a few times, she simply refused to have her motives queried. 'Gentlemen, I beg you not to pursue this. Why are you bringing this up now? I'm not prepared for this.'[72] More often, she behaved like a schoolchild who has to retake an examination, having failed the first round: whenever previous answers had dissatisfied her judges, she promised them a better motive next time. Her promise to think about a motive for her mother's and her daughter's murders, her hesitant statement that she poisoned her father because, possibly, she feared his objections to her marrying Gottfried, her uncertain declaration that she killed Wilhelmine Rumpff because – maybe – she wanted her house back all indicate that she did her best to placate her increasingly bewildered judges by making up reasons that she thought might appear credible to them. On the surface, however, none of these motives make sense, although they were eagerly seized upon by later writers unwilling to grant Gottfried the mystique of a motiveless killer.[73] As a wealthy widow, Gottfried hardly needed her parents' consent to remarry, and her stated reason for killing her children – that she believed Michael Gottfried would not marry her with them – is belied by his demonstrated affection for them. Her motive for poisoning Michael Gottfried shortly before their wedding (they married at his deathbed), stated as revenge for his long hesitation in proposing to her, seems unconvincing, given the lengths to which she had gone (including murdering her parents and children) to force his hand. How Wilhelmine Rumpff's death might have enabled Gottfried to reclaim her house remains mysterious. And most of her other murders are explained by – very often minimal – financial gain.[74] Most interesting in this context is the rationale Senator Franz Friedrich Droste, the ruling judge, advanced in his written substantiation of Gottfried's death sentence: he ruled that the apparent lack of credible motives did not

---

Henriette Alberti, her friend Lucie Block, the nurse of Rumpff's child, the maid of a visitor, Wilhelm Suhling, Johanne Greden and Rumpff. In each case, she was able to provide exact details of the dish and dosage used. See *Protokolle*, i 197, 533–8, 545–8.

[72] 'Ich bitte sie, meine Herren, dies nicht zu berühren. Wie kommen sie auch gerade darauf. Darauf bin ich nicht vorbereitet' (*Protokolle*, i 123).

[73] See, for example, the rather unconvincing list of motives in *Der neue Pitaval* (Hitzig and Häring ii 256–359) and Gribble (99–128).

[74] Voget's *Verteidigungsschrift* sarcastically dismisses these purported motives as utterly contrived and inadequate, see *Giftmörderin*, 56–9.

constitute sufficient evidence of mental disturbance and hence diminished responsibility. He pronounced her able to judge the consequences of her actions, in the sense that she knew that those poisoned by her would die,[75] and dismissed all further questions about her motives as immaterial to the case.

Not everyone was as content as Droste to let sleeping dogs lie. If Gottfried's crimes could not be considered the interpretable acts of a human being, the only explanation left was to see them as acts of magic, fate, or God. The question of motive is only relevant in a context in which the perpetrator acts with volition, intent and self-determination; where these are absent, a motive is no longer required. Gottfried herself was one of the first to pounce upon this option. She described herself as the victim of an inexorable fate, attributing her crimes to the fact that she was suckled by a wetnurse with bad milk,[76] or to Providence, which she often cited as mysterious and inescapable,[77] or to prophesies. One oracle told her that 'her entire family would die out, leaving her alone to lead a very good life';[78] another pronounced that she would be lucky to live beyond the age of forty (she was executed at forty-six), that there would be many deaths in her family, that she would marry twice, and that the last part of her life would be spent in a small room.[79] That these all came true may not explain her crimes, unless one shares the suspicion of her defender and later biographer Friedrich Leopold Voget that she felt compelled to fulfil these predictions herself. It does, however, constitute a diminished-responsibility defence – for who can struggle against fate? – that is not entirely dissimilar to that launched by Voget, who pleaded diminished responsibility due to what he

---

[75] 'Entscheidungsgründe', transcribed by Voget, *Giftmörderin*, 123: 'Die Inquisitin wußte vollkommen, was sie that, indem sie ihren Eltern, Kindern, Gatten u.s.w. das Gift gab. Sie *wußte*, daß es Gift sey, *wußte*, daß sie damit tödten könne, was sogar bei einem großen Theile der Vergifteten ihre entschiedene Absicht war, und *wußte* endlich, daß sie sich damit gegen göttliche und menschliche Gesetze auf das frevelhafteste auflehnte' (emphases original).

[76] Related in Voget, *Giftmörderin*, 221.

[77] Numerous sources quote her expressions of resigned submission to God's will, for example: '"Gott schaut in das Verborgene!" "wir müssen die dunkeln Wege der Vorsehung in Demuth verehren," "was Gott thut, das ist wohlgethan"' (all cited in Voget, *Lebensgeschichte*, 150); see also Niehaus, 'Die Figur', 167.

[78] '"*ihre ganze Familie werde aussterben und sie allein übrig bleiben, um dann sehr gut leben zu können*"' (Voget, *Lebensgeschichte*, 125, emphasis original). Elsewhere she laments that she was destined, according to a prophesy, to lose all of her children: 'es sey ihr prophezeihet, *sie werde alle ihre Kinder verlieren*' (Voget, *Lebensgeschichte*, 150, emphasis original). The prediction is further discussed in Voget's description of Gottfried's interrogation on 29 April 1828, *Giftmörderin*, 269–71; see also Voget, *Lebensgeschichte*, 37, 81, 111, 125, 150, on various predictions that Gottfried claimed to be life-determining.

[79] Meter 72–3.

called her 'monomaniacal addiction to poisoning'.[80] Even though Voget repeatedly belittled Gottfried's views on predestination,[81] his insanity defence echoes it precisely. He even cites the fact that her mother, 'contrary to the laws of nature', was three years older than her father, and that baby Gesche had to share the vital energy provided by her mother *in utero* with her twin brother, as indicators that Gottfried's life of crime was preordained.[82]

If this sounds weak, it is because Voget himself, by his own admission, did not believe a single word of it. As Gottfried's *defender*, he considered it his duty to attempt everything that might spare his client the death penalty; as Gottfried's *biographer*, he clearly states that he considered the psychological basis for his own insanity defence an 'unholy theory imported from France and incompatible with our Christian religion', which he cited 'only with the greatest reluctance', of which he 'disapprove[d] from the bottom of my heart', and due to which, in his estimation, 'many a criminal … has actually escaped his just punishment'.[83] Elsewhere he marvels at the expense, time, and trouble invested in his client's case, given his conviction that 'within a few days of its beginning, common sense had already declared the criminal guilty and meriting death'.[84]

---

[80] Voget's diagnosis of Gottfried's 'giftmordsüchtige Monomanie' is outlined in his *Verteidigungsschrift* in *Giftmörderin*, 17–99, particularly 56–61, 90, 99, 228, as well as in his biography of her (*Lebensgeschichte*, 250–1), where he compares her addiction to poisoning to addictive gambling.

[81] See, among others, his critical remarks in *Giftmörderin*, 239: 'so war es allerdings ihr Plan, sich als das Opfer eines unabänderlichen Geschicks darzustellen'.

[82] 'Ohne gerade eine etwanige Seelenstörung der Inquisitin bloß organisch erklären zu wollen, möchte Defensor hier doch auch manche *physische* Eigenthümlichkeit der unbegreiflichen Giftmörderin an diesem Orte nicht unberührt lassen. Dahin läßt sich zuerst zählen, daß, gegen die eigentliche Ordnung der Natur, ihre Mutter um drei Jahre älter war, als ihr Vater. Sie war ferner Zwillingskind, mußte also in der ersten Zeit ihrer Entstehung das Maß von Lebens- und Geisteskraft, welches regelmäßig für ein einzelnes Individuum bestimmt ist, mit ihrem Zwillingsbruder theilen. Wie schon hiernach zu vermuthen, so findet es sich ausdrücklich bezeugt, Inquisitin war, wie *geistig*, so auch körperlich (f.109) nie recht *kräftig*' (Voget, *Giftmörderin*, 93–4).

[83] Voget's note on his own defence brief, cited in *Giftmörderin*, 54: 'Nur mit dem innersten Widerstreben sah sich der Verfasser, als Defensor, zur Entwicklung der unter obiger Rubrik nachfolgenden Ansicht über Zurechnungsfähigkeit genöthigt. Diese Ansichten gehören zum Theil einer heillosen, unserer christlichen Religion widerstreitenden, aus Frankreich zu uns herüber gekommenen Theorie an, deren [sic] der Verfasser von Herzen gram ist. Aber dieselbe hat sich nun einmal, besonders durch ihre gerichtsärztlichen Anhänger, auf deren Gutachten die peinliche Gerichtsordnung hinweiset, so sehr in die Deutschen Gerichte eingedrängt; es ist so mancher Verbrecher in neuerer Zeit dadurch seiner verdienten Strafe wirklich entgangen, daß es einem gerichtlichen Vertheidiger, als solchem, pflicht- und amtsmäßig obliegt, wenn die Umstände es irgend zulassen, jene sogenannten wissenschaftlichen Fortschritte unserer Zeit für seinen Schützling zu reclamiren.'

[84] Voget, *Giftmörderin*, 206: 'Zwar ist das Todesurtheil gesprochen, bestätigt und am 21. April vollzogen worden; allein nach welchem Aufwande von Zeit und Arbeit wurde endlich dies Ziel erreicht, in einer

If Gottfried's guilt was apparent within a few days, her motives remained obscure even after years of investigation and interrogation. As an unsolved criminological and psychological mystery, she became the subject of examination, observation and study – and big business. The *Bremer Zeitung*, reporting on her arrest on 12 March 1828, already noted (only six days after her arrest!) that the case had caused 'quite a stir' and suspected that it would be every bit as thrilling as the 'most interesting criminal stories'.[85] It was an accurate prediction: fourteen years later, *Der neue Pitaval* elaborated upon her usefulness for scientific study, apparently without the slightest sense of embarrassment:

Since avenging Justice would, in any event, not be deprived of its rights, it was now possible to accommodate scientific and humanitarian interests, to engage in detailed study of this terrible riddle of such a perverted human being. Jurists, theologians, and physicians experimented on this curiosity.[86]

Reporting on her case was not limited to Bremen, but extended all over Europe, even reaching as far as North America and China.[87] At the *Bremer Freimarkt* in October 1828, fantasy portraits of her were sold, and the merchant Johann Dietrich Fagen applied to the City Senate, apparently in all seriousness, for permission to exhibit Gottfried publicly for money, offering the city a fee of 200 *pistolen* for the privilege.[88] On the day of her death sentence, which meant the release of the court records and the end of the censorship regarding her case, no fewer than three books about her appeared – books which had been printed for weeks and were just waiting to

---

Sache, wo schon nach den ersten Tagen ihres Beginns der gesunde Menschenverstand die Verbrecherin des Todes schuldig erklärte.' – Voget's twofold role as Gottfried's defender and biographer has been excellently analysed by Marzahn; see also Peer Meter on Voget's exploitation of his position as Gottfried's defender in order to collect material for his lucrative biography of her (127, 134–9, 146–50).

[85] 'Durch die gefängliche Einziehung eines Frauenzimmers, welches in den Verdacht der Giftmischerei gerathen war, ist unsere Stadt seit einigen Tagen in lebhafte Aufregung versetzt. Es verbreiten sich darüber die seltsamsten Gerüchte, mit welchen man eine Menge ungewöhnlicher Todesfälle von Personen, welche mit ihr in nähere Berührung gekommen waren, zusammenstellt. Es würde nicht passend sein schon jetzt etwas darüber sagen und der eingeleiteten Untersuchung vorgreifen zu wollen; nach allem aber, was man davon hört, möchte dieser Fall eine der merkwürdigsten psychologischen Erscheinungen darbieten und dürfte er den interessantesten Criminalgeschichten an die Seite zu stellen sein' (quoted in Meter 36).

[86] 'Man durfte vielmehr, da der rächenden Gerechtigkeit auf jeden Fall ihr Recht ungeschmälert blieb, den wissenschaftlichen und humanioren Rücksichten nachgeben, um das furchtbare Räthsel eines so entarteten menschlichen Wesens gründlich zu studiren. Rechtsgelehrte, Theologen, Mediciner experimentirten an dieser Rarität' (Hitzig and Häring II 266). On the exploitation of Gesche Gottfried as a scientific experiment and as a cash cow for Voget and others, see Meter 36, 119, 125, 127, 134–9, 146–51; see also Voget's own highly revealing announcement of his second book on her in *Lebensgeschichte*, 296 n.58.

[87] Meter 105–6.   [88] Meter 119.

be distributed to the eagerly awaiting public on that same Friday.[89] The one authorised portrait of her (fig. 10) was drawn by Professor Rudolf Friedrich Karl Suhrland, a well-known portrait painter, and sold for the benefit of the local Institute for the Deaf-Mute at the *Freimarkt* in October 1829. To persuade her to sit for him, Suhrland skillfully played on Gottfried's reputation for charity and her – presumed – guilty conscience: 'Just think how much misery you have brought upon others. Surely you now want to do some good for these poor wretches, don't you?'[90] Within weeks of the first printing, the press plate had to be renewed: demand for Gottfried's picture had outstripped even Suhrland's wildest dreams.

The object of all this fascination was less the murderous career of Gesche Gottfried than her character, which, in the minds of contemporaries, came to replace the missing motive. Since her crimes could not be successfully explained by what she did, thought or wanted, the solution was sought in who she was. The idea that her character, her self, was the source of her crimes is advanced by Senator Droste in his justification of the death penalty:

All of these terrible crimes have their origin and centre in a selfishness unbridled by any deep religious feeling or moral energy, and no particular astuteness is needed to understand how this worst of all poisoned plants could sprout from the soil that had brought forth so much evil.[91]

Droste's argument, which diagnoses Gottfried's selfishness as the root of all evil, neatly does away with the need for individual motives *and* the idea that Gottfried was not responsible for her actions. But there is evidence that he was not entirely comfortable with his own explanation. His straightforward declaration in this passage that Gottfried's character poses no mystery sits badly with his letter to Pastor Rotermund, in which he admits that Gottfried's paradoxical character baffled him to the end:

To describe the delinquent's character seems to me, even now, a task bordering on the impossible. A woman who nurses the sick, feeds the hungry, to whom charity

[89] The books that appeared that day are the ones by Georg Jöntzen, Franz Feilner – which claimed to have used court records that had been unavailable until that day – and Voget's *Lebensgeschichte*. See Meter 147–51.

[90] 'Denken Sie doch, wie viel Unheil Sie den Menschen zugefügt haben; nicht wahr, da mögten Sie auch gern einmal den armen Unglücklichen etwas Gutes thun' (quoted in Meter 135).

[91] From Senator Droste's 'Entscheidungsgründe', cited in Voget, *Giftmörderin*, 125: 'Alle diese groben Verbrechen haben ihre Quelle und ihren Mittelpunct in einem Egoismus, der durch kein tiefer dringendes religiöses Gefühl, durch keine sittliche Kraft gezügelt wird, und es bedarf keines sonderlichen Scharfsinns, um zu begreifen, wie aus demselben Boden, der so viel des Schlechten erzeugte, auch jene ärgste der Giftpflanzen entsprießen konnte.'

Fig. 10 Gesche Margarethe Gottfried. Stone-print by Rudolf Friedrich Karl Suhrland (1829).
Courtesy of the Focke-Museum Bremen

and bounteousness have become, as it were, an inner necessity, and who never the less poisons her friends; a woman who weeps over a line by Goethe but murders her children; a woman who is capable of such a degree of love that she sacrifices to it the lives of her nearest relatives, only to offer the poisoned chalice next to the object of her love … A woman who refuses the hand of a respectable man … in saying that he is too good for her, who today falsely accuses her own father of murder but tomorrow anxiously and meticulously tries to prevent even the shadow of suspicion from falling upon another, taking all guilt upon herself; a woman who steals today that which she will give in charity tomorrow … – who could dare to describe her character?[92]

Droste's inability to reconcile Gottfried's selfish character – to him the cause of her crimes – with her frequent acts of selflessness is understandable. His dilemma arose from his decision to take both sides of her personality seriously, rather than – as her defender Voget did – summarily dismissing her good works as an act designed to fool the world.

Voget's explanation of Gottfried is simultaneously more simplistic – because unlike Droste, he answers all questions, rather than allowing for their potential unanswerability – and more complex – because his answer resorts to the very psychological approaches for which he had professed so much disdain. He describes Gottfried as selfless in the most literal sense imaginable: as void of character, self or soul, as *empty*. To him, Gottfried is a chimera whose inner core consists of nothing but 'a gruesome emptiness', a 'dead character', 'a dead wasteland inside'.[93] Echoing Gottfried's own reported statement that she had never really lived,[94] he describes her entire life as a 'sham life':[95] 'her entire character was … nothing but a *great lie*, an *appearance without reality*'.[96] The appearance that masks Gottfried's lack of

---

[92] Senator Droste to Pastor Rotermund, 24 July 1828, cited in Meter 114: 'Eine Charakteristik der Inculpatin zu geben, scheint mir bis jetzt eine Aufgabe, die ans Unmögliche gränzt. Ein Weib, was Kranke pflegt, Arme speiset, dem Geben und Schenken, ich mögte sagen, zum Bedürfniß geworden, und die doch ihre Freundinnen vergiftet; was über einem Wort von Göthe weint, und ihre Kinder ermordet, ein Weib, was einer Liebe fähig ist in solchem Maaße, daß sie ihr das Leben der nächsten Angehörigen zum Opfer bringt, und die dann eben diesem Gegenstande ihrer Liebe die Gift Schaale reicht … Ein Weib, was die Hand eines achtungswerthen Mannes ausschlägt … indem sie ihm selbst erklärte, er sey ein zu guter Mensch für sie, die heute ihren eigenen Vater fälschlich als Mörder anklagt, und morgen vielleicht mit ängstlicher Sorgfalt strebt, daß jeder üble Schein von einem Dritten genommen werde, und sie allein als die Schuldige erscheine, die heute stiehlt, was sie morgen verschenkt … – wer kann es wagen, ihren Charakter zu schildern?'

[93] Voget, *Giftmörderin*: 'eine grausige Leere' (317); 'Den todten Charakter ihres Geistigen überhaupt' (384); 'die *letzten* Thränen zur Verbergung der todten Oede ihres Innern' (460).

[94] Voget quotes her as saying: 'Ach, ich fühle es immer mehr, ich habe eigentlich noch gar nicht gelebt; es ging immer in einer unruhigen Hast fort, so lange ich denken kann' (*Giftmörderin*, 352).

[95] Voget, *Lebensgeschichte*, 114: 'Schein-Leben'; *Giftmörderin*, 290: 'Scheinleben'.

[96] Voget, *Lebensgeschichte*, 211: 'Ihr ganzes Wesen war ja geistig und körperlich nur *eine* große *Lüge*, ein *Schein* ohne *Wesen*' (emphases original).

reality becomes one of the most prominent subjects in his biography. Trained in deception by her love of play-acting as a child,[97] she grows up to embody perfectly the devoted daughter, virtuous wife, affectionate mother and charitable member of the community: an 'angel of light, a paragon of pious sufferance and benefaction'.[98] Small wonder that she was prayed for publicly when she lost her children,[99] and that even in the course of her trial, numerous witnesses appeared to testify to her good character.[100] Gottfried's selflessness, understood as an *absence of self*, and the flawlessly performed selflessness with which she gave to the poor, aided women in labour and tenderly nursed many of her own victims to their deaths, are thus centrally connected in Voget's account. Unlike the rest of the world, though, Voget is not fooled by her acting talents: the purpose of his biography is less to provide readers with an account of her life and crimes than to establish himself as the only person who successfully looked into the void. He professes himself qualified to answer questions that baffled others involved in the case to the end. Voget, looking behind the façade of Gottfried's publicly performed selflessness, sees literally nothing – a great gaping emptiness where so many others, most of whom he quotes with considerable glee, have struggled desperately and vainly to grasp her innermost self.

Gottfried's essential selflessness is most often illustrated through the appearance that conceals it. Her name change from the lowly 'Gesche' to the more elegant 'Gesina', for example, is presented not only as a sign of her vanity, but also as a telling obliteration of her own identity.[101] At the theatre, Gottfried is unable to identify with the characters or to be moved by the drama; throughout, she remains dry-eyed and coldly aware that 'they're only *pretending*!'[102] This tale, told several times in Voget's biography, aims to convince his readers that while Gottfried was incapable of experiencing

---

[97] On Gottfried's love for the theatre and her play-acting as a child, see Voget *Lebensgeschichte*, 27, 80, 291 n. 20, 247 and *Giftmörderin*, 66, 257.

[98] On Gottfried's reputation, see Voget, *Lebensgeschichte*, 1–2, 194–5; the citation ('der … Ruf die Frau zum Engel des Lichts, zum Vorbild frommer Duldung und thätiger Liebe machte') in *Lebensgeschichte*, 194.

[99] Related in Voget, *Lebensgeschichte*, 2.

[100] Cited and quoted at length in Voget, *Giftmörderin*, 59–61.

[101] Voget, *Lebensgeschichte*, 37, 289 n. 1.

[102] According to Voget, Gottfried only ever attended the theatre 'zur Beobachtung der Verstellungskunst. Denn, was dies letztere Interesse anbetrifft, bei jeder, noch so schönen Stelle war sie sich vorherrschend der Wahrheit bewußt: "*sie thun ja nur so!*"' (*Lebensgeschichte*, 80). Another occasion is described as follows: 'Als man sich gegen sie darüber verwunderte, daß Trauerspiele sie stets so kalt gelassen, erwiederte sie, fast empfindlich darüber, daß man sie so einfältig halten könne: "ich wußte ja, daß sie *nur so thaten!*" – Wenn ihre Freundinnen bei Aufführung jener Stücke häufig Thränen vergossen, pflegte sie von Zeit zu Zeit zu erinnern: "denkt doch, *sie thun ja nur so!*"

an inner response to drama, she did recognise good acting, an art at which she herself was exceptionally accomplished. In prison, Gottfried repeatedly refused spiritual counsel,[103] but her letters to others are full of pious stock phrases,[104] and a policeman who observed her through the keyhole confirmed what Voget had suspected all along: that Gottfried felt no inner yearning to read the Bible, only snatching it up whenever she heard someone approaching her cell.[105] Immediately preceding her execution, she actively avoided spiritual counsel by hiding on her chamber pot until the clergyman was forced to leave, but then obsessed endlessly about her dress for her final performance on the scaffold.[106]

Possibly the most expressive illustration of the recurring idea that Gottfried's carefully contrived outward appearance concealed no inner core but a *void* is a discovery at her arrest: 'With horrified amazement, the women [in charge of undressing her] removed *thirteen corsets*, and thus soon uncovered, in place of the red-cheeked and stout lady, a pale skeleton twisted in terror.'[107] Gottfried's metamorphosis from the jovially chubby, apple-cheeked *burgher* widow to a colourless carcass is a physical manifestation of her character. Earlier examples – her appreciation of acting combined with an inability to be moved by a play, or her constant citation of religious sentiments combined with her profound disinterest in religion – have already unmasked this character, on a psychological and spiritual level, as a *negative*, as a void. Gottfried's self, to borrow a simile from religious philosophy, is not the Kierkegaardian apple, but Murray's onion.[108] Her true self resides not in the core but in the peels: once her layers of defence, and pretence, are peeled off, there is nothing left.

(*Lebensgeschichte*, 291 n.20). Several further incidents of this nature are cited in Voget, *Lebensgeschichte*, 27, 42, 247 and *Giftmörderin*, 66, 257; see also Hitzig and Häring II 275. On the influence of theatre or plays on her crimes, see also Voget, *Lebensgeschichte*, 125–6, 139, 153.

[103] See Voget, *Giftmörderin*, 330–45, 358–64, 434, 439, 455–6 and Meter's interpretation of these scenes, 134.

[104] See, among others, her letters to her friend Marie Heckendorf, her erstwhile lover Kassow, her landlord Rumpff and Voget himself, cited in *Lebensgeschichte*, 168, 190, 228, 237, 264 and *Giftmörderin*, 405–7.

[105] On Gottfried pretending to read the Bible, see Voget, *Giftmörderin*, 228–9, 318; the story of the policeman's observation on 457–8; see also Voget's comments on Gottfried's lack of interest in religion as a child in *Lebensgeschichte*, 21, 33, 63.

[106] See Voget, *Lebensgeschichte*, 357–8 and *Giftmörderin*, 351–2, 450, 457, 460; see also Kohut 118.

[107] 'Mit schauderhaftem Erstaunen zogen die Frauen ihr *dreizehn Corsette* aus, und so stand bald an der Stelle der rothwangigen wohlbeleibten Dame ein blasses, angstvoll verzerrtes Gerippe da' (Voget, *Giftmörderin*, 211–13, the citation 212–13, emphasis original); see also *Lebensgeschichte*, 96; the story is retold in Hitzig and Häring II 282; Meter 62; Niehaus, 'Die Figur', 168, among others.

[108] See Russell on Søren Kierkegaard and Process Theology.

In Voget's entire account, in two volumes and on a total of 768 pages devoted to his client, there is only one single scene in which he purports to have glimpsed a trace of humanity in her.

Asked which of her crimes she regretted the most, she wept and said: 'Alas! my father! …' … I asked – truly? so it is your *father*'s killing – that you regret the most? Not your mother's? Not that of your children? – At first she only shook her head, the she said aloud: 'no, my father!' in a tone that to me seemed to express more pain than remorse.[109]

Up to this point, all of Voget's evidence, every conversation he records with her, every witness, every case description, every analysis was devoted to one single goal: to establish that Gottfried was unable to feel anything, either at the theatre or in real life. In this one scene, however, she is not only endowed with a remorse she did not experience for any of her other victims, but with a far more immediate sensation, that of *pain*. To readers, this may appear as a flagrant contradiction; to the author, however, Gottfried's pain made perfect sense:

In this confession, the truth of which nobody will question and which she later often repeated to her defender [Voget],[110] there lies a deep religious meaning. A *mother's* love for her *children* is more innate, instinctual; even an *animal* loves its young. A *child's* love for his *parents* contains more spiritual power, it fulfills a divine commandment. Amongst his children, from whom he can demand unquestioning obedience, the *father* represents the divine to a greater extent than the mother. – This author admits readily that this confession of our criminal has always given him some comfort, as if it represented a trace of humanity in a nature that had otherwise become so diabolical.[111]

In the court records, as well, Gottfried's interrogators kept returning to the missing motive for the murder of her father, indicating that this one crime troubled them more than any other she had committed. In both cases, the rationale appears to be that breaking the laws of patriarchy by

---

[109] Voget, *Giftmörderin*, 235–6: 'Auf die Frage, welche That sie am meisten drücke? sagte sie weinend: "Ach mein *Vater*! …" … Dann fragte ich – so? also der *Vater*? – drückt sie am meisten? nicht die Mutter? nicht die Kinder? – Sie schüttelte erst bloß mit dem Kopfe, dann sagte sie laut: "nein der Vater!" mit einem Tone, den ich eher für Schmerz, als für Reue, halten mußte' (emphases original).

[110] Throughout his account, Voget consistently speaks of himself in the third person.

[111] Voget, *Giftmörderin*, 236, emphases original: 'Es liegt in diesem, später auch dem Defensor oft wiederholten Bekenntnisse, dessen Wahrheit niemand bezweifeln wird, eine tiefe religiöse Bedeutung. Die Liebe der *Mutter* zu ihren *Kindern* ist mehr eine angeborne, instinktartige; auch das *Thier* liebt seine Jungen. Mehr der geistigen Kraft, der Erfüllung eines göttlichen Gebotes, liegt in der Liebe des *Kindes* zu seinen *Eltern;* und wieder repräsentiert der *Vater* unter seinen Kindern, von denen er unbedingten Gehorsam fordern darf, die Gottheit mehr, als die Mutter. – Der Verfasser gesteht, daß jenes Bekenntniß der Verbrecherin für ihn stets das Tröstliche gehabt hat, als wäre es in einer sonst so teuflisch gewordenen Natur ein Rest von Menschlichkeit.'

murdering a man who should be both father and God to her is the worst of all crimes. The 'trace of humanity' that Voget was so relieved to discover in his client is nothing more than the last vestiges of Gottfried's *femininity*. Under 'normal' circumstances, this femininity would find expression in the unquestioning obedience to God and Father; in Gottfried's corrupted world, it is manifest as the residual knowledge that parricide is a crime beside which matricide or the murder of her own children pale by comparison.

In the end, it was Gottfried's *crimes against her femininity* that led to her arrest. At the time of her arrest, at least thirty people in her immediate vicinity had become severely ill and/or died; her landlord Rumpff had already accused her of poisoning him; the piece of pork that she had given him had been tested by a doctor and found to contain arsenic. None of this, however, seemed sufficient to arrest her. What finally tipped the balance was a police officer's comment on her sexual conduct:

Police Commissarius T[onjes], asked what he knew of Mrs Gottfried's conduct, declared:

She has a bad reputation. It is said that she lived in adultery with her second husband while her first was still alive; there has also been much talk about the frequent fatalities in her house, but without hard facts.

At this, the officers of the court decided to betake themselves immediately to the house of the widow Gottfried.[112]

Tonjes's inventory of suspicious details is revealing: her reputation as an adulteress comes first, gossip about the many deaths in her house second – not only in sequence, we might suspect, but also in importance. Perhaps this does not mean that one count of adultery weighed more heavily on the court's mind than multiple murders, but it does show that Gottfried only came under real suspicion as a *criminal* once her reputation as a *woman* was undermined. The fact that it only occurred to the police to arrest her for murder once she was suspected of sexual misconduct unwittingly proves that Gottfried had been quite right in wearing her thirteen corsets. What protected her from discovery for over fourteen years, even as people in her

---

[112] Voget, *Giftmörderin*, 9: 'Polizeicommissair T., befragt, was ihm aus dem Lebenswandel der Gottfried bekannt sey, erklärte: / Sie steht in üblem Rufe. Man glaubt, daß sie mit dem zweiten Manne beim Leben des ersten im Ehebruche gelebt habe; auch ist viel über die häufigen Todesfälle dort im Hause gesprochen worden; jedoch ohne bestimmte Data. / Das Gericht beschloß darauf, sich sofort zu der Gottfried Wittwe zu begeben.' Officer Tonjes's declaration as recorded in the court records corresponds verbatim: 'Sie steht in üblem Ruf. Man glaubt, daß sie mit dem zweyten Mann beym Leben des ersten im Ehebruch gelebt habe; auch ist viel über die häufigen Todesfälle dort im Haus gesprochen worden; allerdings ohne bestimmte Daten' (*Protokolle*, 1 8).

immediate vicinity continued to die, was her successful impersonation of feminine *roles*: the obedient daughter and wife, the devoted mother, the decent, God-fearing, charitable provider of alms to the poor and comfort to the sick. Her real crime was not limited to the fact that she murdered fifteen people, most important among them, as Voget would have it, her father. Her real crime lay in what the murder of her parents, children, husbands, fiancé, friends and neighbours *symbolised*, namely her rejection of the roles of daughter, wife, mother and woman of good repute – the exact roles on whose successful impersonation her social, and also her physical, survival depended. This may also be the true reason why Gottfried's crimes remained incomprehensible to her judges, her defender, her contemporary community and virtually everyone who wrote about her during and after her life. What makes her crime inexplicable is not the number of her victims (Zwanziger, Ursinus and Brinvilliers were also serial killers), or her lack of empathy (Zwanziger and Brinvilliers also found it in themselves to nurse their own victims to their deaths), or her successful impersonation of a Good Woman (which the three other women also consummately achieved). But Gottfried, in eliminating from her life, slowly, deliberately and consecutively, every single role permissible to women of her time, placed herself beyond analysis or explanation. To her contemporaries, Gottfried's refusal of these roles must have appeared as inexplicable as Zwanziger's desperate desire to reassume them seemed perfectly under-standable. Zwanziger's wish to usurp for herself a feminine role as *burgher* wife to which she, the lowly servant, was not entitled was deemed more than sufficient to motivate her many murders. Conversely, we might take the lack of motive for Gottfried's crimes as indicative of the extent to which her refusal to be the woman that she was mandated to be was beyond contem-porary comprehension.

It is not my intention to celebrate Gesche Gottfried as an early 'feminist', or to excuse her crimes, or to solve the mystery of her motives, or to allege that it was her conscious intention to refuse her socially prescribed role, or even to assign to her an unconscious desire to do so. The simple fact, however, is that that is precisely what she did. In eliminating every member of her family, she broke the ties that bound her personally, but also eliminated the *only* functions permitted to her by her society. This may very well not have been the motive for her murders, but it certainly was their effect. That Gesche Gottfried continued to play these roles even as she no longer fulfilled them throws a different light on many aspects of the case. It might, for instance, prompt us to reconsider her own claim that her life was preordained: Voget presents this as a preposterous excuse for her crimes and as a sign of her superstition and irreligiousness. And yet, in a social sense, she was undoubtedly correct. We might moreover consider this relevant in the context of the debate about Gottfried's ability or inability to exercise 'free will'. In the court documents, including Senator Droste's justification for her death sentence, the term is taken to mean the intellectual ability to decide whether or not to break society's rules. Nowhere does it mean the ability to create a life beyond what society offered to women in the early 1800s, a life beyond the roles of daughter, wife, mother and charitable widow. We will never know if Gesche Gottfried desired such a life, but if she did, it might have been so unthinkable even to herself – despite the 'selfishness' of which she so regularly stood accused – that she would probably have been unable to describe it, thus driving her interrogators to distraction with her monotonously repeated 'Why I did this God only knows.'

Finally, the case of Gesche Gottfried confronts us with a new understanding of the relationship between individual and society that developed in the early 1800s. In describing his client's life, crimes and death, Voget unwittingly also describes a society in which it was possible for at least one individual to exist *entirely* as a social being and have no personal life, to be all appearance and no reality, all peels and no core. His theory of Gottfried's selflessness, the 'dead wasteland inside her',[113] obviously begs the question why Gottfried's social roles as daughter, mother, wife and benefactress were not enough to fill this emptiness. But even in explaining this in rather conventional ways – by Gottfried's lack of religiousness, her carnal desires, her vanity and, above all, her selfishness – he inadvertently alludes to the unthinkable: the *possibility* that for some women, the path to self-fulfilment might lie beyond their socially prescribed existence, and that some women might literally walk over dead bodies to get there.[114]

SELF-ASSERTION: CHAMISSO'S GESCHE GOTTFRIED (1828)

There is my grave and here the block of death.
One last time in my life, let me draw breath

---

[113] Voget, *Giftmörderin*, 460 ('todte Oede ihres Innern').

[114] What remains indirect in Voget's account is made quite explicit in the works of subsequent writers on female poisoners. In the introduction to his book on female poison murderers, Adolph Kohut, to cite just one example, spends considerable time on girls' education. He recommends strict and exclusive training for their future duties as housewives and mothers and elimination of all intellectual instruction unrelated to this goal – for the express purpose of safeguarding girls from future careers as serial poisoners (5–7).

And hold a funeral speech in my own cause.
Why look at me with horror and disgust?
I waged a war, as we all do and must,
    Against a hostile force.
I only did what you all do as well,
Just better. Thus if you send me to hell
    You will do well.

Violence and deceit are all that humans dream,
What then shall, what will, what can justice mean?
The powerful alone have rights on earth.
The strong write laws for their own benefit,
They are the hangman's noose, the prison's pit
    For those of lesser worth.
But money turns a beggar into a king,
Poison and gold: the best that life can bring,
    There is no better thing.

I have ascended from the depths of shame,
I've vanquished fairy tales of guilt and blame,
The fear of ghosts and phantoms I've withstood.
Poison's dark pow'r brings wealth, supremacy,
I made it my helpmeet, suitable to me,
    And saw that it was good.
I sent my husband, brothers, to their death,
My father – and rewarded was my stealth
    By honour and by wealth.

Three children still were loathsome to my eyes,
Three children of my womb, whom I despised,
Because they were a barrier to my will.
I poisoned them, heard them cry out to me,
I watched them sink into despondency,
    Soon corpses, cold and still.
I held their corpses until evensong,
And gazing at them dry-eyed for so long,
    I felt sublime and strong.

Now all my secret pleasures were secure,
Poison saved me from all discomfiture,
And poison sent all witnesses to hell.
That I took joy in murder, in the deed,
He, who can fathom, comprehend my feat,
    Will understand me well.
Like alms my gifts of venom I increased,
And stayed to see where, like a wanton beast,
    Death held his feast.

My sense of safety was my only flaw.
For this, my head will fall into the straw,
Just payment for my rashness soon arrives.
For this alone I can't myself forgive,
To blot it out, how gladly would I give
    So many of your lives!
You! Slaughter me, since you can do no less.
Unyieldingly I gaze from life's egress
    Deep into Nothingness.[115]

Adelbert von Chamisso's poem 'The Female Poisoner' ('Die Giftmischerin') was written in 1828, the year of Gottfried's arrest, and thus his poisoner mounts the scaffold three years before her real-life original. That he based his poem on Gesche Gottfried is not in question, even if he erred on the number of brothers and husbands she dispatched; it is clearly indicated by the murder of three children and his double entendre about the poisoner distributing venom like/as alms. His poem contains, *in nuce*, some of the major contemporary theories developed about venomous women in general and Gesche Gottfried in particular. Like Voget, Chamisso portrays her as someone utterly incapable of compassion or mercy; he even prefigures Voget's reluctant defence that she was 'addicted' to poisoning in his character's admission that she took pleasure in her crimes. The struggle between individual and society that emerges briefly and without consequence in Feuerbach's motivation of Zwanziger resurfaces here as well, but

---

[115] Adelbert von Chamisso, 'Die Giftmischerin': 'Dies hier der Block und dorten klafft die Gruft. / Laßt einmal mich noch atmen diese Luft, / Und meine Leichenrede selber halten. / Was schauet ihr mich an so grausenvoll? / Ich führte Krieg, wie jeder tut und soll, / Gen feindliche Gewalten. / Ich tat nur eben, was ihr alle tut, / Nur besser; drum, begehret ihr mein Blut, / So tut ihr gut. // Es sinnt Gewalt und List nur dies Geschlecht, / Was will, was soll, was heißet denn das Recht? / Hast du die Macht, du hast das Recht auf Erden. / Selbstsüchtig schuf der Stärkre das Gesetz, / Ein Schlächterbeil zugleich und Fangenetz / Für Schwächere zu werden. / Der Herrschaft Zauber aber ist das Geld: / Ich weiß mir Beßres nicht auf dieser Welt, / Als Gift und Geld. // Ich habe mich aus tiefer Schmach entrafft, / Vor Kindermärchen Ruhe mir geschafft, / Die Schrecken vor Gespenstern überwunden. / Das Gift erschleicht im Dunkeln Geld und Macht, / Ich hab es zum Genossen mir erdacht, / Und hab es gut befunden. / Hinunter stieß ich in das Schattenreich / Mann, Brüder, Vater, und ich ward zugleich / Geehrt und reich. // Drei Kinder waren annoch mir zur Last, / Drei Kinder meines Leibes; mir verhaßt, / Erschwerten sie mein Ziel mir zu erreichen. / Ich habe sie vergiftet, sie gesehn, / Zu mir um Hülfe rufend, untergehn, / Bald stumme, kalte Leichen. / Ich hielt die Leichen lang auf meinem Schoß, / Und schien mir, sie betrachtend tränenlos, / Erst stark und groß. // Nun frönt ich sicher heimlichem Genuß, / Mein Gift verwahrte mich vor Überdruß / Und ließ die Zeugen nach der Tat verschwinden. / Daß Lust am Gift, am Morden ich gewann, / Wer, was ich tat, erwägt und fassen kann, / Der wird's begreiflich finden. / Ich teilte Gift wie milde Spenden aus, / Und weilte lüstern Auges, wo im Haus / Der Tod hielt Schmaus. // Ich habe nun zu sicher nur geglaubt, / Und büß es billig mit dem eignen Haupt, / Daß ich der Vorsicht einmal mich begeben. / Den Fehl, den einen Fehl bereu ich nur, / Und gäbe, zu vertilgen dessen Spur, / Wie viele eurer Leben! / Du, schlachte mich nun ab, es muß ja sein. / Ich blicke starr und fest vom Rabenstein / Ins Nichts hinein.'

without Feuerbach's clearly unshakable faith in society's inevitable and justified victory.

Chamisso's poem takes the problem of Gesche Gottfried a step further than anyone – her judges, her defender and the many subsequent 'explainers' – have dared. He does this by *changing perspective*, by providing the answers to the mystery of the poisoner, simultaneously stating that these are not answers we can bear to hear. For once in the long history of bewildered writers searching in vain for the poisoner's motives, the reader is put in the precise place where all questions are answered – into the poisoner's mind. Chamisso's move forces the reader to abandon the perspective of the one who interrogates, examines or studies the poisoner; we are no longer on the outside looking in, but on the inside looking out. And let the reader beware: reproducing the poisoner's worldview beyond the barest minimum of comprehension, identifying with it, emulating it, would exact the loss of all ties binding the individual to society, humanity, religion or morality.

Like Feuerbach's character, Chamisso's is defined, or rather defines herself, as someone at war with her society. Whereas Feuerbach's Zwanziger, however, vainly rebels against a fundamentally moral society, Chamisso's poem permits the rebel to defy her opponent as 'a hostile force' defined by the very characteristics that Voget employed to describe Gottfried: violence and deceit. In the might-makes-right philosophy of Chamisso's character, survival necessitates strength and strength necessitates brutality; ethical considerations (the fairy tales, ghosts and phantoms of the third stanza) merely stand in the way of survival. It is this that makes her most inhumane, in the sense of amoral: beyond the carelessness that leads to her capture, she can regret nothing. But it is also this that makes her most human: her war is the one that all individuals, to the extent that they wish to *be* individuals, wage against society, and she claims, in the penultimate stanza, that she *can* be understood. There is no irresolvable mystery here.

Joachim Linder and Jörg Schönert have claimed, and rightly, that Chamisso's poem allows for both a moralistic and a socially critical reading.[116] Its portrayal of the poisoner echoes Voget's interpretation of Gottfried as 'empty' of all recognisable human emotion, but it also allows her to indict her society. 'I only did what you all do as well, / Just better.' Not everyone might be able to uphold a career as a serial killer while remaining an honoured and respected member of the community, untouched by the slightest suspicion, for decades. Clearly, however, the fulfilment of any social role, however defined, mandates self-representation,

---

[116] Linder and Schönert 347.

social affectation, and hence a measure of deception, and the less suitable the individual perceives that role to be, the greater the deception required to perform it. In the poem, the title character's equation of her crimes with social 'normality' is ostentatiously justified by her Hobbesian definition of the world. But again, Chamisso takes this theme one step further, further perhaps than readers might wish to follow. What appears in Voget's text as an indirect allusion – a woman's refusal to accept the life prescribed by her gender and by her society – mushrooms, in Chamisso's poem, into the usurpation of the act of creation. For his poisoner not only destroys (lives), she also creates an alternative life for herself, made possible by enlisting poison as her 'helpmeet'. Like God, she creates and functions as the only possible judge of her own creation: she 'saw that it was good'.

To contemporary readers, this blasphemous passage might well have been the most shocking part of the poem; within the world of the poem, however, it is the poisoner's ultimate act of self-assertion. In assuming the divine prerogatives to create life and to take it away, Chamisso's poisoner not merely rejects rules, she rewrites them, and it is this that makes the ultimate difference between a loss of self, as diagnosed by Voget, and the creation, and assertion, of self. Chamisso's poisoner needs no further justification for this than the sense of her own power, for 'The powerful alone have rights on earth.' It is only logical that her own death is as inconsequential to her at the end as the deaths of her victims; with her power, she has lost all right to self-assertion, and thus she accepts that she has forfeited her self to the war she wages. But this is no tearful surrender as portrayed in the 'scaffold literature' of the time,[117] no acknowledgment of society's rights over her (beyond that granted by pure power), and certainly no return to God. 'Unyielding' to the end, she once more links her own behaviour with social 'normality' by labelling her own execution as much a 'slaughter' as her own slaughter of innocents, and her glance beyond mortal life shows her neither the Gardens of Paradise nor the Gates of Hell. What Chamisso's poisoner sees, looking outside herself, is precisely what Voget saw looking inside Gesche Gottfried: a void. She was nothing – and to nothingness she returned.

---

[117] For a more extensive discussion of this, see the following chapter.

CHAPTER 7

The end: the etiquette of execution

On the surface, executions do not seem to be a gendered affair. The death penalty in German-speaking countries was tied to the nature of the crime, not the gender of the criminal, and thus female offenders as well as male were executed throughout both centuries. Histories of the death penalty mention no gender-specific difference that was generally applied to men and women on the scaffold, unless the form of execution itself was gender-specific. However, 'male' forms of punishment such as breaking on the wheel,[1] disembowelling and quartering, and 'female' ones such as drowning, sacking and live burial disappeared in practice, and eventually also in legislation, in the late eighteenth to early nineteenth centuries. Thereafter, most capital offenders, male or female, were either beheaded – which was considered the less pain- and shameful form of execution – or hanged.[2] Histories of the death penalty seem to assume, and certainly convey the impression, that the manner of women's state-imposed deaths was gender-blind.[3] Why this should be so, given women's different civic, legal, social and political status in life, is

---

[1] Women were also occasionally subjected to this form of execution (see the case of Maria Katharina Wächtler, chapter 4).

[2] See, among others, Evans, *Rituals*, 238–50; Foucault 7–13; van Dülmen, 'Schauspiel', 207. The two most common forms of execution, beheading and hanging, had strong associations with gender and class: common thieves were hanged, members of the aristocracy beheaded; 'mercy' meant, in many cases, commutation from a painful or dishonourable sentence like hanging, drowning or breaking on the wheel to beheading (van Dülmen, 'Schauspiel' 212). Hanging was considered a more disgraceful death than beheading possibly because of its associations, since antiquity, with femininity. In ancient Rome, it was called 'the death of women' (Naish 81–2). Women are commonly associated with the earth, and thus hanging, as a way of 'separating her from the earth' (Cantarella, quoted in Naish 82), was considered a symbolically 'feminine' death. It was also a highly undignified death involving kicking and writhing and blackened and distorted faces.

[3] See, among others, van Dülmen, 'Das Schauspiel' and *Theater des Schreckens*; Evans; Martschukat; Lewandowski; Härter; Möller; Rusche and Kirchheimer; Radbruch, 'Ars moriendi'; Rossa.

a question not even posed in works focusing on the criminality of women.[4]

Considerable evidence, much of it perhaps too unsavoury to be touched by serious historians,[5] mitigates against this presumed gender-blindness of punishments. Common knowledge as well as common sense indicate that the rape of women prisoners by their guards was widespread. During the French Revolution, incidents are documented involving 'judges in Brest, for example, copulating with the bodies of decapitated girls in a dissecting theatre, in full view of the public'.[6] And the titillating quality of executions seems to have been considerably stronger when the person to be executed was female. There are sordid stories of Charlotte Corday's breasts being ogled as she was drenched by a torrential downpour immediately before execution, seedier ones of a delighted crowd looking up a hanged woman's skirts: in brief, 'there is the problem of public lust'.[7] None of this, however, is *state-imposed*, and thus these examples are of limited value in showing up the gendered aspect of execution as a process planned and implemented by the State. It is therefore hardly surprising that most execution histories do not profess a particular interest in gender.

If the character of execution, as far as its historical representation is concerned, is not gendered, it certainly is *theatrical*. Theatre and drama seem irresistible metaphors for historians of the death penalty, supplying their titles – *Staged Killing*; *Theatre of Horror*; 'The Drama of Death'; *The Spectacle of Suffering*, 'Theatres of Cruelty'; *The Dramaturgy of State Executions*[8] – and shaping their findings.[9] The undeniable theatricality of

---

[4] The now considerable literature on gender-specific legal norms and women's different treatment before the law (among others: Schnabel-Schulte; Hull, 'Sexualstrafrecht'; Weber-Will; Warren-Sabean) is not matched by parallel studies on the different treatment of women on the scaffold, beyond stating the existence of gender-specific punishments (see, among others, Naish; van Dülmen, *Frauen vor Gericht*; Ulbricht, 'Kindsmörderinnen vor Gericht', *Kindsmord* and *Von Huren und Rabenmüttern*; Wächtershäuser). Evans's misleadingly titled chapter 'Gender and the Representation of Punishment' (*Rituals*, 159–67) deals with the gendered representation of criminals rather than that of their punishments.

[5] Evans, for example, professes considerable worry about being classed with those historians who write with 'sensational or titillating intent', trade 'in the pornography of suffering and death', or 'appeal mainly to the reader with sadistic inclinations' (see his 'Preface' to *Rituals*, xiii).

[6] Naish 247.

[7] On the Corday story, see Naish 117–18; on the incidents involving hanged women, Naish 83–4; the quotation Naish 246.

[8] Jürgen Martschukat, *Inszeniertes Töten*; Richard van Dülmen, *Theater des Schreckens* and 'Das Schauspiel des Todes'; Pieter Spierenburg, *The Spectacle of Suffering*; Richard Evans, 'Theatres of Cruelty' (in *Rituals*, 27–64); John Lofland, *The Dramaturgy of State Executions*; see also Zelle's definition of the execution as the 'theatrical fulfillment of torture' ('Autorität', 58: 'die Funktion der öffentlichen Hinrichtung ..., in der die Folter ihre theatralische Erfüllung fand').

[9] For example, with respect to the 'power of the people' motif; see the second part of this chapter.

executions seems to beg the apparently irrelevant gender question yet again: as we know from bourgeois tragedies, dying women make good drama. 'The death of a beautiful woman is, unquestionably, the most poetical topic in the world',[10] pronounced Edgar Allan Poe, who must be considered an expert on women's poetical deaths. And here is Camille Naish's dramatisation of women's executions, introducing a chapter named 'Tragedy, Romance':

Dramatically, the situation is a simple one: a woman is condemned to death. There will be characters: a judge, perhaps an executioner; a victim too; and possibly spectators, or witnesses of some kind. There will be a cause – why is she condemned? – and an outcome: the sentence is or is not carried out. Then, the human feelings. The victim may deplore her fate, or she may welcome it – may actually have chosen it, as a necessary consequence of self-defining deeds. Perhaps she has broken laws; if she admits that she was wrong, she may be spared. Then again, her sense of self may not permit this. Depending on the religious or philosophical context of events, her choice gives rise to tragedy or martyrdom. A happy outcome will be relatively rare.

With bleak beginnings such as this, what scope is there for poetry? Great scope.[11]

This, rather ambiguously, seems to allow for two interpretations. On the one hand, it points to the obvious fact that executions, particularly of women, have inspired literary works.[12] On the other – and this is the aspect that shall interest me below – it alludes to the poetic and dramatic aspects of real-life executions, which are rife in non-literary as well as literary texts and far transcend the predominantly metaphorical meaning that historians of the death penalty have assigned them.

There are two questions that, although largely unanswerable, are also unavoidable for anyone writing on the subject. Specifically: *What can their poetic and dramatic aspects tell us about executions?* And more generally: *What can executions tell us about gender, humanity and civilisation?* I would consider these questions unanswerable for precisely opposite reasons. To the first, there are many good specific answers (specific, that is, to epoch, philosophy, theology, nationality and culture), none of which, however, are universally applicable. To the second, there can only be a universal answer, which cannot, however, be convincingly supported by specific evidence. Rather than attempting an answer to either, I will therefore take both questions as guides. The specific question – *what does its theatrical side tell us about*

---

[10] In *The Philosophy of Combustion*, quoted in Naish 185.   [11] Naish 185.
[12] Including, but certainly not limited to, the copious infanticide literature of the 1770s and 1780s (see chapter 5). On literary executions, see Ballester.

executions? – will inform my reading of specific cases in the first part of this chapter. The general question – *what do executions tell us about gender, humanity and civilisation?* – will inform my reading, in the second part, of those historians and sociologists who have bravely attempted to answer it.

FINAL SCENES: WILLING CONFESSIONS, GOOD DEATHS AND GRATEFUL CORPSES

Eighteenth- and early nineteenth-century punishments were founded on the idea of justice made visible; hence, there was a strict correlation between crime and punishment, initially theorised by Hobbes, demanded by Beccaria and Montesquieu, and worked out to the last detail by Bentham.[13] This is why arsonists were burned alive, thieves had their hands chopped off and blasphemers their tongues cut out or pierced.[14] The purpose of executions was to appease God and avert his wrath, to eliminate the crime by eliminating the criminal, and to repair the rift in the social fabric that had occurred through the commission of the crime.[15] An execution, in other words, was less about punishing a crime than about *taking it back*.

For this reason, all efforts focused on making the criminal take it back, or rather – the next best thing – to make her say that she would if she could. Her 'willing' confession – defined as a confession not made under torture, although confessions made immediately preceding, following or under threat of torture were deemed voluntary – provided not only the foundation for the death sentence, but also the first step on her journey from sinner to saint.[16] Formerly a criminal, now a 'poor sinner', she was expected to mount the scaffold exuding humility and grace. From there, she would meekly state that she deserved death for her crimes, beg forgiveness of the people she had harmed, take leave of her family, thank the authorities for her mild sentence, admonish the people not to follow her wicked example, kiss the staff that was broken over her or the sword about to behead her, and die, praying loudly until the final moment, a Christian death.[17]

To produce this kind of behaviour, a certain amount of time – ranging from the legally required three days to, in some cases, several months – was

[13] See the discussion in Rusche and Kirchheimer 73–4.   [14] van Dülmen, 'Schauspiel', 225.
[15] See, among others, van Dülmen, 'Schauspiel', 244 and *Theater*, 11; Willems 20.
[16] Among others, Martschukat, *Inszeniertes Töten*, 33, 37–9; Evans, *Rituals*, 84–5.
[17] van Dülmen, 'Schauspiel', 241–2 and *Theater*, 22; Foucault 43–6, 65–7.

allowed to elapse between sentencing and execution.[18] During this time the clergy were permitted unlimited access to the condemned. The role of the clergy was not to console the 'poor sinner' or to aid her psychologically, but to exhort her confession, forestall all temptations to retract it – even if her innocence was known or suspected – and ensure that her behaviour on the scaffold conformed to the expectations of the authorities and her awaiting public.[19] A retracted confession compelled cancellation or rescheduling of the execution, which meant public embarrassment for the authorities and a resumption of interrogation and torture for the condemned.[20]

Historians of the death penalty have unanimously stated that very few offenders ever resisted this process of public penitence or their prescribed role in it.[21] The extraordinary collaboration of the condemned throughout several centuries can be explained, as historians have, with an understandable fear of renewed torture; the desire to die with dignity, in a state of grace and public acceptance, may also have played its coercive part. Most likely, their own execution was the first and only time that the condemned were permitted to 'star' in the production of their own deaths and, seen from the retrospective of the scaffold, that of their 'sinful' lives.[22] Whatever the reasons:

Almost without exception, the condemned gave the impression of being penitent Christians who went straight to heaven after making a 'good death' … The 'good death' of the malefactor purged the community of its blood-guilt and cancelled out the 'bad death' – sudden, unprepared, and bereft of the opportunity to make peace with God and the world – of the malefactor's murdered victim.[23]

The criminal's 'willing confession' was the only possible path to her 'good death' and Life Everlasting. Executions were public in part because they were charged to visualise this transition. And the sinner's loudly expressed thanks for the mild and just sentence enabling her swift reunion with God must have been reassuring in an age when customs like the 'Hangman's Meal' (*Henkersmahlzeit*) and the oath of non-retribution (*Urfehde*) were seen as a guarantee that the

---

[18] Van Dülmen, *Theater*, 81–91 and 'Schauspiel', 209. The three-day minimum, reminiscent of the three days between Christ's death and resurrection, already symbolised the religious, rather than legal, character of this custom (see Evans, *Rituals*, 65–6).

[19] van Dülmen, 'Schauspiel', 214: 'Im Zuge der Entstehung des frühmodernen Strafwesens jedoch fungierte der Geistliche zunehmend als obrigkeitlicher Beauftragter, der den Delinquenten von der Urteilsverkündung bis zur Hinrichtung nicht mehr allein zu lassen und so auf den Tod vorzubereiten hatte, daß er ihn willfährig annahm. Er mußte sich jeder Stellungnahme zum Verbrechen enthalten und durfte keinesfalls den Verurteilten – auch wenn er eventuell von seiner Unschuld überzeugt war – ermutigen, ein Geständnis zurückzuhalten; dieses zu erhalten war im Gegenteil vordringliche Pflicht … Ziel war ein Schuldbekenntnis und womöglich eine Entschuldigung des Delinquenten.'

[20] van Dülmen, *Theater*, 83, 206; Evans, *Ritual*, 115.

[21] Among others, van Dülmen, *Theater*, 34, 145, 162; Evans, *Ritual*, 83–4.

[22] van Dülmen, 'Schauspiel', 242 and *Theater*, 84–5, 162.   [23] Evans, *Rituals*, 85.

condemned would not incite others to avenge their deaths, or even come back from the dead to haunt the community.[24] In all, this procedure

guaranteed the peace of society by ensuring a 'grateful corpse'. And it reassured those who witnessed it that they had done a good deed. They had paved the way to eternal life for a soul seemingly beyond redemption. If it was possible for an evil criminal to go to heaven in this way, then it was surely possible for the ordinary people who witnessed the execution to do the same.[25]

Various means of dissemination ensured that this moral was not lost on the public. Broadsheets depicting the sinner's evil life and blessed death in song and story were sold at executions;[26] wandering balladeers (*Bänkelsänger*) sang the ditty of their sin and redemption and sold printed versions;[27] priests published accounts of the 'blessed final hours' of the condemned, purportedly taken down from personal observation.[28] At the close of the eighteenth century, the public staging of executions reached a pinnacle of pomp, solemnity and grandeur undreamed of in the sixteenth[29] (fig. 11).

An example of what has now become known as 'scaffold literature' (*Schafottliteratur*) is Johann Jakob Moser's collection of *Blessed Final Hours of Persons Executed (Selige letzte Stunden hingerichteter Personen)*. Originally published in 1740, it was reissued in 1861 – at a time when the death penalty experienced a lull in most German states between its abolition in 1848/9 and its reintroduction in the 1880s[30] – by a clergyman who saw Moser's many examples of true conversions in the face of death as the best answer to opponents of the death penalty.[31] Moser himself, who was known for his juridical as well as theological writings, might have concurred. While the jurist Moser does not comment on the death penalty *per se*, the theologian Moser clearly appreciates its usefulness in preventing the relapse of converts:

---

[24] *Urfehde* was an oath required by all accused, including those who were released as innocent, not to avenge themselves or invite revenge for their captivity and interrogation under torture (see van Dülmen, *Theater*, 49–50); the Hangman's Meal was the final meal in which all who participated in the judgment and execution (judge, jurors, executioner and malefactor) partook. The collaboration of the condemned in this, their act of 'breaking bread' with their own judges and executioners, was likewise seen as an act of forgiveness and hence a guarantee against future vengeance for their deaths (see Evans, *Ritual*, 67; van Dülmen, 'Schauspiel', 216).

[25] Evans, *Rituals*, 86.   [26] Evans, *Rituals*, 150–90.

[27] Many of them are collected in Braungart, *Bänkelsang*.

[28] See, for example, the collections by Moser; for individual reports of this kind, see Patzke and the anonymous 'Auferbauliches Lebens-Ende der Agatha Laimerinn'.

[29] Most histories agree that the public pageantry of death reached an unparalleled height and complexity immediately before the abolition of the death penalty. See, among others, van Dülmen, 'Schauspiel', 207 and *Theater*, 103.

[30] Evans, *Rituals*, 240–395.   [31] See F. M. Kapff, 'Vorwort' 3 to the 1861 edition.

Fig. 11 The 'Galgenfeld' (Gallow's Field), the execution site in Frankfurt am Main in the eighteenth century, in today's Bahnhofsviertel. The drawing depicts an execution by breaking on the wheel (1741)

Sorrowful experience teaches us that revivals are blossoms of which the greatest number fall off the tree without ever bearing fruit; even those reborn not only can relapse, but at times actually do so … This gives rise to the justified concern whether the foundation within such a person is laid deep and firm and whether it can be hoped that he would remain faithful if released. However: this is not something we need to worry about.[32]

Moser's collection is filled with examples of successful conversions, for which the story of Marie Salome Hausmann, executed on 16 August 1715 for infanticide, can stand as paradigmatic. Her story begins with her confession, which relates not only the crime, but also the life of sin that led to it. She pleaded guilty to

---

[32] 'Erweckungen sind, wie die betrübte Erfahrung lehrt, Blüthen, davon der größte Theil abfällt, ohne Frucht, ja auch Wiedergeborene können nicht nur wieder zurückfallen, sondern thun es auch wirklich zuweilen … Mithin entsteht die nicht unbillige Besorgniß, ob der Grund bei einem solchen Menschen auch tief und fest gelegt sei und ob zu hoffen wäre, daß er auch treu verbliebe, wenn er loskäme. Allein dafür haben wir gar nicht zu sorgen' (Moser, 'Vorrede', 1861 edition, v–vi).

having been a frivolous, brazen, and haughty worldling who cared nothing for the word of God … 'Therefore', she said, 'I only ever took to worldly matters of the flesh … In church my thoughts wandered and I was more interested in gazing at persons to whom I was partial than paying attention to the word of God.' … In such blindness she sowed for the flesh and from it she soon reaped her doom. She fell pregnant in dishonour and was brazen enough to deny and blaspheme when confronted, and so haughty that she, in order to escape worldly shame, unnaturally laid hands on her newborn and well-formed little boy, miserably choking him to death with her handkerchief.[33]

In Moser's account, both theological and juridical aspects make an appearance. Hausmann's irreligious and insubordinate character disallows viewing her as the innocently seduced maiden of infanticide poetry. Moser also makes clear that the child was alive and healthy and that she killed it not in a state of despair but due to her characteristic 'haughtiness'. Thus rendered ineligible for worldly mercy, Hausmann is reduced to throwing herself on that of God.

Hausmann's story is emblematic for others in Moser's compilation. Not a single one of the numerous murderesses whose stories he tells were seduced or despairing; without exception, they began their lives of crime with misdemeanours such as disobedience to their parents, haughtiness, laziness, worldliness and carnality.[34] From there it is only a tiny step, to hear Moser tell it, to major crimes like infanticide or murder. In the near-complete absence of biographical information or remarks on Hausmann's origins, education, situation, motivation or state of mind at the time of the crime, all of which Moser apparently considers irrelevant, Hausmann's motives for conversion remain as obscure as the motives for her crime. 'In prison she soon recognised and wept over her sin and understood in particular the *origin* of her terrible crime, that is: her *contempt for the word of God*.'[35]

---

[33] 'daß sie ein leichtsinniges, freches, hochmüthiges Weltkind gewesen sei und nach Gottes Wort Nichts gefragt habe … "Daher bin ich auch," sagte sie, "nach dem fleischlichen Weltsinn dahingegangen … In der Kirche hatte ich andre Gedanken und ließ meine Augen mehr hinschießen auf die Personen, die ich gern sah, als daß ich auf GOttes Wort Acht hatte." … In dieser Blindheit säete sie auf das Fleisch und mußte bald von demselben das Verderben ernten. Sie wurde in Unehren schwanger und war so frech, zu leugnen und zu lästern, wenn man sie zur Rede stellte und so hochmüthig, daß sie, um der zeitlichen Schande zu entgehen, wider die Natur an ihr neugebornes, wohlgebildetes Knäblein die Hand legte und es mit ihrem Taschentuch elend um's Leben brachte' (Moser, 1861 edition, 11–12).

[34] Examples of hardened sinners (all from the 1861 edition) are the stories of Else Klicken, drowned in 1735 (17–27); Katharina Elisabethe Uhl, beheaded in 1736 (27–9); Anna Martha Hungerland, executed for infanticide in Sachsen-Weimar (33–9); Gertrud Magdalene Bremmel from Westerhausen (39–50); Anna Elisabetha Cumm, executed in 1747 in Wernigerode (50–7); Anna Margarethe Renner, executed in 1752 in Ebersdorf (58–66); Christiane Ruthardt, executed in 1845 in Stuttgart (164–70); and Anna Regina Töpler, executed in 1744 (178–81).

[35] Moser (1861 edition) 12: 'Im Gefängnisse erkannte und beweinte sie ihre Sünde bald und kam namentlich auf die *Quelle* des schrecklichen Verbrechens, nemlich auf die *Verachtung des Worts GOttes*' (emphases original).

Hausmann's conversion, while peculiarly unmotivated, is intense and verbose. For her former haughtiness, she now compensates with volubly expressed penitence; her earlier disregard for the word of God is counter-balanced by her constant invocation of Scripture, which she quotes fluently, unfailingly providing chapter and verse. Spending her time preaching copiously to family, friends, acquaintances and bystanders, admonishing all to take warning from her example, she impatiently awaits the day of execution. One brief excerpt shall stand as representative for her many elaborate expressions of anticipation, which make up most of Moser's account:

'When', she cried, 'will the day come when I can rejoice towards Zion? When shall it happen that I shall suffer the stroke of the sword and then see my Jesus in Heaven and my dear child's soul in Abraham's bosom? My heart leaps for joy in my body when I think of Heaven in the assurance that my poor child, murdered by me, is nevertheless certainly in Paradise. O my dear little angel, how I will embrace and kiss you! How I will clasp you to my heart and love you all the more, for ever and in all eternity!'[36]

Small surprise, then, that she receives her death sentence with great joy: 'She thanked the dear authorities for the merciful sentence and blessed them for it.'[37] Her final day is described as follows:

When her pastor greeted her on Friday morning in the name of Jesus with the words: Truly, I say unto you, this very day you shall be in Paradise with Me, she answered: Oh yes, oh yes! Up to Heav'n I shall be raised, evermore shall God be praised. With this joyful spirit she walked the grave course, through shaming and taunting, to the bitter pillory ... She prayed diligently and sang joyously all the way to the scaffold ... Then she hurriedly mounted the scaffold, sat down on the chair and called out with a clear voice, on her own impulse: 'Lord Jesus, raise my spirit up!' And with the word: *up* – her head fell. Head *down* and spirit *up* were one and the same.[38]

---

[36] '"Wann kommt doch," rief sie, "der Tag, daß ich gen Zion jauchzen kann? Wann soll es denn geschehen, daß ich den Schwertstreich soll ausstehen und meinen JEsum d'rauf im Himmel und meines lieben Kindleins Seele in Abrahams Schooße sehen? Mein Herz im Leibe hüpft mir vor Freuden, wenn ich an den Himmel denke und versichert bin, daß mein armes, von mir ermordetes Kindlein dennoch gewiß im Himmel ist. O liebes Engelein, wie will ich dich herzen und küssen! Wie will ich dich an mein Herz hinandrücken und dich desto brünstiger lieben immer und ewiglich!'" (Moser, 1861 edition, 13).

[37] 'Sie bedankte sich für das gnädige Urtheil und wünschte dafür der lieben Obrigkeit allen Segen' (Moser, 1861 edition, 14).

[38] 'Als ihr Seelsorger Freitag Morgens sie im Namen JEsu mit den Worten begrüßte: Wahrlich Ich sage dir, heute wirst du mit Mir im Paradiese sein, antwortete sie: Ei ja, ei ja! Himmlisch Leben wird GOtt geben Mir dort oben; Ewig soll mein Herz Ihn loben. Mit diesem freudigen Geiste trat sie auch den *ernsten Gang* an durch Schmach und Spott nach dem sauern Prangerstand ... Den ganzen Weg hinaus betete sie eifrig und sang freudig ... Darauf bestieg sie eilend das Schaffot, setzte sich gutwillig auf den Richtstuhl und rief mit heller Stimme aus eigenem Antrieb: 'HErr JEsu, nimm meinen Geist auf!' Und unter dem Wort: *auf* – fiel ihr Haupt. Kopf *ab* und Geist *auf* war Eines' (Moser, 1861 edition, 14–15, emphases original).

For an account that purports to be an accurate description of Hausmann's execution exactly as it occurred, this story contains some astonishingly undisguised literary elements. To speak with Naish, it is lyrical; to speak with the historians of executions, it is theatrical. Hausmann, not content with merely displaying her recently acquired biblical erudition, speaks in rhymed verse. The final line – *down* falls the head, *up* flies the spirit – provides Hausmann's life and death with a highly satisfying symmetry that is merely the apex of the juxtapositions related earlier in the story: that between her initial impiety and her fervent faith after conversion, for example, or that between the cold-blooded murder of her child and the love she lavishes on his memory. Such symmetry, while in itself highly poetic, indicates an instance of catharsis that is more easily attainable in dramatic literature than in real life: it is not only the head we see falling, it is also the curtain.

The other conversion stories in Moser's compilation all show remarkable similarities with Hausmann's. Godlessness, haughtiness, worldliness and carnality set his infanticides irrevocably on the path to crime; seduction, rape, despair, poverty or coercion of any kind play no part in their stories. Even from the meagre biographical information Moser provides, it is clear that most of these women hailed from the servant class. And yet, these women, for whom little or no formal schooling must be assumed, turn into veritable biblical scholars in prison, sometimes in a matter of days, routinely employing a vocabulary and stylistic register betraying far more education than seems believable. Many of them, like Hausmann, practically speak in tongues, incorporating verses taken from hymns or the catechism effortlessly into their everyday speech.[39] Others state they would refuse clemency even if offered, echoing Moser's idea in his foreword that swift death was the only way to ensure the permanence of a conversion: 'I don't want to live, but would much rather die so I can go to Christ … I do not trust in my evil heart. If I live, I might sadden Him again; this way, however, I know I will nevermore aggrieve Him.'[40] In the throes of remorse, they exaggerate their criminal histories, accusing themselves of 'many millions of

---

[39] One example of many is a servant maid's rhymed statement: 'A heart steeped in remorse's flood, A heart drenched in my Christ's dear blood – that is what God has granted me. This is the source of my joy, so that I am not afraid to offer up my head tomorrow' ('Ein Herz mit Reu' und Leid getränkt, Mit Christi theurem Blut besprengt – ist, was mir GOtt gegeben hat. Daher rührt meine Freude, daß ich mich auch nicht fürchte, morgen meinen Kopf hinzugeben', Moser, 1861 edition, 17).

[40] 'Ich will nicht leben, sondern viel lieber sterben, daß ich zu Christo komme, dem Heilande, der die Sünder annimmt und mit ihnen ißt. Ich traue meinem bösen Herzen nicht. Bleibe ich leben, so möchte ich Ihn von Neuem betrüben; so aber weiß ich, daß ich Ihn nicht mehr betrübe' (Moser, 1861 edition, 16).

gruesome sins'[41] or calling themselves the 'most godless person in the whole world'.[42] They rush towards the scaffold,[43] several of them dying, as Hausmann did, in mid-prayer: the head of Anna Martha Hungerland, executed for the same crime twenty-two years later and in a different part of the country, falls at her exclamation 'Lord Jesus, take my spirit up!' – which was also, word for word, Hausmann's final sentence.[44]

The similarity of these stories, the recurring motifs, the complete absence of distinguishing biographical characteristics, the identical endings point to the obvious fictitiousness of these purported eyewitness accounts. Near-indistinguishable final declarations, often identical down to the precise wording, supposedly uttered by women who died over the course of 130 years, do not attest to the actuality of these statements, but rather to the limited imagination of the person who wrote them and put them in the mouths of the condemned. One hardly needs a major thinker like Michel Foucault to point out that such speeches are 'too close, even in the turn of the phrase, to the morality traditionally to be found in the broadsheets and pamphlets … not to be apocryphal'.[45] Like the broadsheets and pamphlets of the *Bänkelsang* tradition,[46] Moser's compilation is a collection of fictional, certainly unabashedly fictionalised, conversion stories whose relationship with the criminal cases on which they are based is hazy at best. As already indicated by the absence of biographical material, however, these are not intended to be individual stories: they are variations of a single story, the story of the hardened criminal turned penitent sinner and dying a martyr's death. The martyrdom of the sinner provided her with saint-like status and turned her body and blood into relics, to which were attributed miraculous healing powers until well into the nineteenth century. Fine ladies dipped their handkerchiefs into the blood spurting from the neck; heads and body

---

[41] Else Klicken thinking of God, 'welchen sie so lange Jahre mit so vielen Millionen greulicher Sünden beleidigt und erzürnt habe' (Moser, 1861 edition, 21).

[42] Anna Margaretha Renner: 'Ich bin die gottloseste Person in der ganzen Welt' (Moser, 1861 edition, 62).

[43] Examples (from Moser, 1861 edition): Else Klicken ('rushed towards the scaffold': 'eilte dem Gerüst zu', 27); Gertrud Magdalene Bremmel ('at once rushed towards the chair on which she was to be beheaded': 'eilte sogleich zum Stuhl, auf welchem sie enthauptet werden sollte', 50); Anna Elisabetha Cumm ('rushed towards the chair': 'eilte dem Stuhle zu', 57).

[44] 'Herr JEsu, nimm meinen Geist auf!'; Moser, 1861 edition, 15 (Hausmann) and 39 (Hungerland). Hausmann was executed in 1715 in Nördlingen in Bavaria; Hungerland in 1737 in Saxe-Weimar.

[45] Foucault on the final speech of bandit leader Marion Le Goff, 66.

[46] Evans makes the same point about the farewell songs of malefactors as related in street ballads: 'These were not, of course, the words uttered by the malefactors themselves on the scaffold. They were made up by the street balladeers in their entirety. Indeed, the texts often changed little from one execution to another. They were cast in formulaic, stereotypical, and above all pious language, much of it taken from sermons, hymns, psalms, prayers, or phrases from the Bible' (*Rituals*, 153).

parts were routinely stolen, and as late as 1820, epileptics, drinking mugs in hand, gathered around the scaffold.[47] Faith in the medicinal virtues of the 'grateful corpse' and in the sainthood of criminals who died a 'good death' was so resolute that Moser felt compelled to issue a caution in the foreword to the second edition of 1752, warning that anyone who committed murder in an attempt to attain sainthood through execution would surely go to hell.[48]

Moser's moral tales distinguish themselves from similar stories told in pamphlets or in the songs of balladeers only through their length and their exact and protracted quotations of every hymn sung and every biblical passage cited by the condemned. Balladeers and pamphleteers told the same tale of the sinner's wicked life and blessed death, but usually made shorter work of it. A pamphlet entitled 'The Story, Intermixed with Moral Admonishments, of the Child-Murderess M. H. of T., Who was Executed by the Sword on 2 March 1779 in Aarau'[49] tells of the life and death of Margaritha Härdin of Thalheim, who was indeed executed for infanticide on that date.[50] At the outset, she appears different from the series of hardened sinners described by Moser: a servant girl, she was 'innocently seduced' by her master[51] and thus became pregnant. However, the reader's sympathies are soon dispelled by the fact that she denied her pregnancy, 'proud and accustomed to lying', and that she murdered her child in 'haughty self-confidence in her own worldly cunning and in her lies, which had been successful for too long'.[52] She threw her dead child in the

---

[47] These and several other examples in Evans, *Rituals*, 92–6. On the medicinal uses of executed persons, see also Härter, *Policey*, II 728.

[48] See Moser's foreword to the 1752 edition, reprinted in the 1861 edition, x: 'May the Lord forfend that anyone be so blind, foolish and reckless to misuse these examples in such a way that he would commit a crime punishable by death in order to die such an uplifting death! For this is neither within the power of a poor sinner nor in that of a preacher, be he ever so honest and inspired. In Romans chapter 6, verse 1.2 it is written: "Shall we then continue in sin so that Mercy be ever the greater? Far be this from us!" And Romans 3,8 makes horrifying mention of those who say: "Let us do evil so that good may issue from it! *The damnation of such is fitting and just!*"' ('Der HErr verhüte es, daß Niemand so blind, thöricht und verwegen sei, diese Exempel dahin zu mißbrauchen, daß er Etwas, worauf die Todesstrafe gesetzt ist, zu dem Ende begehe, damit er auch so erbaulich sterben möge! Das steht ja nicht weder in eines armen Sünders, noch in eines Predigers Macht, er sei so redlich und begabt als er wolle. Röm. 6, 1.2 heißt es: "Sollen wir denn in der Sünde beharren, auf daß die Gnade desto mächtiger werde? Das sei ferne!" Und Röm. 3, 8. lautet es erschrecklich von Denen, welche sprechen: "Lasset uns Uebels thun, auf daß Gutes daraus komme? *Solcher Verdammnis ists ganz recht!*"') – Moser was not the only one to voice such fears: *Der neue Pitaval* tells the story of a woman who commits murder in order to die a 'good death' (Hitzig and Häring XII [1847], 420–1).

[49] 'Mit Belehrungen vermischte Geschichte der Kinds-Mörderin M. H. von T. / Welche zu Aarau den 2. Merz 1779 mit dem Schwerd ist hingerichtet worden', reprinted in Braungart (44–50).

[50] See Braungart's commentary (333–4).   [51] Braungart 44 ('unschuldig gelocket').

[52] 'stolz und des Läugnens gewohnt' (Braungart 44); 'stolze Zuversicht auf Welt-Klugheit und aufs zu lange gelungene Läugnen' (45).

river and was swiftly arrested following its discovery. She steadfastly refused to confess to the crime, even under torture, until she was threatened with the pillory and lifelong imprisonment. 'It was at this point that she was reformed to renounce her worldliness, to acquiesce to God's will and to desire her own salvation and redemption.'[53] Initially hoping that her life might be spared, she soon realised that this would stand in the way of salvation and thus became willing 'to surrender herself joyously to the will of God and the authorities'.[54] The four clergymen who incessantly worked on her 'still count the hours they spent conversing with this sinner among the most instructive and pleasant of their lives'.[55] Her execution is turned into a celebration of martyrdom: 'O beautiful morn of her execution', exclaims the narrator, 'never shalt thou depart my memory!'[56]

The story of Margaritha Härdin exists in two additional versions: one the comparatively dispassionate song accompanying the broadsheet, the other the even more clipped version in Christian Oelhafen's *Chronicle of the City of Aarau from its Foundation to 1798* (1840). Oelhafen, drawing on the original prison records (*Thurmbuch*), offers no explanation for Härdin's sudden desire to confess following her steadfast denials even under torture. He links her confession chronologically, but not causally, to the threat of a lifelong prison sentence. 'She was sentenced to lifelong imprisonment and standing in the pillory, but freely confessed the deed shortly thereafter and showed sincere remorse, upon which she was sentenced to death by the sword.'[57] Likewise, the song states that her confession followed immediately upon the threat of permanent imprisonment but does not hint that this may have been its direct cause.

> Twelve witnesses confronted her,
> Each of them swore an oath,
> But nothing did her lies deter,
> To own it she was loath.
>
> Under torture she did bleed,
> But she did not confess the deed,

---

[53] 'Da wurde sie nun zur Verläugnung der Irdischgesinntheit – zu Ergebung in Gottes Willen und zum Verlangen nach Heil und Rettung umgearbeitet' (Braungart 46).

[54] 'sich dem Wille Gottes und der Oberkeit freudig zu überlassen' (Braungart 47).

[55] 'und diese zählen die Stunden, in denen sie sich mit dieser Sünderin unterhalten, noch jezt unter die lehrreichsten und angenehmsten ihres Lebens' (Braungart 47).

[56] 'Ja, o schöner Morgen ihrer Hinrichtung – nie müssest du meinem Andenken entfallen!' (Braungart 47).

[57] 'Sie wurde zu lebenslänglicher Gefangenschaft und ans Bloch zu Schließen verurtheilt, bekannte dann aber nach kurzer Zeit darauf freiwillig die That und bezeugte aufrichtige Reue darüber, worauf sie zum Tode durchs Schwert verurtheilt wurde' (Christian Oelhafen, *Chronik der Stadt Aarau, von deren Ursprung bis 1798*, cited in Braungart 333–4, the quotation 334).

In gaol they threw the lass therefore,
To languish there for evermore.

Then finally she did confess,
Sincere and free of all duress,
And showed remorse and sadness there,
And well she did for death prepare.[58]

The tacit omission of the obvious – that Härdin's confession did not merely follow chronologically upon, but was compelled by the decision to imprison her until she either confessed or died – is manifest in all sources, as is the claim that she confessed freely and of her own accord. To cast doubt on the voluntary nature of Härdin's confession would have been tantamount to invalidating the death sentence, effectively not only attacking the legitimacy of the legal proceedings, but also eliminating the basis for Härdin's conversion and subsequent martyrdom.

Regarding these varied text types (ballads, pamphlets, eyewitness accounts of 'final hours' and chronicles), two points are worth noting. The first is that they can all, to a greater or lesser extent, legitimately be considered *literary* texts, regardless of genre differences or the varying degrees of truth-claims. Oelhafen's account, which is based on court records, and Moser's, which purports to be taken from eyewitness reports, would certainly lay greater claim to historical accuracy than broadsheets or ballads, which are more blatantly financially motivated and hence imply a primary purpose to entertain. But like these more obviously 'literary' sources, Moser's stories are deeply indebted to lyrical and dramatic motifs and conventions, and all four text types seem to pursue the same goal, namely, to corroborate the official version of events as specified by the 'authorities'. Thus all four – this the second aspect that connects these text types – also fulfil a *legal* function, namely to broadcast this version to the public and provide evidence in support of the death sentence to which the public had no other access: to function, as it were, as literary post-trial witnesses for the State. At a time when executions were public but trials were not, the justification of the death sentence to the community must have seemed imperative to sovereigns constantly worried about public uprisings at executions.[59] It is thus

---

[58] 'Ein Lied', Braungart 49–50: 'Zwölf Zeugen gegen ihr gestellet / Welche sie eidlich han verfället, / Doch wollt sie es gestehen nicht, / Und läugnete vor dem Gericht. // Man thät sie an die Folter schlagen, / Doch wollt sie den Mord nicht aussagen; / Da thät man sie hart sperren ein / Daß sie ihr Lebtag da sollt seyn. // Endlich hat sie sich doch ergeben / Alles bekennet frey und eben, / Bezeugte auch recht Reu und Leid / Und hat sich wohl zum Tod bereit.'

[59] Evans, *Rituals*, 107, 202–25, 246, 257–64; van Dülmen, 'Schauspiel', 204, 213, 217–18, 229–40 and *Theater*, 9–10, 147–59, 183; Martschukat, *Inszeniertes Töten*, 29–30, 113–14; Foucault 52–61.

hardly surprising that the presence of pamphleteers and balladeers at executions was not only condoned but often actively supported. It is unclear, for example, how the authors of songs or broadsheets would have obtained the details of the malefactor's life, crime and trial which appear in their products, unless such details were leaked to them by the 'authorities' – with sufficient lead-time prior to the execution to allow songs to be composed, stories to be written and pamphlets to be printed.[60]

Scaffold literature, then, is literature that, while employing lyrical or dramatic conventions and motifs, at times denies its own fictitiousness and fulfils a legal function. It is characterised largely through its harmonious marriage of legal and literary aspects, expressing no conflict between its legal purpose as a mouthpiece of the State and its literariness. Many legal documents, as well, display manifestly literary characteristics by casting, as historians have tended to point out in their titles, the execution as a drama,[61] with the malefactor as the star of the production, the populace as its audience and the State as its director.

Nothing demonstrates this more clearly than the documents rehearsing what was known either as *Halsgericht* (Capital Trial) or *Endlicher Rechtstag* (Final Judgment Day). Written, on average, between three and fifteen days before execution, they constitute a dress rehearsal for the execution, setting the stage and laying down the roles, including speaking parts, for all actors in the drama: lay assessors, judges, jurors, bailiffs, executioner and the condemned.[62] The scripts normally contained meticulous instructions for the erection of execution sites and the procedure at executions, including the timing and progression of events, the size and placement of a militia or other protective military force, a precise description of the scaffold and the procession, the dress code, the placement of necessary instruments, the seating order of judges, jurors and lay assessors, the exact placement of executioner and malefactor, and instructions regarding the 'speaking roles' of judge, jurors and executioner. In a highly formulaic fashion, the court's

---

[60] Evans, *Rituals*, 151–2: 'Street singers required licences to perform. So they were obliged to adhere remarkably closely to official attitudes as far as crime and criminals were concerned, otherwise they fell foul of the censorship which was virtually universal in Germany until the middle of the nineteenth century' (152). And: 'It was clear that there was considerable cooperation in this between the authorities and the authors of these broadsheets, with the former making details of the case available to the latter' (155).

[61] My point here is distinct from, although related to, that made by Zelle, who is more interested in formal and psychological aspects than generic ones. See particularly his essay 'Strafen und Schrecken', in which he links 'the theatre of tragedy' directly with 'the tragedy of execution'.

[62] The procedure is described at length in van Dülmen, 'Schauspiel', 209–10 and *Theater*, 40–58, 102–8, 205 n. 40; Evans, *Rituals*, 70–80; Härter, *Policey*, 1 416–515.

authority was confirmed, after which the condemned was obliged to make a formal confession of her guilt and assent to the verdict; often, formulae were repeated three times, signifying irrevocability.[63] This was followed by the official reading of the death sentence, the formal dissolution of the court and turning over of the condemned to the executioner, the ceremonial procession to the place of execution (in the precise order stated[64]), and the execution itself. Even the audience, if invited to participate in the 'hue and cry' (*Zeter und Mordio*), was occasionally given a kind of limited 'speaking role', consisting of the licence to yell assertively in the right places.[65] There was nothing impromptu about these performances: the drama of execution was strictly choreographed, orchestrated down to the last minute detail, such as in what way or how fast the malefactor was permitted to walk in the procession.[66] Like most other plays of the period, these execution dramas were written for performance, configured for maximum dramatic effect and intended to convey a moral lesson to the audience. They comprised everything that makes up a literary drama: monologues for the malefactor, dialogues between judges and executioner, and precise stage directions.

One example I would like to offer by way of illustration is the formal script of the show trial of a malefactor we encountered in chapter 5: that of Johanna Catharina Höhn. Her 'Capital Trial' (*Halsgericht*) was written ten days before and performed on a stage on the market square in Weimar immediately preceding her execution for infanticide on 28 November 1783. The document contains formulaic affirmations of the legitimacy of the court and its sentence, questions directed at Höhn and her presumed answers, and a formal interrogation in which she was obliged to repeat her confession in public. W. Daniel Wilson, who discovered the document among the effects of the Weimar publisher Friedrich Justin Bertuch,[67] sums up the document's significance as follows: it gives 'a stark impression of the intimidating atmosphere at the "Halsgericht" [and represents] an important instrument in the effort to justify the execution to a public that seems to have been fairly sceptical, if not … downright outraged'.[68]

---

[63] Evans, *Rituals*, 70–2.

[64] If school classes attended, they too were given precise instructions as to where they were to march in the procession (Evans, *Rituals*, 74–5).

[65] Evans, *Rituals*, 71.   [66] van Dülmen, *Theater*, 106.

[67] See Košenina's short article on Wilson's discovery ('Staatsmord') in *Frankfurter Allgemeine Zeitung*.

[68] Wilson, 'Goethe, His Duke and Infanticide', 31. In the following, descriptions of the document will refer to the manuscript; it will be quoted in my translation of Wilson's transcription ('The "Halsgericht'''). The original document is written in right and left columns; in my transcription, a single / represents a new paragraph, a double // a new paragraph and text on the opposite side of the

The stage directions, with which the drama opens, take up the first four manuscript pages. They set the stage for Höhn's execution, determining the setting of place and time and the precise placement of props and characters. They call for the erection of a black board, a black table and fourteen black chairs, seven to the right of the table, six on the left and one at its head, in the pre-dawn hours of 28 November. At eight o'clock in the morning, this stage was to be surrounded by the militia, which was to form an outer circle composed of armed peasants and an inner circle composed of armed soldiers. At 8.30 a.m., the actors in the drama were to assemble for the formal procession to the stage,

to wit, the Right Honourable Commissarius,[69] *the Right Honourable Actuarius,*[70] *and the twelve judges and members of the jury, specifically: the eight members of the jury and the four judges, all clad entirely in black, the first two bearing swords, shall assemble in the D[ucal] court chamber, and then proceed, as soon as the clock has struck nine, preceded by the bailiff, his rifle at his side, bearing before him in both hands the sword of execution and the white staff, followed, in the following sequence, in pairs, by*

> *the Right Honourable Commissarius and the First Juror*
> *the Right Honourable Actuarius and the Third Juror*
> *the Second Juror and the Fifth Juror ...*[71]

and so on down to the last juror. The following passage outlines the seating arrangement of these officials and the precise cross-wise placement on the table of the staff that was to be broken over the condemned and the sword that was to behead her (fig. 12).

---

manuscript. The left column was reserved for the judge, so that the scribe assumed everything on the left-hand side of the manuscript (speech or directions) to pertain to him. For this reason, the judge's speech is not attributed to him in the manuscript, other than by virtue of placement on the page. Stage directions are distinguished from spoken parts by means of italics; the use of italics here does not represent emphases in the original manuscript.

[69] Commissarius = the investigating police officer.

[70] Actuarius = the court secretary or court scribe, popularly known as *Blutschreiber* (blood scribe). He would have been present at all interrogations to record questions posed to Höhn as well as her answers. He was also the keeper of court records and responsible for their accuracy. Like the judge, he must have had legal training, otherwise he would not have been able to vouch for the legality of the proceedings he recorded. See the entry in Jagemann and Brauer 23.

[71] '... *nehmlich der H[err] Amts-Commissarius, H[err] Amts Actuarius, und die 12. Schultheisen und Schöppen, nehmlich 8. Schöppen und 4 Schultheisen allerseits in schwarzer Kleidung [2ʳ] auch erstere beyde, mit dem Degen an der Seite in Hiesiger F[ürstlichen] Amts-Stube, und verfügen sich sodann aus solcher, wenn es 9. Uhr geschlagen, unter Vortretung des Amts-Frohns, welcher sein Gewehr an der Seite habend, das Richter Schwerd, und den weisen Stab, Creuzweiß gelegt, in beyden Händen haltend vorträgt, in folgender Ordnung, paarweise, als*

> *H[err] Amts Commissarius und Erster Schöppe*
> *H[err] Amts Actuarius und Dritter Schöppe*
> *Zweiter Schöppe und Fünfter Schöppe'.*

(Wilson, 'The "Halsgericht"', 34–5)

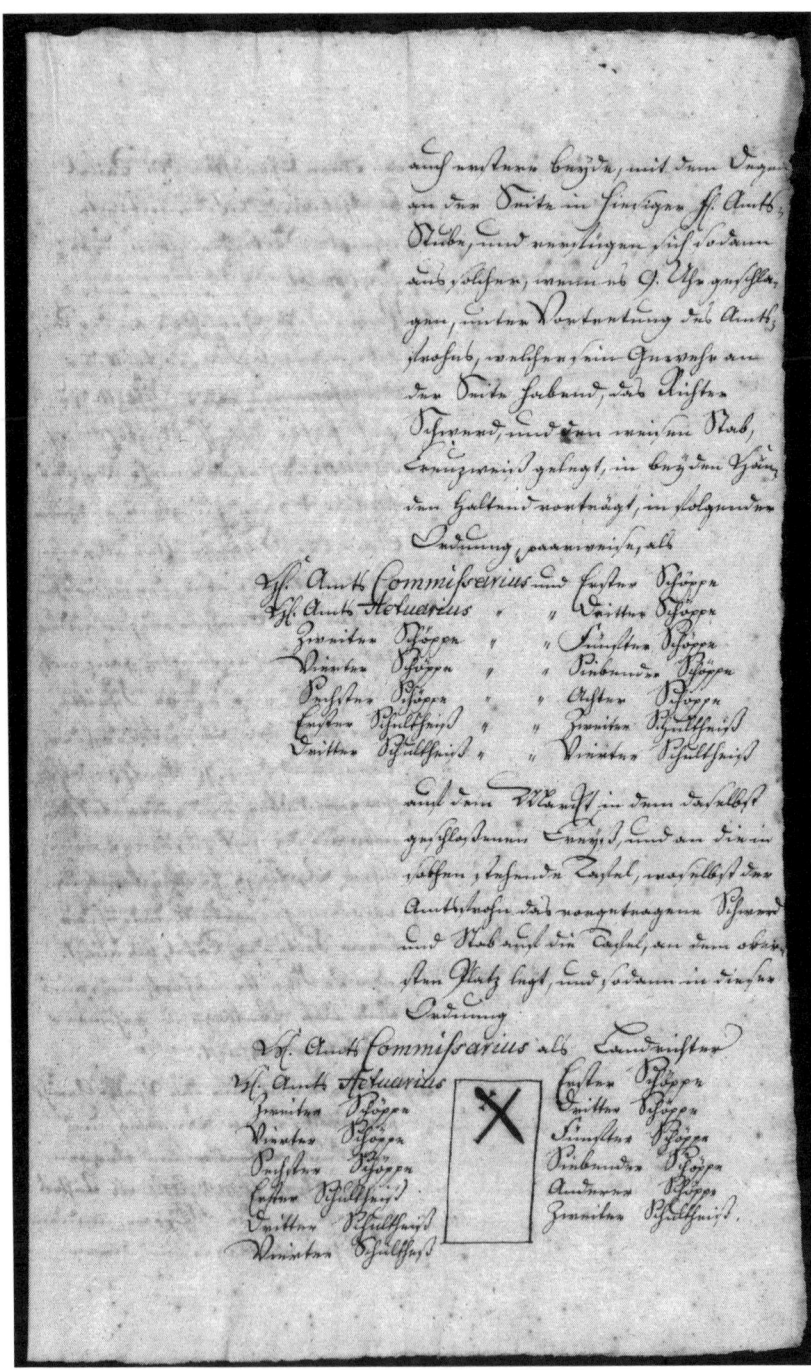

Fig. 12 A page from the 'Halsgericht' of Johanna Höhn, 28 November 1783, showing the seating arrangements for judges and jury, and the cross-wise placement of the staff to be broken over the offender and the sword that was to behead her. Courtesy of the Klassik Stiftung Weimar, Goethe- and Schillerarchiv

Behind this impressive assembly of black-clad nobles lurked the executioner, whose initial role in the play was that of accuser. Before he could proceed, however, there are four and a half more manuscript pages of question-and-affirmative-answer exchange between judge and jury, establishing officially the legitimacy of the court – in performance, this sombre dialogue would have taken approximately twenty minutes. Dramatic tension mounts as the document finally progresses to the official accusation and sentencing:

Here the executioner, as official accuser, comes forward, takes his place at the foot of the table, opposite the judge, and addresses him as follows:

[EXECUTIONER:]   Honoured Judge, I humbly ask permission that I may address this High Criminal Court, speak and accuse.

[JUDGE:]   Permission is granted to thee.

EXECUTIONER AS ACCUSER: Honoured Judge, I humbly ask permission that I may voice my accusation three times in one, so that it may endure before the law.

[JUDGE:]   Permission is accorded thee.

At this point, the poor sinner, who has meanwhile been conducted within the circle, accompanied by two clergymen, one by each side, and accompanied by guards, will be led onto the stage and placed at the foot of the table, to the right of the executioner. The executioner then continues in his role as accuser:

Honoured Judge, I accuse unto death for the first time, I accuse unto death for the second time, I accuse unto death for the third time the here present poor sinner, Anna Catharina Höhn from Tannroda, to have broken the fifth commandment and purposefully murdered and deprived of life a child brought into the world by herself. Honoured Judge, I ask whether I have brought my three accusations in such a manner as befits the law and criminal justice?

[JUDGE:]   Fourth Juror, I ask you whether the accuser has brought his three accusations in a manner befitting the law and criminal justice?

FOURTH JUROR, ON THE RIGHT: Yes, Honoured Judge, his accusation, as voiced, may be endowed with the authority of law and criminal justice.

[JUDGE:]   You have brought three accusations against Anna Catharina Höhn in such a manner as befits law and criminal justice.

EXECUTIONER AS ACCUSER: Honoured Judge, then I ask to interrogate the poor sinner Anna Catharina Höhn, on trial for her life, with regard to her deed, and confront her with her voluntary confession as well as the just sentence, and hear if she will once more confess her evil deed or not?

[JUDGE:]   So it shall be done. *(to the Actuarius:)* Actuarius, remind the poor sinner, Anna Catharina Höhn, once more of her previous confession of her evil deed and ask her if she still confesses to this crime? and then read to her the sentence and its confirmation by our Most Exalted Duke.

At this point, the Actuarius addresses the poor sinner as follows: Anna Catharina Höhn, I ask you whether:

(1)   have you not confessed and do you not now confess that you did, on the eleventh of April of this year 1783, lying in your bed between twelve and one o'clock, give birth to a child?

(2)   have you not confessed and do you not now confess that you left this child hanging from its umbilical cord for a quarter hour, thereafter severing the cord with a knife, and that the child cried and moved as you did this?

(3)   have you not confessed and do you not now confess that thereafter, you administered three stab wounds to the child's throat, first one and then two more in quick succession, with the same knife that you used to cut the umbilical cord, while holding down the child with one hand, and that the child cried a little and moved its hands?

(4)   have you not already confessed and do you not confess again that you pushed the child into the bed straw in order to suffocate it utterly in case it was not yet completely dead?

If, as is to be hoped, the poor sinner answers each individual question with a Yes!, the Actuarius will continue as follows: Since you, Anna Catharina Höhn, have again confessed the sin of which you stand accused, and the murder of your child with which you have been charged before the present criminal court, so shall now be publicly read unto you the well-founded judgment and sentence upon you, along with its confirmation by our Most Exalted Duke.

Thereafter, the Actuarius will read the complete text of the sentence, along with the Duke's rescript ordering that the sentence be carried out, loudly and clearly, and at the end of this reading, the Commissarius, in his capacity as county judge, will break the white staff, which he has heretofore held in his hands, into three pieces and throw them behind him. At this point, the executioner in his role as accuser will resume as follows: Honoured Judge, since the poor sinner Anna Catharina Höhn stands here before God under an open sky and has willingly confessed her evil deed, so I now ask who shall execute the final sentence upon her that has just now been made known and read?

Judge: This you shall perform.[72]

---

[72] '*Hier tritt der Scharfrichter, als peinlicher Ankläger gar herein stellet sich unten vor die Tafel dem Richter gegen über und redet diesen also an.* / Herr Richter ich bitte er wolle mir vergönnen, daß ich vor dieses gehegte hochnothpeinliche HalßGerichte treten, reden und anklagen möge. // Es sey dir erlaubt. // *Scharfrichter als peinlicher Ankläger.* / Herr Richter ich bitte er wolle mir erlauben, meine dreyfache Anklage in einer vollbringen zu laßen wie sie zu Recht beständig seyn möge. // Es sey dir vergönnet. // *Hier wird die inzwischen an den Creyß gebrachte arme Sünderin, welche von denen Herrn Geistl[ichen], so sie in der Mitte führen, begleitet, und von der Wache invocpiret wird in den Creyß geführet, und unten quer vor die Tafel, zur rechten Hand des Scharfrichters gestellet. // Der Scharfrichter als peinlicher Ankläger sagt sodann* [5ᵛ] / Herr Richter ich klage peinlich an zum erstenmahle, ich klage peinlich an zum andernmahle, ich klage peinlich an zum drittenmahle gegenwärtige arme Sünderin, Annen Catharinen Höhnin aus Tannroda, daß sie wieder das fünfte Geboth gehandelt, und das von ihr zur Welt gebohrne Kind vorsetzlich ermordet und um das Leben gebracht habe. Herr Richter ich frage, ob ich meine drey Anklagen in einer so vollbracht habe wie sich solches zu Recht und nach peinlicher Art gebühret? // Vierter Schöppe ich frage euch, ob der peinliche Ankläger seine drey Anklagen in

This is followed by a further two manuscript pages – approximately ten more minutes of performance – in which the executioner is formally guaranteed free passage by the court, in which the population is exhorted not to avenge Höhn's death upon the executioner, followed by a call for further accusations, followed by the formal dissolution of the court, followed by precise instructions regarding preparations to be made at the place of execution. The final sentences of the document read as follows:

After the execution has been completed, the executioner calls out: Honoured Judge, hear me!

[*JUDGE:*]   What wilt thou?
EXECUTIONER: Have I done right?
[*JUDGE:*]   Thou hast done that which justice and decree required.

einer also vollbracht habe, wie sich solches zu Recht und nach peinlicher Art gebühret? // *Vierter Schöppe zur rechten Hand.* / Ja Herr Richter wie er sie vollbracht hat, mag sie gar wohl zu Recht und nach peinlicher Art Krafft haben. // Du hast deine drey Anklagen wieder Annen Catharinen Höhnin, in einer also vollbracht, wie es sich zu Recht und nach peinlicher Art gebühret. // *Scharfrichter als peinlicher Ankläger* / Herr Richter, so bitte ich man wolle die peinlich angeklagte arme Sünderin Annen Catharinen Höhnin, darüber vernehmen, und derhalben ihre gütliche Aussage, nebst wohlbehauptet gesprochenen Urtel vorhalten, und hören, ob sie ihre Mißethat nochmahlen geständig oder nicht? // Ja, es soll geschehen /: *sich gegen den H[errn] Actuarium wendend*: / Herr Actuarius halte er, gegenwärtiger armen Sünderin, Annen Catharinen Höhnin, ihr bereits vorhin gethanes Geständniß ihrer Mißethat, noch[6ʳ] mahlen vor, befrage er selbige ob sie deren auch jetzt noch geständig? und verlese er hierauf das eingeholte Urthel, samt deßen gnädigster Confirmation. // *Hierauf redet der H[err] AmtsActuarius, die arme Sünderin also an:* / Anna Catharinen Höhnin ich frage dich / (1) Hast du nicht bereits bekannt und gestehest nochmahlen, daß du am 11. April des jetzigen 1783sten Jahres Mittags zwischen 12 u[nd] 1. Uhr im Bette liegend ein Kind gebohren? / (2) Hast du nicht eingeräumet und bekennest nochmahlen daß du dieses Kind auf eine Viertel Stunde lang an der Nabelschnur hängen lassen, nachhero aber solches mittelst eines Messers von derselben abgelöset hast, und daß das Kind dabey geheulet und sich gereget habe? / (3) Hast du nicht gestanden, und bekennest nochmahlen, daß du hierauf dem Kinde mit dem nehmlichen Messer, mit welchen du es von der Nabelschnur abgelöset gehabt, drey Stiche in den Halß, und zwar vorerst einen und dann noch zwey hintereinander gegeben, auch solches dabey mit der einen Hand gehalten, das Kind aber einwenig geschrien, und sich mit den Händen gereget habe? / (4) Hast du nicht bereits bekannt und gestehest nochmahlen, daß du das Kind in das Bettstroh gedruckt, um solchergestalt dasselbe wenn es etwan noch nicht ganz todt seyn sollte, vollends zu ersticken? // *Wenn nun wie zu verhoffen die arme Sünderin jede Frage einzeln mit einen Ja! beantwortet, so fähret hierauf der H[err] Actuarius also fort.* / Dieweil denn du, Anna Catharina Höhnin, vor gegenwärtig gehegten hochnothpeinlichen Halß Gerichte, der beschuldigten Missethat, und des an deinem [6ᵛ] Kinde verübten Mords, dessentwegen du anjetzo peinlich angeklagt worden, nochmahlen allenthalben geständig gewesen, so soll dir auch nunmehro, das diesfalls wohlbehauptet gesprochene Urthel, samt deßen höchster Confirmation nochmahlen vorgelesen, und öffentlich publiciret werden. // *Hierauf wird von [?] dem H[errn] Actuario das eingelangte Urtel ganz, samt dem gnädigsten Confirmation Rescript, in welchem, daß dem Urthel nachgegangen werden solle, befohlen worden, deutlich vorlesen [sic], und bey Endigung des letztern, von dem H[errn] AmtsCommissarius, als Landrichter, der bis hieher in der Hand gehaltene weise Stab in 3. Stücken zerbrochen und sich zurück geworfen. Worauf denn / der Scharfrichter als peinl[icher] Ankläger sich folgendergestalt vernehmen läßet.* / H[err] Richter, dieweil die arme Sünderin Anna Catharina Höhnin hier stehet vor Gott und männiglichen unter freyen Himmel, und geständig ist ihrer begangenen Missethat, so frage ich, wer das jetzt publicirte letzte Endurtheil an ihr zur Execution bringen solle? // *Der Richter* / Das solst du thun' (Wilson, 'The "Halsgericht"', 38–41).

> *This concludes trial and execution, the militia is disbanded, the circle of peasants disperses, everyone goes home, and the decapitated poor sinner will be laid in a coffin and either buried or taken to the school of anatomy at Jena.*
> *Given at Weimar, 18 November 1783.*[73]

W. Daniel Wilson, who is, so far, the only interpreter of this document, views it as an indication that the death penalty was more controversial in eighteenth-century Weimar than previously believed, and that the authorities had to take considerable precautions – evidenced, for example, in the presence of a substantial militia at the execution – to pre-empt popular unrest.[74] While Wilson uses the document to make an important socio-historical point about Goethe's Weimar, I am most interested in its double life as a legal *and* a literary document, its *dramatic* aspects, which I hold to be just as pronounced as they might be in any other eighteenth-century drama. They include the solemn procession of black-clad figures onto a black stage, the formalised call-and-response dialogue, the ritualised action and the precise stage directions. Stylistic aspects include the hauntingly evocative style marked by repetitions – 'murdered and deprived of life', for example, or 'I accuse unto death for the first time, I accuse unto death for the second time, I accuse unto death for the third time', or 'have you not confessed and do you not now confess'. The dark solemnity evoked here is further buttressed by cabbalistic numbers: there are three accusations, seven pronouncements of the court's legitimacy, and twelve judges and jurors. Even the painstaking precision of times, places and facts that may have been required for legal reasons – the precise time and place of the birth, the exact time of the murder fifteen minutes later, the identification of the murder weapon as the knife used to cut the umbilical cord, the meticulous relation of the modus operandi – assume an unmistakably elegiac tone in the Actuarius's interrogation of Höhn.

Reading this document as the script of a play, we are reminded that drama, by almost all major writers of eighteenth-century Germany, was not considered pure entertainment, but was charged to fulfil the two great Horatian functions: *prodesse et delectare*, to instruct and amuse. Clearly,

---

[73] '*Nach vollendeter Execution rufet sodann // Der Scharfrichter / Herr Richter hör! // Was ist dein Begehr? // Scharfrichter / Habe ich recht gerichtet? // Du hast gethan, was Urthel und Recht mit sich gebracht. / Hiermit ist das ganze Halß Gericht und Execution beschloßen, die bewehrte Mannschaft wird wieder abgeführt, der Creyß der Bauern gehet aus einander, und jedermann verfügt sich nach Hauße, die enthauptete arme Sünderin aber wird in einen Sarg gelegt und entweder begraben oder [8'] auf die Anatomie nach Jena geschaffet. / Gefertiget Weimar den 18ten Novmbr. 1783*' (Wilson, 'The "Halsgericht"', 44).

[74] 'Goethe, His Duke, and Infanticide'.

both are a factor in this document: the ritualistic role-play, the formulaic back-and-forth, transcend their originally legal origins and turn the 'theatre of horror' into a solemn tragedy of redemption, able to fulfil the obligation of *delectare* on a more philosophical level than the baser pleasure derived from observing the actual beheading. We can also assume that the *prodesse*, clearly directed at the population bearing witness to Höhn's execution and to her publicly repeated confession, targeted particularly the women and girls in the audience who were considered potential perpetrators of Höhn's crime. Compared to the elaborate prayers, blessings and contrite speeches delivered by literary and real-life infanticides at the foot of the scaffold,[75] Höhn's participation was reduced to a minimum – all that was required of her was a simple Yes!, repeated four times. But the performative aspects of this purportedly legal document, its high drama and its intended effect on the spectator, clearly link it with other genres of scaffold literature – the broadsheets, the ballads, the witness reports of the malefactors' 'final hours' – published throughout the century.

One wonders what would have become of the hoped-for salutary effect of this drama, or of other dramas starring condemned women on the scaffold, if these women had refused to observe the etiquette of execution, in other words: if they had withheld the statements of confession and contrition that justified their deaths. One among the exceedingly rare documented instances, recorded in *Der neue Pitaval*, relates the anonymous eyewitness account of the beheading of a twenty-year-old girl for murder, a girl whose last name was Koch and whose first name is not recorded, in Appenzell, Switzerland in 1849. The execution of Girl Koch shows us what happens when the performance is a flop. Her execution, far from the dignified tragedy able to impart its edifying moral, became a grotesque horror show, a theatre of cruelty, and for one simple reason: Girl Koch refused to cooperate. Our witness relates that Girl Koch 'was visited diligently by the local priests in order to prepare her for her near end. Nevertheless, the unhappy woman … was so little able to accept the thought of death that, in her despair, she refused the solace of religion and declared being unable to die.'[76] Girl Koch was dragged by four strong men to the place of execution, fighting tooth and nail all the way to the scaffold, drowning out both the priest's attempts to console her and the public reading of the sentence with her screams.

---

[75] See chapter 5.

[76] 'Sie wurde … von der hiesigen Geistlichkeit fleißig besucht, um auf ihr nahes Ende vorbereitet zu werden. Allein die Unselige, weniges über zwanzig Jahre alt, konnte sich mit dem Gedanken, sterben zu müssen, so gar nicht vertraut machen, daß sie alle Tröstungen der Religion verzweifelnd von sich wies und erklärte, nicht sterben zu können' ('Eine Hinrichtung in Appenzell', unpag.).

Because she refused to hold still, the executioner was unable to chop off her head. At this point, the senior judge presiding over the execution hastily conferred with the city council, asking whether the execution should still go ahead, and received the laconic reply that it was now the executioner's job to deal with her. This astonishing interruption of an execution in progress indicates two things: it shows the extent to which a successful execution depended on the cooperation of the condemned – so much so that Girl Koch's tumultuous resistance actually raised the question whether it would not be better to postpone her beheading or cancel it altogether. And it eloquently documents, once again, that the authorities saw the execution as far more than merely punishment of the culprit: in their view, the primary purpose of the execution was its effect on the witnesses, its *prodesse*, as it had been to the officials of Weimar who had executed Höhn sixty-six years earlier. The story ends as it must: after further protracted struggling and screaming, a man from the audience advised the executioner to tie Girl Koch's long braid to a staff and then force her head upward while holding her body down, and thus Girl Koch was finally beheaded.

Clearly, this was not the dignified spectacle of contrition and justice that the town fathers had had in mind. Our eyewitness, too, commented acerbically on this judicial drama gone wrong. 'Should we not at least and above all demand', he writes,

that such revolting and dehumanising spectacles, as happened yesterday before thousands of spectators of every age and both sexes, not be performed? And should we not give voice to our indignant astonishment that a council (a Catholic one, at that) dares … to have a human being mercilessly executed, without repentance or solace, without any preparation whatsoever and under chaotic conditions? … Is this truly part of the ethical education of the populace, and can such a scene really increase its abhorrence of crime?[77]

Four points here seem worthy of our attention: first, our witness clearly recognises this spectacle as a performance, evidenced in his use of theatre words such as *spectacle* (*Schauspiel*, which means both spectacle and play), *performed* and *scene* (*Auftritt*, which can mean both a hysterical scene and a scene in a drama). Second, he worries about the effect of this botched

---

[77] 'Soll man … vor allem wenigstens darauf dringen, daß dergleichen empörende, entmenschende Schauspiele nicht, wie gestern geschah, vor vielen Tausenden, jedes Alters und Geschlechts, aufgeführt werden? Oder soll man seinem entrüsteten Erstaunen Worte leihen, daß ein Rath (zumal ein katholischer) es wagt und über sich nimmt, einen Menschen ohne Bekehrung, ohne Trost, ohne alle Vorbereitung unter tumultuarischen Formen erbarmungslos hinrichten zu lassen? … Gehört das vielleicht zur sittlichen Erziehung des Volks oder kann ein derartiger Auftritt dazu dienen, seinen Abscheu vor dem Verbrechen zu vermehren?' ('Eine Hinrichtung in Appenzell', unpag.).

performance on the spectator, who will not receive the requisite moral that crime doesn't pay. Third, he hints at a possible mutinous response on the part of the audience: they might voice their *indignation* or even *demand* the discontinuation of such spectacles – both terms that hint at the outright rebellion that a properly conducted public execution was charged to suppress. And finally, he perceives the execution as 'dehumanising' and merciless not because of its injustice but because of its chaos: it becomes recognisable as inhumane only once it is divested of its order, its tidiness and organisation. His objection, in other words, is more aesthetic than juridical, he objects not to a miscarriage of justice but a botched performance, not to its *legal* illegitimacy but to its dramatic failure and hence its failure to impart what every good drama is charged to provide, namely: the 'ethical education of the populace'.

It is this requirement for good theatre, imbued with tragic necessity and adorned with touching final monologues, that is the foundation of the etiquette of execution. Historians have long recognised that executions were not merely legal occasions, that they also fulfil a social function. The social function of execution can be seen, as van Dülmen and Martschukat have done, as expressed through its *structure* (theatre), or, as Evans has done, through its *quasi-religious aspects* (ritual), or, as I have done here, in its *coercion and enforcement of behaviours* (etiquette).

What has been less recognised than the social role of executions, even by scholars who have recognised their theatrical aspects in the metaphorical sense, is that they were, in a much more literal sense, profoundly literary events, spectacles that relied heavily on the dramatic conventions of their day. Executions could not proceed until someone – a balladeer, a chronicler, a pamphleteer, a priest documenting the last days of his convertees, or, as in Höhn's case, an official of the court – had written The End. As did every playwright of the century, these writers of the End worried primarily about their audience's response. As did many theatres, they relied on an armed presence to maintain order. In the mid nineteenth century, shortly before the temporary abolition of the death penalty in the course of the German Revolution of 1848/9, they arrived at the same conclusion as many playwrights, namely that one possible response to the audience's displeasure might be rewriting the ending – as indicated by the witness to Girl Koch's execution, who, in bringing up the possibility of last-minute clemency, clearly hints at an alternative ending. And while he objects to the violence of the proceedings, he stops short of attacking its legitimacy, a legitimacy validated by many earlier texts ranging from legal works (the dress rehearsal script for Höhn's execution) to theological (Moser's compilation) to literary ones (contemporary pamphlets and ballads). Scaffold literature of the age, the many 'final scenes' recorded in genres both literary and (purportedly) non-literary, played a significant legal, social and cultural role, a role illustrated most clearly by its effortless fusion of the flexibility of literature and the rigidity of law.

FINAL THOUGHTS: THE POWER OF THE PEOPLE, THE GENDER OF THE MOB AND THE PROGRESS OF CIVILISATION

The 'successful' execution of Johanna Catharina Höhn and the botched execution of Girl Koch plainly imply a question that has occupied historians for some time, namely: what power resided with the 'people' – either the condemned, who could feasibly withhold cooperation, or the audience, who could potentially disturb the course of events?

The answer most historians tend towards is: considerable power. Overwhelmingly, they agree that the malefactor could thoroughly unnerve an executioner or, worse, judicial authorities, by struggling, resisting, rejecting the sentence, cursing the judges, or exercising other means of refusing to die.[78] Delinquents could not escape death, but they could destroy its symbolic meaning as the restitution of the world order that they had disturbed through their crimes. 'Without the subjective consent of the poor sinner a dignified execution was hardly achievable.'[79] The moment of execution, in other words, is finally the moment of the delinquent's power. Some thinkers have surmised that this is what the crowd came to see, that it came 'to hear an individual who had nothing more to lose curse the judges, the laws, the government and religion'.[80] The power of the condemned is presumed to lie in exciting the people's compassion for the victim, or the people's anger at the cruelty or injustice of the execution.

The power of the people, in turn, presumably lay in expressing its direct opposition to the proceedings, by attacking the executioner, by requesting mercy for or the freedom of the condemned or even by freeing them by force. Foucault has famously described this potential by reference to Bakhtin's concept of the carnivalesque: 'In these executions, which ought to show only the terrorizing power of the prince, there was a whole aspect of the carnival, in which rules were inverted, authority mocked and criminals

---

[78] For example in van Dülmen, *Theater*, 9–10, 83–5, 96, 148 and 'Schauspiel', 213; Evans, *Rituals*, 259–60.
[79] van Dülmen, *Theater*, 83: 'ohne die subjektive Einwilligung des Armen Sünders war eine würdevolle Hinrichtung kaum durchführbar'.
[80] Foucault 60.

transformed into heroes.'[81] It is a sentiment echoed by many historians[82] and critiqued by few.[83] Many of them even credit the power of the people with bringing about major social and legal changes: first the replacement of public executions with public trials and the removal of executions indoors,[84] finally the abolition of the death penalty altogether.[85] To say that 'shifts in penal policy in the late eighteenth and early nineteenth centuries were brought about in the end, despite everything, from below, both by broad social changes, to which governments had to react, and by the resistance of popular culture to the interpretations of crime and punishment forced on it from above'[86] presupposes that the power residing 'below' is extraordinary indeed.

Nevertheless, the history of executions, which now spans millennia and comprises innumerable staged killings, yields comparatively little evidence to support this. To ascribe power to the condemned on the scaffold means to attribute to them a choice that very few were able to exercise. Historians routinely refer to the malefactors' 'willing' compliance with the behaviour expected of them on the scaffold[87] *while* elaborately describing the massive coercion – through torture, psychological pressure and religious 'preparation' – through which this compliance was secured. To speak of 'voluntary' confessions and 'willing' cooperation in such a context is clearly inappropriate to the point of cynicism. Documented instances of the malefactor's opposite choice, that of resistance, are few and far between, indicating that, however much it was feared by the authorities, it was only sporadically exercised.[88]

And what of the power of the people, the audience for whose benefit those rare resisters expressed their defiance on the scaffold? Again, stories abound in which an executioner's clumsiness caused the malefactor undue

---

[81] Foucault 61.

[82] van Dülmen, *Theater*, 147, 183 and 'Schauspiel', 204; Evans, *Rituals*, 9–10: 'public punishments themselves were far from effective as demonstrations of state power; the crowd could just as easily applaud as assail the malefactor at the pillory, while in public executions "there was a whole aspect of the carnival, in which rules were inverted, authority mocked and criminals turned into heroes" [quoting Foucault]. The crowd, sometimes aided and abetted by the malefactor on the scaffold, frequently ridiculed the authorities, attacked the executioner, and celebrated the transgressions of everyday life in a saturnalian orgy of bloodlust, riot, and revelry.'

[83] Elsewhere in the same work, Evans denies that the Bakhtinian carnivalesque was a factor at executions, portraying them as celebrations of order and hierarchy rather than its subversion, as carefully scripted and choreographed rather than improvised events (104, 147). 'The traditional execution in Germany was no outburst of unbridled mob violence, no carnivalesque celebration of mob power, but an elaborate ritual' (Evans, *Rituals*, 104–7, the quotation 107).

[84] Evans, *Rituals*, 257–8, 262–6.   [85] Evans, *Rituals*, 247–8; van Dülmen, *Theater*, 183.

[86] Evans, *Rituals*, 148–9.   [87] For example Evans, *Rituals*, 83–4; van Dülmen, *Theater*, 145.

[88] Evans, *Rituals*, 84.

suffering and provoked the wrath of the crowd, who then sometimes attacked or even killed the executioner;[89] other stories relate how the crowd successfully demanded the release of a prisoner, either because someone offered to marry the delinquent or because the execution had been carried out, sometimes repeatedly, without resulting in the offender's death.[90] But can we assume from these incidents, as Foucault does, that they express a universal or at least regularly recurring popular anger against the authorities, or even compassion with the condemned? While these stories of popular unrest take up an extraordinary amount of space in histories of the death penalty, they have one thing in common with the examples of the resistance of the condemned: they were exceedingly rare. Conflicts at executions occurred no more frequently than 'now and again', admits van Dülmen, who places the last attacks on executioners in the late sixteenth to early seventeenth centuries.[91] There were at least six botched executions in the 1820s, none of which led to riots; in Bavaria between 1814 and 1823, we know of six further messy executions that were 'repulsive to the public' but did not result in unrest.[92] Conversely, Vienna's last public execution in 1868 was disrupted to such a degree that the authorities had to intervene, but the 'carnivalesque' atmosphere at this event was not generated by popular outrage but by singing, gambling and drunkenness.[93] We also know that in the rare cases in which the people did attack inept executioners, they usually waited until he had finally managed to kill the condemned,[94] and not a single assault on executioners that van Dülmen has described was motivated by public disagreement with the verdict.[95] This does not seem to indicate the political opposition that Foucault and others have, perhaps hopefully, attributed to these incidents: they document neither anger at the authorities, compassion with the condemned, nor a principal doubt that the death sentence represented justice, but merely contempt for the sloppy way in which justice was being done. Given the extreme rarity of riots, claims that the crowd 'controlled the orderly process

---

[89] Evans, *Rituals*, 220; van Dülmen, *Theater*, 153 and 'Schauspiel', 217–18, 229; Martschukat, *Inszeniertes Töten*, 29–30, 113–17.

[90] Examples in van Dülmen, 'Schauspiel', 234–5 and *Theater*, 151–2. Van Dülmen places the last known case of a malefactor being released through marriage into the sixteenth century (*Theater*, 151).

[91] van Dülmen, 'Schauspiel', 239, the citation 'hier und da' on 233, and *Theater*, 153.

[92] Evans, *Rituals*, 223–5.   [93] van Dülmen, 'Schauspiel', 232.   [94] van Dülmen, 'Schauspiel', 240.

[95] van Dülmen, *Theater*, 153–9. See also Evans's conclusion in *Rituals*, 207: 'public disturbances at German executions were mostly triggered not by overt popular resistance to the state's punishment of offenders with whom people sympathized, but by departures from the pre-ordained ritual process'.

of executions'[96] or even that 'legal authorities, in collaboration with the clergy, were ultimately powerless when confronted with the interests and practices of the people'[97] appear overstated. And if the power of the people was limited, as we must assume based on documented instances, then we must conclude that the offender's power to disturb his or her own execution was also limited, since the only possible addressee of this alternative drama could be the crowd.

While it seems dubious that the 'power of the people' existed in a historical sense to the formidable degree that has often been claimed, there is no question that it had a lively *discursive* existence in the writings of 'the authorities', who seem to have feared it greatly. 'Fear of the mob' became an obsessive topic of judicial writing throughout the centuries, leading to changes in procedure and inspiring reforms.[98] Lawmakers routinely expressed their worries regarding a particular aspect of popular unrest decades after the last documented incident. A century after the last occurrence of the 'right to mercy' (*Gnadenrecht*), by which any spectator of an execution could obtain the offender's release by offering marriage, jurists continued to write about the possibility that condemned malefactors might escape their just sentence in this fashion.[99] Thus there is some evidence to suggest that the historical view of the 'power of the people' is indebted to the fear expressed in official documents, which furnished historians with much of their material. From the elaborate security measures employed at executions, for example, we cannot really conclude, as historians have at times done, that the crowd was actually dangerous:[100] we can merely conclude that the authorities *assumed* this and prepared accordingly. It seems conceivable, then, that many historians of the death penalty emulated contemporary officials in massively overestimating the power of the people, mistaking a history of fear for a history of events.

---

[96] van Dülmen, *Theater*, 145: 'Aber auch das Volk bestand auf der Öffentlichkeit der Hinrichtung. Einerseits kontrollierte es den ordnungsgemäßen Ablauf, andererseits wollte es den Todesgang eines Delinquenten mit Gebet begleiten, d.h. ihm ein christliches Sterben ermöglichen und schließlich wollte es Zeuge eines Rechtsaktes und Reinigungsaktes sein, der geradezu erlösende Bedeutung haben konnte.'

[97] van Dülmen, *Theater*, 183: 'Dennoch war die richterliche Obrigkeit im Zusammenwirken mit den Geistlichen letztlich machtlos gegenüber den Interessen und Praktiken des Volkes.'

[98] For example, the reforms of the Prussian criminal code of 1805; Evans, *Rituals*, 200–2.

[99] van Dülmen, *Theater*, 152: 'Wenngleich seit dem 17. Jahrhundert kaum noch eine Chance bestand, daß das Volk dieses Gnadenrecht tatsächlich durchsetzen konnte – die Obrigkeit ließ in den uns bekannten Fällen meistens erneut hängen –, blieb das Problem doch bis ins 18. Jahrhundert Gegenstand der juristischen Diskussion.'

[100] For example Martschukat, *Inszeniertes Töten*, 30: 'Paradoxerweise war ausgerechnet der Scharfrichter ... das gefährdetste Element im "Theater des Schreckens" – freilich nach den "Armen SünderInnen". Dies dokumentiert nicht zuletzt der umfangreiche Sicherheitsaufwand, der auch zu dessen Schutz vor einem eventuell aufgebrachten Publikum betrieben wurde.'

We can thus assume the history of discourse and images and the history of events to be related, but not identical, and we can further assume fear to be a powerful motivator of discursive history. Fear, in other words, plays a significant part in how we interpret events of the past and in how we describe the historical characters who participated in them. What, for example, is the difference between 'the people', 'the crowd' and 'the mob'? Clearly, in 'real life', all of these appellations could be applied to the same assembly of people, but it is equally clear that *discursively*, these are three distinct entities. 'The people', for example, deserve respect; they are endowed by many writers, not least of them Foucault, with certain inalienable rights, among them the right to dissent and resistance. 'The crowd', on the other hand, describes a relatively neutral mass of spectators with a potential for hostility and violent behaviour, associations which are considerably intensified when the 'crowd' becomes a 'mob', whose further unsavoury attributes include bloodlust, sadism and – worryingly, in the context of executions – a high propensity for insanity and criminality.[101]

One of the characteristics that distinguishes the 'people' from the 'mob' is the *gender* of the mob: whereas the 'people' and the 'crowd' lead a relatively gender-neutral discursive life,[102] the mob is unquestionably female.[103] Eighteenth- and early nineteenth-century writers have consistently assumed this when describing women's 'irresistible craving to gaze upon hideous scenes, executions, operations, wounds and the like, and to listen to horrible tales of murder – things to which the less effeminate man responds with disgust'.[104] Literary examples of such feminine behaviour abound: we need only remind ourselves of Schiller's poetic metamorphosis of women into hyenas,[105] or of Kleist's description of St Jago's fine ladies jostling for the best places at Josephe's execution.[106] Sociologists from Le Bon to Sighele to Tarde have described the mob as female, 'even if, as is normally the case, it is composed of men'.[107] Le Bon assumed that the mob's irrationality, its tendency for exaggeration, its limited understanding, its enslavement to its own physical urges, and its simultaneous capacity for extremes of

---

[101] See Le Bon; Baschwitz; Dornhof 209–51.
[102] See, among others, Moscovici; Koepke; Polišenský; Golby; Angeli.
[103] See, among others, Le Bon, Blättler.
[104] Knigge II 75: 'Auch die mitleidigsten Seelen unter ihnen [Frauen] empfinden zuweilen einen unbezwinglichen Trieb, schreckliche Scenen, Executionen, Operationen, Wunden und dergleichen anzuschaun, jämmerliche Mordgeschichten zu hören – Gegenstände, denen sich der weniger weichliche Mann nicht ohne Widerwillen gegenüber sieht.'
[105] Schiller, 'Das Lied von der Glocke', 819.   [106] Kleist, 'Das Erdbeben in Chili', 145.
[107] Gabriel Tarde quoted in Martschukat, *Inszeniertes Töten*, 199.

sentimentality and extremes of cruelty were quintessentially female.[108] This idea also presupposes its reverse, namely, the quintessential masculinity of the State, which expressed itself, in the writings of renowned eighteenth-century philosophers like Kant and Fichte, in the principal exclusion of women from all civic rights.[109] Drawing on the old juxtaposition of the symbolic and the semiotic, order and chaos, male and female, the fickle mob is identified as female; the 'authorities', like authority itself, as male. Conceptually, then, the mob observing a woman's execution, staring up her skirts and ogling her breasts, is always female, even if the crowd consists largely of men, and the execution, the spectacle that affirms the authority of the masculine State, becomes, in no small measure, an exercise in subduing the feminine mob. As is the case with the 'power of the people', it is fear that drives this discourse – perhaps as much fear of the uncontrollable female as fear of the unruly masses.

Since the eighteenth century, Western cultures have tended to think of civilisation, at least to some extent, as entailing a continuous expansion of the power of the people, who can be trusted to rule themselves – this a legacy of the Enlightenment – and as necessitating a heightened sensitivity to issues of inequality, including those produced by state power or gender difference. Thus the questions raised above – how the State interacts with 'the people', how male interacts with female and how humans are compelled by fear – eventually lead us to the most nagging question of all, namely, what the history of executions has to tell us about the progress of civilisation, and how concepts of civilisation are indebted to, or expressed in, executions and methods of execution.

Two formidable thinkers, Norbert Elias and Michel Foucault, have sought to answer this question. Both have considered the same historical evidence – that public executions and public torture tended to vanish by the end of the nineteenth century – and come to opposite conclusions: the final curtain in the 'theatre of horror' means successive humanisation to one and successive self-imprisonment to the other. Elias saw a greater degree of self-control and self-restraint, to him an integral aspect of 'the civilizing process', and welcomed it; Foucault saw 'the birth of the prison', in both the literal and the metaphorical sense, and deplored it.[110]

---

[108] See Le Bon; Martschukat, *Inszeniertes Töten*, 199; Moscovici, *The Age*, 71–2.
[109] See Frevert, 'Unser Staat ist männlichen Geschlechts'; Martschukat, *Inszeniertes Töten*, 200.
[110] Elias, *The Civilizing Processes*; Foucault; see also discussion in Evans, *Rituals*, 12–24. For a recent interpretation of the theme of violence in Elias and Foucault, see Kuzmics (Elias) and Sarasin (Foucault).

Elias's optimistic thought that these historical developments imply the process of conscience formation has been received with misgivings. Evans, for example, has pointed out that attendance at public executions reached a peak in the period immediately preceding their abolition; that the initiative for their abolition did not come from 'below' but from 'above'; and that the primary motivation for this initiative was the maintenance of order, not the avoidance of pain or cruelty.[111] More disturbingly, Martschukat has surmised that 'civilisation' is an understanding of self, and that in modern societies that understanding does not express itself by eliminating violence but by eliminating the *appearance* of violence.[112] In turn, Foucault's vision of successive self-imprisonment obviously relies heavily on the assumption of greater popular dissent before the nineteenth century, which can also be questioned, as we have seen.

What Elias and Foucault have in common is that they see a significant change occurring in the penal practices of the nineteenth century compared with those of the eighteenth. In the history of events, such a development undoubtedly took place: torture was almost universally abolished; executions followed; the penal system moved from an emphasis on retribution to a focus on rehabilitation. In the realm of *ideas*, however, history appears to be more static: forms have changed more rapidly than content. The most basic and unchanging content is the manner in which the State exercises authority over its undesirables: *by enlisting their collaboration.*[113] Whether that authority is exercised in the public killing of criminals, coercing their cooperation to avoid further torture, or whether it is exercised by promising them early release for good behaviour, matters a great deal to the individual affected, but it may not, in and of itself, describe a greater degree of 'civilisation', if civilisation is understood as the relative absence of state-induced coercion or a relatively high degree of individual determination.

Executions, as we have seen, are highly theatrical events, but this only partly explains why theatre has become the prime metaphor to describe

---

[111] Evans contra Elias, *Rituals*, 147.

[112] Martschukat, *Inszeniertes Töten* contra Elias, 5–6, 11. See also Reemtsma's recent study on sanctioned forms of violence in modern (twentieth-century) civilisation.

[113] This principle can be said to apply, to a greater or lesser degree, to all state subjects, but is particularly perceptible in the case of those who have forfeited their civic rights, those who have never been granted them, or those who have been granted them to an inadequate degree – including, but not limited to, women criminals, criminals in general and women in general. Many concrete examples for this coerced collaboration could be cited, some from criminal history, others from social life. Public executions figure as prominently in this history of coercion as, for example, eighteenth-century inheritance or marriage laws. For an analysis of this principle with respect to women in modern societies, see Thürmer-Rohr, Emme and Wildt.

them. The other reason for this persistent simile may be simply that executions are attended by an audience, and the power of that audience has been routinely overestimated. This is the main reason why, while fully recognising the manifestly dramatic aspects of the event, I prefer to speak of an *etiquette* of execution, rather than the dramaturgy of killing or the theatre of horror. 'Theatre' describes the form of execution, 'etiquette' its substance. 'Etiquette' indicates a code of civilised behaviour imposed from 'above' that everyone who wants to belong has to follow. And very nearly everyone wants to belong. Thus executions appeal to the most basic social instincts in humans. Executions, in other words, are hardly antithetical to the concept of 'civilisation'; if anything, they indirectly *define* it. They do this in two ways: by expressing society's code of acceptable behaviour through the punishment of those who have broken this code, and, more significantly, by mobilising the 'willing' collaboration of all involved in the execution – its perpetrators, victims and bystanders – as the price of their membership in civilised society.

Works cited

Note: For the reader's convenience, I have elected not to divide archival materials, primary and secondary literature into separate sections. Anonymous publications are integrated alphabetically by title, disregarding articles and prepositions.

Abermalige wahrhafte Aussagen der Inquisitin Wächtlern als Dieselbe den 10. October wiederum zum Verhör in der Raths-Stube geführet wurde. Hamburg, 1788.

Abhandlung des Daseyns der Gespenster, nebst einem Anhange vom Vampyrismus. Augsburg, 1768.

'Acta, Inquisition, Urtheil u. dessen Vollstreckung wider Maria Catharina Wächtler geb. Wunsch pcto. Ermordung ihres Ehemannes. Nebst div. Nebenacten. 1786–1788. Adj. Correspondenz de A°1844 betr. Benutzung dieser Acten für den "neuen Pitaval"'. Staatsarchiv Hamburg. Cl. VII. Lit Me no. 8 vol. 10.

Acten-mäßige und Umständliche Relatio von denen Vampiren oder Menschen-Saugern, Welche sich in diesem und vorigen Jahren, im Königreich Servien herfür gethan. Nebst einem Raisonnement darüber und einen Hand-Schreiben eines Officiers, des Printz-Alexandrischen Regiments, aus Medvedia in Servien, an einen berühmten Doctorem der Universität Leipzig. Leipzig: August Martin, 1732.

Aechte und vollständige Akten der berüchtigten Inquisitin Wächtler zu Hamburg. Hamburg, 1787.

Ahrendt-Schulte, Ingrid. 'Hexenprozesse'. *Frauen in der Geschichte des Rechts. Von der frühen Neuzeit bis zur Gegenwart.* Ed. Ute Gerhard. Munich: Beck, 1997. 199–220.

Alewyn, Richard. 'Die literarische Angst'. *Aspekte der Angst.* Ed. Hoimar von Ditfurth. Munich: Kindler, 1977. 38–52.

'Die Lust an der Angst'. *Probleme und Gestalten: Essays.* Frankfurt/M.: Insel, 1974. 307–30.

Alexander, Sally. 'The Witch and the Child: Women's Historical Writing and the Unconscious'. *Women: A Cultural Review* 18.3 (2007), 327–44.

Alexis, Willibald. *Ruhe ist die erste Bürgerpflicht. Historischer Roman.* 4 vols. Berlin: A. Weichert, n.d.

Anders, Katrin. *Sara, Ester, Thobe und Hanna: Vier jüdische Frauen am Rande der Gesellschaft im 18. Jahrhundert. Eine mikrohistorische Studie unter Verwendung*

Flensburger Gerichtsakten. Flensburg: Gesellschaft für Flensburger Stadtgeschichte, 1998.

Angeli, Oliviero. *Volk und Nation als 'Zukunftsbegriffe': Politische Leitbilder im begriffsgeschichtlichen Kontext der Aufklärung.* Münster: Lit, 2004.

Ankarloo, Bengt, and Stuart Clark. 'Introduction'. Marijke Gijswijt-Hofstra, Brian P. Levack and Roy Porter, *Witchcraft and Magic in Europe: The Eighteenth and Nineteenth Centuries.* London: Athlone Press, 1999. vii–xii.

'Anna Göldi bleibt Hexe'. *20 Minuten* (4 September 2007). www.20min.ch/news/kreuz_und_quer/story/12213631 (last accessed 23 September 2007).

'Anna Göldin – letzte Hexe. Die Geschichte von Europas "letzter Hexe". Biografie'. Documentary Film. Switzerland/FRG/France, 1991.

Arnold-de Simine, Silke. 'Wiedergängerische Texte: Die intertextuelle Vernetzung des Vampirmotivs in E. T. A. Hoffmanns "Vampirismus"-Geschichte (1821)'. *Poetische Wiedergänger: Deutschsprachige Vampirismus-Diskurse vom Mittelalter bis zur Gegenwart.* Ed. Julia Bertschik and Christa Agnes Tuczay. Tübingen: Franke, 2005. 129–45.

'Auferbauliches Lebens-Ende der Agatha Laimerinn, welche den 21 July 1761 allhier durch das Schwerdt vom Leben zum Tod hingerichtet, und von jedermann wegen ihren auserordentlichen Geistes, und Gemüthsfassung dann der annoch auf der Richtstätte gehaltenen Anrede bewundert worden. Auf das neue in Versen vorgetragen'. Hauptstaatsarchiv Munich (unpag.).

Ausführliche Lebensbeschreibung der Wächtlerin geborne Wunschin, Inquisitin zu Hamburg, worinne deren Erziehung und merkwürdigsten Lebensumstände von ihrer Geburt an erzählet werden. N.p., n.d.

Aussage der Inquisitinn Wächtlern in Hamburg bey dem am 25ten Januar 1788 erhaltenen Ersten Grade der Tortur. Nebst Bemerkungen über die Zulässigkeit dieses Beweismittels. N.p., n.d. [Hamburg, 1788].

Aust, Stefan. *Der Baader Meinhof Komplex.* 13th edn. Munich: Wilhelm Goldmann, 1998.

Bader, Guido. *Die Hexenprozesse in der Schweiz.* Affoltern: Weiss, 1945.

Baerlocher, René Jacques. 'Anmerkungen zur Diskussion um Goethe, Todesstrafe und Kindsmord'. *Goethe-Jahrbuch* 119 (2002), 208–17.

'Goethes Schuld an der Hinrichtung von Johanna Höhn?' *Goethe-Jahrbuch* 120 (2003), 332–9.

'Nachwort'. *'Das Kind in meinem Leib': Sittlichkeitsdelikte und Kindsmord in Sachsen-Weimar-Eisenach unter Carl August. Eine Quellenedition 1777–1786.* Ed. Volker Wahl. Weimar: Hermann Böhlaus Nachfolger, 2004. 331–504.

Bahr, Hans-Dieter. *Sätze ins Nichts. Versuch über den Schrecken.* Tübingen: Konkursbuchverlag, [1985].

Baldauf, Dieter. *Die Folter. Eine deutsche Rechtsgeschichte.* Cologne, Weimar and Vienna: Böhlau, 2004.

Ballester, Carmen Pinilla. *Erzählte Hinrichtungen: Zum literarischen Diskurs über Verbrechen und Strafe um 1800.* Frankfurt/M.: Peter Lang, 1992.

Barber, Paul. 'Staking Claims: The Vampires of Folklore and Fiction'. www.csicop.org/si/9603/staking.html (last accessed 17 September 2007).

Vampires, Burial, and Death: Folklore and Reality. New Haven and London: Yale University Press, 1988.

Baring-Gould, Sabine. *The Book of Were-Wolves; Being an Account of a Terrible Superstition.* London: Smith, Elder & Co., 1865.

Barkhoff, Jürgen. 'Female Vampires, Victimhood and Vengeance in German Literature around 1800'. *Women and Death: Representations of Female Victims and Perpetrators in German Culture 1500–2000.* Ed. Anna Linton and Helen Fronius. Rochester, NY: Camden House, 2008. 128–43.

Barndt, Kerstin. '"Mein Dasein ward unvermerkt das allgemeine Gespräch." Anna Louisa Karsch im Spiegel zeitgenössischer Popularphilosophie'. *Anna Louisa Karsch (1722–1791): Von schlesischer Kunst und Berliner 'Natur'. Ergebnisse des Symposiums zum 200. Todestag der Dichterin.* Ed. Anke Bennholdt-Thomsen and Anita Runge. Göttingen: Wallstein, 1992. 162–76.

Baschwitz, Kurt. *Du und die Masse: Studien zu einer exakten Massenpsychologie.* Amsterdam: Feikema, Caarelsen & Co., 1938.

Bauer, Anton. *Strafrechtsfälle.* 4 vols. Göttingen: Vandenhoeck & Ruprecht, 1835.

Bauer, Werner M. 'Zwischen Galgen und Moral – Kriminalgeschichte und Spätaufklärung im österreichischen Raum'. *Die österreichische Literatur. Ihr Profil im 19. Jahrhundert (1830–1880).* Ed. Herbert Zeman. Graz: Akademische Druck- und Verlagsanstalt, 1982. 381–99.

Beattie, J. M. 'The Criminality of Women in Eighteenth-Century England'. *Journal of Social History* 8 (1975), 80–116.

Beccaria, Cesare. *Dei delitti e delle pene. Con una raccolta di lettere e documenti relativi alla nascita dell'opera e alla sua fortuna nell'Europa del Settecento.* Ed. Franco Venturi. Turin: Giulio Einaudi, 1973.

An Essay on Crimes and Punishments, translated from the Italian; with a commentary, attributed to Mons. De Voltaire, translated from the French. 3rd edn. London: F. Newberry, 1770.

Des Herren Marquis von Beccaria unsterbliches Werk von Verbrechen und Strafen. Auf das Neue selbst aus dem Italiänischen übersezet mit durchgängigen Anmerkungen des Ordinarius zu Leipzig Herren Hofrath Hommels. Breslau, 1778.

Becker-Cantarino, Barbara. '"Belloisens Lebenslauf": Zu Dichtung und Autobiographie bei Anna Louisa Karsch'. *Gesellige Vernunft: Zur Kultur der literarischen Aufklärung.* Ed. Ortrud Gutjahr, Wilhelm Kühlmann and Wolf Wucherpfennig. Würzburg: Königshausen & Neumann, 1993. 13–22.

'"Meine Mutter, die Hur, die mich umgebracht hat … ": Die Kindsmörderin als literarisches Sujet'. *Verklärt, verkitscht, vergessen. Die Mutter als ästhetische Figur.* Ed. Renate Möhrmann. Stuttgart and Weimar: J. B. Metzler, 1996. 108–29.

'Witch and Infanticide: Imaging the Female in Faust I'. *Goethe-Yearbook of North America* 7 (1994), 1–22.

Begemann, Christian, Britta Herrmann and Harald Neumeyer, eds. *Dracula Unbound: Kulturwissenschaftliche Lektüren des Vampirs.* Freiburg: Rombach, 2008.

Behringer, Wolfgang. 'Der "Bayerische Hexenkrieg". Die Debatte am Ende der Hexenprozesse in Deutschland'. *Das Ende der Hexenverfolgung.* Ed. Sönke Lorenz and Dieter R. Bauer. Stuttgart: Franz Steiner, 1995. 287–313.

Hexenverfolgung in Bayern: Volksmagie, Glaubenseifer und Staatsräson in der Frühen Neuzeit. Munich: Oldenbourg, 1988.

'Weibliche Kriminalität in Kurbayern in der Frühen Neuzeit'. *Von Huren und Rabenmüttern: Weibliche Kriminalität in der Frühen Neuzeit.* Ed. Otto Ulbricht. Cologne, Weimar and Vienna: Böhlau, 1995. 63–82.

Witchcraft Persecutions in Bavaria: Popular Magic, Religious Zealotry and Reason of State in Early Modern Europe. Trans. J. C. Grayson and David Lederer. Cambridge: Cambridge University Press, 1997.

Witches and Witch-Hunts: A Global History. Cambridge: Polity Press, 2004.

ed. *Hexen und Hexenprozesse in Deutschland.* Munich: dtv, 1988.

Beirne, Piers, ed. *The Origins and Growth of Criminology: Essays on Intellectual History.* Aldershot: Dartmouth, 1994.

Bekenntniß der Inquisitinn Wächtlern in Hamburg. Nebst fortgesetzten Bemerkungen über die Tortur und diesen Kriminalproceß. Eingesandt dem Herausgeber des Archivs der Schwärmerey etc. N.p., n.d. [Hamburg, 1788].

Bekenntnisse einer Giftmischerin. Von ihr selbst geschrieben. Vienna, Prague and Leipzig: Eduard Strache, n.d.

Berger, Renate, and Inge Stephan, eds. *Weiblichkeit und Tod in der Literatur.* Cologne and Vienna: Böhlau, 1987.

Berichtigungen und Anmerkungen über den schrecklichen Mord der an J. R. [sic] Wächteler [sic] einem Bürger in Hamburg im Februar 1786 begangen wurde. N.p., n.d. [Hamburg, 1786].

Bernstein, Daniel. *Dissertatio Juridica de Judicum Circa Torturam Excedentium Emenda, Oder: Was für Satisfaction ein Richter demjenigen / mit dem er in der Folter allzustrenge verfahren / zu geben schuldig sey / Quam Deo benedicente & Illustr. Facult. Jurid. Ordine Annuente in Academia Patria Moderante Dn. Gothofr. Nicol. Ittigio, Phil. & J.U.D. Celeberrimo.* Leipzig: Daniel Bernstein, 1716.

Bertschik, Julia, and Christa Agnes Tuczay, eds. *Poetische Wiedergänger: Deutschsprachige Vampirismus-Diskurse vom Mittelalter bis zur Gegenwart.* Tübingen: Franke, 2005.

Bettelheim, Bruno. *The Uses of Enchantment: The Meaning and Importance of Fairy Tales.* London: Penguin, 1991.

Bewegliche Abschieds-Worte, Womit Johanna Susanne Riedeln (Als solche wegen verübten Kinder-Mords nach Urthel und Recht mit dem Schwerdt vom Leben zum Tode gebracht wurde,) Am Tage ihrer Execution war der 7. Januar 1726. Ihre hertzliche Reue wehmüthigst bezeuget. Dresden, 1725.

Birch, Helen, ed. *Moving Targets: Women, Murder and Representation.* London: Virago Press, 1993.

Birkhäuser-Oeri, Sibylle. *Die Mutter im Märchen.* Stuttgart: Bonz, 1976.

Birkner, Siegfried. *Leben und Sterben der Kindsmörderin Susanna Margaretha Brandt, dargestellt von Siegfried Birkner.* Frankfurt/M.: Insel, 1973.

Birnstiel, Heinrich. *Versuch, die wahre Ursache des Kindsmords aus der Natur- und Völkergeschichte zu erforschen, und zugleich daraus einige Mittel zur Verhinderung dieses Staatsverbrechens zu schöpfen.* Frankfurt and Leipzig, 1785.

Black, Joel. *The Aesthetics of Murder: A Study in Romantic Literature, and Contemporary Culture.* Baltimore: Johns Hopkins University Press, 1991.

Blackbourn, David, and Richard J. Evans, eds. *The German Bourgeoisie: Essays on the Social History of the German Middle Class from the Eighteenth Century to the Early Twentieth Century.* London: Routledge, 1991.

Blanke, Dieter. 'Die Kindstötung in rechtlicher und kriminologischer Hinsicht'. Jur. diss. Kiel, 1966.

Blättler, Sidonia. *Der Pöbel, die Frauen etc.: Die Massen in der politischen Philosophie des 19. Jahrhunderts.* Berlin: Akademie Verlag, 1995.

Blumenberg, Hans. *Die Lesbarkeit der Welt.* Frankfurt/M.: Suhrkamp, 1981.

Bockelmann, Paul. *Das Problem der Kriminalstrafe in der deutschen Dichtung.* Karlsruhe: Müller, 1967.

Boehm, Gottfried. '"Mit durchdringendem Blick": Die Porträtkunst und Lavaters Physiognomik'. *Im Lichte Lavaters: Lektüren zum 200. Todestag.* Ed. Ulrich Stadler and Karl Pestalozzi. Zurich: Neue Zürcher Zeitung, 2003. 21–40.

Bolte, Christian, and Klaus Dimmler. *Schwarze Witwen und eiserne Jungfrauen: Geschichte der Mörderinnen.* Berlin: Aufbau, 2000.

Bösken, Clemens-Peter. *Hexenprozeß Gerresheim 1737/38: Die letzte Hexenverbrennung im Rheinland.* Düsseldorf: Grupello, 1996.

Bouton, Christophe. *Dieu de la nature: la question du panthéisme dans l'idéalisme allemand.* Hildesheim: Olms, 2005.

Braungart, Wolfgang, ed. *Bänkelsang: Texte – Bilder – Kommentare.* Stuttgart: Reclam, 1985.

Breithaupt, Fritz. 'Anonymous Forces in History: The Case of Infanticide in Sturm und Drang'. *New German Critique* 79 (Winter 2000), 157–76.

Brinker-Gabler, Gisela, ed. *Lexikon deutschsprachiger Schriftstellerinnen 1800–1945.* Munich: dtv, 1986.

Bronfen, Elisabeth. *Over Her Dead Body: Death, Femininity and the Aesthetic.* Manchester: Manchester University Press, 1992.

'The Vampire: Sexualizing or Pathologizing Death'. *Disease and Medicine in Modern German Cultures.* Ed. Rudolf Käser and Vera Pohland. Ithaca, NY: Cornell University Press, 1990. 71–90.

Bronfen, Elisabeth, and Sarah Webster Goodwin, eds. *Death and Representation.* Baltimore: Johns Hopkins University Press, 1994.

Buckley, T., and A. Gottlieb. *Blood Magic. The Anthropology of Menstruation.* Berkeley: University of California Press, 1988.

Bunson, Matthew. *The Vampire Encyclopaedia.* London: Thames & Hudson, 1993.

Bürger, Gottfried August. *Gedichte.* Afterword by Jost Hermand. Stuttgart: Reclam, 1981.

Butler, Judith. *Bodies that Matter: On the Discursive Limits of 'Sex'.* New York and London: Routledge, 1993.

Calmet, Augustine. *Treatise on Vampires & Revenants: The Phantom World. Dissertation on those Persons who Return to Earth Bodily, the Excommunicated, the Oupires or Vampires, Vroucolacas, &c. by Dom Augustine Calmet.* Trans. Rev. Henry Christmas, ed. Dr Clive Leatherdale. Brighton: Desert Island, 1993.

Campe, Joachim Heinrich. *Väterlicher Rath für meine Tochter. Ein Gegenstück zum Theophron. Der erwachsenern weiblichen Jugend gewidmet.* Braunschweig: Schul-Buchhandlung, 1796.

[Caprez, Pancratius]. *Astorgia Meretricia: Oder: Ausgelöschte natürliche Mutter-Liebe Der Leichtsinnigen Huren / Welche Ihre getriebene Unzucht und Hurerey zu verbergen / ihre eigene Leibesfrucht abtreiben oder entleiben.* Nuremberg: Michaelles, 1716.

Cassirer, Ernst. *Kant's Life and Thought.* Trans. James Haden. New Haven and London: Yale University Press, 1981.

The Philosophy of the Enlightenment. Trans. Fritz C. A. Koelin and James P. Pettegrove. Oxford: Oxford University Press, 1951.

Cauz, Constantin Franz. *Constantini Francisci de Cauz in Academia Roboretana Quireni de Cultibus Magicis eoreumque perpetuo ad ecclesiam et rempublicam habitu. Libri duo cum adjunctis quibusdam eo pertinentibus ad Jurisprudentiae legumlatoriae illustratorem.* Vienna: Johann Thomas Trattner, 1767.

Chambers, Helen, ed. *Violence, Culture and Identity: Essays on German and Austrian Literature, Politics and Society.* Oxford, etc.: Peter Lang, 2006.

Chamisso, Adelbert von. 'Die Giftmischerin'. *Sämtliche Werke.* Ed. Volker Hoffmann. Munich: Winkler, 1975. I 318–19.

Chézy, Helmina von. 'Meine Großmutter Anna Louisa Karschin'. *Unvergessenes: Denkwürdigkeiten aus dem Leben.* 2 vols. Leipzig: F. A. Brockhaus, 1858.

Christliche Betrachtungen über die wunderbarliche Begebenheit mit den Blutsaugenden Todten in Servien. Leipzig, 1732.

Cocalis, Susan L. 'Der Vormund will Vormund sein: Zur Problematik der weiblichen Unmündigkeit im 18. Jahrhundert'. *Gestaltet und Gestaltend: Frauen in der deutschen Literatur.* Ed. Marianne Burkhard. Amsterdam: Rodopi, 1980. 33–55.

Conrad, Herrmann. *Deutsche Rechtsgeschichte.* Vol. II: *Neuzeit bis 1806.* Karlsruhe: Müller, 1966.

Cosmar, Alexander. *Der Vampyr: Trauerspiel in 5 Abtheilungen; nach einer Spindlerschen Erzählung bearbeitet.* Berlin: Cosmar & Krause, 1828.

Coss, Richard G. 'Reflections on the Evil Eye'. *The Evil Eye.* Ed. Alan Dundes. New York and London: Garland, 1981. 181–91.

Curieuse Relation von denen sich in Servien erzeigend habenden Blutsaugern. Leipzig, 1732.

Curieuse und sehr wunderbarliche Relation von denen sich neuer Dinge in Servien erzeigenden Blutsaugern oder Vampyrs, aus authentischen Nachrichten mitgetheilet und mit historischen und philosophischen Reflexionen begleitet, von W.S. G.E.A. Leipzig, 1732.

Cyrus, Hannelore. 'Das "vorsäzlich verheimlichen von Schwangerschaft und Niederkunft" oder von Frauen, die ihre "Geschlechtsehre" bewahren wollten'. *Criminalia: Bremer Strafjustiz 1810–1850. Beiträge zur Sozialgeschichte Bremens* II (1988), 91–131.

Dainat, Holger. '"Wie wenig irgend ein Mensch für die Unsträflichkeit seiner nächsten Stunde sichre Bürgschaft leisten könne!": Kriminalgeschichten in der deutschen Spätaufklärung'. *Erzählte Kriminalität: Zur Typologie und Funktion von narrativen Darstellungen in Strafrechtspflege, Publizistik und Literatur zwischen 1770 und 1920*. Ed. Jörg Schönert in collaboration with Konstantin Imm and Joachim Linder. Tübingen: Max Niemeyer, 1991. 193–204.

Damm, Sigrid. *Christiane und Goethe: Eine Recherche*. 3rd edn. Frankfurt/M.: Insel, 1998.

Damrow, Hildegard. *Frauen vor Gericht. Ein Bericht über weibliche Kriminalität. Mit einem Vorwort von D. Dr. Gustav W. Heinemann*. Frankfurt/M. and Berlin: Ullstein, 1969.

Danker, Uwe. 'Vom Malefikanten zum Zeugen Gottes: Zum christlichen Fest der staatlichen Strafgewalt im frühen 18. Jahrhundert'. *traverse* 1 (1995), 83–98.

Davies, Owen. 'The Decline in the Popular Belief in Witchcraft & Magic'. Diss. University of Lancaster, 1995.

Witchcraft, Magic and Culture, 1736–1951. Manchester: Manchester University Press, 1999.

Davies, Owen, and Willem de Blécourt, eds. *Beyond the Witch Trials: Witchcraft and Magic in Enlightenment Europe*. Manchester: Manchester University Press, 2004.

Deligiorgi, Katerina. *Kant and the Culture of Enlightenment*. Albany: State University of New York Press, 2005.

Demel, Christoph Friedrich. *Philosophischer Versuch, ob nicht die merckwürdige Begebenheit derer Blut-sauger in Nieder-Ungern, A. 1732. geschehen, aus denen principis naturae, ins besondere aus der sympathia rerum naturalium und denen tribus facultatibus hominis können erleutert werden etc., von Christoph. Frid. Demelio*. Vienna, 1732.

Dieckmann, Hans. *Twice-Told Tales: The Psychological Use of Fairy Tales*. Wilmette, IL: Chiron, 1986.

Dieckmann, Herbert. 'Das Abscheuliche und Schreckliche in der Kunsttheorie des 18. Jahrhunderts'. *Die nicht mehr schönen Künste: Grenzphänomene des Ästhetischen*. Ed. Hans Robert Jauß. Munich: Fink, 1968. 271–317.

Dietrick, Linda. 'Women Writers and the Authorization of Literary Practice'. *Unwrapping Goethe's Weimar: Essays in Cultural Studies and Local Knowledge*. Ed. Burkhard Henke, Susanne Kord and Simon Richter. Rochester, NY: Boydell & Brewer, 1999. 213–32.

Dilcher, Gerhard. 'Die Ordnung der Ungleichheit. Haus, Stand und Geschlecht'. *Frauen in der Geschichte des Rechts. Von der frühen Neuzeit bis zur Gegenwart*. Ed. Ute Gerhard. Munich: Beck, 1997. 55–72.

Dippel, Horst. *Germany and the American Revolution, 1770–1800: A Sociohistorical Investigation of Late Eighteenth-Century Political Thinking*. Trans. Bernhard A. Uhlendorf. Chapel Hill: University of North Carolina Press, 1977.

Dondorf, Christoph. *C. D. Dissertationem Inauguralem, de Confessione Tormentis Extorta, vulgo Von der Uhrgicht, Indultu Magnifici JCtorum Ordinis Lipsiensis pro summis In utroque Jure obtinendis honoribus ac privilegiis Doctoralibus*. Leipzig: Andreas Martin Sched, 1717.

Dornhof, Dorothea. *Orte des Wissens im Verborgenen: Kulturhistorische Studien zu Herrschaftsbereichen des Dämonischen.* Königstein/Ts.: Ulrike Helmer, 2005.

Dotzler, Bernhard J. '"Seht doch wie ihr vor Eifer schäumet…" Zum männlichen Diskurs über Weiblichkeit um 1800'. *Jahrbuch der deutschen Schillergesellschaft* 30 (1986), 339–82.

Drei Preisschriften über die Frage: Welches sind die besten ausführbarsten Mittel, dem Kindermorde abzuhelfen, ohne die Unzucht zu begünstigen? Mannheim, 1784. [Respondents: Pfeil, Klippstein and Kreuzfeld.]

Dreves, Georg. *Resultate der philosophierenden Vernunft über die Natur des Vergnügens, der Schönheit und des Erhabenen.* Leipzig: Crusius, 1793.

Dubos, Jean-Baptiste. *Réflexions critiques sur la Poësie et sur la Peinture.* 2 vols. Geneva: Slatkine, 1967 [rpt of 7th edn., 1770].

Dudeck, Jochen. *Gesellschaftliche Ursachen des Kindsmordes, dargestellt an der Reichsstadt Nürnberg von der Einführung der Carolina bis zum Ausgang des 18. Jahrhunderts.* Erlangen, 1980.

Duden, Barbara. 'Das schöne Eigentum: Zur Herausbildung des bürgerlichen Frauenbildes an der Wende vom 18. zum 19. Jahrhundert'. *Kursbuch* 47 (1977), 125–40.

Dülmen, Richard van. *Frauen vor Gericht: Kindsmord in der frühen Neuzeit.* Frankfurt/M.: Fischer, 1991.

'Das Schauspiel des Todes: Hinrichtungsrituale in der frühen Neuzeit'. *Volkskultur: Zur Wiederentdeckung des vergessenen Alltags.* Ed. Richard van Dülmen and Norbert Schindler. Frankfurt/M.: Fischer, 1984. 203–45.

Theater des Schreckens: Gerichtspraxis und Strafrituale in der frühen Neuzeit. 4th edn. Munich: Beck, 1995.

ed. *Hexenwelten: Magie und Imagination vom 16.-20. Jahrhundert.* Frankfurt/M.: Fischer, 1987.

Dundes, Alan, ed. *The Evil Eye.* New York, London: Garland, 1981.

Durant, Will. *The Story of Philosophy: The Lives and Opinions of the Greater Philosophers.* New York: Simon & Schuster, 1927.

Dürkop, Marlis, and Gertrud Hardtmann. 'Frauenkriminalität'. *Kritische Justiz* 7 (1974), 219–36.

Eakin, Paul John. *How Our Lives Become Stories: Making Selves.* Ithaca, NY: Cornell University Press, 1999.

Ebel, Friedrich, ed. *Gemeinwohl, Freiheit, Vernunft, Rechtsstaat: 200 Jahre Allgemeines Landrecht für die Preussischen Staaten.* Berlin: de Gruyter, 1995.

Ebeling, Gerhard. 'Genie des Herzens unter dem genius saeculi – J. C. Lavater als Theologe'. *Das Antlitz Gottes im Antlitz des Menschen: Zugänge zu Johann Kaspar Lavater.* Ed. Karl Pestalozzi and Horst Weigelt. Göttingen: Vandenhoeck & Ruprecht, 1994. 23–60.

Efthimiou, Costas J., and Sohang Gandhi. 'Ghosts, Vampires and Zombies: Cinema Fiction vs. Physics Reality'. *arXiv: physics/0608059* v. 1 (5 August 2006), 1–10.

Ehlers, Martin. *Betrachtungen über die Sittlichkeit der Vergnügungen.* 2 vols. Flensburg and Leipzig: in der Kortenschen Buchhandlung, 1779.

Eigler, Friederike, and Susanne Kord, eds. *The Feminist Encyclopedia of German Literature*. Westport, CT: Greenwood Press, 1997.

Elias, Norbert. *The Civilizing Process: Sociogenetic and Psychogenetic Investigations*. Trans. Edmund Jephcott, ed. Eric Dunning, Johan Goudsblom and Stephen Mennell. 3rd edn. Oxford: Blackwell, 1994.

Elsberg, R. A. von [pseud for Ferdinand Strobl von Ravelsberg]. *Die Blutgräfin. (Elisabeth Báthory)*. Breslau: Schlesische Buchdruckerei, 1894.

Elworthy, Frederick Thomas. *The Evil Eye: An Account of this Ancient and Widespread Superstition*. London: John Murray, 1895.

Engelbrecht, Ernst, and Leo Heller. *Kinder der Nacht: Bilder aus dem Verbrecherleben, von Kriminalkommissar Ernst Engelbrecht und Leo Heller*. Berlin: Hermann Paetel, 1925.

Eschenburg, Johann Joachim. *Entwurf einer Theorie und Literatur der schönen Wissenschaften. Zur Grundlage bey Vorlesungen*. 2nd edn. Berlin and Stettin: Nicolai, 1789.

Evans, Richard J. 'Öffentlichkeit und Autorität. Zur Geschichte der Hinrichtungen in Deutschland vom Allgemeinen Landrecht bis zum Dritten Reich'. *Räuber, Volk und Obrigkeit: Studien zur Geschichte der Kriminalität in Deutschland seit dem 18. Jahrhundert*. Ed. Heinz Reif. Frankfurt/M.: Suhrkamp, 1984. 185–258.

Rituals of Retribution: Capital Punishment in Germany, 1600–1987. Oxford and New York: Oxford University Press, 1996.

Evidences of the Kingdom of Darkness: Being a Collection of Authentic and Entertaining Narratives of the Real Existence and Appearance of Ghosts, Demons, and Spectres: Together with Several Wonderful Instances of the EFFECTS of WITCHCRAFT. To which is prefixed, an Account of HAUNTED HOUSES, and subjoined a Treatise on the Effects of Magic. London: T. Evans, 1770.

Farin, Michael, ed. *Heroine des Grauens: Wirken und Leben der Elisabeth Báthory in Briefen, Zeugenaussagen und Phantasiespielen*. Munich: Kirchheim, 1989.

Fassbinder, Rainer Werner. *Bremer Freiheit: Blut am Hals der Katze*. Frankfurt/M.: Verlag der Autoren, 1983.

Faust, Günther. 'Die Kindestötung. Eine kriminalbiologische Betrachtung aus der Sicht der Persönlichkeit und der Konfliktlage der Täterin'. Med. diss. Mainz 1967.

Favret-Saada, Jeanne. *Deadly Words: Witchcraft in the Bocage*. Cambridge: Cambridge University Press, 1980.

Fee, Dwight. 'The Broken Dialogue: Mental Illness as Discourse and Experience'. *Pathology and the Postmodern: Mental Illness as Discourse and Experience*. Ed. Dwight Fee. London: Sage, 2000. 1–17.

ed. *Pathology and the Postmodern: Mental Illness as Discourse and Experience*. London: Sage, 2000.

Feilner, Franz. *General-Geschichte der fürchterlichsten Giftmischerin Gesche Margarethe Gottfried gebornen Timm. Aus den besten Quellen geschöpft, in Gemässheit Beschluss den Hohen Senats vom 17. Dezember 1830 zur Herausgabe bestätigt*. Bremen: Franz Feilner, 1831.

Felber, Alfons. 'Unzucht und Kindsmord in der Rechtssprechung der freien Reichsstadt Nördlingen vom 16. bis zum 19. Jahrhundert'. Jur. diss. Bonn, 1961.

Fessler, J. A. *Die Geschichte der Ungern und ihrer Landsassen*. 24 vols. Leipzig: J. F. Gleditsch, 1815–25.

Feuerbach, Anselm Ritter von. *Aktenmäßige Darstellung merkwürdiger Verbrechen von Anselm Ritter von Feuerbach, Staatsrath und Präsidenten*. 2 vols. in 1. Gießen: Georg Friedrich Heyer, 1828–9.

Lehrbuch des gemeinen in Deutschland geltenden Peinlichen Rechts. Gießen: Georg Friedrich Heyer, 1801.

Fichte, Johann Gottlieb. 'Erster Anhang des Naturrechts: Grundriß des Familienrechts'. *Johann Gottlieb Fichtes sämmtliche Werke*. Leipzig: n.p., n.d. III 304–68.

Finkelnburg, Karl Maria. '"AUCH ICH…" Kindesmord-Justiz und Strafrecht unter Goethe'. *Berliner Tageblatt* 161 (5 April 1931), 1. Beiblatt.

Flach, Willy. 'Goethe und der Kindesmord'. *Das Thüringer Fähnlein: Monatshefte für die mitteldeutsche Heimat* 3 (1934), 599–606.

'Der Kindesmord der Anna Katharina Höhn und die grundsätzliche Frage der Strafe bei Kindesmord'. *Beiträge zum Archivwesen, zur thüringischen Landesgeschichte und zur Goetheforschung*. Ed. Volker Wahl. Weimar: Hermann Böhlaus Nachfolger, 2003. 263–70.

Flocke, Petra. *'Ich schaue in den Spiegel und sehe nichts': Die kulturellen Inszenierungen der Vampirin*. Tübingen: Konkursbuchverlag, 1999.

Fort, Garrett. *Dracula*. Screenplay. 1931. Transcribed by B. J. Kuehl. www.horrorlair.com/scripts/draclugo.txt (last accessed 11 September 2007).

Foucault, Michel. *Discipline and Punish: The Birth of the Prison*. Trans. Alan Sheridan. London: Penguin, 1991.

Fragmente über die Frage, welches sind die besten ausführbaren Mittel, dem Kindermorde Einhalt zu thun? Frankfurt and Leipzig, 1782.

'Frauen im Untergrund – Etwas Irrationales'. *Der Spiegel* 33/1977.

Frede, Lothar. 'Kindesmord und Kirchenbuße bei Goethe'. *Zeitschrift für die gesamte Strafrechtswissenschaft* 78 (1966), 420–31.

Frederiksen, Elke, ed. *Women Writers in German Speaking Countries*. Westport, CT: Greenwood Press, 1998.

Freedman, Jeffrey. *The Poisoned Chalice*. Princeton: Princeton University Press, 2002.

French, Lorely. *German Women as Letter Writers: 1750–1850*. Madison and London: Associated University Press, 1996.

Frenschkowski, Marco. 'Keine spitzen Zähne. Von der interkulturellen Vergleichbarkeit mythologischer Konzepte: Das Beispiel des Vampirs'. *Poetische Wiedergänger: Deutschsprachige Vampirismus-Diskurse vom Mittelalter bis zur Gegenwart*. Ed. Julia Bertschik and Christa Agnes Tuczay. Tübingen: Franke, 2005. 43–59.

Frenzel, Elisabeth. 'Verführer und Verführte'. *Motive der Weltliteratur: Ein Lexikon dichtungsgeschichtlicher Längsschnitte*. Stuttgart: Kröner, 1980. 723–6.

Freuler, Kaspar. *Anna Göldin*. Glarus: Baeschlin, 1947.

Frevert, Ute. 'Unser Staat ist männlichen Geschlechts'. *'Mann und Weib, und Weib und Mann': Geschlechter-Differenzen in der Moderne*. Munich: Beck, 1995. 61–132.

Frey, Jakob, ed. *Gartengesellschaft*. Stuttgart: Bibliothek des literarischen Vereins, 1897.

Friend, John Albert Newton. *Demonology, Sympathetic Magic and Witchcraft. A Study of Superstition as It Persists in Man and Affects Him in a Scientific Age*. London: Charles Griffin & Co., 1961.

Fritsch, Johann Christian. *Eines Weimarischen Medici Dr. Ioh. Christ. Fritschii muthmaßliche Gedanken von den Vampyren oder Blutsaugenden Todten*. Leipzig, 1732.

Fronius, Helen. 'Images of Infanticide in Eighteenth-Century Germany'. *Women and Death: Representations of Female Victims and Perpetrators in German Culture 1500–2000*. Ed. Helen Fronius and Anna Linton. Rochester, NY: Camden House, 2008. 93–112.

Gaiman, Neil. 'Snow, Glass, Apples'. *Smoke and Mirrors: Short Fictions and Illusions*. London: Headline Feature, 1999. 371–84.

Gallas, Helga, and Anita Runge, eds. *Untersuchungen zum Roman von Frauen um 1800*. Tübingen: Niemeyer, 1990.

Gardner, Sam. 'UCF Professor Drives Scientific Stake into the Heart of Ghost, Vampire Myths'. *News and Information: The official news source for the University of Central Florida* (20 October 2006). www.arxiv.org/abs/physics/0608059 (last accessed 29 August 2007).

Geitner, Ursula. 'Passio Hysterica – Die alltägliche Sorge um das Selbst: Zum Zusammenhang von Literatur, Pathologie und Weiblichkeit im 18. Jahrhundert'. *Frauen – Weiblichkeit – Schrift*. Ed. Renate Berger, Monika Hengsbach, Maria Kublitz, Inge Stephan and Sigrid Weigel. Berlin: Argument, 1985. 130–44.

Gerhard, Ute, ed. *Frauen in der Geschichte des Rechts. Von der frühen Neuzeit bis zur Gegenwart*. Munich: Beck, 1997.

Gerhardt, Volker, Rolf-Peter Horstmann and Ralph Schumacher, eds. *Kant und die Berliner Aufklärung*. Berlin: de Gruyter, 2001.

Gestrich, Andreas. 'Pietismus und Aberglaube: Zum Zusammenhang von popularem Pietismus und dem Ende der Hexenverfolgung im 18. Jahrhundert'. *Das Ende der Hexenverfolgung*. Ed. Sönke Lorenz and Dieter R. Bauer. Stuttgart: Franz Steiner, 1995. 269–86.

'Gewalthandlungen und Gewaltbetroffenheit von Frauen und Männern'. Gender-Datenreport. Kommentierter Datenreport zur Gleichstellung von Frauen und Männern in der Bundesrepublik Deutschland. Report published by the Bundesministerium für Familie, Senioren, Frauen und Jugend. www.bmfsfj.de/Publikationen/genderreport/10-Gewalthandlungen-und-gewaltbetroffenheit-von-frauen-und-maennern/10–2-Daten-aus-dem-hellfeld-polizeilicher-kriminalstatistik-strafverfolgungs-und-strafvollzugsstatistik/10–2–1-zur-aussagekraft-der-daten.html

Geyer-Kordesch, Johanna. 'Whose Enlightenment? Medicine, Witchcraft, Melancholia and Pathology'. *New Perspectives on Witchcraft, Magic and*

Demonology. Vol. 6: *Witchcraft in the Modern World*. Ed. Brian P. Levack. New York and London: Routledge, 2001. 131–47.

Gibson, Mary. *Born to Crime: Cesare Lombroso and the Origins of Biological Criminology*. Westport, CT: Praeger, 2002.

Die Giftmischerin Gesina Timm in Bremen. Bremen, 1828. [broadsheet]

Die Giftmörderin Wittwe Gottfried in Bremen. Amtliche Mittheilungen. 2 vols. *Besonderer Abdruck aus Hitzigs Annalen für deutsche und ausländische Criminal-Rechtspflege*. Vols. 21–2 (Berlin, 1831).

Gijswijt-Hofstra, Marijke. 'Witchcraft after the Witch-Trials'. Marijke Gijswijt-Hofstra, Brian P. Levack and Roy Porter, *Witchcraft and Magic in Europe: The Eighteenth and Nineteenth Centuries*. London: Athlone Press, 1999. 95–189.

Gijswijt-Hofstra, Marijke, Brian P. Levack and Roy Porter. *Witchcraft and Magic in Europe: The Eighteenth and Nineteenth Centuries*. London: Athlone Press, 1999.

Goddard, Linda. 'Aesthetic Hierarchies: Interchange and Rivalry between the Visual Arts and Literature in France, c. 1890–c. 1920.' PhD diss., University of London, 2005.

Goethe, Johann Wolfgang. 'Die Braut von Korinth'. *Goethes Werke: Hamburger Ausgabe*. Ed. Erich Trunz. 14 vols. Munich: Beck, 1981–. I 268–73.

Clavigo. Goethes Werke: Hamburger Ausgabe. Ed. Erich Trunz. 14 vols. Munich: Beck, 1981–. IV 260–306.

Faust. Der Tragödie erster Teil. Goethes Werke: Hamburger Ausgabe. Ed. Erich Trunz. 14 vols. Munich: Beck, 1981–. III 1–145.

Faust. Der Tragödie zweiter Teil. Goethes Werke: Hamburger Ausgabe. Ed. Erich Trunz. 14 vols. Munich: Beck, 1981–. III 147–364.

Goetzinger, Germaine. 'Männerphantasien und Frauenwirklichkeit: Kindermörderinnen in der Literatur des Sturm und Drang'. *Frauen – Literatur – Politik*. Ed. Annegret Pelz, Marianne Schuller, Inge Stephan, Sigrid Weigel and Kerstin Wilhelms. Berlin: Argument, 1988. 263–86.

Golby, J. M. *The Civilisation of the Crowd: Popular Culture in England 1750–1900*. London: Batsford, 1984.

Gorgoni, Christine Bukowska. 'Die Strafe des Säckens: Wahrheit und Legende'. *Forschungen zur Rechtsarchäologie und rechtlicher Volkskunde* 2 (1979): 144–62.

Gössmann, Elisabeth, ed. *Das wohlgelahrte Frauenzimmer*. Munich: iudicium, 1984.

Göttsch, Silke. '"Vielmahls aber hätte sie gewünscht, einen andern Mann zu haben": Gattenmord im 18. Jahrhundert'. *Von Huren und Rabenmüttern: Weibliche Kriminalität in der Frühen Neuzeit*. Ed. Otto Ulbricht. Cologne, Weimar and Vienna: Böhlau, 1995. 313–34.

Graben zum Stein, Otto. *Unverlorenes Licht und Recht derer Todten unter den Lebendigen*. Wittenberg, 1732.

Graham, John. *Lavater's Essays on Physiognomy: A Study in the History of Ideas*. Berne, etc.: Peter Lang, 1979.

Gray, Richard T. *About Face: German Physiognomic Thought from Lavater to Auschwitz*. Detroit: Wayne State University Press, 2004.

'Aufklärung und Anti-Aufklärung: Wissenschaftlichkeit und Zeichenbegriff in Lavaters "Physiognomik"'. *Das Antlitz Gottes im Antlitz des Menschen: Zugänge zu Johann Kaspar Lavater.* Ed. Karl Pestalozzi and Horst Weigelt. Göttingen: Vandenhoeck & Ruprecht, 1994. 166–78.

Gribble, Leonard R. *Queens of Crime.* London: Hurst & Blackett, 1932.

Grießhammer, Birke, ed. *Drutenjagd in Franken, 16. – 18. Jahrhundert.* Eyrbaum: Wagner, 1999.

Grimm, Jacob, ed. *Weisthümer, gesammelt von Jacob Grimm.* Co-ed. Ernst Dronke and Heinrich Beyer. 3 vols. Göttingen: Dietrichsche Buchhandlung, 1840–2.

ed. *Weisthümer. Gesammelt von Jacob Grimm.* 7 vols. Göttingen: Dietrichsche Buchhandlung, 1840–78.

Grimm, Jacob, and Wilhelm Grimm. 'Sneewittchen'. *Kinder- und Hausmärchen gesammelt durch die Brüder Grimm.* 3 vols. Frankfurt/M.: Insel, 1984. 1300–11.

Grøn, Frederik. 'Über den Ursprung der Bestrafung in Effigie. Eine vergleichende rechts- und kulturgeschichtliche Untersuchung'. *Tijdschrift voor Rechtsgeschiedenis* 13 (1934), 320–81.

Gross, Hans. *Criminalpsychologie.* Graz: Leuschner & Lubensky's, 1898.

Grosz, Elizabeth. *Jacques Lacan: A Feminist Introduction.* London and New York: Routledge, 1990.

Grütter, Karin. '"weil ich fürchtete, aus der Stadt entfernt zu werden…" Kindstötung in Basel um 1850'. *Auf den Spuren weiblicher Vergangenheit: Berichte des zweiten Schweizerischen Historikertreffens in Basel, Oktober 1984.* Basel: Schwase, 1985. 106–19.

Günther, Christian. *Q.D.B.V. Dissertatio Juridica de Convicto non-Confesso, Quam Consentiente Illustri JCtorum Ordine in Alma Lipsiensi sub moderamine D. Gothofredi Barthii, J.U.D. & Practici Celeberrimi.* Leipzig: Andreas Martin Sched, 1715.

Gustafson, Susan E. 'The Cadaverous Bodies of Vampiric Mothers and the Genealogy of Pathology in E. T. A. Hoffmann's Tales'. *German Life and Letters* 52.2 (1999), 238–54.

Gutbrodt, Fritz. 'Physiognomik, Predigt, Okkultismus: Lavater und die Medien der Kommunikation im 18. Jahrhundert'. *Im Lichte Lavaters: Lektüren zum 200. Todestag.* Ed. Ulrich Stadler and Karl Pestalozzi. Zurich: Neue Zürcher Zeitung, 2003. 117–40.

Habermas, Rebekka, ed., in collaboration with Tanja Hommen. *Das Frankfurter Gretchen. Der Prozeß gegen die Kindsmörderin Susanna Margaretha Brandt.* Munich: Beck, 1999.

Hälschner, Hugo. *Geschichte des Brandenburgisch-Preußischen Strafrechtes. Ein Beitrag zur Geschichte des deutschen Strafrechtes.* Bonn: Marcus, 1855.

Häntzschel, Günter, John Ormrod and Karl N. Renner, eds. *Zur Sozialgeschichte der deutschen Literatur von der Aufklärung bis zur Jahrhundertwende.* Tübingen: Niemeyer, 1985.

Härter, Karl. *Policey und Strafjustiz in Kurmainz: Gesetzgebung, Normdurchsetzung und Sozialkontrolle im frühneuzeitlichen Territorialstaat.* 2 vols. Frankfurt/M.: Vittorio Klostermann, 2005.

'Strafverfahren im frühneuzeitlichen Territorialstaat: Inquisition, Entschei-
dungsfindung, Supplikation'. *Kriminalitätsgeschichte: Beiträge zur Sozial-
und Kulturgeschichte der Vormoderne.* Ed. Andreas Blauert and
Gerd Schwerhoff. Konstanz: UVK, 2000. 459–80.

Hagen, Friedrich Heinrich von der, ed. *Gesamtabenteuer: Hundert altdeutsche
Erzählungen.* 3 vols. Stuttgart and Tübingen, 1850.

Hahn Rafter, Nicole, and Mary Gibson. 'Introduction'. Cesare Lombroso and
Guglielmo Ferrero, *Criminal Woman, the Prostitute, and the Normal Woman.*
Ed. and trans. Nicole Hahn Rafter and Mary Gibson. Durham, NC, and
London: Duke University Press, 2004. 3–33.

Hallissy, Margaret. *Venomous Woman: Fear of the Female in Literature.* New York,
Westport, CT, and London: Greenwood Press, 1987.

Hamberger, Klaus. *Mortuus non mordet: Kommentierte Dokumente zum
Vampirismus 1689–1791.* Vienna: Turia & Kant, 1992.

Über Vampirismus: Krankengeschichten und Deutungsmuster 1801–1899. Vienna:
Turia & Kant, 1992.

Hamilton, Edith. *Mythology.* New York and Scarborough: New American Library,
1969.

Hammer, Elke. *Kindsmord. Seine Geschichte in Innerösterreich 1787 bis 1849.*
Frankfurt/M.: Peter Lang, 1997.

Harenberg, Johann Christoph. *Vernünftige und Christliche Gedanken Über die
Vampirs Oder Bluhtsaugende Todten, So unter den Türcken und auf den
Gräntzen des Servien-Landes den lebenden Menschen und Viehe das Bluht
aussaugen sollen, Begleitet mit allerley theologischen, philosophischen und histor-
ischen aus dem Reiche der Geister hergeholten Anmerckungen Und entworfen Von
Johann Christoph Harenberg, Rect. der Stifts-Schule zu Gandersheim.*
Wolfenbüttel: Johann Christoph Meißner, 1733.

Harmening, Dieter. *Der Anfang von Dracula: Zur Geschichte von Geschichten.*
Würzburg: Königshausen & Neumann, 1983.

*Zauberei im Abendland: Vom Anteil der Gelehrten am Wahn der Leute. Skizzen
zur Geschichte des Aberglaubens.* Würzburg: Königshausen & Neumann, 1991.

Harms-Ziegler, Beate. 'Außereheliche Mutterschaft in Preußen im 18. und 19.
Jahrhundert'. *Frauen in der Geschichte des Rechts. Von der frühen Neuzeit bis
zur Gegenwart.* Ed. Ute Gerhard. Munich: Beck, 1997. 325–44.

Hart, Lynda. *Fatal Women: Lesbian Sexuality and the Mark of Aggression.* London:
Routledge, 1994.

Hasler, Eveline. *Anna Göldin: Letzte Hexe.* 6th edn. Zurich: Benziger, 1991.

Hauff, Gustav. 'Goethe und die Todesstrafe'. *Goethe-Jahrbuch* 4 (1883), 365–8.

Haupt-Auszüge aus der Defension der Inquisitin Maria Catharina Wächtlern.
N.p., n.d.

*Hauptbericht in der Untersuchungssache wider Michael Christoph Gottfried Wittwe
Gesche Margarethe geborne Timm.* Bremen, 1831. Handwritten MS; microfilm,
Staatsarchiv Bremen.

Hauschildt, Ingeborg. 'Feministische Theologie – eine fragwürdige neue Welle'.
Unpublished manuscript, n.d. (probably 1980).

Hausen, Karin. 'Die Polarisierung der "Geschlechtscharaktere" – eine Spiegelung der Dissoziation von Erwerbs- und Familienleben'. *Sozialgeschichte der Familie in der Neuzeit Europas*. Ed. Werner Conze. Stuttgart: Klett, 1976. 363–93.

Hauser, Walter. *Der Justizmord an Anna Göldi: Neue Recherchen zum letzten Hexenprozess in Europa. Mit Dokumenten*. 2nd edn. Zurich: Limmat, 2007.

Haustein, Jörg. 'Bibelauslegung und Bibelkritik: Ansätze zur Überwindung der Hexenverfolgung'. *Das Ende der Hexenverfolgung*. Ed. Sönke Lorenz and Dieter R. Bauer. Stuttgart: Franz Steiner, 1995. 249–67.

Heckscher, J[oseph]. 'Das Ende der Gattenmörderin Maria Katharina Wächtler, geb. Wunsch'. *MHG* 8 (1905), 349–52.

Hegel, Georg Friedrich Wilhelm. *Grundlinien der Philosophie des Rechts: oder Naturrecht*. Frankfurt/M., Berlin and Vienna: Ullstein, 1972.

Hegler, August. *Die praktische Tätigkeit der Juristenfakultäten des 17. und 18. Jahrhunderts in ihrem Einfluß auf die Entwicklung des deutschen Strafrechts von Carpzov ab*. Freiburg: Mohr, 1899.

Helbing, Franz. *Die Tortur: Geschichte der Folter im Kriminalverfahren aller Völker und Zeiten*. 2 vols. Berlin: J. Gnadenfeld & Co., n.d.

Held, Robert, ed. *Inquisition: A Bilingual Guide to the Exhibition of Torture Instruments from the Middle Ages to the Industrial Era*. Florence: Qua d'Arno, 1985.

Hellwig, Albert. 'Volkskundliches und Kriminalpsychologisches aus dem Prozeß der Giftmörderin Gesche Margarethe Gottfried, hingerichtet im Jahre 1831 in Bremen'. *Archiv für Kriminal-Anthropologie* 41 (1911), 54–66.

Henschel, Johann Friedrich. 'Die Strafverteidigung im Inquisitionsprozeß des 18. und im Anklageprozeß d. 19. Jahrhunderts'. Diss. Freiburg 1972.

Herx, Liselotte. *Der Giftmord, insbesondere der Giftmord durch Frauen*. Emsdetten: Lechte, 1937.

Heuser, Edith. 'Die ehrsame Mörderin. Der Fall Gesche Margarethe Gottfried'. *Der neue Pitaval: Justizirrtum*. Ed. R. A. Stemmle. Munich: Desch, 1965. 273–322.

Hinckeldey, Christoph, ed. *Criminal Justice Through the Ages: From Divine Judgement to Modern German Legislation*. Trans. John Fosberry. Heilsbronn: Schulist, 1981.

'Eine Hinrichtung in Appenzell, 1849'. *Der neue Pitaval: Eine Sammlung der interessantesten Criminalgeschichten aller Länder aus älterer und neuerer Zeit. Neue Serie*. Ed. J. E. Hitzig and W. Häring. 24 vols. Leipzig: F. A. Brockhaus, 1866–90. Vol. xv.

Hippel, Theodor Gottlieb von. *On Marriage*. Ed. and trans. Timothy F. Sellner. Detroit: Wayne State University Press, 1994.

Hitzig, J[ulius] E[duard] and [Georg] W[ilhelm Heinrich] Häring, eds. *Der neue Pitaval. Eine Sammlung der interessantesten Criminalgeschichten aller Länder aus älterer und neuerer Zeit. Herausgegeben vom Criminaldirector Dr. J. E. Hitzig und Dr. W. Häring (W. Alexis)*. 12 vols. Leipzig: F. A. Brockhaus, 1842–7.

Hock, Stefan. *Die Vampyrsagen und ihre Verwertung in der deutschen Litteratur.*
Berlin: Alexander Duncker, 1900.

Hoff, Dagmar von. 'Die Inszenierung des "Frauenopfers" in Dramen von
Autorinnen um 1800'. *Frauen – Literatur – Politik*. Ed. Annegret Pelz,
Marianne Schuller, Inge Stephan, Sigrid Weigel and Kerstin Wilhelms.
Berlin: Argument, 1988. 255–62.

Hoffmann, Ernst Theodor Amadeus. 'Eine Vampir-Geschichte'. *E. T. A.
Hoffmanns Sämtliche Werke. Historisch-Kritische Ausgabe*. Ed. Carl Georg
von Maassen. Munich: Georg Müller, 1925. VIII 218–33.

The Serapion Brethren. Trans. Alex Ewing. 2 vols. London: George Bell, 1886–92.

Die Serapionsbrüder. 4 vols. Berlin: Walter de Gruyter, 1957.

Hoffmann, Ludger. 'Vom Ereignis zum Fall. Sprachliche Muster zur Darstellung und
Überprüfung von Sachverhalten vor Gericht'. *Erzählte Kriminalität: Zur Typologie
und Funktion von narrativen Darstellungen in Strafrechtspflege, Publizistik und
Literatur zwischen 1770 und 1920*. Ed. Jörg Schönert in collaboration with
Konstantin Imm and Joachim Linder. Tübingen: Max Niemeyer, 1991. 87–113.

Hoffmann, Volker. 'Elisa und Robert oder das Weib und der Mann, wie sie sein
sollten: Anmerkungen zur Geschlechtercharakteristik der Goethezeit'. *Klassik
und Moderne: Die Weimarer Klassik als historisches Ereignis und Herausforderung
im kulturgeschichtlichen Prozeß*. Ed. Karl Richter and Jörg Schönert. Stuttgart:
Metzler, 1983. 80–97.

Hofmann, V[alentin] F[riedrich]. *Ist das eigene Geständniß eines Delinquenten, zu
seiner Hinrichtung, nach der carolinischen peinlichen Halsgerichtsordnung, und
nach unsern Statuten, durchaus erforderlich? Bey Gelegenheit der Sache der
berüchtigten Mannsmörderin, Wächtern, zu beantworten versucht, und mit
einer kurzen actenmäßigen und wahrhaften Darstellung derselben begleitet von
V. F. Hofmann, hiesigem Advocato und Notario. Zwote, mit dem wiederholten
Geständnisse der Wächtern, gegen den Geistlichen in der Frohnerey, vermehrte
und verbessere Auflage*. Hamburg: Gedruckt bey J. M. Michaelsen, 1789 [orig.
edn. Hamburg, 1788].

Hohlbein, Wolfgang. *Die Blutgräfin: Die Chronik der Unsterblichen 6. Roman*. 4th
edn. Cologne: Ullstein, 2007.

Holzhauer, Heinz. 'Rechtsgeschichte der Folter'. *Folter. Stellungnahmen, Analysen,
Vorschläge zur Abschaffung*. Baden-Baden: Nomos, 1976. 107–24.

Hommel, Ferdinand August. *Q.D.B.V. de Revocatione Confessionis per Tormenta
Extortae, Wiederruffung der Urgicht, permissu Illustris Facultatis Juridicae sub
Praesidio Dn. Christophori Dondorffii, Phil. et. J.U.D. Facult. Jur. Lips. et Cur.
Prov. in Infer. LUS, Assessor*. Leipzig: Andreas Martin Sched, n.d.

Honegger, Claudia. *Die Hexen der Neuzeit: Studien zur Sozialgeschichte eines
kulturellen Deutungsmusters*. Frankfurt/M.: Suhrkamp, 1978.

*Die Ordnung der Geschlechter: Die Wissenschaften vom Menschen und das Weib,
1750–1850*. Frankfurt/M.: Campus, 1991.

Hoof, Dieter. '"Hier ist keine Gnade weiter, bei Gott ist Gnade."
Kindsmordvorgänge in Hannover im 18. Jahrhundert. Ein Beitrag zur historischen Sexualforschung'. *Hannoverische Geschichtsblätter* 37 (1983), 45–84.

Horst, Georg Conrad. *Zauber-Bibliothek, oder von Zauberei, Theurgie und Mantik, Zauberern, Hexen, und Hexenprocessen, Dämonen, Gespenstern, und Geistererscheinungen. Zur Beförderung einer rein-geschichtlichen, von Aberglauben und Unglauben freien Beurtheilung dieser Gegenstände. Von Georg Conrad Horst, Großherzoglich-Hessischem Kirchenrathe.* 6 vols. Mainz: Florian Kupferberg, 1821–26.

Hügel, Hans-Otto. *Untersuchungsrichter, Diebsfänger, Detektive: Theorie und Geschichte der deutschen Detektiverzählung im 19. Jahrhundert.* Stuttgart: Metzler, 1978.

Huizing, Klaas. 'Verschattete Epiphanie. Lavaters physiognomischer Gottesbeweis'. *Das Antlitz Gottes im Antlitz des Menschen: Zugänge zu Johann Kaspar Lavater.* Ed. Karl Pestalozzi and Horst Weigelt. Göttingen: Vandenhoeck & Ruprecht, 1994. 61–91.

Hull, Isabel. *Sexuality, State and Civil Society in Germany, 1700–1815.* Ithaca, NY: Cornell University Press, 1996.

'Sexualstrafrecht und geschlechtsspezifische Normen in den deutschen Staaten des 17. und 18. Jahrhunderts'. *Frauen in der Geschichte des Rechts: Von der frühen Neuzeit bis zur Gegenwart.* Ed. Ute Gerhard. Munich: Beck, 1997. 221–34.

Humboldt, Wilhelm von. 'Über den Geschlechtsunterschied und dessen Einfluß auf die organische Natur.' *Werke.* Stuttgart: Cotta, 1960. I 268–95.

'Über männliche und weibliche Form.' *Werke.* Stuttgart: Cotta, 1960. I 296–336.

'Plan einer vergleichenden Anthropologie.' *Werke.* Stuttgart: Cotta, 1960. I 337–75.

Huyssen, Andreas. 'Das leidende Weib in der dramatischen Literatur von Empfindsamkeit und Sturm und Drang: Eine Studie zur bürgerlichen Emanzipation in Deutschland'. *Monatshefte* 69 (1977), 159–73.

Imm, Konstantin, and Joachim Linder. 'Verdächtige und Täter: Zuschreibung von Kriminalität in Texten der "schönen Literatur" am Beispiel des Feuilletons der *Berliner Gerichts-Zeitung*, der Romanreihe *Eisenbahn-Unterhaltungen* und Wilhelm Raabes *Horacker* und *Stopfkuchen*'. *Zur Sozialgeschichte der deutschen Literatur von der Aufklärung bis zur Jahrhundertwende.* Ed. Günter Häntzschel et al. Tübingen: Niemeyer, 1985. 21–96.

Inquisition gegen die berüchtige Wächtlern mit Fragen und Antwort nebst der fiscalischen Anklage derselben im Gericht. N.p., n.d. [1786].

Jackson, Mark, ed. *Infanticide: Historical Perspectives on Child Murder and Concealment, 1550–2000.* Aldershot and Burlington: Ashgate, 2002.

Jacobi, D[aniel] H. *Geschichte des Hamburger Niedergerichts.* Hamburg: Nolte, 1866.

Jacobs, Helmut, ed. *Gegen Folter und Todesstrafe: Aufklärerischer Diskurs und europäische Literatur vom 18. Jahrhundert bis zur Gegenwart.* Frankfurt/M.: Peter Lang, 2007.

Jacobs, Jürgen. 'Gretchen und ihre Schwestern. Zum Motiv des Kindsmords in der Literatur des 18. Jahrhunderts'. *Ethik und Ästhetik. Werke und Werte in der Literatur vom 18. bis zum 20. Jahrhundert.* Ed. Richard Fisher. Frankfurt/M.: Lang, 1995. 103–20.

Jagemann, Ludwig von, and Wilhelm Brauer. *Criminallexikon. Nach dem neuesten Stande der Gesetzgebung in Deutschland*. Erlangen, 1854.

Jöntzen, Georg. *Schreckliche, unerhörte Mordthaten der berüchtigten Giftmischerin Gesche Marg. Gottfried geb. Timme*. Bremen, 1831.

Jones, Ann. *Women Who Kill*. New York: Fawcett Columbine, 1980.

Jones, Louis C. 'The Evil Eye among European-Americans'. *The Evil Eye*. Ed. Alan Dundes. New York and London: Garland, 1981. 150–68.

Ju, Gau-Jeng. *Kants Lehre vom Menschenrecht und von den staatsbürgerlichen Grundrechten*. Würzburg: Königshausen & Neumann, 1990.

Justi, Johann Heinrich Gottlieb von. *Die Grundfeste zu der Macht und Glückseeligkeit der Staaten; oder ausführliche Vorstellung der gesamten Policey-Wissenschaft*. 2 vols. Königsberg and Leipzig: Hartung, 1760 (vol. i), Woltersdorf, 1761 (vol. ii).

Kaemmerer, Ernst Wilhelm. *Das Leib-Seele-Geist-Problem bei Paracelsus und einigen Autoren des 17. Jahrhunderts*. Wiesbaden: Franz Steiner, 1971.

Kant, Immanuel. *Die Metaphysik der Sitten. Abgefaßt von Immanuel Kant. Erster Theil: Metaphysische Anfangsgründe der Rechtslehre*. Königsberg: bey Friedrich Nocolovius, 1797.

Werkausgabe. Ed. Wilhelm Weischedel. 12 vols. Frankfurt: Suhrkamp, 1968. [In it: *Anthropologie in pragmatischer Hinsicht*, xii 395–690; *Die Metaphysik der Sitten*, xviii 305–636.]

Kapferer, Bruce, ed. *Beyond Rationalism: Rethinking Magic, Witchcraft, and Sorcery*. New York and Oxford: Berghahn, 2003.

Karsch, Anna Louisa. 'Belloisens Lebenslauf'. *Gedichte und Lebenszeugnisse*. Stuttgart: Reclam, 1987. 69–70.

Herzgedanken. Das Leben der 'deutschen Sappho' von ihr selbst erzählt. Ed. Barbara Beuys. Frankfurt/M.: Societäts-Verlag, 1933.

'Mein Bruder in Apoll': Briefwechsel zwischen Anna Louisa Karsch und Johann Wilhelm Ludwig Gleim. 2 vols. Ed. Regina Nörtemann (vol. i) and Ute Pott (vol. ii). Göttingen: Wallstein, 1996.

Kast, Verena. *Wege aus Angst und Symbiose: Märchen psychologisch gedeutet*. Olten: Walter, 1982.

Kastner, Klaus. 'Literatur und Recht – eine unendliche Geschichte'. *Neue Juristische Wochenschrift* 56. 9 (2003), 609–15.

Keller, Adalbert von, ed. *Erzählungen aus Altdeutschen Handschriften*. Stuttgart: Literarischer Verein, 1855.

Kilday, Anne-Marie. *Women and Violent Crime in Enlightenment Scotland*. Woodbridge: Boydell Press, 2007.

'KinderMord in Vevay 1781'. *Stats-Anzeigen* 2 (1782), 115–19.

Kirkpatrick, John. *Lady-Killers, or 'How to Murder Your Husband.' A Farce in One Act for Six Women and an Offstage Man*. New York, Hollywood, London and Toronto: Samuel French, 1949.

Kittredge, Katharine, ed. *Lewd & Notorious: Female Transgression in the Eighteenth Century*. Ann Arbor: University of Michigan Press, 2003.

Klaniczay, Gábor. 'The Decline of Witches and the Rise of Vampires under the Eighteenth-Century Habsburg Monarchy'. *Witch-Hunting in Continental*

Europe: Local and Regional Studies. Ed. Brian P. Levack. New York and London: Garland, 1992. 262–86.

'Historische Hintergründe: Der Aufstieg der Vampire im Habsburgerreich des 18. Jahrhunderts'. *Poetische Wiedergänger: Deutschsprachige Vampirismus-Diskurse vom Mittelalter bis zur Gegenwart*. Ed. Julia Bertschik and Christa Agnes Tuczay. Tübingen: Franke, 2005. 83–111.

The Uses of Supernatural Power: The Transformation of Popular Religion in Medieval and Early-Modern Europe. Trans. Susan Singerman, ed. Karen Margolis. Cambridge: Polity Press, 1990.

Klar, Herma. 'Verbrechen aus verlorener Ehre? Kindsmörderinnen. Eine Untersuchung aufgrund von Material aus der ländlichen Unterschicht Nordwürttembergs im 19. Jahrhundert'. Unpublished MA thesis. Tübingen 1984.

Kleist, Heinrich von. 'Das Erdbeben in Chili'. *Sämtliche Werke und Briefe*. Ed. Helmut Sembdner. 2 vols. 8th edn. Munich: Hanser, 1984. II 144–59.

Penthesilea. Sämtliche Werke und Briefe. Ed. Helmut Sembdner. 2 vols. 8th edn. Munich: Hanser, 1984. I 321–428.

Klemens, Elke. *Dracula und 'seine Töchter': Die Vampirin als Symbol im Wandel der Zeit*. Tübingen: Gunter Narr, 2004.

Klencke, Caroline Luise von. 'Vorberichtender Lebenslauf der Dichterin Anna Louise Karschin, geb. Dürbach'. Anna Louisa Karsch, *Gedichte. Nach der Dichterin Tode herausgegeben von ihrer Tochter Caroline Luise von Klencke*. Ed. Barbara Becker-Cantarino. Karben: Petra Wald, 1996 (rpt of edn Berlin, 1792). 1–128.

Knigge, Adolph Freiherr von. *Ueber den Umgang mit Menschen*. 3rd edn. 3 vols. Frankfurt and Leipzig, 1794.

Knight, Chris. *Blood Relations: Menstruation and the Origins of Culture*. New Haven, CT: Yale University Press, 1991.

Koch, Elisabeth. 'Die Frau im Recht der Frühen Neuzeit. Juristische Lehren und Begründungen'. *Frauen in der Geschichte des Rechts. Von der frühen Neuzeit bis zur Gegenwart*. Ed. Ute Gerhard. Munich: Beck, 1997. 73–93.

Kocka, Jürgen, ed. *Bürger und Bürgerlichkeit im 19. Jahrhundert*. Göttingen: Vandenhoeck & Ruprecht, 1987.

Geschichte und Aufklärung: Aufsätze. Göttingen: Vandenhoeck & Ruprecht, 1989.

Koepke, Wulf. 'Das Wort "Volk" im Sprachgebrauch Johann Gottfried Herders'. *Lessing Yearbook* 19 (1987), 209–21.

Kohut, Adolph. *Berühmte und berüchtigte Giftmischerinnen. Eine culturgeschichtlich-psychologische Studie von Dr. Adolph Kohut. Mit einem Vorwort von Rechtsanwalt Dr. Fritz Friedmann*. Berlin: Bibliographisches Bureau, 1893.

Kopper, Joachim. *Ethik der Aufklärung*. Darmstadt: Wissenschaftliche Buchgesellschaft, 1983.

Kord, Susanne. 'Ancient Fears and the New Order: Witch Beliefs and Physiognomy in the Age of Reason'. *German Life and Letters* 61.1 (2008), 61–78.

Ein Blick hinter die Kulissen: Deutschsprachige Dramatikerinnen des 18. und 19. Jahrhunderts. Stuttgart: Metzler, 1992.

'Der Fall Wächtler: Die Hamburger Flugblattliteratur zur Folter (1788) und die Lust am Lesen'. *Zeitschrift für Germanistik*, new series, 19.2 (2009), 346–60.

Sich einen Namen machen: Anonymität und weibliche Autorschaft, 1700–1900. Stuttgart: Metzler, 1996.

'Unmöglichkeiten: Vater-Tochter-Dramen im 18. und 19. Jahrhundert'. *Familie und Identität in der deutschen Literatur.* Ed. Thomas Martinec and Claudia Nitschke. Frankfurt: Peter Lang, 2008. 105–25.

'Women as Children, Women as Childkillers: Poetic Images of Infanticide in Eighteenth-Century Germany'. *Eighteenth-Century Studies* 26.3 (Spring 1993), 449–66.

Women Peasant Poets in Eighteenth-Century England, Scotland and Germany: Milkmaids on Parnassus. Rochester, NY: Camden House, 2003.

Kord, Susanne, and Ruth Whittle, eds. *Ver/Ordnungen: Re-Thinking the German Enlightenment. A Special Issue in Honour of David Hill. German Life and Letters* 61.1 (January 2008).

Kors, Alan Charles, and Edward Peters, eds. *Witchcraft in Europe, 400–1700: A Documentary History.* Philadelphia: University of Pennsylvania Press, 2001.

Witchcraft in Europe, 1100–1700: A Documentary History. London: Dent, 1973.

Košenina, Alexander. *Literarische Anthropologie: Die Neuentdeckung des Menschen.* Berlin: Akademieverlag, 2008.

'Ratlose Schwestern der Marquise von O…: Rätselhafte Schwangerschaften in populären Fallgeschichten – von Pitaval bis Spieß'. *Kleist-Jahrbuch* (2006), 45–59.

'Schiller und die Tradition der (kriminal)psychologischen Fallgeschichte bei Goethe, Meißner, Moritz und Spieß'. *Friedrich Schiller und Europa: Ästhetik, Politik, Geschichte.* Ed. Alice Stašková. Heidelberg: Winter, 2007. 119–39.

'Staatsmord statt Strafe: Neue Dokumente zur Hinrichtung der Johanna Höhn'. *Frankfurter Allgemeine Zeitung* 93 (21 April 2008), 42.

ed. *August Gottlieb Meißner: Ausgewählte Kriminalgeschichten.* St Ingbert: Röhrig 2003 (2nd edn 2004).

Kramer, Heinrich, and Jakob Sprenger. *Der Hexenhammer: Malleus Maleficarum.* Trans. Wolfgang Behringer, Günter Jerouschek and Werner Tschacher, ed. Günter Jerouschek and Wolfgang Behringer. 4th edn. Munich: dtv, 2004.

Kramer, Sven. *Die Folter in der Literatur: Ihre Darstellung in der deutschsprachigen Erzählprosa von 1740 bis 'nach Auschwitz'.* Munich: Wilhelm Fink, 2004.

Krauss, August. *Die Psychologie des Verbrechens: Ein Beitrag zur Erfahrungsseelenkunde.* Tübingen: H. Laupp, 1884.

Kreuter, Peter Mario. 'Vom "üblen Geist" zum "Vampier": Die Darstellung des Vampirs in den Berichten österreichischer Militärärzte zwischen 1725 und 1756'. *Poetische Wiedergänger: Deutschsprachige Vampirismus-Diskurse vom Mittelalter bis zur Gegenwart.* Ed. Julia Bertschik and Christa Agnes Tuczay. Tübingen: Franke, 2005. 113–27.

Kuzmics, Helmut. 'Violence and Pacification in Norbert Elias's Theory of Civilization'. *Violence, Culture and Identity: Essays on German and Austrian Literature, Politics and Society*. Ed. Helen Chambers. Oxford, etc.: Peter Lang, 2006. 27–46.

Labouvie, Eva. 'Absage an den Teufel'. *Das Ende der Hexenverfolgung*. Ed. Sönke Lorenz and Dieter R. Bauer. Stuttgart: Franz Steiner, 1995. 55–76.

Verbotene Künste: Volksmagie und ländlicher Aberglaube in den Dorfgemeinden des Saarraumes (16.–19. Jahrhundert). St Ingbert: Röhrig, 1992.

Zauberei und Hexenwerk. Ländlicher Hexenglaube in der frühen Neuzeit. Frankfurt/M.: Fischer, 1991.

Lacan, Jacques. *Ecrits: A Selection*. Trans. Alan Sheridan. London: Tavistock, 1977.

[Lamezan, Ferdinand Adrian von.] 'Welches sind die besten ausführbaren Mittel, dem Kindermorde Einhalt zu thun?' *Rheinische Beiträge zur Gelehrsamkeit* 2 (1780), 84–7 [also in *Schlözer's Briefwechsel* 7 (1780), 261–4; *Ephemeriden der Menschheit* (1780), 610–14].

Lammel, Hans-Uwe. 'Kinds-Mord und Historiographie: Ärztlich-forensische Praxis und Reformations-Deutung in der zweiten Hälfte des 18. Jahrhunderts am Beispiel von Johann Carl Wilhelm Moehsen (1722–1795)'. *'Vernünftige Ärzte': Hallesche Psychomediziner und die Anfänge der Anthropologie in der deutschsprachigen Frühaufklärung*. Ed. Carsten Zelle. Tübingen: Niemeyer, 2001. 200–19.

Landesarchiv Glarus: Altes Evangelisches Archiv, Prozess Anna Göldi, Kriminalfälle 1782–1783 AE 15.1781:6; Evangelisches Landsgemeinde Protokoll AG I 92 I.; Evangelisches Ratsprotokoll AG I 145 I.; Vermischtes 5er Gerichts Protokoll AG II 40.

Langbein, August Friedrich Ernst. *Feierabende, von A. J. C. Langbein*. 3 vols. Leipzig: Voß, 1798.

Lange, Sigrid, ed. *Ob die Weiber Menschen sind: Geschlechterdebatten um 1800*. Leipzig: Reclam, 1992.

Laqueur, Thomas. *The Making of the Modern Body: Sexuality and Society in the Nineteenth Century*. Berkeley and London: University of California Press, 1987.

Making Sex: Body and Gender from the Greeks to Freud. Cambridge, MA: Harvard University Press, 1990.

Laslett, Peter, Karla Oosterveen and Richard M. Smith. *Bastardy and its Comparative History*. London: E. Arnold, 1980.

Lavater, Johann Caspar. *Essays on Physiognomy; for the Promotion of the Knowledge and the Love of Mankind, written in the German Language by John Caspar Lavater, and translated into English by Thomas Holcroft. To which are added, One Hundred Physiognomical Rules, A Posthumous Work by Mr. Lavater, and Memoirs of the Life of the Author, Compiled principally from the Life of Lavater, written by his Son-in-Law G. Gessner*. 3 vols. in 4. 2nd edn. London: C. Whittingham, 1804.

Physiognomische Fragmente, zur Beförderung der Menschenkenntniß und Menschenliebe. 4 vols. Leipzig and Winterthur: Weidmanns Erben und Reich, und Heinrich Steiner und Compagnie, 1775–78.

Le Bon, Gustave. *The Crowd: A Study of the Popular Mind*. New York: Penguin, 1977.

Lehmann, Heinrich Ludewig. *Freundschaftliche und vertrauliche Briefe, den so genannten sehr berüchtigten Hexenhandel zu Glarus betreffend, von Heinrich Ludewig Lehmann, Candidat der Gottesgelehrtheit*. 2 vols. Zurich: Johann Caspar Füeßly, 1783.

Lenk, Elisabeth. 'Die sich selbst verdoppelnde Frau'. *Ästhetik und Kommunikation* 25 (1976), 84–7.

Lenz, Jakob Michael Reinhold. *Der neue Menoza oder Geschichte des cumbanischen Prinzen Tandi. Eine Komödie. Werke und Briefe*. Ed. Sigrid Damm. 3 vols. Munich: Carl Hanser, 1987. I 125–90.

Zerbin oder die neuere Philosophie. Eine Erzählung. Gesammelte Schriften. Munich and Leipzig, 1913. V 77–106.

Lessing, Gotthold Ephraim. *Emilia Galotti. Lessings Werke*. Ed. Kurt Wölfel. 3 vols. Frankfurt/M.: Insel, 1967. I 399–466.

Miß Sara Sampson. Lessings Werke. Ed. Kurt Wölfel. 3 vols. Frankfurt/M.: Insel, 1967. I 167–247.

Lessing, Gotthold Ephraim, Moses Mendelssohn and Friedrich Nicolai. *Briefwechsel über das Trauerspiel*. Ed. Jochen Schulte-Sasse. Munich: Winkler, 1972.

Lette, Kathy. *How to Kill Your Husband (and Other Handy Household Hints)*. London, New York, Sydney and Toronto: Simon & Schuster, 2006.

'Die letzte Hexe Europas wird voll rehabilitiert'. *Süddeutsche Zeitung* 201 (8 August 2008), 9.

Levack, Brian P. 'The Decline and End of Witchcraft Prosecutions'. Marijke Gijswijt-Hofstra, Brian P. Levack and Roy Porter, *Witchcraft and Magic in Europe: The Eighteenth and Nineteenth Centuries*. London: Athlone Press, 1999. 1–93.

The Witch-Hunt in Early Modern Europe. London: Longman, 1987.

ed. *Witchcraft in the Modern World*. New York and London: Routledge, 2001.

ed. *Witchcraft, Women and Society*. New York and London: Garland, 1992.

ed. *Witch-Hunting in Continental Europe: Local and Regional Studies*. New York and London: Garland, 1992.

Lewandowski, Horst Harald. 'Die Todesstrafe in der Aufklärung'. Diss. Bonn, 1961.

Liebs, Elke. 'Weiße und schwarze Magie, oder: vom romantischen zum dialektischen Kannibalismus/Vampirismus der Frau'. *Frauen – Literatur – Politik*. Ed. Annegret Pelz, Marianne Schuller, Inge Stephan, Sigrid Weigel and Kerstin Wilhelms. Berlin: Argument, 1988. 242–54.

Lindemann, Mary. *Health and Healing in Eighteenth-Century Germany*. Baltimore and London: Johns Hopkins University Press, 1996.

'Die Jungfer Heinrich: Transvestitin, Bigamistin, Lesbierin, Diebin, Mörderin'. *Von Huren und Rabenmüttern: Weibliche Kriminalität in der Frühen Neuzeit*. Ed. Otto Ulbricht. Cologne, Weimar and Vienna: Böhlau, 1995. 259–79.

'Narratives of Dismembering Women in Northern Germany, 1600–1800'. *Women and Death: Representations of Female Victims and Perpetrators in*

German Culture 1500–2000. Ed. Anna Linton and Helen Fronius. Rochester, NY: Camden House, 2008. 76–92.

Linder, Joachim. 'Deutsche Pitavalgeschichten in der Mitte des 19. Jahrhunderts. Konkurrierende Formen der Wissensvermittlung und der Verbrechens-deutung'. *Erzählte Kriminalität: Zur Typologie und Funktion von narrativen Darstellungen in Strafrechtspflege, Publizistik und Literatur zwischen 1770 und 1920.* Ed. Jörg Schönert in collaboration with Konstantin Imm and Joachim Linder. Tübingen: Max Niemeyer, 1991. 313–48.

Linder, Joachim, and Jörg Schönert. 'Ein Beispiel: Der Mordprozeß gegen Christiane Ruthardt (1844/45). Prozeßakten, publizistische und literarische Darstellungen zum Giftmord'. *Literatur und Kriminalität: Die gesellschaftliche Erfahrung von Verbrechen und Strafverfolgung als Gegenstand des Erzählens. Deutschland, England und Frankreich 1850–1880.* Ed. Jörg Schönert. Tübingen: Max Niemeyer, 1983. 239–359.

Lofland, John. *The Dramaturgy of State Executions.* Monclair: Patterson Smith, 1977.

Lombroso, Cesare, and Guglielmo Ferrero. *Criminal Woman, the Prostitute, and the Normal Woman.* Ed. and trans. Nicole Hahn Rafter and Mary Gibson. Durham, NC, and London: Duke University Press, 2004.

Lorenz, Sönke. 'Die letzten Hexenprozesse in den Spruchakten der Juristenfakultäten: Versuch einer Beschreibung'. *Das Ende der Hexenverfolgung.* Ed. Sönke Lorenz and Dieter R. Bauer. Stuttgart: Franz Steiner, 1995. 227–47.

Lorenz, Sönke, and Dieter R. Bauer, eds. *Das Ende der Hexenverfolgung.* Stuttgart: Franz Steiner, 1995.

Loster-Schneider, Gudrun, and Gaby Pailer, eds. *Lexikon deutschsprachiger Prosa und Dramen von Autorinnen (1730–1900).* Tübingen: Francke, 2006.

Lucht, Friedrich-Wilhelm. *Die Strafrechtspflege in Sachsen-Weimar-Eisenach unter Carl August.* Berlin and Leipzig: Walter de Gruyter, 1929.

Luhmann, Niklas. *Ausdifferenzierung des Rechts: Beiträge zur Rechtssoziologie und Rechtstheorie.* Frankfurt/M.: Suhrkamp, 1999.

Luserke-Jaqui, Matthias. *Medea: Studien zur Kulturgeschichte der Literatur.* Tübingen: Francke, 2002.

Mabee, Barbara. 'Die Kindesmörderin in den Fesseln der bürgerlichen Moral: Wagners Evchen und Goethes Gretchen'. *Women in German Yearbook* 3 (1986), 29–45.

Madland, Helga Stipa. 'Gender and the German Literary Canon: Marianne Ehrmann's Infanticide Fiction'. *Monatshefte* 84.4 (Winter 1992), 405–16.

'Infanticide as Fiction: Goethe's *Urfaust* and Schiller's "Kindsmörderin" as Models'. *German Quarterly* 62.1 (1989), 27–38.

Mah, Harold. *Enlightenment Phantasies: Cultural Identity in Germany and France, 1750–1914.* Ithaca, NY: Cornell University Press, 2004.

Mangham, Andrew. *Violent Women and Sensation Fiction: Crime, Medicine and Victorian Popular Culture.* Basingstoke: Palgrave Macmillan, 2007.

Mantzel, Ernst Johann Friedrich. *Ob wohl noch Hexenprozesse entstehen möchten.* Rostock, 1738.

Marsch, Edgar. *Die Kriminalerzählung: Theorie – Geschichte – Analyse.* Munich: Winkler, 1972.

Martschukat, Jürgen. '*Düsterheit und Barbarey?* Erörterungen zum Verhältnis von Justiz und Gewalt im ausgehenden 18. Jahrhundert anhand des Falles der Hamburger Gattenmörderin Maria Catharina Wächtler'. *Justiz und Gerechtigkeit: Historische Beiträge (16.-19. Jahrhundert).* Ed. Andrea Griesebner, Martin Scheuz and Herwin Weigl. Innsbruck, Vienna, Munich and Bozen: Studien Verlag, 2002. 331–48.

Inszeniertes Töten: Eine Geschichte der Todesstrafe vom 17. bis zum 19. Jahrhundert. Cologne: Böhlau, 2000.

'Die öffentliche Hinrichtung: Ein "Theater des Schreckens"?' *KrimJ* 27.3 (1995), 186–208.

Marzahn, Christian. 'Scheußliche Selbstgefälligkeit oder giftmordsüchtige Monomanie? Die Gesche Gottfried im Streit der Professionen'. *Criminalia: Bremer Strafjustiz 1810–1850. Beiträge zur Sozialgeschichte Bremens* 11 (1988), 195–244.

Mason, David S. *Revolutionary Europe, 1789–1989: Liberty, Equality, Solidarity.* Lanham, MD: Rowman & Littlefield, 2005.

Masters, Anthony. *The Natural History of the Vampire.* London: Rupert Hart-Davis, 1972.

McNally, Raymond T. *Dracula was a Woman: In Search of the Blood Countess of Transylvania.* London: R. Hale, 1984.

Mednyánszky, Alois von. *Erzählungen, Sagen und Legenden aus Ungarns Vorzeit. Von Alois Freiherrn von Mednyánszky.* Pest: Korad Adolph Hartleben, 1829.

Malerische Reise auf dem Waagflusse in Ungern. Pest: Conrad Adolph Hartleben, 1826.

Meerloo, Joost A. M. *Intuition and the Evil Eye: The Natural History of a Superstition.* Wassenaar: Servire, 1971.

Meise, Helga. *Die Unschuld und die Schrift: Deutsche Frauenromane im 18. Jahrhundert.* Berlin and Marburg: Ulrike Helmer, 1983.

Meißner, August Gottlieb. *Ausgewählte Kriminalgeschichten.* Ed. Alexander Košenina. St Ingbert: Röhrig Universitätsverlag, 2003.

Memminger, Anton. *Das verhexte Kloster. Nach den Akten dargestellt.* Würzburg: Memminger, 1904.

Mendelssohn, Moses. *Rhapsodie oder Zusätze zu den Briefen über die Empfindungen.* Geneva and Berlin: Nicolai, 1764.

Merc. den 3 Sept. 1788 [sentence in the case of Maria Katharina Wächtler]. N.p., n.d.

'Merkwürdiger Kindermord zwoer Schwestern'. *Ephemeriden der Menschheit* (1782), 484–99.

Meter, Peer. *Gesche Gottfried: Ein langes Warten auf den Tod. Die drei Jahre ihrer Gefangenschaft.* Langenbruch: Gosia, 1996.

Meyer-Krentler, Eckhardt. '"Geschichtserzählungen". Zur Poetik des Sachverhalts im juristischen Schrifttum des 18. Jahrhunderts'. *Erzählte Kriminalität: Zur*

Typologie und Funktion von narrativen Darstellungen in Strafrechtspflege, Publizistik und Literatur zwischen 1770 und 1920. Ed. Jörg Schönert in collaboration with Konstantin Imm and Joachim Linder. Tübingen: Max Niemeyer, 1991. 117–57.

Michalik, Kerstin. *Kindsmord. Sozial- und Rechtsgeschichte der Kindstötung im 18. und beginnenden 19. Jahrhundert am Beispiel Preußen.* Pfaffenweiler: Centaurus, 1997.

Minois, George. *History of Suicide: Voluntary Death in Western Culture.* Trans. Lydia G. Cochrane. Baltimore: Johns Hopkins University Press, 1999 (first published in French, Paris, 1995).

Mirabeau. *L'Ami des Hommes ou traité de la population.* 4th edn. Hamburg, 1758.

Moeller, Katrin, and Burghart Schmidt, eds. *Realität und Mythos: Hexenverfolgung und Rezeptionsgeschichte.* Hamburg: DOBU, 2003.

Möller, Wilhelm. 'Richtstätten und Hinrichtungen in der Stadt Weimar'. *Beiträge zur Geschichte der Stadt Weimar* 21 (1933), 17–29.

Montanus, Martin, ed. *Der Gartengesellschaft anderer Teil.* Tübingen, 1899.

ed. *Wegkürzer.* Tübingen, 1899.

Moritz, Karl Philipp. 'Fragmente aus dem Tagebuche eines Geistersehers'. *Werke.* Ed. Horst Günther. 3 vols. Frankfurt/M.: Insel, 1981. III 271–322.

Gnothi sauton oder Magazin zur Erfahrungsseelenkunde als ein Lesebuch für Gelehrte und Ungelehrte herausgegeben von Carl Philipp Moritz. 10 vols. Ed. Anke Bennholdt-Thomsen and Alfredo Guzzoni. Lindau: Antiqua, 1978–9 [rpt of edn Berlin, 1783–93].

Moscovici, Serge. *The Age of the Crowd: A Historical Treatise on Mass Psychology.* Trans. J. C. Whitehouse. Cambridge: Cambridge University Press, 1985.

L'Age des foules. Un traité historique de psychologie des masses. Paris: Athème Fayard, 1981.

Moser, Johann Jacob. *Seelige Letzte Stunden Einiger dem zeitlichen Tode übergebener Missethäter; Mit einer Vorrede.* Jena, 1742.

Selige letzte Stunden hingerichteter Personen, gesammelt von Johann Jakob Moser. Nach einem Jahrhundert im Auszug neu herausgegeben und mit neueren vermehrt von F. M. Kapff, Pfarrer in Winterbach. Stuttgart: Belser'sche Buchhandlung, 1861.

Möser, Justus. 'Ueber die zu unsern Zeiten verminderte Schande der Huren und Hurkinder'. *Nützlicher Beylagen zum Osnabrückischen Intelligenz-Blate* (1772), 113–20.

[Müller, Johann Valentin]. 'Kindermord, eine Seelenkrankheit'. *Medicinisches Wochenblatt für Ärzte, Wundaerzte und Apotheker* 6 (1785), 81–91, 145–52, 289–94.

Nachricht von Einer erbärmlich verirrten, mit Liebes-voller Begierde gesuchten, und durch eine wahre Bekehrung erfreulich wiedergebrachten armen Sünderin, namentlich Elisabetha Albrechtin, So in der Kayserl. freyen Reichs-Stadt Ravensburg Anno 1767. D. 4. Junii wegen begangenen grausamen Kindes-Mord ... durch das Schwerdt hingerichtet worden. Biberach, n.d.

Nagy, László. *A rossz hirü Báthoryak.* Budapest: Kossuth Könyvkiadó, 1984.

Naish, Camille. *Death Comes to the Maiden: Sex and Execution 1431–1933*. London and New York: Routledge, 1991.

Naso, Eckart von. *Die Chronik der Giftmischerin*. Potsdam: Gustav Kiepenheuer, 1926.

Neumeyer, Harald. 'Psychenproduktion. Zur Kindsmorddebatte in der Gesetzgebung, Wissenschaft und Literatur um 1800'. *Diskrete Gebote: Geschichte der Macht um 1800*. Ed. Roland Borgards and Johannes F. Lehmann. Würzburg: Königshausen & Neumann, 2002. 47–76.

Neuwirth, Barbara, ed. *Blaß sei mein Gesicht. Vampirgeschichten von Frauen*. Frankfurt/M.: Suhrkamp, 1990.

Niehaus, Michael. 'Die Figur der Giftmischerin als Fall der Literatur'. *KulturPoetik* 5.2 (2005), 153–68.

Mord, Geständnis, Widerruf. Verhören und Verhörtwerden um 1800. Bochum: Posth, 2006.

[Niethammer, Friedrich, ed.] *Merkwürdige Rechtsfälle als ein Beitrag zur Geschichte der Menschheit. Nach dem Französischen Werk des Pitaval durch mehrere Verfasser ausgearbeitet und mit einer Vorrede begleitet herausgegeben von Schiller*. 4 vols. Jena: bei Christ. Heinr. Cuno's Erben, 1792–5.

Niethammer, Ortrun. *Autobiographien von Frauen im 18. Jahrhundert*. Tübingen, Basel: Francke, 2000.

Nolde, Dorothea. *Gattenmord: Macht und Gewalt in der frühneuzeitlichen Ehe*. Cologne, Weimar and Vienna: Böhlau, 2003.

Nörtemann, Regina. 'Verehrung, Freundschaft, Liebe: Zur Erotik im Briefwechsel zwischen Anna-Louisa Karsch und Johann Wilhelm Ludwig Gleim'. *Anna Louisa Karsch (1722–1791): Von schlesischer Kunst und Berliner 'Natur'. Ergebnisse des Symposiums zum 200. Todestag der Dichterin*. Ed. Anke Bennholdt-Thomsen and Anita Runge. Göttingen: Wallstein, 1992. 81–93.

Ockel, Ernst Friedrich. *Ueber die Sittlichkeit der Wollust*. Mietau, Hasenpoth and Leipzig: Hinz, 1772.

Ossenfelder, Heinrich August. 'Der Vampir'. *Der Naturforscher* 48 (25 May 1748), 380–1.

Patzke, Johann Samuel. *Aufrichtige Nachricht von der Bekehrung und den letzten Stunden einer Kindermörderin, Nahmens Anna Elisabeth Blumin, welche den 1. des Maymonaths 1767. den Rothensee mit dem Schwerdte den Lohn ihrer That empfing; aufgesetzt von den beyden Predigern an der Heiligen Geist Kirche. Nebst der Rede, die an der Gerichtsstädte gehalten worden*. Magdeburg, 1767.

Paulowitz, Brigitte. '"Nippen nur darf ich an dir." Vampirtexte der deutschsprachigen Literatur des 19. Jahrhunderts'. Dipl. Vienna, 1997.

Penrose, Valentine. *The Bloody Countess: Atrocities of Erzsebet Bathory*. Trans. Alexander Trocchi. Los Angeles: Solar, 2006.

Perthold, Sabine, ed. *Rote Küsse: Ein sinnliches Frauen-Film-Schaubuch*. Tübingen: Claudia Gehrke, 1990.

[Pestalozzi, Johann Heinrich.] *Ueber Gesetzgebung und Kindermord. Wahrheiten und Träume, Nachforschungen und Bilder. Vom Verfasser Lienhardts und Gertrud. Pestalozzis Gesammelte Werke*. 10 vols. Zurich 1945/6. VII 121–395.

ed. *Ein Schweizer-Blatt* 1 (1782).

Pestalozzi, Karl, and Horst Weigelt, eds. *Das Antlitz Gottes im Antlitz des Menschen: Zugänge zu Johann Kaspar Lavater*. Göttingen: Vandenhoeck & Ruprecht, 1994.

Peters, Kirsten. *Der Kindsmord als schöne Kunst betrachtet. Eine motivgeschichtliche Untersuchung der Literatur des 18. Jahrhunderts*. Würzburg: Königshausen & Neumann, 2001.

Philosophie der Ehe. Ein Beytrag zur Philosophie des Lebens für beyde Geschlechter. Leipzig: bey Roch und Comp, 1800.

Pinkus, Gertrud. *Anna Göldin, letzte Hexe. Screenplay*. Solothurn: G. Pinkus, 1992.

Pitaval, Gayot de. *Causes célèbres et intéressantes avec les jugements qui les ont décidées. Recuillées par Mr. Gayot de Pitaval, Avocat au Parlement de Paris*. 22 vols. La Haye, 1735–45.

Pockels, Carl Friedrich. *Versuch einer Charakteristik des weiblichen Geschlechts. Ein Sittengemählde des Menschen, des Zeitalters und des geselligen Lebens*. 5 vols. Hanover: Christian Ritscher, 1797–1802.

Pohl, Johann Christoph. *Dissert. de hominibus post mortem sanguisugis*. Leipzig, 1732.

Polišenský, Josef. *Aristocrats and the Crowd in the Revolutionary Year 1848: A Contribution to the History of Revolution and Counter-Revolution in Austria*. Trans. Frederick Snider. Albany: State University of New York Press, 1980.

Porter, Roy. 'Witchcraft and Magic in Enlightenment, Romantic, and Liberal Thought'. Marijke Gijswijt-Hofstra, Brian P. Levack and Roy Porter, *Witchcraft and Magic in Europe: The Eighteenth and Nineteenth Centuries*. London: Athlone Press, 1999. 191–274.

Pott, Martin. *Aufklärung und Aberglaube: Die deutsche Frühaufklärung im Spiegel ihrer Aberglaubenskritik*. Tübingen: Niemeyer, 1992.

'Aufklärung und Hexenaberglaube: Philosophische Ansätze zur Überwindung der Teufelspakttheorie in der deutschen Frühaufklärung'. *Das Ende der Hexenverfolgung*. Ed. Sönke Lorenz and Dieter R. Bauer. Stuttgart: Franz Steiner, 1995. 183–202.

Protokolle des Criminalgerichts in Untersuchungssache wider die Giftmischerin Gesche Margarethe Gottfried geborene Timm. 2 vols. Vol. 1: *Protokolle der Verhöre und Zeugenvernehmungen* (Staatsarchiv Bremen 2-D.17.c.5.c.l.; microfilm FB); vol. 11: *Anlagen zu Band* 1 (Staatsarchiv Bremen 2-ad D.17.c.5.c.l; microfilm FB 2217).

Pütz, Susanne. *Vampire und ihre Opfer: Der Blutsauger als literarische Figur*. Bielefeld: Aisthesis, 1992.

Putoneus besondere Nachricht von denen Vampyrs. Leipzig, 1732.

Quanter, Rudolf. *Die Folter in der deutschen Rechtspflege sonst und jetzt*. Dresden: Dohrn, 1900.

Radbruch, Gustav. 'Ars moriendi: Scharfrichter – Seelsorger – Armesünder – Volk'. *Schweizer Zeitschrift für Strafrecht* 59 (1945), 460–95.

ed. *Die Peinliche Gerichtsordnung Kaiser Karls V (1532)*. 6th edn, ed. Arthur Kaufmann. Stuttgart: Reclam, 1984.

Radbruch, Gustav, and Heinrich Gwinner. *Geschichte des Verbrechens: Versuch einer historischen Kriminologie.* Stuttgart: Köhler, 1951.

Rameckers, Jan Matthias. *Der Kindesmord in der Literatur der Sturm- und Drangperiode. Ein Beitrag zur Kultur- und Literatur-Geschichte des 18. Jahrhunderts.* Rotterdam: Nijgh & Van Ditmar's Uitgevers-Maatschappij, 1927.

Ranft, M. Michael. *M. Michael Ranfts Diaconi zu Nebra, Tractat von dem Kauen und Schmatzen der Todten in Gräbern, Worin die wahre Beschaffenheit derer Hungarischen Vampyrs und Blut-Sauger gezeigt, Auch alle von dieser Materie bißher zum Vorschein gekommene Schrifften recensiret werden.* Leipzig: Teubner, 1734.

Rankin, Walter. *Grimm Pictures: Fairy Tale Archetypes in Eight Horror and Suspense Films.* Jefferson, NC: McFarland, 2007.

Rasche, Johann C. *Es ist nöthig, jeden Missethäter durch Geistliche zum Tode vorbereiten und zur Hinrichtung begleiten zu lassen: dem Widerspruch eines Berliners entgegengesetzt.* Hildburghausen, 1770.

Raupach, Ernst. 'Lasst die Toten ruhn'. *Minerva: Taschenbuch für das Jahr 1823* xv (1823), 35–88.

Reemtsma, Jan Philipp. *Vertrauen und Gewalt: Versuch über eine besondere Konstellation der Moderne.* Hamburg: Hamburger Edition, 2008.

Regge, Jürgen. *Kabinettsjustiz in Brandenburg-Preußen. Eine Studie zur Geschichte des landesherrlichen Bestätigungsrechts in der Strafrechtspflege des 17. und 18. Jahrhunderts.* Berlin: Duncker & Humblot, 1977.

Reif, Heinz, ed. *Räuber, Volk und Obrigkeit: Studien zur Geschichte der Kriminalität in Deutschland seit dem 18. Jahrhundert.* Frankfurt/M.: Suhrkamp, 1984.

Richards, Anna. *The Wasting Heroine in German Fiction by Women 1770–1914.* Oxford: Clarendon Press, 2004.

Rickels, Laurence A. *The Vampire Lectures.* Minneapolis and London: University of Minnesota Press, 1999.

Rivers, Christopher. *Face Value: Physiognomical Thought and the Legible Body in Marivaux, Lavater, Balzac, Gautier, and Zola.* Madison: University of Wisconsin Press, 1994.

Robbins, Barney R. *A Dissertation on the Evil Eye.* New York: privately printed, 1934.

Rodegra, Heinrich, Mary Lindemann and Martin Ewald. 'Kindermord und verheimlichte Schwangerschaft in Hamburg im 18. Jahrhundert'. *Gesnerus* 35 (1978), 276–96.

Roetzer, Karl. 'Die Delikte der Abtreibung, Kindstötung sowie Kindsaussetzung und ihre Bestrafung in der Reichsstadt Nürnberg'. Jur. diss. Erlangen, 1957.

Rohner, Markus. 'Von Gewissensbissen geplagte Glarner'. *Werdenberger & Obertoggenburger Zeitung* (8 June 2007), 11.

'Wie eine Hexe wieder aktuell wird'. *St. Galler Tagblatt* (11 September 2007). www.tagblatt.ch/index.php?artikelxml=1393442 (last accessed 23 September 2007).

Roper, Lyndal. 'A Witch in the Age of Enlightenment'. *Witch Craze: Terror and Fantasy in Baroque Germany.* New Haven, NJ: Yale University Press, 2004. 222–46.

'Witchcraft and the Western Imagination'. *Transactions of the Royal Historical Society* 16 (2006), 117–41.

Rossa, Kurt. *Todesstrafen. Ihre Wirklichkeit in drei Jahrtausenden*. Oldenburg and Hamburg: Stalling, 1966.

Rowlands, Alison. *Witchcraft Narratives in Germany: Rothenburg 1561–62*. Manchester: Manchester University Press, 2003.

Rückert, Joachim. 'Zur Rolle der Fallgeschichte in Juristenausbildung und juristischer Praxis zwischen 1790 und 1880'. *Erzählte Kriminalität: Zur Typologie und Funktion von narrativen Darstellungen in Strafrechtspflege, Publizistik und Literatur zwischen 1770 und 1920*. Ed. Jörg Schönert in collaboration with Konstantin Imm and Joachim Linder. Tübingen: Max Niemeyer, 1991. 285–311.

Ruhl, Ludwig Sigismund. *Über den Eindruck des Schrecklichen in Werken antiker und moderner Kunst*. Kassel: Joseph Has, 1876.

Rüping, Hinrich. *Grundriß der Strafrechtsgeschichte*. 2nd edn. Munich: Beck, 1991.

Rürup, Reinhard, ed. *The Problem of Revolution in Germany, 1789–1989*. Oxford: Berg, 2000.

Rusche, Georg, and Otto Kirchheimer. *Punishment and Social Structure*. New York: Columbia University Press, 1939.

Russell, Helene. 'Solitude: A Theological Dialogue. Søren Kierkegaard and Process Theology'. www.ctr4process.org/publications/SeminarPapers/242Russell.rtf (last accessed 20 August 2007).

Ruthner, Clemens. 'Untote Verzahnungen. Prolegomena zu einer Literaturgeschichte des Vampirismus'. *Poetische Wiedergänger: Deutschsprachige Vampirismus-Diskurse vom Mittelalter bis zur Gegenwart*. Ed. Julia Bertschik and Christa Agnes Tuczay. Tübingen: Franke, 2005. 11–41.

Saine, Thomas P. *Black Bread, White Bread: German Intellectuals and the French Revolution*. Columbia, SC: Camden House, 1988.

The Problem of Being Modern, or, The German Pursuit of Enlightenment from Leibniz to the French Revolution. Detroit: Wayne State University Press, 1997.

Sarasin, Philipp. 'Gewalt als Codierung und der Code als Gewalt bei Michel Foucault'. *Die Szene der Gewalt. Bilder, Codes und Materialitäten*. Ed. Daniel Tyradellis. Frankfurt/M.: Peter Lang, 2007. 45–60.

Schaffers, Uta. *Auf überlebtes Elend blick ich nieder: Anna Luisa Karsch in Selbst- und Fremdzeugnissen*. Göttingen: Wallstein, 1997.

Schemme, Wolfgang. 'Goethe *Die Braut von Korinth*. Von der literarischen Dignität des Vampirs'. *Wirkendes Wort* 36 (1986), 333–45.

Schiche, Hans-Joachim. 'Zur Psychopathologie vier berühmter Giftmörderinnen aus dem Pitaval'. Diss. med. Munich, 1954.

Schieth, Lydia. *Die Entwicklung des deutschen Frauenromans im ausgehenden 18. Jahrhundert: Ein Beitrag zur Gattungsgeschichte*. Frankfurt/M.: Peter Lang, 1987.

Schild, Wolfgang. *Alte Gerichtsbarkeit: Vom Gottesurteil bis zum Beginn der modernen Rechtsprechung*. 2nd edn. Munich: Callwey, 1985.

'Relationen und Referierkunst. Zur Juristenausbildung und zum Strafverfahren um 1790'. *Erzählte Kriminalität: Zur Typologie und Funktion von narrativen*

Darstellungen in Strafrechtspflege, Publizistik und Literatur zwischen 1770 und 1920. Ed. Jörg Schönert in collaboration with Konstantin Imm and Joachim Linder. Tübingen: Max Niemeyer, 1991. 159–76.

Schiller, Friedrich. *Kabale und Liebe*. *Werke*. Ed. Herbert G. Göpfert and Gerhard Fricke. 3 vols. Munich: Hanser, 1984. I 263–343.

'Die Kindsmörderin'. *Werke*. Ed. Herbert G. Göpfert and Gerhard Fricke. 3 vols. Munich: Hanser, 1984. I 18–21.

'Das Lied von der Glocke'. *Werke*. Ed. Herbert G. Göpfert and Gerhard Fricke. 3 vols. Munich: Hanser, 1984. II 810–21.

'Zerstreute Betrachtungen über verschiedene ästhetische Gegenstände'. *Schillers Werke. Nationalausgabe*. Ed. Julius Petersen, Gerhard Fricke, Hermann Schneider, Lieselotte Blumenthal, Benno von Wiese, Norbert Oellers and Siegfried Seidel. 42 vols. Weimar: Böhlau, 1943–. XX 222–40.

ed. *Merkwürdige Rechtsfälle als ein Beitrag zur Geschichte der Menschheit. Nach dem Französischen Werk des Pitaval durch mehrere Verfasser ausgearbeitet und mit einer Vorrede begleitet herausgegeben von Schiller*. 4 vols. Jena: bei Christ. Heinr. Cuno's Erben, 1792–5.

Schlosser, Johann Georg. *Die Wudbianer. Eine nicht gekrönte Preißschrift über die Frage: Wie ist der Kindermord zu verhindern, ohne die Unzucht zu befördern?* Basel, 1783.

Schlözer, August Ludwig. 'Summe der *ermordeten Kinder* in Schweden seit 30 Jahren'. *Schlözer's Briefwechsel* 9 (1781), 297–8.

Schmidt, Eberhard. *Entwicklung und Vollzug der Freiheitsstrafe in Brandenburg-Preußen bis zum Ausgang des 18. Jahrhunderts*. Berlin: Guttentag, 1915.

Die Kriminalpolizei Preußens unter Friedrich Wilhelm I und Friedrich II. Berlin: Guttentag, 1914.

Schmidt, Michael. *Genossin der Hexe. Interpretation der Gretchentragödie in Goethes Faust aus der Perspektive der Kindesmordproblematik*. Göttingen: Altaquito, 1985.

Schmoeckel, Mathias. *Humanität und Staatsraison: Die Abschaffung der Folter in Europa und die Entwicklung des gemeinen Strafprozeß- und Beweisrechts seit dem hohen Mittelalter*. Cologne, Weimar and Vienna: Böhlau, 2000.

Schnabel-Schulte, Helga. 'Frauen im Strafrecht vom 16. bis zum 18. Jahrhundert'. *Frauen in der Geschichte des Rechts. Von der frühen Neuzeit bis zur Gegenwart*. Ed. Ute Gerhard. Munich: Beck, 1997. 185–98.

Schneider, Jost. *Sozialgeschichte des Lesens: Zur historischen Entwicklung und sozialen Differenzierung der literarischen Kommunikation in Deutschland*. Berlin and New York: de Gruyter, 2004.

Scholz, Heinrich, ed. *Die Hauptschriften zum Pantheismusstreit zwischen Jacobi und Mendelssohn*. Berlin: Kantgesellschaft, 1911.

Scholz, Ludwig. *Die Gesche Gottfried: Eine kriminalpsychologische Studie*. Berlin, 1913.

Scholz, Rüdiger. 'Die Gewalt dichterischer Ideologie. Das Bild der "Kindsmörderin" in der Literatur und die soziale Wirklichkeit'. *Ideologie nach ihrem 'Ende': Gesellschaftskritik zwischen Marxismus und Postmoderne*.

Ed. Hansjörg Bay and Christof Hamann. Opladen: Westdeutscher Verlag, 1995. 245–68.

'Goethes Schuld an der Hinrichtung von Johanna Höhn'. *Goethe-Jahrbuch* 120 (2003), 324–31.

ed. *Das kurze Leben der Johanna Catharina Höhn: Kindesmorde und Kindesmörderinnen im Weimar Carl Augusts und Goethes. Die Akten zu den Fällen Johanna Catharina Höhn, Maria Sophia Rost und Margarethe Dorothea Altwein.* Würzburg: Königshausen & Neumann, 2004.

Schönert, Jörg. 'Zur Ausdifferenzierung des Genres "Kriminalgeschichten" in der deutschen Literatur vom Ende des 18. bis zum Beginn des 20. Jahrhunderts'. *Literatur und Kriminalität: Die gesellschaftliche Erfahrung von Verbrechen und Strafverfolgung als Gegenstand des Erzählens. Deutschland, England und Frankreich 1850–1880.* Ed. Jörg Schönert. Tübingen: Max Niemeyer, 1983. 96–125.

'Literatur und Kriminalität: Probleme, Forschungsstand und die Konzeption des Kolloquiums'. *Literatur und Kriminalität: Die gesellschaftliche Erfahrung von Verbrechen und Strafverfolgung als Gegenstand des Erzählens. Deutschland, England und Frankreich 1850–1880.* Ed. Jörg Schönert. Tübingen: Max Niemeyer, 1983. 1–13.

ed. *Literatur und Kriminalität: Die gesellschaftliche Erfahrung von Verbrechen und Strafverfolgung als Gegenstand des Erzählens. Deutschland, England und Frankreich 1850–1880.* Tübingen: Max Niemeyer, 1983.

ed., in collaboration with Konstantin Imm and Joachim Linder. *Erzählte Kriminalität: Zur Typologie und Funktion von narrativen Darstellungen in Strafrechtspflege, Publizistik und Literatur zwischen 1770 und 1920.* Tübingen: Max Niemeyer, 1991.

Schönert, Jörg, in collaboration with Wolfgang Naucke and Konstantin Imm. 'Zur Einführung in den Gegenstandsbereich und zum interdisziplinären Vorgehen'. *Erzählte Kriminalität: Zur Typologie und Funktion von narrativen Darstellungen in Strafrechtspflege, Publizistik und Literatur zwischen 1770 und 1920.* Ed. Jörg Schönert in collaboration with Konstantin Imm and Joachim Linder. Tübingen: Max Niemeyer, 1991. 11–55.

Schönhaar, Rainer. *Novelle und Kriminalschema: Ein Strukturmodell deutscher Erzählkunst um 1800.* Bad Homburg: Gehlen, 1969.

Schönitz, Karl Albert von. *Q. D. B. V. Disputatio Juridica de Quaestionibus sev Tortvris Qvam Praeside Dn. Georgio Wernero J. V. D. Canonici Atque Feudalis Professore Publico nec non dica; sterii Gvelpherbytani Assessore Dn. Praeceptore, Patrono et Hospite Omni Honoris Cultu Devenerando.* Helmstadt: Johann Heitmüller, 1767.

Schörkhuber-Drysdale, Cornelia. '*Ich bitt dich umb Gottes willen, mein herr und frau bringen schirr umb einander.* Ehestreitigkeiten und Ehetrennung in der bäuerlichen Gesellschaft Oberösterreichs zu Beginn des 18. Jahrhunderts'. *Justiz und Gerechtigkeit: Historische Beiträge (16.-19. Jahrhundert).* Ed. Andrea Griesebner, Martin Scheuz and Herwin Weigl. Innsbruck, Vienna, Munich and Bozen: Studien Verlag, 2002. 255–68.

Schreiben eines guten Freundes an einen andern guten Freund, die Vampyren betreffend. Frankfurt, 1732.

Schroeder, Aribert. *Vampirismus: Seine Entdeckung vom Thema zum Motiv.* Frankfurt/M.: Akademische Verlagsgesellschaft, 1973.

Schuller, Marianne. 'Gesichter und Gesichte: Lavaters "weibische" Suche nach dem Individuellen'. *Im Lichte Lavaters: Lektüren zum 200. Todestag.* Ed. Ulrich Stadler and Karl Pestalozzi. Zurich: Neue Zürcher Zeitung, 2003. 103–16.

Schulte, Regina. *Das Dorf im Verhör. Brandstifter, Kindsmörderinnen und Wilderer vor den Schranken des Gerichts. Oberbayern 1848–1910.* Reinbek bei Hamburg: Rowohlt, 1989.

'Die Kindsmörderin Anna H'. *Journal für Geschichte* 5 (1981), 20–4.

'Kindsmörderinnen auf dem Lande'. *Emotionen und materielle Interessen. Sozialanthropologie und historische Beiträge zur Familienforschung.* Ed. Hans Medick and David Sabean. Göttingen: Vandenhoeck & Ruprecht, 1984. 113–42.

'Strafrechtlicher Entwurf und Lebenswirklichkeiten von Kindsmörderinnen im 19. Jahrhundert'. *Frauen in der Geschichte des Rechts. Von der frühen Neuzeit bis zur Gegenwart.* Ed. Ute Gerhard. Munich: Beck, 1997. 382–9.

Schumann, Valentin. *Nachtbüchlein.* Ed. Johannes Bolte. Tübingen: Bibliothek des Litterarischen Vereins, 1893.

Schwann, Jürgen. *Vom 'Faust' zum 'Peter Schlemihl': Kohärenz und Kontinuität im Werk Adelbert von Chamissos.* Tübingen: Narr, 1984.

Schwarz, Manfred. *Die Kindestötung.* Berlin: Philo, 1935.

Schwarzwälder, Herbert. 'Gesche Gottfried'. *Reise in Bremens Vergangenheit.* Bremen: Schünemann, 1965. 159–64.

Schwerhoff, Gerd. 'Geschlechtsspezifische Kriminalität im frühneuzeitlichen Köln'. *Von Huren und Rabenmüttern: Weibliche Kriminalität in der Frühen Neuzeit.* Ed. Otto Ulbricht. Cologne, Weimar and Vienna: Böhlau, 1995. 83–115.

'Strafjustiz und Gerechtigkeit in historischer Perspektive – das Beispiel der Hexenprozesse'. *Justiz und Gerechtigkeit: Historische Beiträge (16.-19. Jahrhundert).* Ed. Andrea Griesebner, Martin Scheuz and Herwin Weigl. Innsbruck, Vienna, Munich and Bozen: Studien Verlag, 2002. 33–40.

Seabrook, William. *Witchcraft: Its Power in the World Today.* London: White Lion, 1972.

Seibert, Thomas-Michael. 'Erzählen als gesellschaftliche Konstruktion von Kriminalität'. *Erzählte Kriminalität: Zur Typologie und Funktion von narrativen Darstellungen in Strafrechtspflege, Publizistik und Literatur zwischen 1770 und 1920.* Ed. Jörg Schönert in collaboration with Konstantin Imm and Joachim Linder. Tübingen: Max Niemeyer, 1991. 73–86.

Seifert, Theodor. *Snow White: Life Almost Lost.* Trans. Boris Matthews. Wilmette, IL: Chiron, 1986.

'Selbstmord aus allzugroßer Scham'. *National-Zeitung der Teutschen* (1800), 860.

Seligmann, S., *Der böse Blick und Verwandtes. Ein Beitrag zur Geschichte des Aberglaubens aller Zeiten und Völker.* 2 vols. Berlin: Hermann Barsdorf, 1910.

Seling-Biehusen, Petra. 'Johann Eberhard Noltenius: Gerichtssekretär im Fall Gesche Gottfried'. *Criminalia: Bremer Strafjustiz 1810–1850. Beiträge zur Sozialgeschichte Bremens* 11 (1988), 133–50.

Seling-Biehausen, Petra and Johannes Feest. 'Gesche Gottfried und die Bremer Strafjustiz. Aktenauszüge mit Anmerkungen'. *Criminalia: Bremer Strafjustiz 1810–1850. Beiträge zur Sozialgeschichte Bremens* 11 (1988), 151–94.

Sellert, Wolfgang, and Hinrich Rüping. *Studien- und Quellenbuch zur Geschichte der deutschen Strafrechtspflege.* Vol. 1: *Von den Anfängen bis zur Aufklärung.* Aalen: Scientia, 1989.

Selpert, Georg Matthias. *Rectore Magnificentissimo ac Domino Friderico Avgvsto Principe Regio cetera Praeside D. Mich. Henr. Gribnero P. P JCT. Ord. H. T. Decano pro conseqvendis Svmmis in Vtroqve Jvre Honoribvs de Repetitione Tormentorum confesso Infitiante.* Wittenberg: Prelo Vidvae Gerdensianae, 1714.

Seybold (David Christoph). 'Die Mutter und ihre Zwillingstöchter zu Vevay'. *Magazin für Frauenzimmer* (1782), 316–21.

Shookman, Ellis. 'Pseudo-Science, Social Fad, Literary Wonder: Johann Caspar Lavater and the Art of Physiognomy'. *The Faces of Physiognomy: Interdisciplinary Approaches to Johann Caspar Lavater.* Ed. Ellis Shookman. Columbia, SC: Camden House, 1993. 1–24.

    ed. *The Faces of Physiognomy: Interdisciplinary Approaches to Johann Caspar Lavater.* Columbia, SC: Camden House, 1993.

Sighele, Scipio. *Psychologie des Auflaufs und der Massenverbrechen.* Trans. Hans Kurella. Dresden: Reissner, 1897.

Signori, Gabriela, ed. *Trauer, Verzweiflung und Anfechtung: Selbstmord und Selbstmordversuche in mittelalterlichen und frühneuzeitlichen Gesellschaften.* Tübingen: Edition Diskord, 1994.

Sigrist, Christoph. '"Letters of the Divine Alphabet" – Lavater's Concept of Physiognomy'. *The Faces of Physiognomy: Interdisciplinary Approaches to Johann Caspar Lavater.* Ed. Ellis Shookman. Columbia, SC: Camden House, 1993. 25–39.

Sonnenfels, Joseph von. *Grundsätze der Polizey, Handlung und Finanzwissenschaft.* Part 1. 3rd edn. Vienna: Gedruckt bey Johann Thomas Edlen von Trattnern, 1770.

Spee von Lengenfeld, Friedrich, S J. *Cautio Criminalis oder Rechtliches Bedenken wegen der Hexenprozesse.* 7th edn. Munich: dtv, 1982.

Spierenburg, Pieter. *A History of Murder: Personal Violence in Europe from the Middle Ages to the Present.* Cambridge: Polity Press, 2008.

    The Spectacle of Suffering. Executions and the Evolution of Repression: From a Preindustrial Metropolis to the European Experience. Cambridge: Cambridge University Press, 1984.

    ed. *Men and Violence: Gender, Honor, and Rituals in Modern Europe and America.* Columbus: Ohio State University Press, 1998.

Spindler, Johann. 'Der Vampyr und seine Braut: Nachtstück aus der neuesten Zeit'. *Zwillinge: Zwei Erzählungen, nebst einem Anhange von Originalbriefen.* Hanover, 1826.

Spokiene, Diana. '"Was bleibt … deinem Geschlecht anders übrig, als die List …" *Bekenntnisse einer Giftmischerin. Von ihr selbst geschrieben*: Friederike Helene Unger und die Autorschaftslage'. Diss. University of Alberta, 2004.

Sprenger, Jakob, and Heinrich Institoris. *Der Hexenhammer (Malleus maleficarum)*. Ed. and trans. J. W. R. Schmidt. 13th edn. Munich: dtv, 1997.

Stadler, Ulrich, and Karl Pestalozzi, eds. *Im Lichte Lavaters: Lektüren zum 200. Todestag*. Zurich: Neue Zürcher Zeitung, 2003.

Stehle, Maria. 'Widersprüche: Terror und Angst in westdeutschen Texten der späten 70er Jahre'. *Gelegentlich – Brecht: Jubiläumsschrift für Jan Knopf*. Ed. Birte Giesler, Eva Kormann, Ana Kugli, Joachim Lucchesi and Gaby Pailer. Heidelberg: Universitätsverlag Winter, 2004. 183–95.

Steinbart, Gotthilf S. *Ist es rathsam, durch Geistliche Missethäter zum Tode vorbereiten, und zur Hinrichtung begleiten zu lassen?* Berlin, 1769.

Stephany, C. F. *Charlotte Ursinus die Giftmischerin: Enthüllung ihrer Lebenszüge und Schuld*. Berlin, 1866.

Stock, J. C. *Dissertatio Physica de Cadaveribus sangvisugis i. e. von denen so genannten Vampyren oder Menschen-Saugern. Praeside J. C. Stock, Philos. & Med Doct. habitae Resp. J. W. Noebling, Leutenberga-Schwarzburgico*. Jena, 1732.

Stöckle, Frieder. *… bis er gesteht: Folter und Rechtsprechung*. Würzburg: Arena, 1984.

Stölzel, Adolf. *Brandenburg-Preußens Rechtsverwaltung und Rechtsverfassung, dargestellt im Wirken seiner Landesfürsten*. 2 vols. Berlin: Franz Vahlen, 1888.
Die Entwicklung der gelehrten Rechtsprechung. Berlin: Franz Vahlen, 1901.

Strasser, Peter. *Verbrechermenschen: Zur kriminalwissenschaftlichen Erzeugung des Bösen*. Frankfurt/M. and New York: Campus, 1984.

Sturm, Christoph C. *Ueber die Gewohnheit, Missethäter durch Prediger zur Hinrichtung begleiten zu lassen*. Hamburg, 1784.

Sturm, Dieter, and Klaus Völker, eds. *Von denen Vampiren oder Menschensaugern: Dichtungen und Dokumente*. Munich: Hanser, 1968.

Sulzer, Johann Georg. *Allgemeine Theorie der Schönen Künste. Neue vermehrte zweyte Auflage*. 4 vols. Leipzig: Weidmann, 1792–4.

Summers, Montague. *The Vampire in Europe*. London: Bracken Books, 1929.

[Swieten, Gerard van]. 'Vampyrismus von Herrn Baron Gerhard van-Swieten verfasset, aus dem Französischen ins Deutsche übersetzet, und als ein Anhang der Abhandlung des Daseyns der Gespenster beigerücket'. Bound with: *Abhandlung des Daseyns der Gespenster, nebst einem Anhange vom Vampyrismus*. Augsburg, 1768.

Tallar, Georg. *Visum Repeterum Anatomico-Chirurgicum oder Gründlicher Bericht von den sogenannten Blutsäugern, VAMPIER, oder in der wallachischen Sprache Moroi, in der Wallachey, Siebenbürgen, und Banat, welchen eine eigends dahin abgeordnete Untersuchungskommission der löbl. k.k. Administration im Jahre 1756 erstattet hat, Durch Georg Tallar, Wundarzten*. Vienna and Leipzig, 1784.

Tatar, Maria. *The Hard Facts of the Grimms' Fairy Tales*. Princeton: Princeton University Press, 1987.

Thieser, Bernd. *Gattenmord und Galgenstrick: Kriminalfälle in der Oberpfalz 1519–1522*. Weiden: Stangl & Taubald, 1992.

Thomasius, Christian. *De Crimine Magiae*. Halle, 1701.

Kurtze Lehr-Sätze von dem Laster der Zauberey. Halle, 1705.

De origine ac progressu procressus inquisitorii contra sagas. Halle, 1712.

Über die Folter: Untersuchungen zur Geschichte der Folter. Ed. and trans. Rolf Lieberwirth. Weimar: Böhlau, 1960.

Über die Hexenprozesse. Ed. Rolf Lieberwirth. Weimar: Böhlau, 1986.

Thorne, Tony. *Children of the Night: Of Vampires and Vampirism*. London: Gollancz, 1999.

Countess Dracula: The Life and Times of Elisabeth Báthory, the Blood Countess. London: Bloomsbury, 1997.

Thürmer-Rohr, Christina, Martina Emme and Carola Wildt. *Mittäterschaft und Entdeckungslust*. 2nd edn. Berlin: Orlanda Frauenverlag, 1990.

Topalović, Elvira. *Sprachwahl – Textsorte – Dialogstruktur: Zu Verhörprotokollen aus Hexenprozessen des 17. Jahrhunderts*. Trier: WVT, 2003.

Touaillon, Christine. *Der deutsche Frauenroman des 18. Jahrhunderts*. Leipzig: Wilhelm Braumüller, 1919.

Treitschke, Heinrich von. *Politik. Vorlesungen gehalten an der Universität zu Berlin*. Vol. I. 4th edn. Leipzig: S. Hirzel, 1918.

Trummer, Carl. *Vorträge über Tortur, Hexenverfolgungen, Vehmgerichte und andere merkwürdige Erscheinungen in der Hamburgischen Rechtgeschichte*. 3 vols. Hamburg: Meißner, 1844–50. I 89–93.

Trusen, Winfried. 'Rechtliche Grundlagen der Hexenprozesse und ihrer Beendigung'. *Das Ende der Hexenverfolgung*. Ed. Sönke Lorenz and Dieter R. Bauer. Stuttgart: Franz Steiner, 1995. 203–26.

Turner, Victor. *The Anthropology of Performance*. New York: PAJ, 1986.

Dramas, Fields, and Metaphors: Symbolic Action and Human Society. Ithaca, NY, and London: Cornell University Press, 1974.

Tyradellis, Daniel, and Burkhardt Wolf, eds. *Die Szene der Gewalt: Bilder, Codes und Materialitäten*. Frankfurt/M.: Peter Lang, 2007.

'Ueber die letzte Defension der Inquisitinn Wächtlern in Hamburg'. *Inquisitenblätter für Juristen und Nichtjuristen*.1. Stück. N.p., n.d. 3–8.

Ulbrich, Claudia. 'Weibliche Delinquenz im 18. Jahrhundert: Eine dörfliche Fallstudie'. *Von Huren und Rabenmüttern: Weibliche Kriminalität in der Frühen Neuzeit*. Ed. Otto Ulbricht. Cologne, Weimar and Vienna: Böhlau, 1995. 281–311.

Ulbricht, Otto. 'Einleitung: Für eine Geschichte der weiblichen Kriminalität in der Frühen Neuzeit oder: Geschlechtergeschichte, historische Kriminalitätsforschung und weibliche Kriminalität'. *Von Huren und Rabenmüttern: Weibliche Kriminalität in der Frühen Neuzeit*. Ed. Otto Ulbricht. Cologne, Weimar and Vienna: Böhlau, 1995. I–37.

'Kindsmörderinnen vor Gericht: Verteidigungsstrategien von Frauen in Norddeutschland 1680–1810'. *Mit den Waffen der Justiz: Zur Kriminalitätsgeschichte des Spätmittelalters und der Frühen Neuzeit*. Frankfurt/M.: Fischer, 1993. 54–85.

'Kindsmord in der Frühen Neuzeit'. *Frauen in der Geschichte des Rechts. Von der frühen Neuzeit bis zur Gegenwart*. Ed. Ute Gerhard. Munich: Beck, 1997. 235–47.

Kindsmord und Aufklärung in Deutschland. Munich: R. Oldenbourg, 1990.

ed. *Von Huren und Rabenmüttern: Weibliche Kriminalität in der Frühen Neuzeit.* Cologne, Weimar and Vienna: Böhlau, 1995.

Unger, Joseph. *Die Ehe in ihrer welthistorischen Entwicklung. Ein Beitrag zur Philosophie der Geschichte.* Vienna: Jasper, Hügel & Manz, 1850.

Unverfälschte Nachricht von dem Betragen der Wächtlern in der Frohnerei nebst dem letztern Urtheile des Obergerichts. N.p., n.d.

Urtel in Sachen Fiscalis&c.c. Wächtlern publicirt Veneris d. 14. Nov. 1788. N.p., n.d.

Ussher, Jane. 'Women's Madness: A Material-Discursive-Intrapsychic Approach'. *Pathology and the Postmodern: Mental Illness as Discourse and Experience.* Ed. Dwight Fee. London: Sage, 2000. 207–30.

Vallée, Gérard, ed. and trans. *Die Hauptschriften zum Pantheismusstreit zwischen Jacobi und Mendelssohn.* Lanham, MD, and London: University Press of America, 1988.

Varesi, Andreas. *Das Geheimnis der Báthory. Roman.* Dresden: Felicity Management and Publishing, 2005.

Vierhaus, Rudolf, ed. *Bürger und Bürgerlichkeit im Zeitalter der Aufklärung.* Heidelberg: Lambert Schneider, 1981.

'Vierzehen Schriften über die Preisaufgabe von den Mitteln dem Kindermord Einhalt zu thun'. *Allgemeine juristische Bibliothek, herausgegeben von zweyen Altdorfischen Professoren.* Vol. 11. Nuremberg, 1782. 233–44.

Visus et repertus über die sogenannten Vampyren. Nuremberg, 1732.

Vogel, Ursula. 'Gleichheit und Herrschaft in der ehelichen Vertragsgesellschaft – Widersprüche der Aufklärung'. *Frauen in der Geschichte des Rechts. Von der frühen Neuzeit bis zur Gegenwart.* Ed. Ute Gerhard. Munich: Beck, 1997. 265–92.

Voget, F[riedrich] L[eopold]. *Die Giftmörderin Gesche Margarethe Gottfried, in der Gefangenschaft bis zur Hinrichtung. Nach Vollzug des Todesurtheils herausgegeben von dem Defensor derselben, Dr. F. L. Voget.* 2 vols. in 1. Bremen: C. Schünemann, 1831.

Lebensgeschichte der Giftmörderin Gesche Margarethe Gottfried, geborne Timm. Nach erfolgtem Straferkenntnisse höchster Instanz herausgegeben von dem Defensor derselben, Dr. F. L. Voget. Bremen: Wilhelm Kaiser, 1831.

Vogt, Gottlob Heinrich. *Der eingeschlichene, nun aber Wieder ausgemertzte Dritte Theil des Menschen Nebst angehängter Quelle Vieler Irrthümer, nehmlich der Lehre Von denen Temperamenten Darinnen denn auch die besten und bindigsten Beweißgründe von denen 2. Theilen des Menschen, ingleichen der Unterscheid des Lebens des Menschen oder Thier; und des verworffenen Welt-Geistes und Harmonia Praestabil. vorkommen. Ans Licht gestellet Von Gottlob Heinrich Vogt, Medic. Pract.* Leipzig: August Martin, 1732.

Kurtzes Bedencken Von denen Acten-mäßigen Relationen Wegen derer Vampiren, oder Menschen- und Vieh-Aussaugern, Ingleichen Über das davon in Leipzig heraus-gekommene Raisonnement Vom Welt-Geiste, An gute Freunde gesandt von Gottlob Heinrich Vogt, Medic. Pract. Leipzig: August Martin, 1732.

[Voigt, Christian Gottlob.] 'Manuskript des Aufsatzes von Christian Gottlob Voigt vom 11. Februar 1781: Ueber die Preisfrage: Welches sind die besten ausführbaren Mittel, dem Kindermorde Einhalt zu thun?' *'Das Kind in meinem Leib': Sittlichkeitsdelikte und Kindsmord in Sachsen-Weimar-Eisenach unter Carl August. Eine Quellenedition 1777–1786.* Ed. Volker Wahl. Weimar: Hermann Böhlaus Nachfolger, 2004. 56–60.

'Ueber die Preisaufgabe: Welches sind die besten ausführbaren Mittel, dem Kindermord Einhalt zu thun? Den Chronologen mitgetheilt den 29. März 1781'. *'Das Kind in meinem Leib': Sittlichkeitsdelikte und Kindsmord in Sachsen-Weimar-Eisenach unter Carl August. Eine Quellenedition 1777–1786.* Ed. Volker Wahl. Weimar: Hermann Böhlaus Nachfolger, 2004. 60–8.

Volckmann, Silvia. '"Gierig saugt sie seines Mundes Flammen". Anmerkungen zum Funktionswandel des weiblichen Vampirs in der Literatur des 19. Jahrhunderts'. *Weiblichkeit und Tod in der Literatur.* Ed. Renate Berger and Inge Stephan. Cologne and Vienna: Böhlau, 1987. 155–76.

Volkmar, Friedrich Nathaniel. *Philosophie der Ehe.* Halle: bey Hemmerde und Schwetschke, 1794.

Vorläufiger Bericht in der Untersuchungssache wider Michael Christoph Gottfried Wittwe Gesche Margarethe geborne Timm. Bremen 1830. Handwritten MS; microfilm, Staatsarchiv Bremen.

Wächtershäuser, Wilhelm. *Das Verbrechen des Kindesmordes im Zeitalter der Aufklärung. Eine rechtsgeschichtliche Untersuchung der dogmatischen, prozessualen und rechtssoziologischen Aspekte.* Berlin: E. Schmidt, 1973.

Wagner, Hans, ed. *Sinnlichkeit und Verstand in der deutschen und französischen Philosophie von Descartes bis Hegel.* Bonn: Bouvier, 1976.

Wagner, Heinrich Leopold. *Die Kindermörderin. Ein Trauerspiel.* Ed. Jörg Ulrich Fechner. Stuttgart: Reclam, 1981.

Wagner, Michael. *Beyträge zur Philosophischen Anthropologie und den damit verwandten Wissenschaften.* 2 vols. Vienna: Joseph Stahel und Compagnie, 1794–6.

Wahl, Volker, ed. *'Das Kind in meinem Leib': Sittlichkeitsdelikte und Kindsmord in Sachsen-Weimar-Eisenach unter Carl August. Eine Quellenedition 1777–1786.* Weimar: Hermann Böhlaus Nachfolger, 2004.

Wahre Aussagen der in der Frohnerey zu Hamburg sitzenden Inquisitin Wächtler als dieselbe den 11ten Julius 1788 nach dem Hamburgischen Niedergericht gebracht wurde und daselbst die sogenannte Bürgerfindung erhielt. N.p., n.d. [Hamburg, 1788].

Wahrhafte Aussagen der Inquisitin Wächtlern, als sie den 4ten März auf die Folter gebracht werden sollte. Hamburg, 1788.

Walser Smith, Helmut. *The Butcher's Tale: Murder and Anti-Semitism in a German Town.* New York and London: W. W. Norton & Co., 2002.

Warren-Sabean, David. 'Allianzen und Listen: Die Geschlechtsvormundschaft im 18. und 19. Jahrhundert'. *Frauen in der Geschichte des Rechts. Von der frühen Neuzeit bis zur Gegenwart.* Ed. Ute Gerhard. Munich: Beck, 1997. 460–79.

Weber, Beat. *Die Kindsmörderin im deutschen Schrifttum von 1770–1795.* Bonn: Bouvier, 1974.

Weber-Will, Susanne. 'Geschlechtsvormundschaft und weibliche Rechtswohltaten im Privatrecht des preußischen Allgemeinen Landrechts von 1794'. *Frauen in der Geschichte des Rechts. Von der frühen Neuzeit bis zur Gegenwart.* Ed. Ute Gerhard. Munich: Beck, 1997. 452–9.

Wechsler, Judith. 'Lavater, Stereotype, and Prejudice'. *The Faces of Physiognomy: Interdisciplinary Approaches to Johann Caspar Lavater.* Ed. Ellis Shookman. Columbia, SC: Camden House, 1993. 104–25.

Weigel, Sigrid. *'Die geopferte Heldin und das Opfer als Heldin: Zum Entwurf weiblicher Helden in der Literatur von Männern und Frauen'.* Inge Stephan and Sigrid Weigel, *Die verborgene Frau: Sechs Beiträge zu einer feministischen Literaturwissenschaft.* Berlin: Argument, 1983. 138–52.

'Der schielende Blick: Thesen zur Geschichte weiblicher Schreibpraxis'. Inge Stephan and Sigrid Weigel, *Die verborgene Frau: Sechs Beiträge zu einer feministischen Literaturwissenschaft.* Berlin: Argument, 1983. 83–137.

Weiler, Inge. *Giftmordwissen und Giftmörderinnen: Eine diskursgeschichtliche Studie.* Tübingen: Niemeyer, 1998.

Eines Weimarischen Medici Muthmaßliche Gedancken Von denen Vampyren, Oder sogenannten Blut-Saugern, Welchen zuletzt Das Gutachten Der Königl. Preußischen Societät derer Wissenschaften, Von gedachten Vampyren, Mit beygefüget ist. Leipzig: Michael Blochberger, 1732.

Weißenburg d. ält. *Geschichte der berüchtigten Bremer Giftmischerin Margarete Gesina Gottfried, geb. Timme, und ausführliche Erzählung ihrer schauderhaften Unthaten. Nach authentischen Quellen bearbeitet von Weißenburg d. ält.* Quedlinburg and Leipzig: Gottfried Basse, 1829.

Werner, Oscar Helmuth. *The Unmarried Mother in German Literature. With Special Reference to the Period 1770–1800.* New York: AMS Press, 1917.

Wetzell, Richard F. *Inventing the Criminal: A History of German Criminology 1880–1945.* Chapel Hill and London: University of North Carolina Press, 2000.

Wezel, Johann Karl. *Versuch über die Kenntniß des Menschen.* 2 vols. Leipzig: Dyck, 1784–5.

Wiedemeyer, David. *Disputatio Juridica de Confesso Non Convicto, quam Dei & Superiorem Consensu in Academia Lipsiensi sub Praesidio Viri Prae-Nobilissimi, Aplissimi atque Excellentissimi, Dn. Gothofredi Nicolai Ittigii Assessoris, Dn Patroni, sui Fautoris atque Praeceptoris aetatem devenerandi, Publico Eroditorum Examini placido.* Leipzig: Andreas Martin Sched, 1715.

Wiederholdt, Johann Ludwig. *Christliche Gedancken, Von der Folter oder Peinlichen Frage, Durch welche gezeiget wird / Daß der Gebrauch derselben / so wohl denen Göttlichen Gesetzen / als der gesunden Vernunfft zuwider / und dannenhero / als grausam und betrüglich / von Christlichen Obrigkeiten abzuschaffen / dagegen aber mit denen durch Indicia gravirten Personen auf eine gantz andere Weiße zu verfahren seye. Entworffen von Johann Ludwig Wiederholdt / J.U.Lto, und verschiedener Reichs-Ständen Rath.* Wetzlar: bey Nicolaus Ludwig Winckler, 1739.

Willems, Marianne. 'Der Verbrecher als Mensch: Zur Herkunft "anthropologischer" Deutungsmuster der Kriminalgeschichte des 18. Jahrhunderts'. *Jahrbuch der Aufklärung* 14 (2002), 23–48.

Wilson, W. Daniel. 'Goethe, His Duke and Infanticide: New Documents and Reflections on a Controversial Execution'. *German Life and Letters* 61.1 (January 2008), 7–32.

Das Goethe-Tabu: Protest und Menschenrechte im klassischen Weimar. Munich: dtv, 1999.

ed. 'The "Halsgericht" for the Execution of Johanna Höhn in Weimar, 28 November 1783'. *German Life and Letters* 61.1 (January 2008), 33–44.

Wimmer, Wolf. 'Zum Gedenken an Anna Göldi. Die letzte Hinrichtung einer "Hexe" in Europa'. *Juristenzeitung* (1982), 551–3.

Winteler, Jakob. *Der Prozess gegen Anna Göldi im Urteil der Zeitgenossen.* Glarus: O. Bartel-Hefti, 1951.

Wittkowski, Wolfgang. 'Hexenjagd auf Goethe. November 1783: Hinrichtung einer Kindsmörderin und "Das Göttliche"'. *Oxford German Studies* 31 (2002), 63–102.

Wittrock, Christine. *Abtreibung und Kindsmord in der neueren deutschen Literatur.* Frankfurt/M.: C. Wittrock, 1978.

Wolf, Hans-Jürgen. *Geschichte der Hexenprozesse: Holocaust und Massenpsychose vom 16.–18. Jahrhundert.* Erlensee: EFB, 1995.

Wosnik, Richard. 'Die letzte Anwendung der Folter in Hamburg an einer Frau, Maria Katharine Wächtler, geb. Wunch, aus Plauen an der Havel'. *Beiträge zur hamburgischen Kriminalgeschichte unter besonderer Berücksichtigung des Kriminal-Museums, nach Quellen und Urkunden.* 3 vols. Hamburg: Selbstverlag, 1926–7. I 57–61.

Wulffen, Erich. *Psychologie des Verbrechers. Ein Handbuch für Juristen, Ärzte, Pädagogen und Gebildete aller Stände.* 2 vols. 2nd edn. Berlin: Langenscheidt, 1913 (first published 1908).

Das Weib als Sexualverbrecherin. Flensburg: Orion, 1993.

Wunder, Heide. 'Herrschaft und öffentliches Handeln von Frauen in der Gesellschaft der Frühen Neuzeit'. *Frauen in der Geschichte des Rechts. Von der frühen Neuzeit bis zur Gegenwart.* Ed. Ute Gerhard. Munich: Beck, 1997. 27–54.

'"Weibliche Kriminalität" in der Frühen Neuzeit: Überlegungen aus der Sicht der Geschlechtergeschichte'. *Von Huren und Rabenmüttern: Weibliche Kriminalität in der Frühen Neuzeit.* Ed. Otto Ulbricht. Cologne, Weimar and Vienna: Böhlau, 1995. 39–61.

[Wunderlich, August.] *Die Selbstanklage von Anna Thormählen geb. Schneider zu Hamburg gerichtet auf Gattenmord durch Morphium und deren Freisprechung. Eine critische Studie.* Leipzig: J. M. Gebhardt, 1876.

Zagolla, Robert. 'Die Folter: Mythos und Realität eines rechtsgeschichtlichen Phänomens'. *Realität und Mythos: Hexenverfolgung und Rezeptionsgeschichte.* Ed. Katrin Moeller and Burghart Schmidt. Hamburg: DOBU, 2003. 122–49.

Zelle, Carsten. *'Angenehmes Grauen': Literaturhistorische Beiträge zur Ästhetik des Schrecklichen im achtzehnten Jahrhundert.* Hamburg: Felix Meiner, 1987.

'Autorität der Brutalität – Brutalität der Autorität. Folterpraktiken und Hinrichtungsrituale in der frühen Neuzeit'. *Autorität: Spektren harter*

Kommunikation. Ed. Ralph Kray, K. Ludwig Pfeiffer and Thomas Studer. Opladen: Westdeutscher Verlag, 1992. 56–77.

'Strafen und Schrecken: Einführende Bemerkungen zur Parallele zwischen dem Schauspiel der Tragödie und der Tragödie der Hinrichtung'. *Jahrbuch der Schillergesellschaft* 28 (1984), 76–103.

'Über den Grund des Vergnügens an schrecklichen Gegenständen in der Ästhetik des achtzehnten Jahrhunderts (mit einem bibliographischen Anhang)'. *Schönheit und Schrecken: Entsetzen, Gewalt und Tod in alten und neuen Medien*. Ed. Peter Gendolla and Carsten Zelle. Heidelberg: C. Winter, 1990. 55–91.

Zopf, Johann Heinrich. *Dissertatio de Vampyris Serviensibus, quam Praeside M. Jo. Henrico Zopfio, Gymnasii Assindiensis Directore publice defendit Respondens Christianus Fridericus van Dalen, Emmericensis*. Duisburg, 1733.

Index

Notes: The main entries for names and titles are in the original language, e.g.:
  'Friedrich II, King of Prussia', *not* 'Frederick the Great'
  '*Dei delitti e delle pene*', *not* '*Of Crimes and Punishments*'
Authors better known under their pseudonyms are indexed by their pseudonyms, e.g.:
  'Voltaire', *not* 'Arouet, François Marie'
  'Maler Müller', *not* 'Müller, Friedrich'